Law and Religious Dive
in Education

Religion is a prominent legal force despite the premise constructed and promoted by Western constitutionalism that it must be separated from the State in democracies. Education constitutes an area of human life that leaves ample scope for the expression of religious identity and shapes the citizens of the future. It is also the place of origin of a considerable number of normative conflicts involving religious identity that arise today in multicultural settings.

The book deals with the interplay of law and religion in education through the versatility of religious law and legal pluralism, as well as religion's possible adaptation and reconciliation with modernity, in order to consider and reflect on normative conflicts. It adopts the angle of the constitutional dimension of religion narrated in a comparative perspective and critically reflects on regulatory attempts by the State and the international community to promote new ways of living together.

Kyriaki Topidi is a Senior Research Associate and Head of Cluster on Culture and Diversity at the European Centre for Minority Issues (Germany). Her research focuses on diversity management, religion, education and comparative law. She is the author and editor of a number of volumes, including *EU Law, Minorities and Enlargement* (Intersentia, 2010), *Constitutional Evolution in Central and Eastern Europe: Expansion and Integration in the EU* (Ashgate, 2011), *Transnational Legal Process and Human Rights* (Ashgate, 2013) and *Religion as Empowerment: Global Legal Perspectives* (Routledge, 2016). She has also recently edited a collection on *Normative Pluralism and Human Rights* published by Routledge in 2018.

ICLARS Series on Law and Religion

Series Editors:

Silvio Ferrari
University of Milan, Italy
Russell Sandberg
Cardiff University, UK
Pieter Coertzen
University of Stellenbosch, South Africa
W. Cole Durham, Jr.
Brigham Young University, USA,
Tahir Mahmood
Amity International University, India

The *ICLARS Series on Law and Religion* is a new series designed to provide a forum for the rapidly expanding field of research in law and religion. The series is published in association with the International Consortium for Law and Religion Studies, an international network of scholars and experts of law and religion founded in 2007 with the aim of providing a place where information, data and opinions can easily be exchanged among members and made available to the broader scientific community. The series aims to become a primary source for students and scholars while presenting authors with a valuable means to reach a wide and growing readership.

Other titles in this series:

Religious Rights within the Family
From Coerced Manifestation to Dispute Resolution in France,
England and Hong Kong
Esther Erlings

Religion, Law, Politics and the State in Africa
Applying Legal Pluralism in Ghana
Seth Tweneboah

Law and Religious Diversity in Education
The Right to Difference
Kyriaki Topidi

The Transition of Religion to Culture in Law and Public Discourse
Lori Beaman

For more information about this series, please visit: www.routledge.com/ ICLARS-Series-on-Law-and-Religion/book-series/ICLARS

Law and Religious Diversity in Education

The Right to Difference

Kyriaki Topidi

Routledge
Taylor & Francis Group

LONDON AND NEW YORK

First published 2021 by Routledge

2 Park Square, Milton Park, Abingdon, Oxon OX14 4RN

605 Third Avenue, New York, NY 10017

Routledge is an imprint of the Taylor & Francis Group, an informa business

First issued in paperback 2022

British Library Cataloguing-in-Publication Data
A catalogue record for this book is available from the British Library

Library of Congress Cataloging-in-Publication Data
Names: Topidi, Kyriaki, author.
Title: Law and religious diversity in education : the right to
   difference / Kyriaki Topidi.
Description: Abingdon, Oxon ; New York, NY : Routledge, 2020. |
   Series: ICLARS | Includes bibliographical references and index.
Identifiers: LCCN 2019048883 (print) | LCCN 2019048884
   (ebook) | ISBN 9781138340299 (hardback) |
   ISBN 9780429440748 (ebook)
Subjects: LCSH: Religion in the public schools—Law and
   legislation. | Religious minorities—Legal status, laws, etc.. |
   Multiculturalism—Law and legislation. | Religion in the public
   schools—Law and legislation—Israel. | Religion in the public
   schools—Law and legislation—South Africa. | Religion in the
   public schools—Law and legislation—England.
Classification: LCC K3645 .T67 2020 (print) | LCC K3645 (ebook) |
   DDC 344/.07—dc23
LC record available at https://lccn.loc.gov/2019048883
LC ebook record available at https://lccn.loc.gov/2019048884

ISBN: 978-1-138-34029-9 (hbk)
ISBN: 978-1-03-233599-5 (pbk)
DOI: 10.4324/9780429440748

Typeset in Galliard
by Apex CoVantage, LLC

To Eva-Maria, Alexia and Claire

Contents

Acknowledgments

This book represents, like many books, an attempt to understand the complexities of our super-diverse world. It is based on the desire and intention to approach law in a holistic yet realistic way. To do so, it contributes to the growing literature of comparative public law of 'difference'.

But apart from its scientific and intellectual value, it reflects also a personal journey of growth. I am particularly grateful to Werner Menski, Rene Pahud de Mortanges, Christa Rautenbach, Alexander Morawa, Tove Malloy and Judith Wyttenbach for listening, reading, suggesting and supporting in their own ways my project at various stages. I am also thankful to the audiences at various network conferences and workshops such as ICLARS, JURIS DIVERSITAS, the Berkeley Anti-Discrimination and Equality Network and the MPI law and anthropology researchers at Halle as well as many others across the globe for constructive comments and encouragement.

I need to stress that a book project is also a relational endeavor: apart from its scientific value, the making of this volume has allowed me to meet and get better acquainted with a great number of scholars belonging to various epistemic communities relevant to my topic. This has created precious human connections that I consider equally valuable.

As always, I am indebted to Alison Kirk and Emily Summers at Routledge for their support and efficiency. It truly makes a difference to produce work within a framework that encourages it.

Finally, as a female scholar with a family, which includes three fascinating personalities – my daughters – I have to emphasize how their presence has inspired me to 'keep moving', not so much to serve as a role model to them, but more to demonstrate to them that they need not compromise as our societies will often expect of them. A special thanks goes to my mother in the same spirit.

Preface

Comparative legal scholarship is being developed at present in conditions that give less and less importance to the distinction between national and international law and politics.[1] At the same time, global governance has largely overcome state-centric patterns of growth and evolution and is rather focusing on social sub-systems as affected by particular actors and their interests.[2] These considerations confirm the fragmentation of the normative landscapes that comparative (public) law is encouraged to examine.

Yet the national legal frameworks, typically reflected in constitutions, remain a valuable starting point for comparisons, especially if one approaches them as the 'structural coupling' of law and politics.[3] Patterns of cooperation and/or conflict among actors can be observed, as human agency makes and un-makes law(s). In the meantime, allegiance to national communities is also being transformed: individuals and groups choose to complement their national identity with other identities connected to the local, religious or ideological aspects of their existence, some of which have transnational dimensions.[4]

In a world of multiple and non-exhaustive loyalties, cultural and religious diversity management therefore becomes essential to understand how co-existence in super-diverse societies relies increasingly on negotiation and exchange. This is why 'privatizing' diversity in order to pursue integrationist aims is being challenged as the dominant strategy to manage plurality. And while the task to cope with social and cultural diversity depends and is connected to the State, a closer look at various social spaces of human encounter may suggest otherwise: uniformity in constitutional terms is a fiction, much like James Tully feared,[5] with different groups following diverging culturally grounded norms. Some of them,

---

1 Nico Krisch, *Beyond Constitutionalism: The Pluralist Structure of Postnational Law*, Oxford University Press, 2010, esp. Chapter 2.
2 Krisch (2010).
3 Niklas Luhmann, *Das Recht der Gesellschaft*, Frankfurt am Main: Suhrkamp Verlag, 1993, 468–481.
4 Krisch (2010).
5 James Tully, *Strange Multiplicity*, Cambridge University Press, 1995, in particular chapters 2 and 3.

in fact, go as far as to reject the liberal conception of the 'modern' free individual. But how far can we really push for the universalizing tendencies in constitutionalism? And how does one cope with the absence of uniformity that often leads to inequality?

The main aim of this book is to reflect on how public schools are regulated when attempting to manage the growing religious diversity of learners. Normatively, the analysis is premised on exploring the limits of the right to religious difference against the background of essential rights such as those to equality and non-discrimination or to education. The underlying purpose of the comparative study is also to look at how law shapes actors' preferences and how actors mobilize law to serve their intentions to advance claims.

Ideologically, there is no preconceived determination for the purposes of this analysis on how law may act as a force for progressive social change,[6] although it is clear, as will be further shown, that actors can create new norms (at least content-wise), and courts often simply follow already developed social consensus. The aim here is more modest: the comparison will strive to contribute to more legal empirical research about the 'law in action'. In such a context, state law becomes a tool, not an end in itself. It is therefore worth examining how it is understood, invoked or simply bypassed when interacting with other normative systems and how this interaction can produce legal and non-legal action.[7] In a sense, the rights analyzed (i.e. religious freedom, equality and education) are viewed as tools for the mobilization of forms of both individual as well as collective religious identities.

Within such a quest, schools and systems of education broadly understood function as bridges between the private family sphere and the public space. They also constitute a privileged platform to observe and analyze the linkages between religion and education. Whether one chooses to focus on the secularization thesis, the evolution of citizenship policies, socio-economic empowerment of particular ethno-cultural groups or reflect on the governance of religious diversity, public schools allow us to test whether indeed 'the consequence of modernity is not secularism, but pluralism'.[8] In other words, the school environment represents a relevant locus to study how difference and diversity are practiced in light of the respective legal frameworks within which they operate.

In this direction, the analysis proceeds in three parts: the first concentrates on the method used to analyze and compare, but it also revisits essential normative concepts as well. Chapter 1 specifically identifies the methodological approach for this study. It relies on the synergy between comparative legal methodology,

---

6 See Scott L. Cummings, 'The Social Movement Turn in Law', *Law and Social Inquiry*, 43(2), 2018, 360–416, at 361.

7 Cummings (2018) at 377.

8 Wolfram Weisse, 'Analysis of the Teachers' Responses to Religious Diversity in the Course of the REDCo Project—A Foreword', in Anna van der Want, Cok Bakker, Ina ter Avest and Judith Everington (eds.), *Teachers Responding to Religious Diversity in Europe—Researching Biography and Pedagogy*, Waxmann, 2009, at 7.

with all its flaws, and the conceptual tool of legal pluralism. The chapter posits that they can function complementarily as they both pursue the protection of difference. The starting point of such a 'rapprochement' stems from a doubt: the doubt that state law remains the exclusive or even predominant expression of normativity in multicultural societies. Instead, it is argued that the starting point of the study can be that normative plurality (including religious law) shapes the content and balancing of rights whenever they are found in conflict, including within schools. The chapter unfolds the ways in which legal pluralism overlaps comparative methodology that strives to illustrate and celebrate differences among legal systems. A crucial connecting link between the two concepts is the recognition of the existence and impact of non-state legal orders on a given legal framework. Ultimately, the chapter develops also the range of methodological challenges of protecting religious difference in the context of pluri-normativity.

Chapter 2 looks at key normative elements of the analysis of religious diversity frameworks within education. These are the right to religious freedom, which is central to the inquiry; the notion of secularism and secularization as essential background components of the exercise of religious freedom(s); the connection (and potential for clash) between religious freedom and equality; and finally, the links between the right to religious freedom with education and the principle of equality.

Chapter 3 completes the first part of the study by outlining the international legal standards applicable to religious freedom within public education. While not covering exhaustively the entire breadth of the rights to religious freedom, education and equality, the chapter focuses on the intersection between education and religion against the background requirement of equality. The overview of prevailing international legal standards serves the purpose here of exposing the normative content as a minimum common denominator of the rights studies. Indirectly, it also serves as a relative 'benchmark' not to measure states' performance in the case studies but rather to show how the studied norms (i.e. religion, education, equality) are adjusted at the national level, especially under conditions of normative conflict.

The analysis begins with an overview of the special nature of the right to education as an empowerment 'gateway' right, to then move to its content in connection to its cultural and religious dimensions. Following the legal trajectory, the right is at a second level discussed from a governance perspective in relation to its potential contribution towards societal co-existence while respecting religious differences. Finally, the role of the right to equality within the educational process is introduced, particularly in a context of normative conflict between competing rights/interests. Aware of the ideological variations that govern equality, this section stresses the importance of the identitarian dimension in the exercise of one's fundamental rights, as reflected in international legal texts governing discrimination within education.

The second part of the study shifts from core theoretical considerations to three distinct case studies. These cover the regulation of religious diversity in state-sponsored education in Israel, South Africa and England. The studies in question form the core empirical data on which comparative analysis will be extracted from in the third part of the book. All three case studies, while very different from each other, share a common constitutionally warranted recognition of non-state law, though to different degrees. Additionally, they embrace legally explicit commitments to the management of ethno-religious diversity.

Chapter 4 examines religious diversity in the Israeli public education context. It begins with a background analysis – a common feature of all case studies – on the state of pluri-normativity and legal pluralism in Israel's legal system. The chapter then devotes a separate section to justify the close normative entanglement between the State and the (majority) Jewish faith. The general features of Israeli multicultural public education are described in order to set the basis for a more analytical overview of the characteristics of religious diversity from a constitutional perspective. In that context, particular attention is given to the sui generis understanding of the principle of equality in constitutional terms, coupled and connected with the special role of the State in providing and regulating religious services, including within education. The cases of the Arab Israeli schools and the separate stream of ultra-Orthodox religious education are discussed to demonstrate the variations in the balancing of religious freedom with education and equality. On the basis of the systems examined, the chapter then moves on to assess the implications of the prevailing legal arrangements from the viewpoint of educational pluralism, autonomy and the protection of religious identity, also putting forward some concluding remarks on the ways that the provision of religiously relevant public education affects governance in the country.

The second case discussed in Chapter 5 turns to South Africa. In a country with a heavy historical background, the South African analysis begins with an overview of the type of legal pluralism that prevails in this context. The chapter stresses the prevalence of the principle of equality in the constitutional design of the country's legal system, when contrasted with rights such as that to religion or education. The very sophisticated theorization of equality in constitutional law is explored as a basis to debate the existence of a right to difference. The chapter then moves on to the right to religious freedom, of essence to the study of religious diversity frames in South African public schools. At the difference of Israel, religion is considered a private matter in legal terms in contemporary South Africa and is less prominent in the design of religious diversity laws and policies. It is also often conflated with the notion of culture. The analysis of the essential rights for the focus of this study is completed with discussion on the legal parameters of the right to education in domestic legal terms.

A special section of the chapter is devoted to independent schools that have a religious ethos. This focus is in analogy with the part in the Israeli case that discusses ultra-Orthodox schools and in the English case of 'faith schools'. It is justified by the global rise in religious education establishments and connected to a question of state funding devoted to such educational establishments.

From a diversity governance perspective, the South African case is then placed within the chapter into its socio-historic context: the South African approach to religious diversity in education is analyzed following three axes. The first one looks at the legacy of apartheid in public education in order to build the second axis related to the contemporary profile of the relation between religion and education in contemporary South Africa. The third axis analytically examines the determinant role of (and potential for) desegregation as a process affecting education.

The chapter concludes with a series of remarks on the effects of religious diversity policy in education from the perspective of its achievements and gaps in bringing about societal cohesion.

The final chapter of the second part of the book looks at English public education and religious diversity. As previously, it begins with an overview of the state of legal pluralism in the British context, emphasizing its connection with multiculturalism. In its second part, the chapter provides a brief historical account of the evolution of the relationship between education and faith in curricular development. It also covers the necessary legal framework background on the issue, including the typology of schools in the English educational system in relation to their connection to a religious profile in their educational programmes.

Similar to the previous two case studies, a special part of the chapter is devoted to the principle of equality as it relates to religious freedom. With the help of legislative developments on the evolution of this relationship and using relevant national case law, the ambiguity of the co-existence between the two rights is highlighted, especially in conditions where they are seen to be in conflict. Emphasis is inevitably placed at this point in education-related cases.

The special category of 'faith schools' is then analyzed, echoing the global trend towards more culturally relevant education pursued by parents and their children. An element of intense public debate, yet still with scientifically unclear implications for diversity management, these schools illustrate well the debate on values and co-existence in conditions of religious and cultural diversity.

The next section of the chapter takes up the aspect of citizenship education and its features as it connects to religiously diverse classrooms in England. This part discusses the major dichotomies in scholarship and educational practice with an eye on religious diversity governance.

On the basis of the legal evidence gathered from the English case, the chapter moves on to an analytical assessment of the outcomes of the current policy framework on religious diversity in public education. First, it briefly reverts to the issue of 'faith schools' as a litmus test for diversity in education, and then focuses respectively on the role of teachers as agents of religious diversity management, the use of religious symbols in schools (a topic hotly debated in Europe), and ends with the question of the place of religious education in the national curriculum. All four points are identified here as topics that not only showcase the unique features of the English context (from a comparative perspective) but also as indicators of the main sources of contention in the area.

The chapter concludes with some remarks on the ambiguous role of religious belief in the English public education system that, at the difference of the Israeli and South African cases, chooses to place regulatory weight on the right to education as opposed to the rights to religious freedom and equality.

The third part of the book reflects on the findings from the three preceding case studies on two levels: the first level focuses on how normative conflicts related to religious identity are (or can be) negotiated in multicultural classrooms. It, first, revisits the conceptual tool of legal pluralism, this time measured against its efficiency to understand and explain the reality of competing versions of religious 'truths': it highlights in particular the limits of law to manage religious differences, the necessity to account for power dynamics in any given legislative and policy framework on religious diversity in education and the role of specific actors (e.g. teachers) within the broader process of educating. The chapter then proceeds to focus on religious diversity as a normative conflict regulating factor. To do so, it addresses two points: one concerns the understanding of religious education as a public good in light of the shortcomings observed in the three cases explored. The other focuses on the way that inequalities are de facto (as opposed to de jure) perpetuated in the delivery of public education, despite contrary legislative pronouncements.

The second level of analysis looks at the methods, conditions and challenges that public educational systems face when called to address religious diversity. Three elements are particularly stressed: the role of social and historical context in determining the successes and failures of a public education system to protect religious diversity, the new role of the State in conditions of normative plurality, and the concrete challenges that public education systems encounter in their quest for protection of (religious) difference.

Chapter 8 is the final one and adopts a more optimistic viewpoint. It discusses how religious diversity in schools may become conducive to the legal empowerment of learners both during their time at school but also beyond that, as citizens of multicultural polities. The analysis emphasizes the trend towards a more individualized approach to religious education, as connected to the multiple cultural affiliations of children. At the same time, the chapter notes and debates how public education can be understood as development both on the individual and the community levels, especially in light of the pressing globalizing and transnationalizing dimensions that it has acquired.

Of particular interest to this volume, as testimony of the intense levels of agency that both individuals as well as entire religious groups and communities are exercising in the area of education, 'faith schools' are once more placed in the framework of education.

The last part of the chapter addresses the empowerment dimension of religiously diverse education both from the angle of identity-building (eventually connected to rights-based claims) but also citizenship. This last dimension is particularly debated through the medium of 'common values', provoking intense debates due to the binary interpretations of its position within education for diverse learners.

Ultimately, the book ends with a summary of the common findings among the studied cases in the hope to have shown that religious plurality is, at the end of the day, an opportunity not to be missed in the quest for the protection of difference.

1 The method

Legal pluralism and comparative constitutional law: complementary methodology in the protection of religious difference

"All beings have their laws [and] a greatness of genius consists rather in distinguishing between those cases in which uniformity is a requisite, and those in which there is a necessity for differences".

Montesquieu, *The Spirit of Laws*, xxix, 18

1 Legal hybridity and legal pluralism: state law as one way of imagining the real[1]

Law is never apolitical. Law is never neutral or value-free. Law is often part of the conflict that opposes religious communities, actors within these same communities, or entire ideologies and approaches to diversity management, one against the other. Given the ongoing debates about the difficulties of understanding and handling such complex issues, the broader methodological aim of this study is to show how legal pluralism 'in tandem' with comparative constitutional law can be used as a conceptual device to influence legal and social stability within democracy in multi-ethnic societies towards the recognition of religious difference.

A useful definition for the purposes of this analysis approaches legal pluralism

> as the state of affairs in which a category of social relations is within the fields of operation of two or more bodies of legal norms. Alternatively, if it is viewed not from above in the process of mapping the legal universe but rather from the perspective of the individual subject of law, legal pluralism may be said to exist whenever a person is subject to more than one body of law.[2]

---

1 Expression borrowed from Geertz (1983) and used here with the caveat that law provides standards of permissible behavior and action, yet individuals are influenced by other factors than state law when deciding when to act or abstain from acting [See Clifford Geertz, *Local Knowledge*, New York: Basic Books, 1983].

2 G.R. Woodman, 'Legal Pluralism and Justice', *Journal of African Law*, 40, 1996, 152 at 157. Other definitions of legal pluralism find it to be "generally defined as a situation in which two or more legal systems co-exist in the same social field" (Sally Engle Merry, 'Legal Pluralism', *Law & Soc'y Review*, 22, 1988, 869 at 870) or "a term used to describe and characterise the existence of several distinct legal systems, or perhaps legal sub-systems, within a single independent political community, like a nation-state" (Jeremy Waldron, 'Legal Pluralism and the Contrast Between Hart's Jurisprudence and Fuller's', in Peter Crane (ed.), *The Hart-Fuller Debate in the Twenty-First Century*, Hart: Oxford, 2010, 135 at 136.

While the origins of the term lie in ethnology,[3] it is currently a rapidly grow-ing stream of legal scholarship because it refers to conditions of possible and continued co-existence of non-state legal systems with state-centric ones. This co-existence is far from a new phenomenon in human history.[4] Legal pluralism has, nevertheless, suffered from the conceptual difficulty of not being able to rely on a broadly agreeable definition of 'law',[5] although it cannot be held responsible for this difficulty.

A broad understanding of the term would also suggest a generic use of 'law' comprising a variety of social phenomena that traditionally are not categorized as 'law'. Among others, the concept includes a body of law or legal system, legal rules and principles that are mandatory or optional, expressions of legal cognitive and normative conceptions that are systematized and/or institutionalized, the agents and organizations that generate and maintain bodies of law and even the categorization of legal conceptions under religion, ethics or morals.[6]

In such a plural context, legal pluralism describes the co-existence of more than one body of law within the same social or geographical space[7] but is above all a starting point and not yet an explanatory theory to approach the empirical com-plexities of bodies of law.[8] Just like comparative constitutional law, legal pluralism allows the study of similarities, differences and, as importantly, conflicts between state law and other types of law. While within a given legal system only one body of law may be recognized as state law, others may still run in parallel to that sys-tem but not be considered part of the official law.[9] The cases of constitutional sys-tems discussed in the following chapters, among many others, concede, however, legal validity to other bodies of normative ordering or decision-making entities

---

3 Fore more on this point see Maxime St-Hilaire, 'The Study of Legal Plurality Outside "Legal Pluralism": The Future of the Discipline?' in Shauna Van Praagh and Helge Dedek (eds.), *Stateless Law: Evolving Boundaries of a Discipline*, Routledge, 2015, 115–132 at 116.

4 William Twining uses the examples of medieval Europe and the Ottoman Empire as histori-cal precedents, in W. Twining, 'Normative and Legal Pluralism: A Global Perspective', *Duke Journal of Comparative and International Law*, 20, 2010, 473–517 at 486.

5 See indicatively, Brian Z. Tamanaha, 'A Framework for Pluralistic Socio-Legal Arenas', in M-C. Foblets, J-F. Gaudreault-DesBiens, A. Dundes-Renteln (eds.), *Cultural Diversity and the Law: State Responses from Around the World*, Bruxelles: Bruylant, 2010, 381–401, at 382 et seq. Tamanaha distinguishes between six forms of normative ordering: official legal systems, customary/cultural normative systems, religious/cultural normative systems, economic/capitalist normative systems, functional normative systems and community/cultural normative systems.

6 This brief listing draws from Franz von Benda-Beckmann and Keebet von Benda-Beckmann, 'The Dynamics of Change and Continuity in Plural Legal Orders', *Journal of Legal Plural-ism and Unofficial Law*, 53/54, Special Double Issue, 2006, 1–44, at 13–14, Berlin: LIT Verlag and does not claim to be exhaustive.

7 Franz von Benda-Beckmann, 'Who's Afraid of Legal Pluralism?' *Journal of Legal Pluralism*, 47, 2002, 37–83, at 37.

8 Franz and Keebet von Benda-Beckmann (2006) at 14.

9 Franz and Keebet von Benda-Beckmann (2006) at 18.

(essentially religious or customary), each on its own conditions and reflecting its own trajectory on the nature of law.

From the point of view of religious groups, however, the perception (and expectation) of law within religious groups often differs greatly from a state-centric one: law in these contexts operates commonly as a 'folk concept'[10] suggesting law's role as a regulator of community conduct, tightly connected to the perpetuation of religious customs.[11] This 'vision' of law largely escapes the confines of the private sphere and has moved to the public one, positing questions on the 'legitimate public expression of what [is] legitimate law'.[12] This is why an actor-oriented analysis of how the private individual exercises (or not) religious rights as an expression of power/agency is necessary though particularly complex for the analysis undertaken here.

There is abundant theoretical and empirical argumentation in contemporary socio-legal scholarship that claims that modern state governance can no longer ignore non-state normative commitments and community affiliations, especially when these highlight the (in)-efficiency of state law.[13] In fact, the more critical strands of this type of scholarship, labeled as 'critical legal pluralism', advance that even apparently marginalized actors (e.g. members of a religious minority community) may contribute to shaping the normative frameworks in which they live.[14] Different categories and types of legal subjects, thus, produce law, as much as official law-making instances. The underlying principle in the case studies offered here is thus that "law arises from, belongs to, and responds to everyone",[15] although in different ways and following varied patterns. Hence, community as well as individual dynamics often supersede and bypass the 'official state law' in an attempt to provide solutions to conflicting normative statements.

10 Maleiha Malik, *Minority Legal Orders in the UK: Minorities, Pluralism and the Law*, British Academy Policy Centre, 2012, at 11.
11 Malik (2012) at 11.
12 Malik (2012) at 16.
13 Chiba's tripartite classification distinguishes in this respect between 'official law', defined as "the legal system authorized by the legitimate authority of a country", 'unofficial law', defined as the legal system which is 'not officially authorized by the official authorities but . . . by the general consensus of a certain circle of people', and of 'legal postulates' understood as 'the system of values and ideals specifically relevant to both official and unofficial law'. The focus in this comparative study on religious diversity frameworks in state-sponsored education relates to Chiba's identified dichotomies between official and unofficial law insofar as religious belief influences education and vice versa. It also engages with Chiba's rules versus postulates dichotomy in the sense that within the sample of case studies explored, the State recognizes only some parts of religious legal systems. Yet the unrecognized parts exercise influence on the ways religious identities are protected in public school systems both de facto as well as de jure. [Cf. Masaji Chiba, 'Three Dichotomies of Law in Pluralism', in Peter Sack and Jonathan Aleck (eds.), *Law and Anthropology*, Aldershot, 1992, 171–180, at 173, 178].
14 Angela Campbell, 'Wives Tales: Reflecting on Research in Bountiful', *Canadian Journal of Law and Society*, 23, 2008, 121–141, at 123.
15 Roderick A. Macdonald, *Lessons of Everyday Law*, Montreal: McGill University Press, 2002, at 8.

The wider question as to whether religious law is indeed law remains of course contested,[16] especially if one prefers a state-centric approach.

From a governance perspective and using a more anthropological understanding of law as both an enabling and a constraining tool,[17] especially in scenarios of normative conflict, religious diversity management models reveal indeed the plural nature of law in relation to individuals and religious communities within multicultural societies. They also unveil the impact of the globalization of law and the evolution towards new forms of diversity governance where law is negotiated both internally and externally, in supra-national settings.[18]

Legal pluralism therefore becomes a relevant analytical tool for a comparative constitutional law analysis: it does not consider 'anything' as law but it pushes the quest for looking at similarities and differences of concepts and rights in a consistent way, while providing a more detailed perspective on differences in content, form and function compared to a strictly state-centered concept.[19] At the same time, it raises controversial and thought-provoking questions on the nature of the State, on sovereignty or on equality of citizens, particularly vis-à-vis claims for exemptions. In sum, it represents a 'juridical response' to growing social diversity.[20]

Scholarly literature premised on modernist foundations and using a methodology that identifies categories of law as fully distinguishable, refers to two types of legal pluralism: first, there is 'weak' pluralism that exists when "the sovereign commands different bodies of law for different groups in the population by incorporating their normative orderings into the central administration of law and courts".[21] This type of pluralism is filtered through the state legal system. 'Strong' pluralism, on the other hand, subscribes to the recognition of all normative orderings, irrespective of mutual recognition.[22] In this context, state law is one of several legal orderings. In both cases, legal (or normative) pluralism is more relevant for an enriched understanding of the application of law, as it extends beyond a statement of the state-centric legal doctrine. It is this bond that brings together the selected three case studies of this project insofar as all three engage with legal pluralism in explicit terms.

16 Franz and Keebet von Benda-Beckmann (2006) at 11.
17 Franz and Keebet von Benda-Beckmann (2006) at 3.
18 Von Benda-Beckmann (2002) at 10.
19 Von Benda-Beckmann (2002) 37–83, at 56.
20 Bryan S. Turner, 'Legal Pluralism: Freedom of Religion, Exemptions and the Equality of Citizens', in R. Bottoni et al. (eds.), *Religious Rules, State Law and Normative Pluralism: A Comparative Overview*, Springer, 2016, 61–73, at 63.
21 Yüksel Sezgin, 'Theorizing Formal Pluralism: Quantification of Legal Pluralism for Spatio-Temporal Analysis', *Journal of Legal Pluralism*, 50, 2004, 101–118, at 102. See also John Griffith, 'What Is Legal Pluralism?' *Journal of Legal Pluralism*, 24, 1986, 1–55.
22 Robert Cover, 'Nomos and Narrative', in M. Minow, M. Ryan and A. Sarat (eds.), *Narrative, Violence and Law*, Ann Arbor: The University of Michigan Press, 1995, 95–172. See also J. Griffiths, 'What Is Legal Pluralism', *Journal of Legal Pluralism*, 24, 1986, at 38–39.

But how much plurality can a legal system manage? The answer to the question is by no means a straightforward one. The expectation from the State is at best to facilitate plural normative interactions, but these movements ought to happen in 'dialectical and iterative interplay'.[23] The solution, therefore, of distinguishing between the public and private sphere in order to safeguard the neutrality of the State (and the public sphere) appears artificial, divisive and subjective.[24]

According to Taylor, when the State fails to protect certain values, it undermines concomitantly individual identity and self-worth.[25] Education (and the rights attached to it), which is the field of application of normative conflicts in this study, as a process stands in its normative dimension against undermining identity and self-worth, though it may succumb to the fault of considering cultural attachments as fixed and/or essentialized.[26]

Another reason to use legal pluralism as a basis towards comparison stems from the observation that in a given legal field, state law and non-state normative orderings are no longer two neatly separated entities.[27] They co-exist and shape each other, but just like the boundaries between state and society, they are blurred. Logically, the next question in this sequence of queries would be who decides how the boundaries are placed each time; in other words, who is the ultimate legal actor. The answer to this question would depend on whether one considers the autonomous individual to be the 'consumer' of law or rather the (globally) interconnected and interdependent individual, in which case he/she decides on a case-by-case basis.

Returning to the issue of normative interactions, in order to negotiate conflict it is useful to explore the extent to which there is only conflict between a religious community's perceptions of 'law' and state law 'sovereignty'[28] or whether, instead, there are also points of interaction and cross-referencing.[29] What both structures – the State and religious legal orders – have in common are their respective substantive norms and a certain institutional order that affects enforcement and change.[30] That being said, it should not be assumed that religious legal orders are uniform: to the contrary, they are plural, plurivocal loaded in many

---

23 Paul Schiff Berman, *Global Legal Pluralism: A Jurisprudence of Law Beyond Borders*, Cambridge University Press, 2014, at 25.
24 Selen A. Ercan, 'Democratizing Identity Politics: A Deliberative Approach to the Politics of Recognition', in Dorota A. Gozdecka and Magdalena Kmak (eds.), *Europe at the Edge of Pluralism*, Intersentia, 2015, 13–26, at 16.
25 Charles Taylor, *Sources of the Self*, Cambridge: Cambridge University Press, 1989, at 27.
26 See the work of Alison Dundes Renteln, *The Cultural Defense*, Oxford University Press, 2004.
27 Chiba (1992) and Sezgin (2004) at 102.
28 I am referring here to both the economic, political and symbolic dimensions of state law significance (i.e. the coercive power to enforce norms). [Cf. Malik (2012) at 22].
29 Malik (2012) refers to findings confirming for instance in the UK the dynamic relationship between religious courts and civil law that do not run in parallel but instead shape and impact each other (At 51).
30 Malik (2012) at 16.

cases with intense asymmetries of power leading to the imposition of solutions deemed to become the 'governing norm'.[31]

The risk present in such a case is that legal pluralism may become a victim of instrumentalization in similar ways that state law itself may be 'used': often for political or moral purposes, it may be manipulated to apply pressure for the recognition of legal orders by the State and may invoke in that context intense debate when it implies the recognition of morally intolerable values (e.g. gender inequality).[32]

On a broader disciplinary scale, far from being widely accepted in legal studies as an intellectual reconceptualization of law on the ground, legal pluralism has challenged the modernity of law on a number of levels: first, it doubted H.L.A Hart's assumption that premodern law was founded on morality and habits, not to forget rationality, while modern law relies on interpretation, recognition and consent.[33] Second, legal pluralism has brought back to the forefront legal uncertainty as a way to de- and re-construct law. Finally, and as importantly, the idea that consent is at the basis of obedience to law has been questioned,[34] with legal pluralism bringing to light conflicts between and within normative orders as the source of both obedience and disobedience towards (State) law. More generally, it has also challenged the conventional division between national and international law, private and public, colonial and post-colonial and even territorial and personal laws. Pushing this process further, when combined with the element of globalization, legal pluralism implies today that not only can non-state laws become transnational (e.g. due to immigration), but they can also co-exist with state law outside conflict and competition,[35] through the use of an emerging methodology better suited to the transnational dynamics of societies.

Within this context, the discussion here engages with the ways that religious normative systems affect official State legal systems, with the assumption that religious identity shapes an important part of the social arena of both individuals and communities and is perceived as existential and particularly powerful. In this framework, however, political interactions also shape legal practices. This is particularly evident in conditions of normative clash, such as those explored within this book. Law's (non)-neutrality (often taking the shape desired by hegemonic

---

31 Expression borrowed from Malik (2012) at 25.
32 Von Benda-Beckmann (2002) at 45.
33 H.L.A. Hart, *The Concept of Law*, Oxford University Press, 1961, at 62, 165, 178.
34 On the point, see Gad Barzilai, 'Beyond Relativism: Where Is the Political Power in Legal Pluralism?', *Theoretical Inquiries in Law*, 9(2), 2008, 395–416 at 402.
35 Twining (2010) at 489 labels this as 'interlegality'. He quotes later (at 495) the example of public reasoning in Indonesia in circumstances where adat, shari'a and state law need to be reconciled: the practice in that context focuses on reasoning towards an acceptable-to-all-parties, negotiated resolution of the conflict. See also in that respect J.R. Bowen, *Islam, Law and Equality in Indonesia: An Anthropology of Public Reasoning*, Cambridge University Press, 2003.

groups), combined with the different narratives of law offered by those with different religious and/or cultural identities, is directly affecting the legitimacy of state and non-state law. In that sense, Ramstedt is justified to call for the use of the term 'law' to refer to state law, as a means to emphasize the hegemonic nature of the State's claims, as opposed to 'normativities' used to describe non-state law.[36] Furthermore, according to Tamanaha, the official State legal systems often adopt a posture of declared neutrality when called to manage co-existing communities with clashing normative orders, at least within a liberal political frame.[37] Legal pluralism risks becoming in some of these cases a tool of control over non-ruling communities, including immigrants, by marginalizing them further,[38] instead of just being a hindrance to state law, as usually portrayed. Barzilai states the examples of Canada, India and Israel to demonstrate how legal pluralism "was aimed to furnish non-ruling communities with some legal rights, while hindering demands for changes to the structure of the political regime".[39] In that respect, the circumstances of clash that arise over competing claims for monopoly between different normative orders are revealing.[40]

For the purposes of this study, normative conflicts are deemed inevitable. State law can still be used though as a comparative criterion to analyze religious diversity frameworks within public education. The aim is to show how a legal pluralist lens of state law influences the content and balancing of the right to religious freedom, the right to equality and the right to education in normative conflicts as they occur in public schools. The degree and type of accommodations that state law makes to other normative orders are the background for this inquiry. In the field of education, as well as elsewhere, religious norms often become a primary source of reference for individuals, despite secularist constitutional arrangements in many States seeking to relegate religious rights to the private sphere. This shows the ineffectiveness in the citizens' lived experience of the presumption that modern state law has completely replaced or displaced their earlier or other forms of legal identity.

As some of the case studies will demonstrate, limiting religious freedom exercise to the private sphere does not have the same resonance in non-Christian

---

36 Cf. Martin Ramstedt, 'Anthropological Perspectives on the Normative and Institutional Recognition of Religion by the Law of the State', in R. Bottoni et al. (eds.), *Religious Rules, State Law and Normative Pluralism: A Comparative Overview*, Springer, 2016, 45–59 at 53.

37 Tamanaha (2010) at 392. Indeed the State may adopt a variety of options in dealing with those clashes: ignorance, condemnation, endorsement without support, absorption into the official state system or aggressively seek to eliminate contrary norms and institutions (Tamanaha (2010) at 393).

38 Barzilai (2008) at 409.

39 Barzilai (2008) at 416.

40 It is worth noting that these clashes may occur both among competing versions within a single type of normative ordering (e.g. human rights and state law) or between co-existing normative orderings (e.g. official legal system and religious or community norms). [Cf. Tamanaha (2010) at 387].

contexts.[41] As 'religion' is such a large part of that personal law construct or imagination or identity, state law just is not always pervasive enough to prevail to the exclusion of the other system. The result is a hybrid reconstruction, as theorized by Ballard,[42] through the concept of the 'skilled cultural navigator', shown in this case for Asians in Britain.

In sum, a legal pluralist inquiry on religious diversity in education offers two significant advantages: first, it is committed to non-state normativities, but second, it is also attentive to state law, particularly through the study of scenarios of conflicts of norms.[43] The reality remains that individuals maintain multiple community affiliations,[44] without necessarily embracing universal normative statements akin to human rights in the same ways.

The methodological proposal here is to bring together the 'hermeneutic circle of law' following a legal pluralist analysis with the linear 'ruler' of law, used under classic comparative constitutional law. They are brought together to give a fuller picture on both the substance of law but also the use that its subjects are making of it, when traveling the circle and crossing the lines.[45] The experience of the law is, in that respect, neither the hegemonic 'myth of rights', nor autonomous, apolitical and neutral.[46] The following salient questions, when studying these normative processes in the realm of religion within public education, are worth asking: what are the rules in each context? Which institutions are engaged in the normative exchange? Which are the prevailing processes? What is ultimately the normative outcome when conflict arises?

The discussion focuses not only on the different types of competing norms but also on the use that individuals, religious communities and other legal actors such as teachers, parents or even international organizations, make of the norms that they prioritize and more specifically the content with which they provide them. The latter point is mostly evident when considering the question of which order the legal subject perceives to be acting upon when resisting or sustaining state law.[47] This inevitably leads and connects to the issue of power: if one accepts that power (and its use) is connected to a community's survival, it is useful to

41 Pascale Fournier, 'Halacha, the Jewish State and the Canadian Agunah: Comparative Law at the Intersection of Religious and Secular Orders', *Canadian Journal of Legal Pluralism*, 65, 2012, 165–204 at 180.

42 Roger Ballard, *Desh Pardesh: The South Asian Presence in Britain*, Hurst and Co Publishers, 1994.

43 Fournier (2012) at 189.

44 Typically, people develop hyphenated identities, such as British-Muslim.

45 The graphic representation of these processes belongs to Martha-Marie Kleinhans and Roderick A. Macdonald, 'What Is Critical Legal Pluralism?' *CJLS/RCDS*, 12(2), Fall 1997, 25–46, at 45.

46 Sarat makes this point in the context of the welfare poor in Austin Sarat, 'The Law Is All Over: Power, Resistance and the Legal Consciousness of the Welfare Poor', *Yale Journal of Law and the Humanities*, 2(2), 1990, Art.6, 343–380 at 346.

47 This is a question pertinently asked in Kleinhans and Macdonald (1997) at 36, 38, 39. This sort of question, however, is tightly related to the critical stream of legal pluralism that focuses on citizens-subject as generators of normativity ("law inventing" as opposed to "law abiding"). This focus is outside the scope of the present comparison.

account for both the negative and positive sides of its use towards the creation of normativity.[48] Power, nevertheless, is also connected to the positioning of any individual, not just communities (e.g. an individual teacher teaching religious education in a specific classroom of a given state). In fact, any legal pluralist analysis needs to be more aware of the fact that individual actors are often behind what is normally presented as institutional forms of law, be they socio-cultural manifestations of law as group structures, including huge international corporations as private entities, state laws in their various manifestations, or human rights organizations and international law bodies.

Digging deeper into the theorization of legal pluralism as a relevant frame and background for comparative constitutional analysis, Barzilai has confirmed the need to account for (political) power as a normative concept.[49] He emphasizes the asymmetrical impact of power in legal pluralist frames, as the driving force of the 'internal' mechanisms of legal systems.[50] He identifies three particularly relevant arenas of action of political power: identity politics, non-ruling communities and neo-liberal globalization.[51] For him, "law figures as a factor in the power relationships of individuals and social classes but [it is] also . . . omnipresent in the very marrow of society". [52] The danger remains that pluralist readings of law often deviate from mere observations of the plurality of legal orders to political statements and attitudes leaning towards assertion of autonomy and suspicion towards the State.[53] The dividing line between a pluralist reading of law with power politics then becomes fuzzy, and, depending on cases, may be required to be factored as an actant in its own right.

But legal pluralism is also inherently connected with multiculturalism insofar as contemporary societies struggle with globalization, labor mobility, immigration flows and their pluralizing effects. The discussion around legal pluralism is, therefore, connected to a deeper cause: the perceived or actual erosion of shared values and the threatened or actual fragmentation of the public sphere, both leading to the decline of shared forms of citizenship.[54] Particularly relevant here is the question of the division between public and private realms of religious belonging and exercise already mentioned. Liberal societies and their governments rely on this binary differentiation and claim from the State and its law to act as a 'neutral' presence within society for the common good. But what if state law is seen as an extension of one community (normally, but not always, the demographic majority) or is indeed inseparable from one religious normative ordering

---

48 For more on this nuanced point see Kleinhans and Macdonald (1997) at 40.
49 Barzilai (2008).
50 Barzilai (2008) at 398.
51 Barzilai (2008) at 399.
52 Robert W. Gordon, 'Critical Legal Histories', *Stanford Law Review*, 36, 1984, 57, 109.
53 St-Hilaire (2015), 115–132, at 128.
54 Bryan S. Turner and James T. Richardson, 'The Future of Legal Pluralism', in A. Possamai, James T. Richardson and Bryan S. Turner (eds.), *The Sociology of Shari'a: Case Studies from Around the World*, Springer, 2015, 305–313 at 311–312.

(e.g. in theocracies) and/or is not structured according to the public/private separation?[55]

The legal systems examined here (Israel, South Africa and England) illustrate some of the ways that the exchange and constant normative (re)negotiation between state and society happens while adopting variations of legal pluralist models. The aim of such exchange is predominantly an accommodative one,[56] although not always exclusively so. Decision-makers, therefore, need to revert to a wider range of norms in order to manage plurality: their decisions might carry more variation, while at the same time guaranteeing higher rates of participation from the various communities involved and concerned.[57]

The recurring counter-arguments to the use of legal pluralism for legal analysis and diversity management purposes stress the risk of persistence of illiberal social practices of the law that include the silencing of certain voices within those communities, the toleration of 'abhorrent' or 'intolerable' and 'harmful' normativity and ultimately the side-stepping or avoidance of state-power. Some of these conflicts are shaped through both 'contestation from within',[58] with explicit power hierarchies in action, as well as contestation from the State. Interestingly, in this context, the notion of standards of tolerance by each community is being increasingly replaced by considerations of harm. This 're-labeling' is not without implications: the acceptability of a certain religious (or cultural) practice begs huge questions as to what 'counts' as harm. In a liberal context with no fixed/ imposable conception of the 'good life', juxtaposed with the inadmissibility of debates about fundamental values, harm becomes a new frame for reflecting on pluri-normativity,[59] occasionally blocking the wider vista.

Ultimately, and on a broader policy level, the social efficacy of law is increasingly problematized due to those 'contestations': H.L.A. Hart questioned the nature of law by claiming that the legal nature of a norm is determined by the degree of adherence and recognition that it generates.[60] Earlier, Eugen Ehrlich

---

55 Tamanaha (2010) at 399.
56 Sezgin (2004) at 103. There is a further division between formal and informal plurality in deep legal pluralist scenarios: formal plurality refers to the State's formal response to the reality of state-law pluralism while informal plurality describes situations where the State acquiesces to non-state norms and institutions without formal acknowledgement.
57 Paul Schiff Berman, 'Non-State Lawmaking Through the Lens of Global Pluralism', in Michael A. Helfand (ed.), *Negotiating State and Non-State Law: The Challenge of Global and Local Legal Pluralism*, Cambridge University Press, 2015, 15–40 at 27.
58 Expression borrowed from Judith Resnik, 'Living Their Legal Commitments: Paideic Communities, Courts and Robert Cover (an Essay on Racial Segregation at Bob Jones University, Patrilineal Membership Rules, Veiling and Jurisgenerative Practices)' 17 *Yale Journal of Law and the Humanities*, 17, 2005, 27.
59 For further analysis on this point see Benjamin L. Berger, 'Polygamy and the Predicament of Contemporary Criminal Law', Research Paper Series on Comparative Research in Law and Political Economy, Osgoode Hall Law School, Research Paper No. 36/2012, available at http://ssrn.com/abstract=2081142, at 18–20. Berger adds the question of the magnitude or seriousness of the harm to the discussion.
60 Hart (1961).

had, however, introduced the notion of 'law in action' by explaining how the law that was effective at the borders of the Austro-Hungarian Empire differed from the actual law of the Empire.[61] He argued further the existence of diverse customary laws outside and even prior to the coming into being of the nation-state. Ehrlich's discussion of law was not centered on the bureaucrat/state law relation but on that between the normal citizen and state law, and thus was more anthropological than Hart's. His analysis suggested that a rule does not qualify as law merely by virtue of being adhered to.[62]

Reflecting the same concern, legal sociology has theorized the nature of law on the basis of its functions: law as an instrument in the resolution of disputes may be suggestive of a legal nature, though not in absolute terms; law as a social order tool is also conducive to recognition of a norm as 'law'; finally, the recognition of a norm as law by the State is identified, although there is note of the insufficiency of this criterion.[63] The critique against these assertions is vast, to the point that the search for the answer to the question of what counts as law may need to be abandoned. John Gardner states, in that respect, "law is not, 'whatever resolves disputes' but a special way of resolving disputes".[64] Tamanaha adds – at a particular point of his understanding of this concept – that law is whatever members of a community regard as law,[65] with the caveat that the binary distinction between legal and illegal may not be useful in all contexts.[66] These questions regarding the basis of authority of the law are further stressed and problematized in a legal pluralist context,[67] but while they are important, they relate only indirectly to the analysis provided here.

Another stream of analysis approaches the phenomenon of legal pluralism in contemporary societies from an angle critical of modern conceptualizations of state law. Here the key argument is that territorially defined states are no longer the sole source of legal norms, not that they ever enjoyed exclusivity. A new, fluid norm development track is developing in the global legal arena that acknowledges multiple community affiliations, particularly relevant in the light of current

---

61 Eugen Ehrlich, *Fundamental Principles of the Sociology of Law*, Harvard University Press, 1936. Hart was mainly looking, however, at the tension between state law and potential 'other' influences on bureaucrats.
62 Ralf Michaels, 'What Is Non-State Law? A Primer', in Michael A. Helfand (ed.), *Negotiating State and Non-State Law: The Challenge of Global and Local Legal Pluralism*, Cambridge University Press, 2015, 41–58, at 50.
63 Michaels (2015) at 52.
64 John Gardner, *Law as a Leap of Faith*, Oxford University Press, 2012, at 289.
65 Brian Tamanaha, 'A Non-Essentialist Version of Legal Pluralism', *Journal of Law and Society*, 27, 2000, 296.
66 For example, in Islamic law there are five layers of legality: obligatory, recommended, neutral, abominable and sinful. (Cf. Michaels (2015) at 54.)
67 For Max Weber, the sovereignty of the State forms the basis of authority of law, for Hans Kelsen it is the *grudnorm*, while for Eugen Ehrlich, it is tradition. For more on this point, see Turner and Richardson (2015) at 307.

migratory movements of populations in the European continent and beyond.[68] As Berman argues, however, it is still difficult to ignore the fact that territorial jurisdiction creates political and social identities.[69] The challenge remains to explore how the notion of identity and religious difference can be 'spatialized' in ways that address the complexity of these two seemingly opposing processes.[70]

The role of the State in this context is still essential and depends on how it positions itself in the debate on the need to create demarcating lines between 'us' and 'them'. The process of line drawing, very prominently present in public education systems, involves, apart from power, the questioning of the extent to which the State (just like law) retains its capacity to reflect its conception of membership to the actual community in all its diversity on the ground[71] and at what cost this happens, if at all.

2 The relationship of international and comparative law with legal pluralism

International law, contrary to its portrayed one-dimensionality and the defensive approach on the question as to whether it constitutes 'real' law, is at present well situated in disciplinary terms to engage in dialogue with socio-legal scholarship. Sally Engle Merry notes the gaps in our understanding of the workings of International Law around three important aspects: the study of the dynamics of power (and agency) among legal actors and regimes, the processes of giving meaning to international legal provisions and to 'legal consciousness'[72] and finally the impact of social structures and relationships on informal social processes (e.g. shaming).[73] Similar to state law, international law is constituted in a vast variety of ways. This is particularly evident in the case of human rights conventions and their implementation. As international law 'merges' with national law, states but also non-state actors and communities give to the law and norms at question

---

68 See indicatively, Paul Schiff Berman, *Global Legal Pluralism: A Jurisprudence of Law Beyond Borders*, Cambridge University Press, 2012.

69 Berman (2012) at 63. Quoting Richard T. Ford, Berman notes that "[j]urisdictions define the identity of the people that occupy them".

70 See Austin Sarat and Thomas R. Kearns, 'The Unsettled States of Human Rights: An Introduction', in Austin Sarat and Thomas R. Kearns (eds.), *Human Rights: Concepts, Contests, Contingencies*, Ann Arbor: University of Michigan Press, 2001, at 1 and 13 that argue in favor of a new understanding of culture that takes account of the internal plurality of cultures and their fragmentation.

71 Peter J. Spiro, 'The Boundaries of Cosmopolitan Pluralism', *Wayne Law Review*, 51, 2005, 1261, 1264.

72 The concept of legal consciousness can be defined as "all the ideas about the nature, function and operation of law held by anyone in society at a given time". (Cf. David Trubek, 'Where the Action Is: Critical Legal Studies and Empiricism', *Stanford Law Review*, 36, 1984, 575, 592).

73 Sally Engle Merry, 'International Law and Sociolegal Scholarship: Toward a Spatial Global Legal Pluralism', in M.A. Helfand (ed.), *Negotiating State and Non-State Law: The Challenge of Global and Legal Pluralism*, Cambridge University Press, 2015, 59–80 at 61.

their shape and meaning. Merry pertinently notes that the more communities are fragmented and fluid, operating through networks rather than territories, as, for example, are contemporary immigration movements, the more the law that governs them becomes plural. This plurality is also inherent within international law, especially private international law, due to its ordering and grounding.[74] She further adds that within transnational legal processes this is particularly the case, given that compliance with international law depends on the interactions among international legal actors,[75] with the involvement of individuals, too.

Comparative law backs certain types of similar inquiries by its traditional outlook on the 'diffusion' of norms:[76] the vocabulary of receptions, transplants, transfers, contaminations, migration or transnational and transfrontier mobility of law all suggest precisely that.[77] As a sub-discipline of law but at the same time as a methodology,[78] comparative law is gradually considering how it can contribute towards the creation of 'pluralist legal minds'.[79] This is a process that, among other purposes, can be used as a pathway to better understand one's own set of constitutional values, through analogy, distinction and contrast.[80]

In parallel, Roger Cotterrell has explicitly stated that comparative law can be useful in challenging the inevitability of legal arrangements, in increasing the appreciation of difference, and cultivating knowledge of the social world through the study of its legal aspects but also to express "the awakening of an international legal consciousness".[81] In sum, it is not just a question of theory and/or method but as much an exercise with ethical and political implications.[82] Here,

---

74 Merry (2015) at 62.

75 Merry (2015) at 64. For a resonating analysis of this point see, Harold Hongju Koh, Transnational Legal Processes, *Nebraska Law Review*, 75, 1996, 181, 184.

76 Ran Hirschl, quoting Mary Ann Glendon's *Rights Talk: The Impoverishment of Political Discourse*, 1999 at 158, refers to 'a brisk international traffic in ideas about rights'. (Cf. Ran Hirschl, 'The Rise of Comparative and Constitutional Law: Thoughts on Substance and Method', *Indian Journal of Constitutional Law*, 2008, 11–37 at 11).

77 Sean Patrick Donlan, 'Everything Old Is New Again: Stateless Law, the State of the Law Schools and Comparative Legal/Normative History', in Shauna Van Praagh and Helge Dedek (eds.), *Stateless Law: Evolving Boundaries of a Discipline*, Routledge, 2015, 187–200, at 188.

78 Gunter Frankenberg, *Comparative Law as Critique*, Elgar, 2016, notes at 41 that a narrow conception of comparative law as method runs the risk of limiting the ethical and political considerations that are connected, implied or produced in the context of studying the foreign.

79 See, for example, Jaakko Husa, 'Turning the Curriculum Upside Down: Comparative Law as an Educational Too for Constructing Pluralistic Legal Mind', *German Law Journal*, 2009, 913.

80 Hirschl (2008) at 12.

81 Roger Cotterrell, *Law, Culture and Society: Legal Ideas in the Mirror of Social Theory*, Ashgate: Farnham, 2006.

82 Frankenberg (2016), at ix. One may consider here as an illustration the global expansion of judicial power and how increasingly judges are called upon to decide on issues related to primordial collective identity questions or national-building processes (Cf. Hirschl (2008) at 17).

too, theory and practice go hand in hand and have multiple impacts on each other in constantly changing situational contexts.

In addition, contemporary comparative law is no longer exclusively after the extraction of universally valid legal principles,[83]nor is it seeking 'perceptual and conceptual tidiness' through similarities among systems.[84] It seems increasingly concerned with questions such as whether and how law has a social context that needs to be taken into account or whether law is able to create its own context.[85] It has also become more aware of the presence of difference and does not treat it as a problem, but rather as an asset in reaching more sophisticated conclusions about the nature of law as well as practical solutions in scenarios of conflict. Comparisons that in previous times defied conventional orthodoxy in the sense that they were focusing on systems apparently too remote from each other, now have been attracting attention simply because norms move fast across jurisdictions and in many, often complex, directions. Comparatists are also affording 'equal discursive dignity' to legal traditions beyond the Euro-American axis, like Upendra Baxi called for.[86] The main challenge, however, in this movement stands in the difficulty to map (and reconcile) localized tendencies with the globalization of law.[87]

Without neglecting the reality that comparative legal studies are 'political' in the sense that they produce political effects,[88] it is worth investigating critically the "unwritten story of comparative law's participation in governance".[89] Often accused of eclecticism, the discipline is admittedly facing difficulty to engage with the socio-political implications of legal comparisons from a strictly legal perspective.[90] But in conditions of globalization, it is highly questionable whether it is still possible to maintain Dworkin's assertion that there is "one right answer" to all legal conflicts.[91] Logically, if one accepts that law is indeed political, it becomes

---

83 Roderick Munday, 'Accounting for an Encounter', in Pierre Legrand and Roderick Munday (eds.), *Comparative Legal Studies: Traditions and Transitions*, Cambridge University Press, 2003, 3–28 at 3.
84 Frankenberg (2016) at 11.
85 Munday (2003) at 8, with references to the work of Gunter Teubner, *Law as an Autopoietic System*, Oxford: Blackwell, 1993.
86 See also Werner Menski, 'Beyond Europe', in Esin Orucu and David Nelken, *Comparative Law: A Handbook*, Hart Publishing, 2007, 189–216.
87 Munday (2003) at 12. Hirschl points out that this kind of tension is in the image of the basic tension in modern law schools' mission: a vocational training institution as opposed to a locus of research and reflection with the aim to explain (Cf. Hirschl (2008) at 29).
88 Alan Watson aptly remarks: "Law is power. Law is politics. Law is politics in the sense that persons who have the political power determine which persons or bodies create the law, how the validity of the law is assessed, and how the legal order is to operate". [Cf. Al. Watson, *Roman Law and Comparative Law*, Athens, GA: University of Georgia Press, 1991, at 97.] Again, the doctrinal separation of law and politics remains highly contested (Cf. Hirschl (2008) at 31).
89 Munday (2003) at 19.
90 Hirschl (2008) makes a similar point at 30.
91 Ronald Dworkin, *Taking Rights Seriously*, Cambridge: Harvard University Press, 1978, as quoted in Frankenberg (2016) at 26.

equally problematic to insist that "neutral and apolitical legal reasoning could resolve charged controversies".[92] To further complicate the matter, the possibility that law may be treated as a 'dependent variable' connected to ideology, strategic choice or hegemonic interest is far from being widely acknowledged.[93]

Yet engaging with the seemingly 'different' is one of the preconditions of any comparison, and as such applied comparative legal studies are inherently engaged with alterity, to the point of giving priority to 'difference' over sameness.[94] As much as the future of comparative law seems fluid, it is hard to dispute that research in this area is now more and more concerned with multilateral legal developments, as opposed to its prior uni-directionality.[95]

Returning to the political dimension of comparative law, it becomes gradually clearer how law as a 'political tactic' illustrates power arguments,[96] creating geographies of injustice.[97] It is as clear that, when comparing, it is generally unsafe to assume that the State is neutral in matters of belief, organization or language, for example, [98] or even that in many cases it represents the primary source of normativity.[99] Against this complexity, there is not one single method for comparative law, especially in light of the diverse constitutional settings and policies regulating religious matters. Leaving out, however, one's consideration of history, mores and cultural elements shows ignorance of the fact that legal rules are connected, dependent and constructed upon the local dimensions of the law, where context is crucial.[100] Considering law together with culture (and by extension also religion) in comparative legal studies is a way for the discipline "to modernize

---

92 Mark Kelman, *A Guide to Critical Legal Studies*, Cambridge: Harvard University Press, 1987, as quoted in Frankenberg (2016) at 25.

93 See, for example, Mark Tushnet, 'Political Power and Judicial Power: Some Observations on the Their Relation', *Fordham Law Review* 75, 2006, 755; or Adrian Vermeule, *Judging Under Uncertainty: An Institutional Theory of Legal Interpretation*, Harvard University Press, 2006.

94 Pierre Legrand, 'The Same and the Different', in Pierre Legrand and Roderick Munday (eds.), *Comparative Legal Studies: Traditions and Transitions*, Cambridge University Press, 2003, 240–311.

95 For the neo-colonial argument of this movement, see Upendra Baxi, 'The Colonialist Heritage', in Pierre Legrand and Roderick Munday (eds.), *Comparative Legal Studies: Traditions and Transitions*, Cambridge University Press, 2003, 46–75, at 49 et seq.

96 I am thinking here of Baxi's argument of law as "the convenience of the powerful" in a colonial and post-colonial perspective [Cf. Baxi (2003) at 56].

97 Term borrowed from Baxi (2003) at 59.

98 Patrick H. Glenn, 'The Nationalist Heritage', in Pierre Legrand and Roderick Munday (eds.), *Comparative Legal Studies: Traditions and Transitions*, Cambridge University Press, 2003, 76–99, at 88. Contrast this point with Rodolfo Sacco's point that: "With regard to the unification of the law, comparative science is neutral" [Cf. Rodolfo Sacco, 'One Hundred Years of Comparative Law', *Tulane Law Review*, 75, 2000, 1159, at 1162].

99 Glenn (2003) at 95–96 gives illustration of this through the examples of Islamic, Hindu, Confucian and adat normativity.

100 Michele Graziadei, 'The Functionalist Heritage', in Pierre Legrand and Roderick Munday (eds.), *Comparative Legal Studies: Traditions and Transitions*, Cambridge University Press, 2003, 100–127, at 110.

itself, to come of age, by moving away from its oft-repeated commitment to positivism",[101] admitting the difficulty, nevertheless, to generalize. It also represents a better chance for law and comparative analysis to reflect on how other sources of knowledge, such as the aspiration and experiences of individuals and groups, inform the content of normative provisions.[102]

So, while law may be the product of local conditions,[103] the global phenomenon of migration of legal systems (and people) makes comparative law uniquely placed to reflect on difference. Each culture is largely the product of its own historical experiences and development, but as Graziadei rightfully reminds us "collective identities are established through interaction with others".[104]

In understanding and embracing 'difference', comparative law seeks therefore the understanding of the 'inner' perspective of a given legal system, particularly when aiming at exploring the conscious actions and inactions of individual actors, navigating within that system,[105] but also the unspoken assumptions that motivate legal actions in a given society.[106] Taking the process of observation of both articulated and less explicit assumptions a step further, this 'otherness' or 'alterity' potentially adds another task on the list of aims of comparative law: that of appreciating the depth of differences between legal traditions,[107] including by challenging preconceptions, stereotypes or biases. Legrand is siding with this mission of comparative law when he insists on privileging alterity while arguing that 'law is culture'.[108] After all, law is inherently connected with meaning, identity and communities. And while the risk of relativism is not avoided when one adopts a vision of comparative law as the study of 'difference', it is the context and purpose of comparison that guides us in deciding whether it is more relevant to focus on similarities rather than differences.[109] As the methodology of comparative law,

101 Pierre Legrand, 'John Henry Merryman and Comparative Legal Studies: A Dialogue', *The American Journal of Comparative Law*, 47, 1999, 3, at 65.
102 Frankenberg (2016) at 229.
103 Graziadei (2003, at 119) among others makes the point that law as a local product is linked to the categorization of legal systems into legal families. Alan Watson's *Legal Transplants*, 2nd ed., Athens, GA: University of Georgia Press, 1993 argues further that law is borrowed because it is not always rooted in local conditions and is not in touch with current needs.
104 Graziadei (2003) at 122, his footnote 75.
105 See William Ewald, 'Legal History and Comparative Law', *Zeitschrift fuer Europäisches Privatrecht*, 1999, at 553.
106 For a fuller argument, see indicatively James Q. Whitman, 'Enforcing Civility and Respect: Three Societies', *Yale Law Journal*, 109, 2009, 1387.
107 James Q. Whitman, 'The Neo-Romantic Turn', in Pierre Legrand and Roderick Munday (eds.), *Comparative Legal Studies: Traditions and Transitions*, Cambridge University Press, 2003, 312–344, at 326.
108 See Pierre Legrand, 'The Impossibility of Legal Transplants', *Maastricht Journal of European and Comparative Law*, 1997, 111–124 at 124; Pierre Legrand, *Fragments on Law-as-Culture*, Deventer: W.E.J. Tjeenk Willink, 1999.
109 David Nelken, 'Comparatists and Transferability', in Pierre Legrand and Roderick Munday (eds.), *Comparative Legal Studies: Traditions and Transitions*, Cambridge University Press, 2003, 437–466, at 442. See also Rudolf B. Schlesinger, 'The Past and Future of Comparative Law', *The American Journal of Comparative Law*, 1995, 477, at 477 that posits that the future belongs to 'integrative Comparative law', combining 'contractive' and 'contrastive' terms.

and the debates surrounding it, represent evidence of one's motivations when comparing, comparative law can now be considered as a 'relational practice'.[110]

In the present case, where the center of gravity is placed on religious diversity in education, the study of 'difference' takes priority insofar as ontologically and conceptually the right to (religious) 'difference' may be subject to varied legal interpretations and policies. To be clear, the right to religious freedom in public schools merits protection not merely as a human rights normative statement, sourced from domestic and international legal provisions. It also deserves protection because existing differences require protection on the level of the individual, just like they deserve equivalent protection on the level of legal traditions.

But where does the right to 'difference' stop?[111] And where should it stop if we take note and account of the ways that law is occasionally used as part of a strategy by both individuals and groups to illustrate the changing dynamics of society? An additional argument in favor of an approach to comparative law stressing difference that stretches beyond the ideological coherence between the frame (comparative law) and the content (right to religious difference) of the present analysis would argue that stressing differences may be more conducive to the empowerment of weaker and more vulnerable religious or broader social groups.[112] A study on the range of variations on religious diversity legal schemes in public schools, particularly when juxtaposed to other human rights, such as equality or the right to education, sheds more light on the multiple effects of law on religious individuals and entire communities, if nothing else, at least to show how the lines of inclusion and exclusion are not naturally given.[113] The axis of inquiry stands therefore to be fixed on equality and (the right to) differential treatment, with underlying consideration on the limits of claiming protection for being different.

On this last point, the stream of scholarship that started with sociological jurisprudence[114] to move on to legal realism and reach legal/normative pluralism, reminds us that law is 'a practical matter of balancing, negotiating and managing competing political visions, ideals and outcomes'.[115] Law is not universal in

---

110 Munday (2003) at 20.
111 The same question is asked in Nelken (2003) at 445.
112 Lawrence Rosen, 'Beyond Compare', in Pierre Legrand and Roderick Munday (eds.), *Comparative Legal Studies: Traditions and Transitions*, Cambridge University Press, 2003, 493–510, at 495.
113 Rosen (2003) at 505. In that respect, the study of normative conflicts involving state law and religious normativities, stems from the acceptance that individuals and groups compete for resources and a favorable (to them) distribution of resources (Cf. Michele Graziadei, 'State Norms, Religious Norms and Claims for Plural Normativity Under Democratic Constitutions', in R. Bottoni et al. (eds.), *Religious Rules, State Law and Normative Pluralism: A Comparative* Overview, Springer, 2016, 29–43 at 34.
114 See indicatively Roscoe Pound, 'Scope and Purpose of Sociological Jurisprudence (Part I)', *Harvard Law Review*, 24, 1911, 591.
115 David Kennedy, 'The Methods and the Politics', in Pierre Legrand and Roderick Munday (eds.), *Comparative Legal Studies: Traditions and Transitions*, Cambridge University Press, 2003, 345–433, at 348.

its ideals, as the testimonies of comparison between the Chinese or the Islamic or Hindu legal traditions with the Western ones demonstrate.[116] It has therefore become more difficult for contextual legal comparison to escape entirely ideological debates on the aim of the comparison.[117]

a The value of difference in comparative law and human rights

Pierre Legrand describes 'difference' in comparative law as 'polymorphous' and as "an assertion of being".[118] He also considers it as an "empowering feature" on which comparative legal studies may build a deeper understanding of and among legal cultures.

When stressing the performative features of law, emphasis is placed on the cultivation and promotion of difference in terms that challenge the Platonic, Kantian or even Rawlsian interpretations of difference as inferior, pathologic or negative.[119] The comparative analysis that follows will be accordingly premised on the starting point that 'difference' is not necessarily a hindrance to emancipation or empowerment not only in the methodology of the analysis but also in the discussion of human rights affected in the exercise of religious freedom(s) in public education.[120] Moving away, thus, from a presumption of similarity, the aim is to explore the space that law lays out for religious difference in various settings, ultimately showing how it partakes in religion and vice versa. So, if there is indeed a 'hidden' agenda in the comparison of religious diversity legal frameworks in public schools of the countries selected, it would be precisely to perceive the 'Other' law as a partner, rather than some kind of adversary or enemy, despite comparative law's imperfect methodologies and theorization.

The multiplying effects of the comparisons that follow match the overarching priority to alterity, as already mentioned, as the preferred ground for discussion because it shows that "whatever conclusion [the comparative study of law] comes to must relate to the management of difference not to the abolition of it".[121] Additionally, accepting that individuals may engage with and embrace more than one legal culture in our time, the study of legal culture should explore social differentiation within contextualized comparisons in parallel terms to legal pluralism.

---

116 Kennedy (2003) at 389.
117 See however Rudolf B. Schlesinger (ed.), *Formation of Contracts: A Study of the Common Core of Legal Systems*, Dobbs-Ferry: Oceana, 1968; or Rodolfo Sacco, 'Legal Formants: A Dynamic Approach to Comparative Law', *The American Journal of Comparative Law*, 39, 1991, 1 that both claim 'objectivity' and 'neutrality' in this respect.
118 Legrand (2003) at 241.
119 Legrand (2003) at 257.
120 One may appreciate the anti-mainstream character of this approach at least in a European context. Ian Ward notes: "it is undeniable . . . that in the European scenario, comparative law, at both micro and macro levels is being used as a means of effecting sameness and suppressing difference" [Cf. Ian Ward, 'The Limits of Comparativism: Lessons from UK-EC', *Maastricht Journal of European and Comparative Law*, 2, 1995, 23 at 31].
121 Geertz (1983) at 215–216.

What is expected from such comparisons is a 'visualization' of relationships among individuals, groups and concepts, which will surely emerge as complex and multilayered.[122] 'Official portraits' of legal systems that only represent the state-sanctioned versions of how a legal system operates are as such incomplete.[123]

In sum, the purpose of the comparison in this instance is to compare laws as social phenomena: this aim is mirroring Max Rheinstein's writing in the late 1930s that treated comparative law as a functional comparison of legal rules accepting the broader social functions of law.[124] More specifically, among the many possible aims of comparative law,[125] this study will attempt to provide some perspectives that can contribute to a better understanding of the power of legal cultures while explaining the legal development of religious freedoms in public schools. On a more holistic level, the aim is also to use legal aspects of religious diversity in education to connect them with aspects of the social practices, not usually explored and exposed in legal studies. To do so, the focus will be not just on positive legal rules but also on official action and social practices that give meaning to norms in the experience of individuals and the groups to which they belong. In dogmatic terms (and to fulfill the aims stated), it is assumed that law does not create and lead to an independent discourse, in autopoietic terms.[126] Instead, finding the 'social music' of law[127] in each context transforms comparative law into an attempt towards cross-cultural communication.[128]

Consideration and analysis of legal materials beyond official legal texts is mandated in the form of academic writings or arguments sourced from empirical observations in order to bring the comparison closer to the ground but also to fulfill comparative law's perspective as a relational inquiry in how law is used and communicated by actors who put the legal system in motion on a daily basis.

Yet any attempt to compare the terms described earlier is not without significant impediments: a legal system is far from a monolithic entity but instead a polyvocal one, comprised of infinite elements such as actors, institutions and concepts.[129] There is furthermore the puzzling methodological inquiry about what

---

122 Mitchel De S.-O.L' E. Lasser, 'The Question of Understanding', in Pierre Legrand and Roderick Munday (eds.), *Comparative Legal Studies: Traditions and Transitions*, Cambridge University Press, 2003, 197–239, at 205.

123 Lasser (2003) at 208, echoing the 'law in the books' versus 'law in action' dichotomy.

124 Max Rheinstein, 'Teaching Comparative Law', *University of Chicago Law Review*, 5, 1938, 617, at 619 and 622 as quoted in Roger Cotterrell, 'Comparatists and Sociology', in Pierre Legrand and Roderick Munday (eds.), *Comparative Legal Studies: Traditions and Transitions*, Cambridge University Press, 2003, 131–153, at 133.

125 For an overview of these aims see Cotterrell (2003) at 134–135.

126 Gunther Teubner, 'Legal Irritants: Good Faith in British Law or How Unifying Law Ends Up in New Differences', *Modern Law Review*, 61, 1998, 11–32.

127 Term borrowed from Bernhard Grossfeld, 'Comparatists and Languages', in Pierre Legrand and Roderick Munday (eds.), *Comparative Legal Studies: Traditions and Transitions*, Cambridge University Press, 2003, 154–194, at 168.

128 Grossfeld (2003) at 186.

129 Lasser (2003) at 213.

belongs 'inside' the studied system(s) and what remains 'outside'. Transnational legal processes precisely challenge the dichotomy of the domestic and the foreign, and comparative law is called upon to address the fuzziness of this dividing line.[130]

A third (recurring) obstacle to a convincing legal comparison lies with comparatists' own subjectivity: a comparison requires methodological justification. In the present study, the comparison between Israel, South Africa and the UK is warranted by a two-layered justification: first, all three legal systems have devised patterns of official recognition of non-state law relevant for religious communities in their own individual terms. Second, as the aim is to focus on comparing legal models of religious diversity in public school systems (with the connected intention of inquiring on the legal validity of a right to difference), these cases represent three distinct options that choose to privilege within public schools either the right to equality, that to religious freedom or finally that to education respectively, as not only a means to manage religious diversity in public education but also to deal with conflicts of human rights on the basis of religious identity. In other words, the clear motive of the study is to observe religious diversity patterns in school as a means to preserve diversity and pluralism in increasingly super-diverse socio-legal environments.[131]

The final major concern in adopting a cultural studies approach to legal comparison stems from the questions related to the kinds of sources that can be used as indicators of the measure of comparison. As formal legal texts are insufficient to highlight the patterns of interaction between the judicial system and its users, Lasser's suggestion is "to forge relationships with prior comparative analyses, with the objects of analysis, with other disciplines".[132] This interdisciplinary outlook is designed to fill the gaps, which in the present case would refer to sociology and anthropology of law. Yet, this last concern does not have a golden rule as a response, apart perhaps from one's genuine attempt to reach a 'deep contextually embedded judgement'.[133]

As for human rights, legal scholarship has mostly focused on States, institutions and to some extent social movements, when attempting to explain the normative change relating to the spread and effect of human rights.[134] The connection between comparative law and human rights may not be the obvious one here: the use of comparative law in the context of this study is not to argue that a particular

---

130 See indicatively James Gordley, 'Comparative Legal Research: Its Function in the Development of Harmonized Law', *The American Journal of Comparative Law*, 43, 1995, 555 arguing in favor of a 'trasnational legal science'.

131 The consonance with Pierre Legrand's frame and arguments is clear here.

132 Lasser (2003) at 235.

133 Lasser (2003) at 236.

134 See indicatively Margaret E. Keck and Kathryn Sikking, *Activists Beyond Borders: Advocacy Networks in International Politics*, Cornell University Press, 1998; Sanjeev Khagram, James V. Riker and Kathryn Sikkink (eds.), *Restructuring World Politics: Transnational Social Movements*, University of Minnesota Press, 2002; or Thomas Risse-Kappen, Steve C. Ropp and Kathryn Sikkink (eds.), *The Power of Human Rights: International Norms and Domestic Change*, Cambridge University Press, 1999.

normative interpretation of a right captures a universally valid interpretation.[135] Conversely, it posits that context shapes content, including in human rights and particularly so in conditions of conflict among human rights. So, the analysis proposes to look more closely at the use of some of the human rights explicitly contained in international law to examine how their meaning and content is shaped in their daily practice, relying implicitly on the 'legal consciousness' of right-holders and the complexity of their domestic implementation.

This sort of inquiry draws to some extent from anthropological scholarship, especially when it examines the conflicts that occur as a result of different conceptions of the permissible and the impermissible, the tolerable and the intolerable within the same social field. [136] The 'heritage' of legal anthropology brings to this discussion three essential points: first, the hierarchy among legal systems is not always clear: in most cases,[137] normative systems co-exist within the same legal field. Second, the interaction between systems is bi-directional, often multilateral: each contributes to shaping the other. Third, our understanding of a 'legal system' needs to be broadened to include non-official normative orderings, even within highly industrialized societies and states.[138] These directions are particularly relevant in the study of religious communities and their ongoing tensions with the State and its authorities and illustrate the natural affinities between comparative law and legal pluralist methodology.

Testing the methodological limits of human rights by looking beyond international human rights treaties and the pronouncements of international courts taken together with the implicit assumption that law does not reside only in the acts of state-sanctioned bodies and is no longer the exclusive privilege arising out of state sovereignty (if it ever was),[139] one can be led to the conclusion that a narrow view of how law operates transnationally is no longer sufficient in the context of present discourses about legal pluralism and comparative law. The study of the processes of international norm development also offers accounts of overlapping transnational jurisdictional assertions by states, international bodies, NGOs, religious communities and individuals, not to mention transnational terrorists or

---

135 For an illustration of this line of argument, see Christopher McCrudden, 'Judicial Comparativism and Human Rights', in David Nelken and Esin Örücü (eds.), *Comparative Law: A Handbook*, Hart Publishing, 2007, 371–398, at 371.

136 To illustrate the content of a legal pluralist analysis see, for example, Gunter Teubner, 'The Two Faces of Janus: Rethinking Legal Pluralism', *Cardozo Law Review*, 13, 1992, 1443, where he notes: "[L]egal pluralism is at the same time both: social norms and legal rules, law and society, formal and informal, rule-oriented and spontaneous".

137 See Masaji Chiba (ed.), *Asian Indigenous Law: In Interaction with Received Law*, London: KPI, 1986.

138 All three points are drawn from Berman (2012) at 47.

139 While there is a degree of oversimplification in this point, non-state norm creation is not a new phenomenon, but as Berman argues, it is a growing branch in international law scholarship, conducive in the longer run to the reclassification of international law itself. [Cf. Berman (2012) at 51–52].

networks of activists.[140] Clashes of normativities are also not fully explored within international and comparative law, and this is where there is potential for further conceptualization of conflict within a diversity management context.

If we, therefore, accept that legal systems are both autonomous but also porous and permeable, as Sally Falk Moore suggests,[141] we are not denying state law its coercive power, but instead are taking into account the multiple sites of normative authority in need of management, without considering them as problematic per se. The methodological implication of such an approach is the need for an empirical study of statements of authority. Yet, on the individual level that may not be entirely realistic since individuals rarely 'speak' or leave documents outlining their intentions and the extent to which they are treated as binding in practice.

Within a comparative legal analysis, there is also an evident trap that one must avoid and that Silvio Ferrari pertinently has put elsewhere:[142] we should not ask "what is the State legal system that grants citizens the best chance to live their lives according to their religious (or non-religious) convictions". Instead, we should aim to inquire about what a legal system can do to give its citizens the opportunity to live according to these convictions without resulting in segregation or jeopardizing social cohesion. Traditional human rights theory would call at this point for a dual protection of individual as well as collective rights to meet this particular challenge. Such recognition, though not universally accepted, presupposes the additional task for the State to act as regulator of the space of rights they have devised, subject to the limits set (including on one's autonomy).[143]

The locus of normativities, however, is clearly outside the strict control of the State. Harry Arthurs, when reflecting on polyjuriality noted:

> Civil or common law, religious or secular law, domestic or international law, state law or some other kind, all form part of the open-textured, complex, heterogeneous normative universe which students must learn to inhabit. Law . . . is therefore found not only in statute books and law reports; it is found everywhere, inscribed in private documents, embedded in custom,

---

140 Berman (2012) at 52–53.
141 Sally Falk Moore, 'Law and Social Change: The Semi-Autonomous Social Field as an Appropriate Subject of Study', *Law & Society Review*, 7, 1973, 719, at 720. She defines the idea of "semi-autonomous social field" as one that "can generate rules and customs and symbols internally, but that . . . is also vulnerable to rules and decisions and other forces emanating from the larger world by which is it surrounded. The semi-autonomous social field has rule-making capacities, and the means to induce or coerce compliance; but it is simultaneously set in a larger social matrix which can, and does, affect and invade it, sometimes at the invitation of persons inside it, sometimes at its own instance".
142 Silvio Ferrari, 'Religious Rules and Legal Pluralism: An Introduction', in R. Bottoni et al. (eds.), *Religious Rules, State Law and Normative Pluralism: A Comparative Overview*, Springer, 2016, 1–25.
143 Russell Sandberg, 'Conclusion: In Pursuit of Pluralism', in R. Bottoni et al. (eds.), *Religious Rules, State Law and Normative Pluralism: A Comparative Overview*, Springer, 2016, 395–420 at 412.

extruded from transactions or experienced as conventions of discourse and routines of daily life. Indeed, . . . by acknowledging the infinite varieties of 'law' . . . [it] underscores the need for a 'dialogue with otherness'. It denies students the comfort of the familiar: it asks them to imagine law as if they were someone else. Even law's connection with justice cannot be taken for granted; law sometimes empowers, sometimes oppresses and sometimes seems to do not much at all.[144]

In this passage, Arthurs represents in very vibrant colors the process of learning within law, but he equally focuses on the challenges of learning to deal with otherness. Religious otherness is at the core of many societal debates at present, with education often being one of its battlegrounds.

To sum up, the theme of this study engages directly with the ways that State recognition of religious rules (in the context of a religious rights' exercise) affects the levels of diversity guaranteed by the State to its citizens.[145] The clear-cut transcendence of religious rules in some cases explains the collapse of the boundaries between the private and the public spheres and as such goes to some length in exposing the reason(s) why state law is not obeyed, followed or even regarded.[146] The conflictual relationship between equality and religious liberty is the most visible illustration of the ways that legal pluralism operates, beyond a regulatory system of personal law, in public schools.

The struggle to distinguish religious from cultural rules may also contribute towards conflict insofar as it entails differing degrees of legal legitimacy of accommodation within exemption claims.[147] To complicate the terms of the debate even further, a third layer of normative movements superimposed on the two previous ones merits attention: religious normative orderings have more visibly developed the capacity to supersede national borders as distinct legal spaces and are now proceeding, following migratory movements of populations, to add a transnational layer (or bond) connected to religious identity.[148] This happens often in deliberate opposition to state-centric expectations and rules regarding assimilation of religious minorities.

Returning once more to the importance of the role that power plays in such contexts, the link between legal agency and socio-political empowerment for individuals and religious communities ultimately becomes important, particularly as one observes how rights are shaped in their context and content when learners, teachers and parents use them in public education.

---

144 Harry W. Arthurs, 'Law and Learning in an Era of Globalization', *German Law Journal*, 10, 2009, 629 at 637–638.
145 This type of scholarship is currently in growth. See indicatively Rossella Bottoni, Rinaldo Cristofori and Silvio Ferrari (eds.), *Religious Rules, State Law and Normative Pluralism— A Comparative Overview*, Springer, 2016.
146 Ferrari (2016) at 2.
147 Ferrari (2016) at 6.
148 Ferrari (2016) at 8.

b *The protection of religious difference in times of legal plurality*

The pursuit of pluralism premised on religious norms and identity has served well (and is continuing to do so) the needs of societies to 'let off steam'.[149] States use either group recognition and/or personal laws to address legal pluralism or opt for an individualized treatment of religious claims, usually through exemptions and on an ad hoc basis.

The legal management of religious difference very often follows techniques that rely on the use of personal laws for specific aspects of the individual's relationship with the State (e.g. in family law matters), on the use of exemptions from laws of general application (e.g. within schools on the basis of religion) or through the creation of specific legal tools that regulate the relationship between the State and a specific religion (e.g. conclusion of concordats).[150] Commonly, the State withdraws its supervision from the internal autonomy and self-administration of religious communities, relying on the principle of separation between state and religion. This withdrawal becomes relevant in the present context insofar as it affects the enforcement of equality and non-discrimination.[151]

The terms of the interaction are usually framed according to the binary distinction between legal systems that place emphasis on individual rights and equality as opposed to those that opt for community rights and freedoms,[152] without excluding possibilities for combinations of both. Yet, we are still struggling with the partial theorization of how and why religion becomes part of the public sphere in the first place. Legal pluralism may, in this sense, be both an advantage but also a constraint.[153]

Berman claims that "[e]very legal system shares with religion certain elements – ritual, tradition, authority, and universality – which are needed to symbolize and educate men's legal emotions".[154] Religion, indeed, has resurfaced as a major social signifier with clear implications for law. It has even been overemphasized to the extent that it is possible to argue for a 'religionization of identities', largely in post-modern terms.[155] This process of religionization clearly competes with modernist law-centric visions of state law as the dominant legal authority.[156] It has impacted on the use and management of law in the direction of affecting

---

149   Sandberg (2016) 397.
150   Ferrari (2016) analyzes all three in 12–17.
151   A common example across a number of faiths is the exclusion of women from church/ religious leadership positions or within the realm of schools in matters related to admission, teacher background or materials taught.
152   Ferrari (2016) at 19.
153   Ferrari (2016) at 21.
154   Harold Berman, *The Interaction of Law and Religion*, Nashville and New York: Abingdon Press, 1974, at 49.
155   Term borrowed by D. Gozdecka and S. Ercan, 'What Is Post-Multiculturalism? Recent Trends in Legal and Political Discourse', in D. Gozdecka and M. Kmak (eds.), *Europe at the Edge of Pluralism*, Intersentia, 2015, 27–42 at 33.
156   See John Griffith, 'What Is Legal Pluralism?' *Journal of Legal Pluralism*, 24, 1986, 1–55.

conditions of access to the right of religious freedom and issues connected to the manifestation of religion. Equality, as a legal concept but also as a right, has been trapped in a normative duel between recognition of difference and expectation of cultural sameness.[157] In the meantime, the term 'parallel societies' has become synonymous with illiberal practices in the midst of uneven and asymmetrical power relations that pursue and maintain the essentialization of culture. Are we then faced with new forms of segregation as a result of the assertion of religious identities? Or to what extent are religious communities and identities willing and capable of recognizing the right of other religions to exist, before one even factors in any form of state-centric intervention and/or control or supervision? And if so, what is the role of the right to education in mitigating those effects?

At first glance, legal pluralism does not appear to be a 'natural' strategy to pursue in addressing religious diversity in education because it seems to suggest fragmented legal landscapes. But legal pluralism as an approach also stresses the inevitable connectedness of competing entities of the same genus, such as 'laws' and 'religions'. The dilemma of uniformity versus fragmentation thus appears: If universalism as an approach towards human rights (and diversity management) erases diversity insofar as it aims to combat fragmentation,[158] at the same time it leads to "the silencing of less powerful voices in the global conversation".[159] It also chooses to ignore the emotional ties generated through religious belonging and identity that also happen to be intrinsically linked to agency and the empowerment of the individual.

The real dimensions of the normative dialogue(s) between the local and the universal happen in reality in different terms: local actors employ universalist language in order to interact in strategic terms at the individual, social, national and universal levels.[160] Comparative law has echoed the same debate, between the 'functionalist' and 'contextualist' strands of its scholarship, only to reach the conclusion that it is impossible to answer this kind of dilemma.[161]

The aim in this study is different: the present analysis seeks to explore the ways in which normative conflicts are managed as they arise in the realm of religious diversity claims within education. The goal is to achieve this by reflecting first on how the actors claiming competing norms position themselves into a

---

157 Gozdecka and Ercan (2015) at 37.
158 This is what Schiff Berman claims in Berman (2012) at 131.
159 Berman (2012) at 131.
160 In that respect see, for example, Kyriaki Topidi and Lauren Fielder (eds.), *Religion as Empowerment: Global Legal Perspectives*, Routledge, 2016, for a string of case studies that examine this interaction.
161 This debate is resonating of Marion Iris Young's concept of "unassimilated otherness" that claims that individuals within the ideal "unoppressive city" should be able to belong to a variety of distinct groups but without seeking to assimilate or reject the non-belongers. In this way, there is no hegemonic imposition of sameness and at the same time no complete separation between the groups (See Marion Iris Young, 'The Ideal of Community and the Politics of Difference', in Linda J. Nicholson (ed.), *Feminism/Postmodernism*, Routledge, 1990, 300 et seq., at 317–319.)

shared social space. Would forms of 'flexible citizenship', for instance, based on the understanding that individuals may shift identities (given their plurality of affiliations), be a solution against the 'Us v. Them' normative dualism? To be clear, more flexible forms of citizenship do not include illiberal communities and practices or even a de jure right to autonomy, but pluralist belonging should at least become part of the exchange.[162]

In that respect, the theory and practice of liberalism should have taught us by now that the good life comes in many varieties.[163] Liberalism treats individuals as agents with choice who may choose to lead more valuable lives through religious belonging. The essence of this choice includes, nevertheless, the possibility to leave a religious group to (potentially) join another one, to adopt a more hybrid identity or even to renegotiate the terms of one's membership. It also includes the potentiality of recognizing a variety of 'Others' beyond the believing self as individual agents. In practice, the vulnerability of certain segments within religious groups brings back into the discussion the perceived as 'benevolent' role of the State in protecting citizens from harm, even when they make the choice to become members of non-liberal religious communities.[164] Gray suggests a step further in this discussion: what is new in the modern, complex, multicultural world is not accepting diversity in the form of difference.[165] Rather, it is dealing with a different starting point, namely a situation where otherness or difference is outlawed, hated, resented, disliked, and thus needs to be managed in a liberal manner both from the perspective of religions and States. This type of questioning seeks to curtail or control our hostility towards hierarchies: the goal of co-existence will be attained if we refrain from imposing on each other the 'right' order of things. The strategy of imposing something on others relates to power dynamics and so does the abuse of power in the name of saving souls or avoiding harm to one's own belief system or religion, or state construct, as the case may be. Religions thus act as States in rallying the activist energies of their claimed protectors in the process of outlawing any 'Others' who are too different. The task of an imposed hierarchical vision of identities is not only questionable, but it may also be impossible. Gray continues: "if liberalism has a future, it is in giving up the search for a rational consensus on the best way of life. Nearly all societies today contain several ways of life, with many people belonging to more than one".[166] Demanding absolute sameness therefore is the strategic fault. It runs diametrically counter to any respect for individual human rights, which includes the right to be oneself, and thus different from everyone else. A more nuanced reading of equality may suggest a different implementation approach to the principle. Acceptance of

---

162 Berman (2012) at 151.
163 See, for example, Arif A. Jamal, *Law and the Modern State: (Re)Imagining Liberal Theory in Muslim Contexts*, Routledge, 2018.
164 For more on this point, see Malik (2012) at 28–30.
165 J. Gray, *Gray's Anatomy*, London: Allen Lane, 2009, at 22.
166 Gray (2009) at 22.

difference and an awareness that it needs to be managed, not to be erased, but made tolerable, would appear instead to be the overarching goal.

A more progressive understanding of law would take into consideration the political assertions of marginalized people to power, or a fair share in power, and give channels for them to claim central spaces in life and thought, with the caveat that the right to claim is not synonymous to the possibility to actually reach that aim. Such an approach would nevertheless at least welcome the possibility for one to claim the right to be different.

We live in times when human activity has acquired unprecedented speed and complexity: from global communication technologies to population movements and the movements of capital, it is difficult to imagine that state jurisdictions and assertions of legal authority will remain unaffected. The 'sharing' of legal authority with international courts, regional courts or other regulatory entities and the systematic and deliberate bypassing of national legal authority further demonstrate the need for pluralist readings of normativity. As such, legal pluralism can be conceived as a 'natural companion' to a liberal reading in contemporary comparative constitutionalism.[167] Statements of normativity, even in the absence of formal enforcement power, are more and more common.[168]

Liberalism embraces the rights and freedoms of individuals, often against religious claims. But is liberalism compatible only with state law? Is it useful to link it only to central legal authorities in super-diverse contexts? It is clear that concepts of liberalism do not preclude the consideration of other 'visions of the good life', entailing non-state normative commitments but fail to propose ways of dealing with positions and claims premised on self-righteousness.[169] The dilemmas, however, remain:

> Lacking a conviction in the absolute truth of our own beliefs and practices, we are uncertain how to respond to those who live by different norms. We are all too aware that such differences exist, as we interact with cultures that put different values on life and death, family and society, religion and the state, men and women. We constantly confront the question of whether some of the practices supported by these values are beyond the limits of our own commitment to a liberal moral philosophy and a political practice of tolerance. We worry about moral cowardice when we fail to respond critically, and about cultural imperialism when we do respond.[170]

---

167 Bryan S. Turner, 'Legal Pluralism: Freedom of Religion, Exemptions and the Equality of Citizens', in R. Bottoni et al. (eds.), *Religious Rules, State Law and Normative Pluralism: A Comparative Overview*, Springer, 2016, 61–73, at 62.

168 Berman (2015) at 19.

169 Berman (2015) at 15. Berman cautions, however, against the risk of complete merging, keeping in perspective the fragmented nature of global legal pluralism. (Berman (2015) at 15–16).

170 Paul W. Kahn, *Putting Liberalism in Its Place*, Princeton: Princeton University Press, 2005 at 1.

Critics of liberalism have taken issue with the problem of accommodating cultural diversity, suggesting that the way to respond to the subordinate position of certain disadvantaged groups is to grant them special entitlements[171] in the form of exemptions and exceptions. In fact, and as already mentioned, legal pluralists do not necessarily deny the nature of State power and its ability to enforce norms in a different way compared to non-state entities. At the same time, they note that "not all the phenomena related to law and not all that are law-like have their source in government".[172]

In existing studies linking constitutional law issues to the normative activities of non-state communities, there are two predominant incentives to link the two: either there is a study of the ways in which these communities assert rights in fora specifically created by state authorities, or there is intense focus on the conflict(s) created between the norms that these communities propagate (and apply) with those emanating from the State.[173] In both scenarios, nevertheless, the assessment and inquiry by scholars is predominantly made from the perspective of the State. The present study will adopt a different lens: it will attempt to move closer to a pluralist legal perspective by shedding light onto how such individuals and groups, as legal agents, function, as opposed to the State, when asserting constitutional rights. It will show how their agency is exercised and how, in some cases, individuals are navigating through various normative systems towards strategic aims in the field of education. The complexity of the global legal arena calls for more insight on the use of norms as empowerment tools towards specific interests by qualifying the characteristics of access to state-policy-making apparatus.[174] Guided by the need to 'unpack the idea of state interest',[175] particularly when considering ways to reflect on effective public policy, the right-claimer's conception of justice, perception of strategy towards her/his aim and belief and/ or morality become relevant factors towards a comprehensive assessment of any constitutional right. It is also relevant in addressing instances of 'forum shopping' where despite (or because of) state law being perceived as an instance of state domination, users may instrumentally use it against oppression, or conversely the State itself may use it to establish further its dominant position.[176] Such processes highlight how actors perceive, interpret, use and abuse the law.

171 This strategy has been labeled 'the politics of recognition'. See Charles Taylor, *Multicultur-alism and the Politics of Recognition*, Princeton: Princeton University Press, 1992. There is also abundant literature on multiculturalism which is representative of the same

172 Sally Falk Moore, 'Legal Systems of the World: An Introductory Guide to Classifications, Typological Interpretations and Bibliographical Resources', in Leon Lipson and Stanton Wheeler (eds.), *Law and the Social Sciences*, New York: Russell Sage Foundation, 1986, at 11, 15.

173 Berman (2015) at 17. The essential question asked in the latter respect reverts to how much the State should tolerate the non-normative community, instead of how to manage the conflict created.

174 Berman (2015) at 20.

175 Berman (2015) at 19.

176 Franz and Keebet von Benda- Beckmann (2006) at 28.

If religion (as part of identity) is to be dialogically constructed, state legal systems should recognize religious differences and provide the conditions to facilitate interaction between and transformation of such differences.[177] The sample of cases discussed not only recognize in constitutional terms cultural and religious differences, but they also accept and engage with the existence of interactions between the formal and informal spheres of normative regulation.

Drawing on Foucault's theory on and around "biopower", understood as the management of human life towards health, efficiency and productivity,[178] the assumption is that diversity management allows for differences, but it is likely that it does not tolerate all kinds of differences. Studies like the present one have a clear 'biopolitical' aim, as well as a methodological one: they aim to show the legal empirical limits of toleration[179] towards religious diversity from the perspective of learners in public schools as 'objects' of education. They also show how the government's ability and legal content are shaped depending on the extent to which each society and its legal orders assimilate or exclude religious difference within the education process.

The recognition of formal group rights premised on religious and cultural identity is of course hotly contested in this frame: the institutionalization of group representation appears the antidote to individual representation but does not eliminate the risk of essentializing these religions/cultures.[180] In this sense, forms of cultural imperialism affect our perception of the public-private divide as well as the individual – collective rights' status.[181] From a public policy perspective, the examination of religious diversity legal arrangements in public education within such a framework stresses the extent to which "institutions or policies alone do not shape the politics of recognition".[182]

---

177 Ercan (2015) at 18.
178 The term belongs to Michel Foucault, *The History of Sexuality, Vol. 1: An Introduction*, Penguin Books, 1978; Michel Foucault, *Society Must Be Defended: Lectures at the Collège de France*, 1975–76, New York: Picador, 2003.
179 On the limits and critique of the tolerance discourse see Wendy Brown, *Regulating Aversion: Tolerance in the Age of Identity and Empire*, Princeton and Oxford: Princeton University Press, 2008, emphasizing how tolerance is transformed from a positive moral attitude towards difference to a private therapeutic project that avoids the political dimension of recognition of the 'Other'. Slavoj Zizek has also labeled tolerance as "racism with a distance" insofar as it implies a hierarchy among those marked as objects of tolerance and those with the capacity to tolerate. (S. Zizek, *Living in the End Times*, London: Verso, 2011.)
180 Marion Iris Young elevates group representation to an "important enactment of political inclusion" within multicultural societies. (See I.M. Young, *Inclusion and Democracy*, Oxford: Oxford University Press, 2000, at 123.). Anthropologists engaging with culture accept that 'culture' is not a homogenous concept but instead an evolving process, often the product of negotiation and struggles that follow from inequality (See, for example, A. Appadurai, *Modernity at Large: Cultural Dimensions of Globalization*, Minneapolis: University of Minnesota Press, 1996)
181 L. King-Irani, 'Women's Rights Are Human Rights', *Al-Raida*, 13(74/75), 1996, 11–12.
182 Ercan (2015) at 23.

The conditions laid out for the new 'post-multiculturalist' project emphasize the need to foster collective identity, but coupled with cultural diversity.[183] The actual debate on whether a retreat from multiculturalism should be warranted is explicitly denied by Vertovec and Wessendorf as "overstated and misdiagnosed".[184] This study will ultimately show how and why the (post)-multiculturalist project can be invigorated.

---

183 The term 'post-multiculturalist' is used by Steven Vertovec and Susanne Wessendorf in *The Multiculturalism Backlash: European Discourses, Policies and Practices*, Abingdon: Routledge, 2010.

184 Vertovec and Wessendorf (2010) at 29, with particular emphasis on the challenges posed by immigration as a threat to national values and social cohesion.

2 The concepts

Revisiting religious diversity within multicultural classrooms: religious freedom, education and equality

1 Introduction: human rights and normative conflict

The transformative power of human rights is hard to question. What is less clear, particularly outside the confines of the Western world, is the degree of the authentically universal components of the current body of human rights.[1] This study is not focused on the debate of whether international human rights are the product of a predominantly European perspective of the individual. Admittedly, they are. Nor is it concerned directly with the extent to which this body of rights had been used in both colonial and post-colonial frames as an "instrument of a modern-day civilizing project".[2] Indeed, they have, even within the European space.[3] While human rights have been proposed as a "solution to the normative consequences of legal pluralism",[4] it remains open to debate to what extent these norms 'suffer' merely from jurisdictional conflicts of diverse interpretation or whether they are subjected to a form of normative pluralism in themselves.

In this frame, the interaction between domestic human rights and international human rights is uncontested:[5] while it may be occasionally conflictual or conducive to fragmentation, it is established. The trend towards fragmentation was intensely debated in the last decade. It was premised on the growth of specialized sub-fields of international law after 1989, the rise of non-state actors and the inclusion of new types of international norms beyond those already recognized.

---

1 For a discussion on this point see Srilatha Batliwala, 'When Rights Go Wrong—Distorting the Rights Based Approach to Development', Harvard University: Hauser Center for Non-profit Organizations, 2010, at 1–2, available at www.justassociates.org/WhenRightsGoWrong.pdf.
2 Batliwala (2010) at 2.
3 See, for example, Topidi, Kyriaki EU Law, Minorities and Enlargement, 2010, Intersentia for an account of minority rights standards alignment process addressed to post-communist countries preparing for EU accession.
4 For a discussion of this point see Samantha Besson, 'European Human Rights Pluralism: Notion and justification', in M. Maduro, K. Tuori and S. Sankari (eds.), *Transnational Law: Rethinking European Law and Legal Thinking*, Cambridge University Press, 2014, 170–205, at 173.
5 Besson (2014) at 185.

Such fragmentation can and does create conflicts and incompatibilities arising from diverging rules. Peters argues, however, that we have presently entered into an era of 'systemic harmonization' in international law where this process is gradually being reversed.[6] National law is to a lesser degree affected.

What the exchange is still unclear about, however, relates to cases when international human rights norms conflict among themselves: pluralism embedded within (clashing) normative statements provokes a sense of hierarchy among rights and even among the interpretations of one right, despite the perceived validity of the norms in dispute. This kind of inquiry on normative conflicts presupposes a clearer understanding of the content of the rights to religious freedom, education and equality that are the object of this study. The aim therefore of this chapter is to revisit the conceptual bearings of these central norms in order to then explore their use in the case studies that follow.

One of the latent horizontal concerns of this analysis is the ongoing tension between individualized rights and collective duties and responsibilities.[7] When engaging with the right to equality, the right to religious freedom or the right to education, following a rights-based approach,[8] any proposed strategy adopted by States, defined as duty-bearers in protecting rights, should account for the ways that individuals in their own complexity experience both the affirmation and especially the denial of such rights.[9] The right to education in conjunction with that of freedom of belief is, for example, mediated by intersecting institutions such as local authorities, teachers, parents or religious organizations. In other words, the role of the State in protecting individuals' religious freedom becomes more complex due to the conception of freedoms outside State interference, as connected to individual moral choices.[10]

In recent human rights scholarship, two key issues framing the debate of the present discussion occupy the scene: first, the content of equality. If we understand equality as "the extent to which individuals are in a position actually to exercise . . . rights",[11] then we are using a substantive form of the concept where the duty of the State is heavier as it needs to remove any impediments jeopardizing the exercise of such rights. Equality can be also conceived as "the ability to exercise genuine choice and to act on this choice",[12] or 'agency', extending

6 Anne Peters, 'The Refinement of International Law: From Fragmentation to Regime Interaction and Politicization', *ICON*, 15(3), 2017, 671–704.
7 Obligations appearing as preconditions for rights is as much of a culture-based argument as it is a necessity for survival and development for a number of groups.
8 Borrowed from the analysis of the rights-based approach to development, the UN Office of the High Commissioner defines it as follows: "Essentially, a rights-based approach integrates the norms, standards and principles of the international human rights system into the plans, policies and processes of development" (www.unohchr.org).
9 Batliwala (2010) at 3.
10 Sandra Fredman, *Human Rights Transformed: Positive Rights and Positive Duties*, Oxford University Press, 2008, at 9.
11 Fredman (2008) at 9.
12 Fredman (2008) at 11.

beyond the formal entitlement to act. After all, the exercise of rights, even at the supra-national and global levels requires the involvement of individuals, not just states.

At the same time, and this is the second point, the State can no longer be considered neutral with regard to ethical/moral commitments, merely by virtue of its acceptance to follow and abide by human rights.[13] Autonomy and individualism are, for example, explicit value commitments on behalf of the State, as Rawls has noted.[14] So, the open question becomes when should the State intervene: to defend specific values with which it identifies or to protect a specific plurality of values conducive to maintaining equality?

The complexity of the human rights frame is further highlighted by the fact that other factors, in the form of constraints, affect the exercise of freedoms. Poor health, poverty and lack of education move the analysis beyond the simple consideration of the question on whether there has been state interference with a particular right.[15]

In reality, legal systems often contribute to the enforcement of social stratifications,[16] and any attempt to reverse the social effects of law depends on changes in structure and perception of law as a non-static and heterogeneous phenomenon. It is not uncommon, thus, that a legal system, despite human rights guarantees, allows privileges to persist or maintains the status quo ante of former systems,[17] in more subtle ways.

Within the context of the study of the normative co-existence – and occasional competition – between religious belief and state law, translated most commonly as a conflict between religious freedom and other human rights or communal interests, balancing has acquired a constitutional dimension. More than that, it has become a method of constitutional interpretation,[18] leading to the adjudication of such conflicts in both domestic and supra-national fora.

Such balancing usually happens through an assessment of the limitations of religious freedom invoked with the activation of the principle of proportionality. The method runs, however, in international human rights law an inherent risk: that of legitimizing abuses of political power.[19] It also assumes that international

---

13 Fredman (2008) at 9.

14 John Rawls, *Justice as Fairness*, Cambridge, MA: Harvard University Press, 2001, at 156.

15 This point resonates Amartya Sen's *Development as Freedom*, Oxford University Press, 1999, at 5 where he finds freedom to be conditioned on the removal of major sources of unfreedom: "poverty as well as tyranny, poor economic opportunities as well as systematic social deprivation, neglect of public facilities as well as intolerance or over-activity of repressive states". His approach is framed on development within developing countries.

16 Reva Siegel, 'Why Equal Protection No Longer Protects: The Evolving Forms of Status-Enforcing State Action', *Stanford Law Review*, 49, 1996–1997, 1111–1148, at 1113.

17 Siegel (1997) at 1116, also considering the example of the 1875 US Civil Rights Act on racial discrimination in 1124.

18 Basak Çali, 'Balancing Human Rights? Methodological Problems with Weights, Scales and Proportions', *Human Rights Quarterly*, 29, 2007, 251–270 at 252.

19 Çali (2007) at 253.

adjudicatory bodies may adopt a deferential approach to the assessment of such conflicts, as the example of the European Court of Human Rights illustrates with respect to its Article 9 ECHR jurisprudence.[20] While there is a clear advantage to balancing as a method leading to potentially fairer outcomes, religious freedom in the assessment of the ECtHR is shown to operate, for example, at the antipode of communal interests.[21] In other words, it is translated as a conflict between a right's claim of an individual against the rest of the community.[22] For purposes of diversity management, however, such an approach towards the balancing of interests neglects the diversity of human experience while rejecting any consideration of the context in which human rights claims arise. Reverting to *Hatton v. UK*, the dissenting opinion to the majority judgment was explicit on this point:

> We do not find it persuasive to engage in the balancing exercise employing the proportionality doctrine in order to show that the abstract majority's interest outweighs the concrete 'subjective element of the small minority of people'. . . . Indeed, one of the most important functions of human rights protection is to protect 'small minorities' whose 'subjective element' makes them different from the majority.[23]

Balancing, therefore, as described earlier, seems to lack in precision and consistency, particularly for religious freedom. It shows additional weaknesses too: first, it operates under criteria of sincerity, centrality of belief or seriousness in order to make the belief legally examinable, and second, the legal assessment is more often than not measured against the understanding that it is a private matter of choice.[24] The use of the 'margin of appreciation' for instance in the European context, ultimately strips away any remaining notion of balancing in the European religious rights adjudication landscape, as it shows evidence of judicial restraint on behalf of the Strasbourg Court to even enter the discussion of human rights balancing.

That is not to say, however, that all religious rights' claims should be granted or accommodated. The broader picture that merits some reflection when exercising religious rights in the ECHR framework but also in other 'fora' lies in the unclear demarcation line between the means of balancing and its consequences.[25] The latter paradoxically seem to accentuate rights' inequalities instead of mitigating

---

20 See indicatively *Sahin v. Turkey*, Appl. No. 44174/98 (Grand Chamber), 2005 and *Lautsi v. Italy*, Appl. No. 30814/06 (Grand Chamber), 2011.
21 See, conversely, *Hatton and Others v. UK*, Appl. No. 36022/97, 2003 describing the balance "between the competing interests of the individual and the community as a whole" (at para. 86)
22 Çali (2007) at 259.
23 *Hatton and Others v. UK*, Appl. No. 36022/97 (Grand Chamber), 2003 Joint Dissenting Opinion of Judges Costa, Ress, Turmen, Zupancic and Steiner at para. 14.
24 Günter Frankenberg, *Comparative Law as Critique*, Elgar, 2016, at 121.
25 Çali (2007) at 270.

them. At the moment, for instance, the perception of threat and risk of religious radicalization prevails over any serious attempt to balance rights that are in conflict with each other.[26]

Overall, analyzing normative conflict between state regulation of public education and religious norms calls for both a legal as well as a cultural analytical perspective. Human rights, such as the principle of equality or that of religious freedom, reveal themselves in a different light when viewed in a context of cultural difference, beyond a strict state-centered notion of legality.[27] This different light allows for reflection on what makes (and unmakes) social order or, in simpler terms, what provokes conflict in the first place. Public schools, in that sense, are places filled with manifold layers of normativity where children, parents, teachers, administrators or religious communities and the State get involved in their individual, but also group, identities as agents of order and disorder, giving 'the law' its fluidity and elasticity. Even state law in itself is occasionally far from stable, filled with inner tensions, while it remains a prima facie dominant ordering by virtue of the high amount of resources that it disposes of in comparison to other orders of norms.[28]

At the origin of equality is precisely the need to protect diversity, which is an important point to recall when balancing rights. Equality, like other norms, is challenged as a normative discourse to capture the constant evolution of identity claims in societies where personal autonomy and free consent occupy distinct places, often to the declared detriment of social cohesion.[29] When conflict occurs, therefore, equal status in society becomes contingent not upon competition but rather upon interdependence.[30] Normative pluralism, in this respect, represents the starting point for the quest towards interdependence.

2   The right to freedom of religion in education: religion as a secular blasphemy?

In the beginning of the strong development of human rights in the mid-20th century, rights were interpreted creatively as a tool towards the liberation of people and the protection of human dignity. It quickly became clear that the implementation of this idea was not as simple: human rights can be perverted; they can be translated in the power to maintain the status quo and privileges, as mentioned.

---

26 See indicatively ECtHR Decisions of 4 December 2008 *Dogru v. France*, Appl. No. 27058/05 and *Kervanci v. France*, Appl. No. 31645/04.

27 Michele Graziadei, 'State Norms, Religious Norms and Claims for Plural Normativity Under Democratic Constitutions', in R. Bottoni et al. (eds.), *Religious Rules, State Law and Normative Pluralism: A Comparative* Overview, Springer, 2016, 29–43 at 36.

28 Graziadei (2016) at 38.

29 Graziadei (2016) at 39.

30 Graziadei (2016) at 39.

Engaging with the right to religious freedom presupposes a degree of clarity on the recurring question of the limits (and defense) of religious and inter-connected cultural practices in the process of exercising human rights. Freedom and respect for religious difference depends on one's understanding of religion. Similar to culture,[31] however, religion resists definition because it appears contested, fluid, dynamic and evolving. At the same time, religion has often been perceived within human rights law discourse as premodern, a hindrance to progress, as primitive or as backward, in order to justify lack of human rights exercise, to the exclusion of other political, socio-economic or structural factors.

But as we are gradually moving away from the notion of 'Kultur'[32] as an instrument stressing national boundaries and national identities, and in the light of migratory movements and national and transnational legal processes, it would be more accurate to analyze legal systems as they relate to religious freedom(s) as "unbounded, contested, and connected to relations of power".[33]

In the European space, for instance, the notion and concept of religion as a protected identity marker has known expansive development. A typical illustration of this expansion is evident in the ways in which the European Union (EU) has engaged with religion in law and policy. Despite the lack of an express competence, religious affairs have been affected in the EU by the 1999 Treaty of Amsterdam[34] and the connected directives guaranteeing non-discrimination and other fundamental rights. With the help of alternative strategies, religious identity has entered the frame of EU consideration while connected to employment, education, culture or the integration of third-country nationals.

Essentially, there are three main trajectories through which religion has been gaining a more central position in the Union: (European) citizenship, non-discrimination and immigration.[35] Within the Treaty on the Functioning of the EU (TFEU), Article 17(3) formalized a previously informal exchange by calling the EU to recognize religious groups and maintain an open, transparent and regular dialogue with these churches and organizations.

The increasing importance of religious actors as 'agents' shaping the conditions of the socio-legal exercise of the right to religious freedom is thus acknowledged,

---

31 Sally Engle Merry, 'Human Rights Law and the Demonization of Culture (and Anthropology Along the Way)', in *Polar: Political and Legal Anthropology Review*, 26(1), May 2003, 55–76 at 62.
32 On this point see Merry (2003) at 74.
33 Merry (2003) at 76.
34 See Declaration 11 of the Treaty that "The Union respects and does not prejudice the status under national law of churches and religious associations or communities in the Member States" [EU Declaration on the Status of Churches and Non-Confessional Organizations No. 11 to the Last Act of the Treaty of Amsterdam, O.J. 10/111997, 133].
35 Sergio Carrera and Joanna Parkin, 'The Place of Religion in EU Law and Policy: Competing Approaches and Actors Inside the European Commission', Religare Working Document No. 1, September 2010, at 1.

even in the absence of a firm legal basis for action. Similar to other contexts, religion is lacking here, too, a commonly agreed definition.[36]

The EU Charter of Fundamental Rights includes the relevant Articles 10 (on freedom of thought, conscience and religion), 21 (on non-discrimination) and 22 (on cultural, religious and linguistic diversity). These legally binding provisions reflect the net of protection of religious freedom available in other supranational fora, for example, the Council of Europe's European Convention on Human Rights, imposing the obligation on States and EU institutions to respect their content when acting within the scope of EU law.

It is also interesting to stress how religion was introduced in the EU's public sphere and agenda, as Carrera and Parkin show in their work, in connection with immigration. They argue that this connection signified a treatment of religion as a ground for exemption from recognized European rights and freedoms to third-country nationals.[37] Instead of raising a shield of protection, religious difference was interpreted, especially for non-Christian religions, as an inhibiting factor towards integration, a resistance to liberal democratic values justifying the right of Member States to use integration requirements to limit access to EU legal protection.[38]

Within this framework, the question of what constitutes 'common values' surfaces: 'neutral' liberal norms usually fit the context of the term.[39] The debate on values, as case studies examined later will further confirm, is a recurring one at both the national and supra-national levels. Yet, the notion of values does not spell out the mutual adjustment duties between the Autochthonous European and the Migrant 'Other'.[40]

---

36 With the exception of Article 10(1) of Directive 2004/83/EC on the status of third-country nationals or stateless persons as refugees which approaches religion as "the holding of theistic, non-theistic and atheistic beliefs, the participation in, or abstention from, formal worship in private or in public, either alone or in community with others, other religious acts or expressions of view, or forms of personal or communal conduct based on or mandated by any religious belief".

37 Carrera and Parkin (2010) at 16.

38 Carrera and Parkin (2010) indicatively discuss the transposition of Directive 2003/86/EC on the right to family reunification COM(2008)610, 8 October 2008 and the connected case C-540/03 *Parliament v. Council* (2006) ECRI-5769 that both confirm the requirement for states to meet the general objectives of the directive and those of fundamental rights principles of EU law before imposing restrictions on this category of individuals.

39 The notion of European values appears to hold a central position in the discourse of the European Commission on the integration of migrant communities, without defining what those values are or to what extent they are shared among Member States. See the European Pact on Immigration and Asylum of 2008, Council of the EU, 13440/08, Brussels, 24 September 2008.

40 While it has been mentioned that the EU's religious identity framework acknowledges the growing agency of religious actors, it neglects minority faith groups resulting in the overrepresentation of Christian actors, without due consideration to the overlapping marginalization, poverty and discrimination connected with non-majoritarian faith groups. (Cf. Carrera and Parkin (2010) at 27.)

Returning to religious freedom(s), the 20th century, often called the century of secularization in Europe, proved misleading with respect to religion. Since the late 1970s, a so-called religious revival began and, certainly following 9/11, religion is firmly back on the public agenda as a social force or a source of tensions.

Despite the lack of conceptual clarity as a term, religion appears to work on many levels, including in the present analysis: as a constructed (legal) category, it represents a system of beliefs and norms but also provides the space for one's questions on the nature of human existence and its purpose.[41] The many meanings of religion in contemporary terms lead also to a more nuanced understanding of the evolution of religiosity in Europe: there is a multitude of parallel processes underway in this respect, that, among others, include the transfer of religious property and institutions to the State, the decline of personal religiosity, the transformation of religious views into cultural ones, or the decreasing levels of commitment to religious institutions.[42] Grace Davie's concept of "believing without belonging", for example, adequately describes the low level of church commitment of Britons with the large diffusion of faith in the 20th century,[43] although the opposite – "belonging without believing"- may also apply in conditions where religions lead social networks (e.g. in some Islamic mosque communities in Europe).[44] The work of José Casanova, taken as another example, demonstrated how religious associations seek public presence, taking a more communal form within a process that is labeled 'deprivitization'.[45]

The legal interpretation of religion as a right, however, calls for, at least, an attempt to even indirectly define the term. Across a variety of jurisdictions, we are currently witnessing a phase of use of a variety of criteria to remedy the lack of a universally valid legal definition of the term: sincerity of belief, centrality of contested practice to the faith in question, or shared public understanding, are some of them as mentioned.[46] At the same time, religious influence on law- and policy-making has grown as an independent area of inquiry, with both political as well as socio-economic ramifications. This growth of interest incidentally suggests and confirms that religious actors are in a position to openly influence the formation and implementation of law, including within 'secular' (Western)

---

41 Ryan T. O'Leary, 'The Irony of the Secular: Violent Communication at the Limits of Tolerance', *Journal of Religion, Conflict and Peace*, 3(2), Spring 2010, at 2, available at www.religionconflictpeace.org/volume-3-issue-2-spring-2010/irony-secular.

42 Hans G. Kippenberg, 'Europe: Area of Pluralization and Diversification of Religions', *Journal of Religion in Europe*, 1, 2008, 133–155 at 149.

43 Grace Davie, *Religion in Britain Since 1945: Believing Without Belonging*, Oxford: Blackwell, 1994.

44 Kippenberg (2008) at 151.

45 José Casanova, *Public Religions in the Modern World*, University of Chicago Press, 1994.

46 Veit Bader, 'Post-Secularism or Liberal Democratic Constitutionalism?' *Erasmus Law Review*, 5(1), 2012, 5–26 at 7. He particularly discussed the Canadian case *Syndicat Northcrest v. Anselem* (2004) SCC 47; (2004) 2 S.C.R. 551 where the Court explains 'sincerity of belief' in length.

societies.[47] The power and appeal of religious organizations are based on their mobilization potential, which in turn relies on the level and type of religiosity of their adherents.[48] In the framework of public education, this translates into very specific resources and preferences on the level of religious diversity desired and ways to pursue it, depending on the context of each case.

According to Fink, essential considerations when assessing the broader framework of (in)actions of religious organizations and individuals, and the features of such agency that are determining are the legal provisions regulating church-state relations, as well as the cultural assumptions and developing trends on the socially expected role of religion in public life.[49] Although often, particularly in relation to strategic decisions, religious actors' decisions are tightly linked to their organizational survival,[50] the dimension of their role as social and corporate actors implies broader involvement than that of a cultural variant. This is particularly so in a climate of increasing visibility of religious divides,[51] with clearer linkages articulated between attitudes to immigration, value orientation and religiosity.[52]

Within this context, religious education in the 21st century is struggling to address conflicting trends: educating students towards religious diversity may entail a religious pluralization of the curriculum in the direction of a post-religious comparative introduction to the various religious traditions and other worldviews and at the same time a deepening of the knowledge of one's own faith.[53] In light of the overlap between faith and culture, the task is not a minor one in a constantly evolving landscape of our relation to both faith and secularization. [54] The option of 'educating into religion' as opposed to that of 'educating about religion(s)' attempts to find the right balance in the quest for a better understanding of religious plurality, with or without the use of confessional religious education courses. Ultimately, the goal remains to address the religious illiteracy of learners as an alternative to confrontation or mere tolerance.[55]

47 Simon Fink, 'Churches as Society Veto Players: Religious Influence in Actor-Centred Theories of Policy-Making', *West European Politics*, 32(1), 2009, 77–96 at 77.

48 Fink (2009) refers to these adherents as 'voters' at 78. He defines "mobilization potential", as "the ability of a church to mobilize its adherents for political action, such as collective action in the form of protests or voting behaviour".

49 Fink (2009) at 84, despite diverging opinions in literature discussed on whether a closed or more remote connection to the State may increase the impact of religious actors in governance.

50 Fink (2009) at 90.

51 Hajo G. Boomgaarden and André Freire, 'Religion and Euroscepticism: Direct, Indirect or No Effects?' *West European Politics*, 32(6), November 2009, 1240–1265, at 1240.

52 Boomgaarden and Freire (2009).

53 Lieven Boeve, 'Religious Education in a Post-Secular and Post-Christian Context', *Journal of Beliefs and Values*, 33(2), August 2012, 143–156 at 144.

54 Boeve (2012) refers to these parallel dynamics as "post-Christian" and "post-Secular".

55 Mike Castelli, 'Faith Dialogue as a Pedagogy for a Post Secular Religious Education', *Journal of Beliefs and Values*, 33(2), August 2012, 207–216 at 208.

Institutional actors, such as teachers and faith organizations themselves, operationalize policy and legal frameworks while bringing in their own agendas and predispositions. The trifold role of teachers, in particular, as experts in religious knowledge, as witnesses to the one tradition where they belong/believe, and as moderators of the interreligious exchange in the classroom,[56] in the context of a development of reflexive religious identities appears paramount for the successful implementation of any policy. It is also often the part of the equation that is most neglected in both secular and 'faith schools'.

Contemporary approaches to education in general in the Western world, but very evident in Europe, tend to emphasize the creation of a frame for the integration of diversity and promote social instruments that allow them to exist within super-diverse societies.[57] In many cases, it is possible to argue for the need of a paradigm shift that treats immigrant learners as 'resources', instead of 'liabilities'.[58] This paradigm shift, however, based on an intercultural approach to education, continues to pose a number of challenges, beyond Europe as well, on how to transform religious otherness (as often connected to migration) to an "object of knowledge".[59]

Teaching religion in government-funded education represents thus a challenge in a variety of ways: depending on the approach privileged in each setting, every teacher has to engage with notions of tolerance and respect, with values, with her/his own self-restraint in order to not exploit the learners' vulnerability and with sensitivity to objectivity and against indoctrination.[60] A post-secular interpretation of religious education would suggest treating religious identity as 'a matter of faith rather than knowledge', leading implicitly, however, to the treatment of religious beliefs as controversial.[61] As crucial, in multicultural contexts, it is the expectation that the learning process on religion will yield an understanding of how to share social space with those holding different or no beliefs and with whom one disagrees.[62]

3 Secularization, secularism and the right to religious freedom

A conceptual overview of the normative processes of religious diversity in public education would be incomplete without a brief account of how religious freedom

---

56 Boeve (2012) at 154.
57 Nathalie Muller Mirza, 'Civic Education and Intercultural Issues in Switzerland: Psychosocial Dimensions of an Education to "Otherness"', *Journal of Social Science Education*, 10(4), 2011, 31–40 at 31.
58 Mirza (2011) at 32.
59 Mirza (2011) at 32.
60 In the words of Trevor Cooling: "To teach as settled something that is controversial is indoctrination and to teach as controversial something that is settled is irrational". [Cf. Trevor Cooling, 'What Is a Controversial Issue? Implications for the Treatment of Religious Beliefs in Education', *Journal of Beliefs and Values*, 33(2), August 2012, 169–181 at 170.]
61 Cooling (2012) at 174.
62 Cooling (2012) at 177.

has been affected by the secularization and secularism trends. The secularization thesis can be understood in four distinct, yet heavily contested, ways: as the decline of religion in our societies; as the individualization of religion; as the privatization of religion; or finally, as the separation of politics/states from organized religions.[63] Of particular relevance and connection to this study are the dimensions of individualization and privatization of religion: religiosity in contemporary terms is belief-centered, subjectified as a personal and authentic expression of identity as well as a largely voluntary one,[64] while at the same time emerging as a useful resource for organization and mobilization, as will be later illustrated.

Using as a point of departure the observation that it is hard to claim convincingly that religion is strictly private or neatly separated from the State, post-secularism has become synonymous to the vitality of religion in our societies (instead of its predicted decline) and the increase of its public influence.[65] The pluralization of the religious landscape has often put pressure on the State and religions organizations alike, where membership is declining, at least in the European context. But the scope of the present discussion reveals a more complex situation, beyond the binary logic of choice between a fully secularized state and a pillarized regime of selective cooperation between states and organized religions:[66] in the form of equal associational freedoms, non-discrimination and individual freedoms.

Alternative forms of secularism, not to be confused with secularization, whether constitutional,[67] 'inclusive', or moderate, demonstrate the unclear contours of the notion, often to the point of disguising, essentializing or withholding questions of religious identity.[68] In Charles Taylor's terms, secularism (as opposed to religion treated as "one human possibility among others"),[69] denotes a situation where public space becomes "religiously neutral", within a "context of understanding in which our moral, spiritual, or religious experience and search takes place".[70] The possibility, however, that the public space may not be realistically conceived as neutral, remains a valid concern. For Talal Asad, for instance,

---

63 Bader (2012) at 11.

64 Bader (2012) at 12.

65 Juergen Habermas, 'Notes on a Post-Secular Society', 2008, available at, www.signandsight. com/features/1714.html, at 5–7. Bader (2012) disputes whether religions have ever lost their public role in secular societies and also the novelty of immigration as a factor conducive to post-secularity (at 14).

66 Bader (2012) proposes a third model called "associational governance" of religious diversity based on non-establishment but with wider possibility for recognition of smaller religious minorities.

67 A. Sajó, 'Preliminaries to a Concept of Constitutional Secularism', *Int'l Journal of Constitutional Law*, 6, 2008, 617.

68 Bader (2012) develops this point by suggesting that it is conceivable to perceive states with imbalances between the rule of law and democracy, in particular militant democracies such as India and Turkey (at 22).

69 Charles Taylor, *A Secular Age*, Cambridge: The Belknap Press of Harvard University Press, 2007, at 3.

70 Taylor (2007) at 2–3.

secularism suggests status rather than space. He invokes, in his work, citizenship as a means to avoid religious conflict through the "unifying experience" of secularism.

The commonality in both approaches hints at the difficulty to construct and accept the sharp division between the public and private spheres: while secularism is commonly perceived as the requirement that religious institutions do not interfere with civil government, it is commonly known (and accepted) that religious organizations have access to and influence on political action.[71]

Religion, taken as a private concern, artificially assumes the division of the human existence in distinct spheres, which incidentally belongs to Western thought and can be traced to Plato and his classification between being and becoming, the rational and the material or the eternal and the temporal.[72] The implication of this approach is that religion becomes an individual right located within one's conscience, and therefore in one's private sphere of existence.[73] This view is problematic for believers in faiths that do not distinguish religious obligations from socio-political and civic organizations as sharply (for example, Sunni Muslims where 'secular' activities are accounted for as acts of worship).[74]

The complexity and paradoxical nature of secularism can be therefore described as follows: on the one hand, secularism lays the basis for religious pluralism and co-existence, by designating the public space as 'neutral', but on the other hand, when faced with religiously contested claims, the secular space negates its tolerance and becomes exclusivist,[75] as the European experience post-9/11 has illustrated.

Secularization, understood as the "systematic erosion of religious practices, values and beliefs",[76] faces analogous challenges: there is evidence suggesting a steady decline in religiosity in Western Europe since the 1960s (though not matched in the USA), with great variation in the patterns of faith from one country to the other.[77] Secularization is not, however, accepted without contestation from other theoretical frames that aim to explain contemporary religious trends.

---

71 O'Leary (2010) refers to "accepted channels" of such influence.

72 O'Leary (2010) at 4.

73 The connection of this point with the Christian emphasis on Orthodox belief and the individual's equal relation to God as conditions for salvation are unavoidable (Cf. O'Leary (2010) at 9).

74 For instance, Islamic law distinguishes legal acts between *ibadat* and *muamalat*. *Ibadat* dictates that acts such as prayer or fasting are not susceptible to innovation or change. *Muamalat* covering acts involving interaction and exchange among people, in sales or sureties, for example, suggests more room to facilitate interaction while promoting justice. Both categories are nevertheless regulated by Islamic law. [Oxford Islamic Studies Online, available at www.oxfordislamicstudies.com/article/opr/t125/e1564].

75 O'Leary (2010) at 9.

76 O'Leary (2010).

77 Pippa Norris and Ronald Inglehart, 'Uneven Secularization in the US & Western Europe', in Thomas Banchoff (ed.), *Democracy and the New Religious Pluralism*, Oxford University Press, 2007, 31–57 at 33 et seq.

Religious market theory, prompted as an alternative explanatory framework, is put forward, for example, to claim that levels of religious participation are shaped by the competition among denominations taken together with the degree of state regulation of religious institutions.[78] In other words, the variance of the 'top-down' religious supply explains the variation in patterns of religiosity more than the secularization thesis. In a sense, the religious market approach to religiosity variation resonates with and reflects the growing field of studies that focuses on the agency of religious actors. It claims that the competition between faith organizations (often to fill gaps or space left by the State) creates religious activism.[79] One of the fields where the competition is particularly evident in Western states is education.

The social class dimension may also potentially be affecting secularization dynamics. Put simply, if the poor are almost twice as likely to be religious compared to the rich,[80] socio-economic equality and human development may hold a stronger connection to religiosity than initially foreseen. Norris and Inglehart argue further that secularization and cultural change are path-dependent: secularization brings cultural changes that move in the direction of less allegiance to culture/tradition and more tolerance.[81] A post-secularist vision of society relies instead on the co-existence of the religious and the non-religious but also suggests the possibility for individuals to determine the degree and type of 'religious' faith to which they adhere. [82] Habermas's solution in that respect is that "[b] oth religious and secular mentalities must be open to a complementary learning process if we are to balance shared citizenship and cultural difference".[83]

An empirically grounded understanding of religion as connected to (post)- secular dynamics and statehood in modern legal systems calls also for at least some understanding of the distributions of religious power within a community. This dimension of secular statehood is necessary in order to establish realistically how religions influence 'secular' governance and law in their quest to become considerable social actors.[84] Conversely, this also shows that secularism currently

---

78 Norris and Inglehart (2007) at 40–41. The theory remains contested, however, due to the inconclusive findings connecting religious pluralism to religious participation, both empirically and geographically.

79 The phenomenon is most evident in the US, where the survival of these actors depends on their efforts to attract volunteers as much as financial resources (Norris and Ingelhart (2007) at 41).

80 Norris and Ingelhart (2007) at 47.

81 Norris and Ingelhart (2007) at 47–48.

82 Hazel Bryan, 'Reconstructing the Teacher as a Post Secular Pedagogue: A Consideration of the New Teachers' Standards', *Journal of Beliefs and Values*, 33(2), 2012, 217–228 at 222. For a critique of the concept, see David Carr, 'Post-Secularism, Religious Knowledge and Religious Education', *Journal of Beliefs and Values*, 33(2), 2012, 157–168.

83 Juergen Habermas, 'Notes on a Post-Secular Society', *New Perspective Quarterly*, 25(4), 2008, 17–29.

84 Matthias Mahlmann, 'Religion, Secularism and the Origins of Foundational Values of Modern Constitutionalism', Paper presented at the VII World Congress of Constitutional Law: Rethinking the Boundaries of Constitutional Law, 11–16 June 2007, at 2 [in file with the author].

is not independent from religious actors, particularly due to the importance that faith(s) have in the life of many individuals.

In addition, the *stricto sensu* constitutional dimension of secularism calls for the non-endorsement of a particular faith by the State but may in fact diversify greatly in the position that States take when regulating religion in the public sphere. While some States may conceive their legal role in abstentionist terms (i.e. complete separation between state and religion), other states may interpret their task in more liberal terms, as non-intervention or by means of giving space to all religions without discrimination (i.e. open neutrality). The implications of any of the earlier mentioned are particularly felt in education, with emphasis often given, for example, to the issue of the presence of religious symbols in public schools. A liberal humanist perspective, reflecting the principle of equality, would endorse an understanding of the role of the secular state as one that extends room for action of religious communities, even when the core of the faith is criticized as unacceptable, perhaps even intolerable. Such an individualistic approach requires, nevertheless, some qualification: it is often recalled that religious practices that violate human rights unjustifiably reach the limits of this approach, requiring actions on behalf of the (secular) State. The current difficulty in such scenarios is to decide what these limits are, when human rights happen to collide among them in the exercise of religious belief.

Against a declared resistance by State legal systems to create a 'hierarchy' among human rights to solve such conflicts, and the great difficulty to separate the values contained within human rights from their religious roots, secularism ends up as a paradoxical configuration: as the secular state leaves aside its religious influences in their constitutional dimension, these influences claim their presence through human rights-based claims and their underpinning values.[85]

An illustration of the fallacy of the principle of neutrality, perceived as the legal reflection of secularism, can be observed within Europe in the case law developed by the European Court of Human Rights on religious symbols. With the intention to approach religion on the basis of objective methods of what can be considered an 'appropriate' manifestation of religious belief, and with exclusive focus on the 'forum externum', the Court has often used Article 9 ECHR as a tool of repression of religious liberties.[86] The role of the State is described in the decisions of the ECtHR as being "to reconcile the interests of the various groups" (Sahin, at para. 106), act even-handedly "in exercising its regulatory power in this sphere and in its relations with the various religions, denominations and beliefs" (*Metropolitan Church of Bessarabia and Others v. Moldova*, at para. 116) and as a "neutral organizer of religious life within the state" (Sahin, at para. 107). Similarly, in *Refah Partisi v. Turkey*, secularism dictated the ban of a political party because some forms of religious expression are not deemed compatible

---

85 Mahlmann (2007) makes a similar point at 8.
86 See, for example, the case of *Sahin v. Turkey*, Appl. No. 44174/98 (Grand Chamber), 2005 on the prohibition of students wearing headscarves in universities.

with secularism.[87] Evans and Petkoff make the same point using the wearing of religious symbols as an example: it is an inherent exercise of individual choice; that of being different in a pluralistic society.[88]

Human rights are, therefore, primarily legal tools, but neutrality, at least in its European legal dimension, has often transformed them into normative statements of what is perceived as politically correct in a given time and space.[89] The perspective of interaction and interdependence between religious identities is a radically different one, however: "it is essential to our humanity that there should always be foreigners, human beings from another community who have an alternative way of organizing the task and privilege of being human, so that our imaginations are refreshed and so our sense of cultural possibilities renewed'.[90]

4 Educational autonomy, religious freedom and equality

Religion is a global new priority for public policy. It is a 'cultural fact' with tremendous emotional and political power. Since 9/11, the vast majority of States within and beyond the European continent have been confronted, many times in brutal ways, with the role that religion plays in good community and personal relations, including within public education.

In Europe, there is a broad policy tendency to teach religion in public schools as a subject that is designed to prepare students to live within multicultural societies. Both within, but also beyond Europe, however, alternative arrangements of religious education dispensed by religious communities within the framework of a given national curriculum are present and growing.[91] How religion is taught is linked to how religion is perceived in the "imagination of the nation",[92] but also depends on the legal arrangements that prevail at a given time and space, not neglecting the complementary efforts towards religious education undertaken by the family and the school.

In this framework, the question of religion in education has been gaining in importance in multicultural societies for a variety of reasons. One common angle to perceive the issue is the one that argues that education represents an ideal path to maintain and develop one's identity, especially when belonging to a religious minority. It is also a legitimate way to promote tolerance and respect for the

---

87 See para. 123 of the Refah Partisi judgment stating: "The Court concurs in the Chamber's view that sharia is incompatible with the fundamental principles of democracy".
88 Malcolm Evans and Peter Petkoff, 'A Separation of Convenience? The Concept of Neutrality in the Jurisprudence of the European Court of Human Rights', *Religion, State and Society*, 36(3), September 2008, 205–223, at 209.
89 Evans and Petkoff (2008) at 216.
90 Oliver O'Donovan, *The Desire of the Nations: Rediscovering the Roots of Political Theology*, Cambridge University Press, 1996, at 268.
91 Peter Van der Veer, 'Religion and Education in a Secular Age: A Comparative Perspective', *Extrême Orient Extrême Occident*, 33/2011, 235–245, at para. 3.
92 Expression borrowed from Van der Veer (2011) at para. 3.

Other, and difference more broadly, the aim being to foster social cohesion while combating ignorance, often the cause of hostility towards religion(s).

At times, there is reluctance to acknowledge issues related to religion as a mode of discourse within the public sphere. A fresh approach to this 'old' question may require us to leave to the side the traditional distinction between the private and public sphere when it comes to considering the role of religion in public affairs, as already explained. Habermas has been debating this point post 9/11, arguing that while it is legitimate for political institutions to remain neutral vis-à-vis religion, the use of religious language and discourse may in fact now be required in order to establish streams of dialogue between the different communities.[93] The central role of dialogue and exchange is of course not aimed at reinventing religion or secularity: it is aimed at averting the escalation of conflicts. The art of politics is, after all, not the suppression of conflict, but rather the mediation of it.[94]

Publicly funded schools are microcosms of these debates and the theatres of daily exchanges about religions. Public international law has now recognized these playgrounds of intercultural activity but has limited itself to insist on social cohesion arguments and human rights protection. What we are still missing is the element of interaction: the engagement with each other in a way that will prevent violence.

There is great wealth in educational approaches that cultivate this missing interactivity: some approaches are more 'interpretive' and insist on the skills of interpretations and critical self-reflection. At the same time, they recognize the inner diversity of religions, the contested nature of religious traditions and even the complexity of cultural change, as religious traditions operate as identity markers and reference points. Other approaches are relying on 'dialogical' experiences. These start from the understanding that all individuals are relatively autonomous but at the same time influenced by social groupings to which they simultaneously belong (family, peers, ethnic and religious groups). Students become collaborators in teaching and learning, and dialogue happens on the acceptance of diversity, on the need to be positive about difference, and finally, on the actual verbal exchange between students. Such an approach may be complemented with elements of historical background when trying to understand one's 'roots', together with citizenship training and/or comparing and contrasting one's background to that of another fellow student.[95]

Educating 'about' religion is clearly a distinct approach, however, from that of educating 'into' religion (a single religious tradition is taught by insiders as part of a socialization project) or educating 'from' religion (pupils consider different

---

93 Habermas (2008).

94 Jonathan Sacks, *Not in God's Name*, London: Hodder and Stoughton, 2015, at 228.

95 Both broad approaches are analyzed in more detail in Robert Jackson, 'Is Diversity Changing Religious Education? Religion, Diversity and Education in Today's Europe', in Geir Skeie (ed.), *Religious Diversity and Education: Nordic Perspectives*, Muenster: Waxmann, 2009, 11–28, at 23–25.

responses to religious and moral issues in order to develop their own point of view).[96] All three approaches, however, may be the subject of manipulation for ideological or political purposes, raising issues of excessive agency/autonomy or bias.

The link between education and religious diversity is, however, not a new one: the United Nations Educational, Scientific and Cultural Organization (UNESCO) has been involved in human rights and intercultural education since the mid-1970s.[97] *The UNESCO Dakar Framework for Action 2000–2015*, more recently, referred to the role and potential of schools in promoting understanding among religious groups, emphasizing the crucial contribution of education in that respect. Also echoing the general concern about religion in Europe, the Council of Europe has gradually shifted its agenda towards the acknowledgement that religion should be given a cautious place in education in order to enable students to develop the necessary competences of critical empathy. Religion as culture, therefore, has been utilized as the most sensible way forward on the basis of a lowest common denominator approach.[98] The Organization for Security and Cooperation in Europe (OSCE)'s Office for Democratic Institutions and Human Rights (ODIHR) similarly produced a set of principles that describe religious diversity in education as a project that should stress the positive value in the teaching of respect for everyone's right to freedom of religion and that should acknowledge that education 'about' religion can avert harmful stereotypes.[99]

From a diversity management perspective, however, religious diversity education frameworks are against two kinds of factors in multicultural settings: in the first case, there is a struggle for the control of the principal institutions of the State (and predominance in steering the direction of the law and political culture within that given State), and in a second one, the main issue is how the central institutions of a State should let minority groups live, particularly when their lifestyle contradicts some of the important values of that state as reflected in its law and political culture.[100] Both of these processes are interlinked and influence how public education is organized, with more emphasis on the second aspect.

---

96 Jackson (2009) at 20.
97 See, for example, the UNESCO Recommendations Concerning Education for International Understanding, Co-operation and Peace and Education Relating to Human Rights and Fundamental Freedoms (1974), available at www.unesco.org/education/nfsunesco/pdf/Peace_e.pdf.
98 The point justifying this reliance was the diversity of arrangements in European states on the place of religion in schools and the public space more broadly.
99 OSCE Office for Democratic Institutions and Human Rights (ODIHR), Toledo Guiding Principles on Teaching About Religions and Beliefs in Public Schools, OSCE-ODIHR, Warsaw, 2007.
100 Menachem Mautner, 'The Immanuel Affair and the Problems of Intercultural Encounter', *Democratic Culture in Israel and the World*, 15, 2013, at 19, available at http://ssrn.com/abstract=2257217.

Constitutionally, the question of autonomous religious education, recognized as a right to religious groups,[101] creates the background for the potential conflict between three subjects of rights/duties: the child-learner, who enjoys a right to (meaningful) education and equal opportunities, the right of parents to educate their children according to their own community's religious values, and finally, the State, whose duty is to provide education for all under the understanding that its existence, within democratic parameters, depends on its citizens' participation and peaceful co-existence, as cultivated through education. In legal theory, liberal thinkers have been unable to provide a uniform position on how the balance between these three sources of normativity should be struck. Indicatively, Brian Barry[102] places emphasis on the right and duty of the State to control the education of children, in an attempt to protect both the interests of the State and the rights and interests of children. Through separated schools on the basis of religious identity, he fears that refusal to admit non-believer learners or resistance to teach the core curriculum will disintegrate society further. Religion in public education will also frontally attack what he sees as the triple aim of education to equip children to function in society, to understand the world and obtain a job with the help of aesthetic appreciation and critical capacity, and to develop a capacity for personal autonomy.[103]

At the other end of the liberal spectrum, Chandran Kukathas argues that as the core principles of liberalism are diversity and limited government, therefore, religious education should be outside the State's scope of action and control.[104] Connected to this last point, the question of state funding of religious education, for example, appears to be most controversial, as the case-study on Israel in Chapter 4 will illustrate.

The perpetuation of the religious identities of citizens often comes at the cost of civic education, and by extension the continued existence of the liberal democratic state in itself. The lack of exposure to diversity and the lack of cultivation of common citizenship remain pending question marks on the issue.[105] The relationship between state funding and state supervision is clearly spelled out in many legal systems, insofar as no contradiction is allowed to subsist between cultural development and the liberal democratic state. In fact, there is no incompatibility expressed or legally sanctioned between state control and the right to religious education. The emphasis on the civic duty of the State to ensure that

---

101 For more on this point, see Chapter 3 of this book.
102 Brian Barry, *Culture and Equality*, Harvard University Press, 2001.
103 Barry (2001) at 212–225.
104 Chandran Kukathas, 'Education and Citizenship in Diverse Societies', *International Journal of Educational Research*, 35, 2001, 319, 321–322; Chandran Kukathas, *The Liberal Archipelago: A Theory of Diversity and Freedom*, Oxford University Press, 2003.
105 For an excellent analysis of these points, see Gila Stopler, 'The Right to an Exclusively Religious Education—The Ultra-Orthodox Community in Israel in Comparative Perspective', *Georgia Journal of International and Comparative Law*, 42, 2014, 743–796 in particular 754–781.

all children receive some form of civic education is a constant concern in most case studies discussed here, with the exception of Israel. At the same time, an interesting emerging trend to observe is the shifting emphasis of parents' choice from providing a religiously relevant education to their children to one that also addresses the need to find good jobs later on, with the deracializing effects that this carries.[106]

5 The neutrality of education and the principle of equality

In the context of this comparative study, and within the wider discussion of the perennial conflict between the preservation of cultural identity and the enforcement of shared citizenship (and values), the case studies offered in the following chapters will investigate how the balance is struck between the sets of interests of different actors, with the additional consideration of how the principle of equality and non-discrimination becomes operationalized and even determines the balancing act between the other two competing rights.

Critical streams of the sociology of education have noted in relation to the right to equality in the past that "Education was not about equality, but inequality. . . . Education's main purpose of social integration of a class society could be achieved only by preparing most kids for an unequal future, by ensuring their personal underdevelopment".[107] In other words, public education may be a process that maintains societal divisions along class, gender, culture, religion or ethnic lines. If that is so, it clearly challenges the principle of equality, understood as the possibility of every child to access education in order to fulfill her/ his potential.

The example of religious dress at schools is indicative of the controversial terms of the debate: States owe a special duty of protection towards children due to their vulnerability.[108] At the same time, international law treats children as 'incomplete' right holders when compared with adults.[109] The implications of this categorization are clear in terms of agency: their ability to act is conditioned by and legally subjected to the will of their parents/guardians,[110] subject to the

---

106 Stopler (2014) at 782–783. See also the case study on the UK in Chapter 6 of this book.
107 P. Willis, 'Cultural Production and Theories of Reproduction', in L. Barton and S. Walker (eds.), *Race, Class and Education*, London: Croom Helm, 1983, 106–110, at 110.
108 UN International Covenant on Civil and Political Rights 1966, Article 14(1).
109 Committee on the Rights of the Child, CRC General Comment No. 12: The Right of the Child to Be Heard, UN Doc. CRC/C/GC/12, 2009, at para. 1.
110 The limitations imposed on their agency decrease as their 'evolving capacity' defined as "processes of maturation and learning whereby children progressively acquire knowledge, competencies and understanding, including acquiring understanding about their rights and about how they can be best realized" unfold. [Cf. Committee on the Rights of the Child, CRC General Comment No. 7: Implementing Child Rights in Early Childhood, UN Doc. CRC/C/GC/7/Rev.1, 20 September 2006, para. 17.

limitations of fundamental rights.[111] It is clear that all decisions made for or on behalf of the child should be made in her/his best interest.[112] It is up to the State, however, to determine what those interests are in each case.[113]

Indicatively, in *Hasan and Eylem Zengin v. Turkey*, the European Court of Human Rights found that: "in a democratic society, only pluralism in education can enable pupils to develop a critical mind with regard to religious matters in the context of freedom of thought, conscience and religion".[114] In striking the balance between the best interests of the child while justifying the rights of parents, the same Court further noted that dealing critically with plurality in society justifies the limitation of parental rights based on the exercise of the right to religion.[115] Is it then accurate to claim that community affiliation may limit autonomy? Are the two mutually exclusive, and is there any possibility for balancing? Mustasaari claims that it is possible to be simultaneously high in autonomy and in 'relatedness':[116] all that is required is that one approaches autonomy "not [as] a matter of sheer independence but of what one does with one's dependence".[117]

Connected to autonomy, the parameters of the discussion concerning religious diversity in schools call for reflection on another common phenomenon: the existence and limits of religious exemption claims in public schools, especially in circumstances where religious norms conflict with school policy and/or the broader legal framework. The wider implications of such accommodative practices have repercussions on the content of the principle of equality.

Increasing religious diversity in public education, understood as any "government-funded and/or government-regulated educational activity",[118] is therefore a complex task that has an inherently reflective and reflexive dimension. Robert Wuthrow's notion of "reflective pluralism" highlights the nature of this reflection by first recognizing that both within (but also beyond the school environment)

---

111 In *Kjeldsen, Busk Madsen and Pedersen v. Denmark* (Cases No. 5095/71, 5920/72, 5926/72), Judgment of 7 December 1976, paras. 53–54 and *Dojan and Others v. Germany* (Cases No. 319/08, 2455/08, 7908/10, 8152/10, 8155/10), Judgment of 13 September 2011, the ECtHR ruled on the conflict between parental authority against public interest on the issue of sexual education and where the latter prevailed, without nevertheless considering the opinion or best interests of the children concerned.

112 Article 3 CRC.

113 John Eckelaar, *Family Law and Personal Life*, Oxford: Oxford University Press, 2007, at 13.

114 *Zengin v. Turkey*, Appl. No. 1448/04, Judgment of 9 October 2007, para. 5.

115 *Dojan and Others v. Germany* (Cases No. 319/08, 2455/08, 7908/10, 8152/10, 8155/10), Judgment of 13 September 2011, at para. 2(a).

116 Sanna Mustasaari, 'Law, Agency and the Intimate Relationships of Young People: From Rights to Duties and Back?' in Dorota A. Gozdecka and Magdalena Kmak (eds.), *Europe at the Edge of Pluralism*, Intersentia, 2015, 133–145, at 142–143.

117 This definition belongs to Robert C. Roberts and W. Jay Wood, *Intellectual Virtues: An Essay in Regulative Epistemology*, Oxford: Oxford University Press, 2007, at 257–258.

118 David Basinger, 'Religious Diversity in Public Education', in Chad Meister (ed.), *The Oxford Handbook of Religious Diversity*, New York: Oxford University Press, 2011, 277–288 at 277.

our opinions are shaped by our beliefs, which we should not assume to be 'inherently superior' and second, that religious plurality within schools requires "a principled willingness to compromise . . . in order to arrive at a workable relationship with another person".[119] The practice of adjudicating on exemption claims on the basis of religious belief emerges much more complex in practice, as will be demonstrated in the following chapters.

---

119 Robert Wuthrow, *America and the Challenge of Religious Diversity*, Princeton University Press, 2005, in particular 286–307 and 292.

3 The standards

Interpreting the content of rights: the legal interaction of religious freedom, education and non-discrimination

1 Introduction: the relevance of religion in education

The rationale and triggering factor for international bodies to turn their attention to the role of religion in education is related to concerns of maximizing social cohesion with implications and real risks connected to the shift from integration to assimilation. At the same time, states in multicultural societies are struggling to achieve the 'right' balance among human rights, including religion and equality, in the public sphere.[1]

In this context, the right to education has been described as a multiplier right that operates as an instrument for individuals to enhance their freedom.[2] Yet, it is also a highly contextual right: the ability of right holders to access education, on equal terms, is highly dependent on a series of other factors such as gender, poverty, conflict, ethnicity or geographical location.

Within a global climate of intense competition for scarce resources, it is therefore worth considering the value of education also beyond a rights-based perspective, as an instrument of social mobility, while also accounting for its potential as a policy factor connected to economic growth.[3] The instrumental character of education, as a right, is emphasized when it is presented as an essential precondition to create empowered citizens.[4] Incidentally, it is also conducive to increasing levels of income as well as democratic citizenship.[5]

---

1 Robert Jackson, 'Is Diversity Changing Religious Education? Religion, Diversity and Education in Today's Europe', 2009, 11–28, at 11, available at www.waxmann.com/?id=20&cHash=1&buchnr=2154.
2 Amartya Sen describes the benefits of education as follows: "A person may benefit from education – in reading, communicating, arguing, in being able to choose in a more informed way, in being taken more seriously by others and so on. The benefits of education, thus, exceed its role as human capital in commodity production". [Cf. Sen, Amartya, *Development as Freedom*, Anchor Books, 2000, at 294.]
3 Joanna Bourke Martignoni, *Echoes from a Distant Shore: The Right to Education in International Development*, Schulthess—Editions Romandes, 2012, at 17.
4 See, for example, R. Brian Howe and Katherine Covell, *Empowering Children: Children's Rights Education as a Pathway to Citizenship*, University of Toronto Press, 2007. Empowerment rights in this context can be defined as those that "provide the individual with control over the course of his or her life, and in particular, control over . . . the state". Jack Donnelly and Rhoda E. Howard, 'Assessing National Human Rights Performance: A Theoretical Framework', *Human Rights Quarterly*, 10(2), 1988, 214–248, at 234–235.
5 The connection between education and civil and political rights is well established through case law as well. The example of US jurisprudence is characteristic: *Wisconsin v. Yoder* (1972)

On a more global scale, educational models sourced from the West were selectively transplanted in non-European and colonial education systems during the 19th and 20th centuries. But while in Europe education was becoming gradually more secular, in the colonies missionaries were responsible for educating children.[6] The seeds of religious evangelism, imperialism and racial superiority are still visible in the educational systems of some post-colonial states. In the more recent past, and after World War II, there has also been a clear shift in the type of actors who are involved in the education process: "transnational networks and international organizations played a particularly influential role in the development of mass schooling in Asia, Africa, and Latin America . . . insofar as they impelled modernizing elites to facilitate the circulation, emulation and adoption of Western educational models and the adaptation of these to local customs".[7]

Within international law, the right to education in itself is laid out in well-defined terms within at least three distinct international legal documents that set the standard:[8] the Universal Declaration of Human Rights (UDHR), the International Covenant of Economic, Social and Cultural Rights (ICESCR) and the Convention on the Rights of the Child (CRC).[9] In each one of these documents, the duty of the State is to provide primary education "compulsory and available free to all". For secondary education, the State's duty is more restricted insofar as it is required to make it "available and accessible to every child", with a progressive introduction of free secondary education. Further to the duty of availability, the CRC requires states to "make educational and vocational information and guidance available and accessible to all children" and to "take measures to encourage regular attendance and the reduction of drop-out rates". It should,

---

406 US 205, 221 where it is found that "some degree of education is necessary to prepare citizens to participate effectively and intelligently in our open political system"; *San Antonio Independent School District v. Rodriguez* (1973) 411 US 1, 63 where the Court stated that "there can be no doubt that education is inextricably linked to the right to participate in the electoral process".

6 Bourke Martignoni (2012) at 39.

7 Aaron Benavot and Julia Resnik, 'Lessons from the Past: A Comparative Socio-Historical Analysis of Primary and Secondary Education', in Joel E. Cohen, David E. Bloom and Martin B. Malin (eds.), *Educating All Children: A Global Agenda*, MIT Press, 2006, 123–229, at 125.

8 There is abundant legal literature that discusses the right to education as a human right. See indicatively, Klaus Dieter Bieter, *The Protection of the Right to Education by International Law*, Martinus Nijhoff Publishers, 2005; Katerina Tomasevski, *Education Denied: Costs and Remedies*, London: Zen Books, 2003; Mieke Verheyde, *Commentary to the UN Convnetion on the Rights of the Child—Article 28: The Right to Education*, Martinus Nijhoff, 2006; Douglas Hodgson, *The Human Right to Education*, Ashgate, 1998.

9 Other regional legal instruments guaranteeing the right to education are the Council of Europe 1950 European Convention for the Protection of Human Rights and Fundamental Freedoms, ETS No. 5, 213 U.N.T.S. 222; Article 2 of the 1952 First Protocol to the European Convention, ETS No. 9, 213 U.N.T.S. 262; Council of Europe 1961 European Social Charter, ETS No. 35, Article 10; Organization of African Unity, 1981 African (Banjul) Charter on Human and Peoples' Rights, OAU. Doc. CAB/LEG/67/3Rev.5, 1520 U.N.T.S. 217, Article 17(1); Organization of American States, 1988 Additional Protocol to the American Convention on Human Rights in the Area of Economic, Social and Cultural Rights—Protocol of San Salvador, OAS Treaty Series No. 69, Article 13.

however, be noted that "the role of legal obligations per se remains often a weak reed on which to lean. Non-legal factors such as perceptions of self-interest, including the notion of reciprocity, and culturally established notions like self-image, are often more important".[10] The focus of this study will be limited to primary and secondary education, where the duty of the State is at its strongest.

2 The nature of the right to education

Article 26 of the UDHR reads:

"1   Everyone has the right to education. Education shall be free, at least in the elementary and fundamental stages. Elementary education shall be compulsory. Technical and professional education shall be made generally available and higher education shall be equally accessible to all on the basis of merit.

2   Education shall be directed to the full development of the human personality and to the strengthening of respect for human rights and fundamental freedoms. It shall promote understanding, tolerance and friendship among all nations, racial or religious groups, and shall further the activities of the United Nations for the maintenance of peace".

According to Article 26 UDHR and Article 13 ICEPCR, education is a gateway right: not only is it a human right in itself, but it also represents a means towards the realization of other rights, a vehicle of empowerment that assists economically and socially marginalized groups to achieve fuller means of participation in their communities.[11] It is connected to the dignity and equality of individuals that are inherently important for the protection of diversity.

The element of participation in society is combined with an entitlement for all ethnic groups as well as national and religious groups to enjoy the right in question. The link between education and particular religious and cultural groups is spelled out in Article 15 ICESCR that is interpreted as striving for education that must be "culturally appropriate, include human rights education, enable children to develop their personality and cultural identity and to learn and understand cultural values and practices of the communities to which they belong, as well as those of other communities and societies".[12]

---

10   Forsythe, David P., 'Human Rights Studies: On the Dangers of Legalistic Assumptions', in Fons Coomans, Fred Gruenfeld and Menno T. Kamminga (eds.), *Methods of Human Rights Research*, Intersentia, 2009, 59–75 at 74.

11   UN ICESCR, General Comment No. 13, Article 13: The Right to Education, UN Doc. E/C.12/1999/10, 8 December 1999, at para. 1. See also Articles 17 and 22 of the African Charter on Human and Peoples' Rights recognizing the right to education for advancement, as connected, however, to participation in the cultural life of one's community as a means for development.

12   UN Committee on Economic, Social and Cultural Rights, General Comment No. 21: The Right of Everyone to Take Part in Cultural Life, UN Doc. E/C.12/GC/21, 2009, at para. 26.

Content-wise, the right to education within the International Covenant on Economic, Social and Cultural Rights (ICESCR) includes four essential features: 'availability', denoting that functioning educational institutions must be available in sufficient numbers, as well as facilities and learning resources, including adequate numbers of qualified teachers;[13] 'accessibility', requiring that education be accessible to everyone without discrimination, including the positive measures that may be required from duty bearers in this direction;[14] 'acceptability', stipulating that the form and substance of education offered must be culturally relevant and appropriate;[15] and finally, 'adaptability', adding the prerequisite that education be flexible enough to adjust to the needs of changing societies, both macroscopically in response to global realities but also microscopically in connection with the local ethnic, religious and linguistic groups.[16]

Additionally, the right, in itself, carries three normative dimensions: the right to receive education, the right to choose freely the most appropriate form of education and the right to equal access to education without discrimination. This plurality creates a context of interaction with regard to educational provision and funding as well as the freedom of right holders to choose the context and form of education that suits them within a broader frame of equality. The interests of the various rights holders and duty bearers often conflict, however, largely as a direct

13 In practice this translates into satisfactory numbers of adequately trained and remunerated teachers, sustainable funding, facilities such as classrooms, electricity and toilets, as well as physical accessibility defined as "within safe physical reach, either by attendance, at some reasonably convenient geographic location (e.g. a neighbourhood school) or via modern technology (e.g. access to a 'distance learning' programme)". Cf. UN Committee on Economic, Social and Cultural Rights, General Comment No. 13: The Right to Education, UN Doc. E/C.12/1999/10, 1999, para. 6)

14 The positive obligations of duty bearers to guarantee educational accessibility span over three 'overlapping dimensions' namely non-discrimination, physical as well as economic accessibility (Cf. UN Committee on Economic, Social and Cultural Rights, General Comment No. 13: The Right to Education, UN Doc. E/C.12/1999/10, 1999, para. 6(b)). In this context, non-discrimination concerns both the theoretical availability of education as the nature of access to education (Cf. Office of the High Commissioner for Human Rights, Report on Indicators for Promoting and Monitoring the Implementation of Human Rights, UN Doc. HRI/MC/20, 2008, at para. 20.

15 This requirement concerns the content of education in terms of its quality and with the aim of providing satisfactorily for 'basic learning needs'. The usual indicators in this respect are literacy, numeracy and problem-solving skills. Additionally, school materials must respect the dignity of the students while furthering the aims of education such as promotion of human rights, tolerance and an understanding of cultural diversity. It is also important to include here the degree to which religious and other convictions of both learners and their parents are respected in the teaching syllabus. For more, see Tomasevski (2003).

16 UN Committee on Economic, Social and Cultural Rights, General Comment No. 13, The Right to Education, UN Doc. E/C.12/1999/10, 1999, para. 6. For a translation of these criteria into rights-based indicators see Katerina Tomasevski, Annual Report of the Special Rapporteur on the Right to Education, UN Doc. E/CN.4/2002/60, 13, 2002. See also Katerina Tomasevski, Preliminary Report of the Special Rapporteur on the Right to Education, UN Doc. E/CN.4/1999/49, 1999, at para. 71.

consequence of the plurality found within the right itself. This web of rights that increasingly connects children, their parents, the State and teachers, as well as private educational providers, relies on an understanding of the right to education as a mechanism for child protection from harm, as a tool for the provision of basic goods and services as well as a pathway towards the participation of children as independent social actors in our diverse societies.[17]

The right to education has often been qualified as a 'progressive' right: this signifies that states, by becoming parties to international agreements that pertain to this specific right, commit themselves to take steps to the maximum of their available resources to realize those rights. In this regard, the right to education should be contrasted with the right to equality: the Committee on Economic, Social and Cultural Rights has stated that "the prohibition against discrimination enshrined in Article 2(2) of the ICESCR is subject to neither progressive realization nor the availability of resources; it applies fully and immediately to all aspects of education and encompasses all internationally prohibited grounds of discrimination". A state will be violating the prohibition of discrimination (in education) both with direct action (e.g. introduction of discriminatory laws) but also when failing to take measures "which address de facto education discrimination". States must also ensure that their respective legal systems provide "appropriate means of redress, or remedies . . . to any aggrieved individual or groups".[18]

The Convention against Discrimination in Education[19] defines discrimination in education as follows:

> any distinction, exclusion, limitation or preference which, being based on race, colour, sex, language, religion, political or other opinion, national or social origin, economic condition or birth, has the purpose or effect of nullifying or impairing equality of treatment in education and in particular . . . limiting any person or group of persons to education of an inferior standard.

The Convention sanctions "any differences of treatment by the public authorities between nationals, except on the basis of merit or need . . . and in any form or assistance granted by the public authorities to educational institutions, any restrictions or preferences based solely on the ground that pupils belong to a particular group".[20]

Despite the clear framing of non-discriminatory approaches to the enjoyment of the right to education, it remains a challenge to measure the extent of inequality within education on a global scale, especially when accessing schools. This is why it becomes correspondingly difficult to monitor the patterns of discrimination in

---

17 Bourke Martignoni (2012) at 120.
18 UN Committee on Economic, Social and Cultural Rights, General Comment No. 13: The Right to Education, UN Doc. E/C.12/1999/19, 1999 at para. 59.
19 UNESCO, Convention Against Discrimination in Education, Adopted by the General Conference at its 11th Session, 14 December 1960, Paris, available at www.unesco.org/educa tion/pdf/DISCRI_E.PDF
20 Article 3(c)-(d) of the Convention.

that respect in order to then address the phenomenon at its source.[21] Some of the usual indicators used refer to the socio-cultural setting, the gender dimension or the family status of students. Statistical evidence is increasingly used by courts to bring to light specific obstacles in accessing education.[22]

The collective dimension of the right to education is of equivalent relevance: education becomes a 'public good' insofar as it may contribute towards the increase of the skills of a given population with repercussions on its social welfare, per capita income but also the dignity and autonomy of its members.[23] The UN Human Rights Committee has connected this collective dimension of the right with Article 27 ICCPR by finding that while the right to education is individually exercised, it is crucial for the capacity of the members of certain groups to maintain their language and culture and to practice their religion in community with others of the same group.[24] The typical illustration of the collective dimension of the right to education is found in the freedom to establish and run alternative educational institutions which in themselves form part of the framework for the creation of conditions appropriate towards multicultural types of citizenship. The international legal framework and, in particular, the Convention against Discrimination in Education allows the establishment of separate educational systems for religious or linguistic reasons, provided that the education offered is "in keeping with the wishes of the pupil's parents or legal guardians", is framed according to national policy that "ensure[s] that the standards of education are equivalent in all public education institutions of the same level, and that the conditions relating to the quality of education provided are also equivalent".[25] Conflicts are not rare in this context: educational rights of individuals belonging to a particular group may run counter to the imperatives of the collective. The US case of *Wisconsin v Yoder* is diachronically illustrative of the scenario.[26]

The general trend in international human rights law with respect to education appears to be to balance the rights of the individuals concerned to receive an education on the basis of norms laid out in international and national law with the collective rights of the group affected.[27] In extension of this recognition, Article

---

21 See indicatively, Tomasevski (2003), in particular 57.
22 See the landmark decision of the European Court of Human Rights, *D.H. and Others v. Czech Republic*, Appl. No. 57325/00 of 2007, which established that "reliable and significant" statistics can be used to establish discriminatory impact concerning the practice of the city of Ostrava to place Romani schools in special schools disproportionately.
23 Bourke Martignoni (2012) at 154.
24 UN Human Rights Committee, General Comment No. 23: The Rights of Minorities, UN Doc. CCPR/C/21/Rev.1/Add.5, at para. 62.
25 Article 2(b) and Article 4(b) of the Convention.
26 US Supreme Court, *Wisconsin v. Yoder* (1972) 406 US 205.
27 Article 5(1)(c) of the UNESCO Convention Against Discrimination in Education recognizes the rights of national minorities to "carry on their own educational activities" provided that individual group members are not prevented from "understanding the culture and language of the community as a whole and from participating in its activities" and that the standard of education is not lower, with attendance to those schools remaining optional.

13 (4) ICESCR awards the right to everyone to found private schools, subjected to national government regulation and meeting minimum educational and human rights standards. As such, private school institutions can also be considered right-holders in education with an equivalent right to autonomy and equal treatment, covering among others their own curricula, admission criteria and methods of instruction.[28] The question as to whether such schools are entitled to public funding remains open and highly controversial, as the evidence from the case studies covered here will further illustrate. The reality is often such that the right to establish private schools can be rarely realized without the financial support of the State, making meaningless any rights of education granted to minority groups on the basis of culture, religion, language or nationality when the State withdraws financially.[29] To the extent, however, that governments subsidize such schools, they "must do so without discrimination on any of the prohibited grounds".[30]

Particularly for migrants and their families, international human rights law provides specific guarantees in relation to access to education through Article 30 of the Migrant Workers' Convention, covering both regular and 'irregular' migrants.[31]

3 The content of the right to education in its religious/cultural dimension

Article 29(1) of the Convention on the Rights of the Child states clearly the aims of education for children. These are:

(a) the development of the child's personality, talents and mental and physical abilities to their fullest potential;
(b) the development of respect for human rights and fundamental freedoms, and for the principles enshrined in the Charter of the United Nations;

---

28 See Manfred Nowak, 'The Right to Education', in A. Eide et al. (eds.), *Economic, Social and Cultural Rights: A Textbook*, Martinus Nijhoff, 2001, 245–271 at 264.
29 Yoram Rabin, 'The Many Faces of the Right to Education', in Daphne Erez-Barak and Aeyal Gross (eds.), *Exploring Social Rights—Between Theory and Practice*, Hart Publishing, 2008, 265–288, at 272.
30 UN Committee on Economic, Social and Cultural Rights, General Comment No. 13: The Right to Education, UN Doc. E/C.12/1999/19, 1999, at para. 54.
31 Article 30 stipulates "Each child of a migrant worker shall have the basic right of access to education on the basis of equality of treatment with nationals of the State concerned. Access to public pre-school educational institutions or schools shall not be refused or limited by reason of the irregular situation with respect to stay or employment of either parent or by reason of the irregularity of the child's stay in the State of employment". [UN International Convention on the Protection of the Rights of All Migrant Workers and Members of Their Families, G.A. Res. 45/158, 45 UN GAOR Supp. (No. 49A) at 262, UN Doc. A/45/49, 2220 U.N.T.S. 93, 1990. The text has nevertheless received few ratifications.

(c) the development of respect for the child's parents, his or her own cultural identity, language and values, for the national values of the country in which the child is living, the country from which he or she may originate, and for the civilizations different from his or her own;

(d) the preparation of the child for responsible life in a free society, in the spirit of understanding, peace, tolerance, equality of the sexes, and friendship among all peoples, ethnic national and religious groups and persons of indigenous origin; and

(e) the development of respect for the national environment.

The interpretative force of the provision lies in its attempt to strike a balance between education as a means for instruction on the State's national values and respect for cultural difference. It places emphasis on the state authorities' duty to harmonize national curricula with lessons on the child's own cultural identity. To this effect, the Committee on the Rights of the Child has emphasized, while commenting on Article 29(1) CRC, the child's "individual and subjective right to a specific quality of education" that is "child-centered" and based on a "curriculum . . . of direct relevance to the child's social, cultural, environmental, and economic context".[32] It has further added that the right to education is not limited to access but covers also content and processes.[33] Similarly, the UN Committee on Economic, Social and Cultural Rights has stated that "the form and substance of education, including curricula and teaching methods, have to be acceptable (e.g. relevant, culturally appropriate and of good quality) to students" and states must "fulfill (facilitate) the acceptability of education by taking positive measures to ensure that education is culturally appropriate for minorities and indigenous peoples".[34]

The qualitative dimension of Article 29(1) proposes a right to education that is "child-centered, child-friendly and empowering".[35] Two conclusions may be drawn from this dimension: first, the concept and content of education clearly extends beyond formal schooling towards affording children the possibility to develop their personalities, talents and experiences, and second, this dynamic perception of education ultimately entails an empowering dimension that conditions the content of the right. Driven by the changes and challenges brought as a result of globalization and new technologies, and taking into account the tensions that arise between the global and the local, the individual and the collective, tradition and modernity, a meaningful education, according to Article 29(1) CRC,

32 UN Convention on the Rights of the Child, General Communet No. 1, Article 29(1): The Aims of Education, UN Doc. CRC/GC/2001/1, 17 April 2001.

33 UN Convention on the Rights of the Child, General Communet No. 1, Article 29(1): The Aims of Education, UN Doc. CRC/GC/2001/1, 17 April 2001, at para. 2.

34 UN Committee on Economic, Social and Cultural Rights, General Comment No. 13: The Right to Education, UN Doc. E/C.12/1999/10, 1999, at para. 50.

35 UN Convention on the Rights of the Child, General Communet No. 1, Article 29(1): The Aims of Education, UN Doc. CRC/GC/2001/1, 17 April 2001, at para. 2.

must be based on a broad range of values that extend beyond the boundaries of religion, nation and culture as they are understood in many parts of our world.[36] The stated goal and ambition of the right is to utilize Article 29(1) as a 'bridge' reuniting groups that have been separated on account of their different perceptions of values. The noted difference between individuals and groups with respect to important values in education and more broadly social life may be sourced from within the child's own community. Hence, there is a prioritization of multidisciplinary approaches to achieve the goal of integrated and holistic education.[37]

Such a contextualized approach to the content of education would, however, dictate the consideration of the broader ethical framework described in Article 29(1), with clear emphasis on human rights. The General Comment notes in that respect: "Children do not lose their human rights by virtue of passing through the school gates".[38] Specifically for children belonging to ethnic, religious or linguistic minorities, or who are indigenous, the CRC finds in Article 30 that such a child "shall not be denied the right, in community with other members of his or her group, to enjoy his or her own culture, to profess and practice his or her own religion, or to use his or her own language". In cases of children living in situations of conflict or emergency, educational programmes must be organized with particular emphasis on tolerance and mutual understanding so as to prevent violence and conflict as much as possible.[39]

The right to relevant education extends, however, beyond children as learners to their parents. The right of parents and guardians to decide what is in a child's best interest with respect to his/her education is well established.[40] This right operates and is connected to the cultural context in which the child lives. Articles 5 and 12 of the Convention on the Rights of the Child state that these rights decrease as the child's capacity to make independent decisions increases.[41] The

---

36 UN Convention on the Rights of the Child, General Communet No. 1, Article 29(1): The Aims of Education, UN Doc. CRC/GC/2001/1, 17 April 2001, at paras. 3–4.

37 UN Convention on the Rights of the Child, General Communet No. 1, Article 29(1): The Aims of Education, UN Doc. CRC/GC/2001/1, 17 April 2001, at para. 13.

38 UN Convention on the Rights of the Child, General Communet No. 1, Article 29(1): The Aims of Education, UN Doc. CRC/GC/2001/1, 17 April 2001, at para. 8.

39 UN Convention on the Rights of the Child, General Communet No. 1, Article 29(1): The Aims of Education, UN Doc. CRC/GC/2001/1, 17 April 2001, at para. 16.

40 UDHR, Article 26(3); ICESCR, Article 13(4); UN CRC, Article 29(2).

41 Article 12 of the CRC stipulates: "State Parties shall assure to the child who is capable of forming his or her own views the right to express those views freely in all matters affecting the child, the views of the child being given due weight in accordance with the age and maturity of the child".

Article 5 of the CRC states: "States Parties shall respect the responsibilities, rights and duties of parents or, where applicable, the members of the extended family or community as provided for by local custom, legal guardians or other persons legally responsible for the child, to provide, in a manner consistent with the evolving capacities of the child appropriate direction and guidance in the exercise by the child of the rights recognized in the present Convention". [UN Convention on the Rights of the Child, UN Doc. A/44/49, 1577 U.N.T.S. 3, 1989.

spirit of the provisions here aims at treating parents as 'agency rights' holders that act on behalf of their children to protect their rights, under the understanding that in case of conflict between the parental freedom and the rights of the child, the latter shall prevail.[42]

Religious instruction is singled out for special consideration under Article 13(3) ICESCR that grants parents the right to ensure the religious and moral education of their children. The Committee on Economic, Social and Cultural Rights has stated that the ICESCR:

> permits school instruction in subjects such as the general history of religious and ethics if it is given in an unbiased and objective way, respectful of the freedoms of opinion, conscience and expression. . . . [P]ublic education that includes instruction in a particular religion or belief is inconsistent with article 13(3) unless provision is made for non-discriminatory exemptions or alternatives that would accommodate the wishes of parents and guardians.

Article 18 of the International Covenant on Civil and Political Rights (ICCPR)[43] also states that:

> The States Parties to the present Covenant on Civil and Political Rights have respect for the liberty of parents . . . to ensure the religious and moral education of their children in conformity with their own convictions.

A parallel provision of the Convention Against Discrimination in Education also stipulates that "no person or group of persons should be compelled to receive religious instruction inconsistent with his or their conviction". In this sense, the parental right to determine the education of his/her child functions as a counterweight to potential state indoctrination, and by extension its exercise is designed to reinforce pluralism.[44] Very similarly, Article 2 of Protocol 1 of the European Convention on Human Rights and Fundamental Freedoms stipulates that:

> No person shall be denied the right to education. In the exercise of any functions which it assumes in relation to education and to teaching, the State shall respect the right of parents to ensure such education and teaching in conformity with their own religious and philosophical convictions.

---

42 See indicatively ECtHR *Neulinger and Shuruk v. Switzerland*, Appl. No. 41615/07, 2010 and ECtHR *Kjeldsen, Busk Madsen and Pedersen v. Denmark* (Cases No. 5095/71, 5920/72, 5926/72), Judgment of 7 December 1976.
43 International Covenant on Civil and Political Rights, Article 18, 16 December 1966, U.N.T.S. 171.
44 Rabin (2008) at 276.

In yet another context, in the realm of EU law, the European Charter of Fundamental Rights, which has become legally binding since December 2009, stipulates in Article 14 that:

> 1. Everyone has the right to education and to have access to vocational and continuing training
>
>   1. The freedom to found education establishments with due respect for democratic principles and the right of parents to ensure the education and teaching of their children in conformity with their religious, philosophical and pedagogical convictions shall be respected, in accordance with the national laws governing the exercise of such freedom and right.

A clear limit established from the perspective of the State in the exercise of parental power in abusive terms lies, for example, in the prohibition against corporal punishment or the choice of an education stream that hinders the child's integration in society. The real terms of the balancing exercise between parental preferences and state intervention, however, are rarely as clear: if parents wish to remain part of the minority religious groups that require such practices, the exercise of parental rights comes second to the requirements of group membership, which, incidentally, may be violating the essence of the right of individual members (children) to receive an appropriate education.

4 The right to religious freedom within education: a path towards co-existence?

Contemporary studies on religious pluralism have accepted that the governance of religious pluralism under conditions of globalization and international migration have to address directly or indirectly the point on the definition of the public sphere, outside and beyond the nation-state format.[45]

In broad terms, freedom of religion in international law is a fundamental right that allows the individual to have a certain religion (or none) and to manifest it,[46]

---

45 Matthias Koenig, 'How Nation-States Respond to Religious Diversity', in P. Bramadat and M. Koenig (eds.), *International Migration and the Governance of Religious Diversity*, Montreal: McGill–Queen's University Press, 2009, 293–317, at 300. See also Chapter 1 of this book.

46 See, for example, Article 18 of the Universal Declaration of Human Rights that stipulates:
18. Everyone has the right to freedom of thought, conscience and religion; this right includes freedom to change his religion and belief, and freedom, either alone or in community with others and in public or private, to manifest his religion or belief in teaching, practice, worship and observance.

A corresponding right is recognized in Article 18 ICCPR in greater length as follows:

"18.1 Everyone shall have the right to freedom of thought, conscience and religion. This right shall include freedom to have or to adopt a religion or belief of his choice, and freedom, either individually or in community with others and in public or private, to manifest his religion or belief in worship, observance, practice and teaching.

2 No one shall be subject to coercion which would impair his freedom to have or to adopt a religion or belief of his choice.

extending to children and their parents.[47] Yet religion as a social phenomenon and as an object of legal protection remains a notoriously challenging concept to define. There are three mainstream options to the effect of framing legislation protecting (non)beliefs: the first follows Emile Durkheim's definition of religion, which describes the concept as "[a] unified system of beliefs and practices relative to sacred things, that is to say, things set apart and forbidden – beliefs and practices which unite into one single moral community called a Church, all those who adhere to them".[48] The second proceeds according to a list of recognized religions (including the outline of the process and criteria for recognition).[49] Within that option, certain religions are given the status of a legal person in public law. The third option leaves the task of defining religion to courts, as it relates to a statute or any other legal instrument.

In general legal terms, the scope of the right covers both the freedom to adopt a religion or belief but also the freedom from coercion in religious matters.[50] While separation of the State and religion is not part of public international law

---

3 "Freedom to manifest one's religion or beliefs may be subject only to such limitation as are prescribed by law and are necessary to protect public safety, order, health, or morals or the fundamental rights and freedoms of others". See also indicatively Article 8 of the African Charter on Human and Peoples' Rights that stipulates "Freedom of conscience, the profession and free practice of religion shall be guaranteed. No one may, subject to law and order, be submitted to measures restricting the exercise of these freedoms".

47 See Article 18 (4) ICCPR that states:

"4 The States Parties to the present Covenant undertake to have respect for the liberty of parents and, when applicable, legal guardians, to ensure the religious and moral education of their children in conformity with their own convictions".

Article 24 ICCPR further adds: "24.1 Every child shall have, without any discrimination as to race, colour, sex, language, religion, national or social origin, property or birth, the right to such measures of protection as are required by his status as a minor, on the part of his family, society and the State".

48 Emile Durkheim, *The Elementary Forms of Religious Life, 1915*, J.W. Swain (trans.), New York: Free Press, 1962, at 62.

49 These criteria can be related, for example, to internal organization, financing and historical presence on the territory of the State. It leaves scope, however, for discretion with regards to new religious movements.

50 Article 6 of the Declaration on the Elimination of All Forms of Intolerance and of Discrimination Based on Religion and Belief defines religion as follows:

"6 In accordance with Article 1 of the present Declaration, and subject to the provisions of Article 1, paragraph 3, the right to freedom of thought, conscience, religion or belief shall include, inter alia, the following freedoms:

(a) to worship or assemble in connection with a religion or belief, and to establish and maintain places for these purposes;

(b) to establish and maintain appropriate charitable or humanitarian institutions;

(c) to make, acquire and use to an adequate extent the necessary articles and materials related to the rites or customs of a religion or belief;

(d) to write, issue and disseminate relevant publications in these areas;

(e) to teach a religion or belief in places suitable for these purposes;

(f) to solicit and receive voluntary financial and other contributions from individuals and institutions;

(g) to train, appoint, elect, or designate by succession appropriate leaders called for by the requirements and standards of any religion or belief;

or customary law per se, it has become over time the preferred policy option in order to preserve the core of the right of freedom of religion, subject to limitations prescribed by law such as public safety, order, health, morals and the rights and freedoms of others. The Convention on the Rights of the Child[51] explicitly guarantees freedom of religion for children in Article 14,[52] with a broader duty of non-discrimination on State parties included in Article 2 of the same Convention. There is nevertheless no right for children to receive teaching about one specific religious or belief system within a public school.

Current initiatives in public education and religion stemming from UNESCO,[53] the UN,[54] the Council of Europe, the EU[55] or the Organization for Security and Cooperation in Europe have set the goals of promoting respect for freedom of religion in the public sphere while encouraging social cohesion through tolerance. The United Nations Educational, Scientific and Cultural Organization (UNESCO) in its Dakar Framework for Action 2000–2015 highlighted the role of schools in fostering understanding among religious groups in and through education.[56] In a similar spirit, the 2005 'Alliance of Civilizations' initiative

---

(h) to observe days of rest and to celebrate holidays and ceremonies in accordance with the precepts of one's religion or belief;

(i) to establish and maintain communications with individuals and communities in matters of religion and belief at the national and international levels".

51 Into force on 2 September 1990.

52 Article 14 states:

"14.1 States Parties shall respect the right of the child to freedom of thought, conscience and religion.

2 States Parties shall respect the rights and duties of the parents and, when applicable, legal guardians, to provide direction to the child in the exercise of his or her right in a manner consistent with the evolving capacities of the child.

3 Freedom to manifest one's religion or beliefs may be subject only to such limitations as are prescribed by law and are necessary to protect public safety, order, health or morals, or the fundamental rights and freedoms of others".

53 UNESCO, The Dakar Framework for Action, Education for All: Meeting our Collective Commitments, 2000–2015 is the current UNESCO programme that aims to promote in schools understanding among religious groups with emphasis on the role of institutions in developing partnerships with religious bodies in educational contexts. [Cf. www.unesco. org/education/nfsunesco/pdf/Peace_e.pdf].

54 The UN Secretary launched in 2005 the *Alliance of Civilizations* Programme co-sponsored by the Prime Ministers of Spain and Turkey with a similar goal to "provide students with a mutual respect and understanding for the diverse religious beliefs, practices and cultures in the world". [Cf. Report of the High-Level Group of the Alliance of Civilizations, 13 November 2006, Chapter VI, para. 6.8, available at www.unaoc.org/repository/HLG_Report.pdf]

55 In 2005 the Council adopted a resolution on the response of educational systems to racism and xenophobia which includes the value of teaching materials for religious diversity purposes. [Cf. Resolution of the Council on the Response of Educational Systems to the Problem of Racism, 23 October 2005, O.J. C312, 23 November 2005.]

56 UNESCO, The Dakar Framework for Action, Education for All: Meeting Our Collective Commitments, adopted at the World Education Forum, Dakar, Senegal, 26–28 April 2000, available at http://unesdoc.unesco.org/images/0012/001211/121147e.pdf.

launched by the UN Secretary-General referred to education systems as hubs of "mutual respect and understanding for the diverse religious beliefs, practices and cultures in the world".[57]

At the Council of Europe level, beyond Article 9 of the ECHR and Article 12 of the Framework Convention for the Protection of National Minorities (FCNM), the policy trajectory on intercultural education has mainly gained impetus as a means to develop respect for the rights of others as well as a predisposition and appreciation for dialogue with others of different backgrounds. The shift towards intercultural education ends a relatively long period of ignoring religion due to the different relationships between religion and State across European countries.[58] The common locus for such debates was not set on the personal and societal aspects of religion, but instead on the recognition of religion as a legitimate factor of public policy.[59] The OSCE's contribution to the issue, post-9/11, the Toledo Guiding Principles on Teaching about Religions and Beliefs in Public Schools (OSCE 2007),[60] focuses primarily on education 'about' religion, as a means to bridge cultural gaps of ignorance and misunderstanding while allowing for the exercise of the right to religious freedom.

From the perspective of the individual's right to freedom of religion, religious education can under no circumstances influence students in the direction of embracing a particular belief. The Council of Europe Recommendation on education and religion is clear in that respect:

> each person's religion, including the option of having no religion, is a strictly personal matter. However, this is not inconsistent with the view that a good general knowledge of religions and the resulting sense of tolerance are essential to the exercise of democratic citizenship.[61]

Related to the exercise of religious freedom in public schools is the often-overlooked aspect of the rights of teachers. As the case studies in this discussion will demonstrate in the following chapters, teachers hold a pivotal role in translating

---

57 Report of the High Level Group of the Alliance of Civilizations, 13 November 2006, Chapter VI, para. 6.8 available at www.unaoc.org/repository/HLG_Report.pdf.

58 Jackson (2009) at 14.

59 The Council of Europe established a Steering Committee on Education that went further and submitted a recommendation to the Committee of Ministers on the management of religious diversity in schools urging governments to take into account the religious dimension of intercultural education, as a basis for the development of tolerance and a culture of "living together". See Final Recommendation CM/Rec (2008) 12, as approved by the Committee of Ministers in December 2008, available at https://search.coe.int/cm/Pages/result_details.aspx?ObjectID=09000016805d20e8.

60 OSCE Office for Democratic Institutions and Human Rights (ODIHR), Toledo Guiding Principles on Teaching About Religions and Beliefs in Public Schools, OSCE-ODIHR, Warsaw, 2007.

61 Recommendation 1720 (2005).

law into practice but also remain themselves the holders of socio-economic rights, including the one to individual religious freedom.

The starting point of this section claims that within increasingly globalized settings, it is dangerous, if not unsustainable, to claim that any given national model on the co-relation of secular and religious values in education can serve as a blueprint for a universal model of human rights education in multicultural societies. One immediate effect of this assumption is that constitutional traditions should not operate as legal justifications for the limitations of religious human rights exercised in the public sphere.[62] Challenges to the established models of state-church relations stem from the growing role of religious communities that are increasingly involved in social activities, such as education, with immediate impact and repercussions on the shaping of national identities.

In cases where due to the absolute separation of religion and the State, no religious instruction in public schools is offered, the paradigm of religious 'otherness' cannot be sufficiently connected to the principles of equality and religious pluralism. Yet such content is necessary in multicultural and multi-religious societies, as will be shown.[63]

There is little doubt that the introduction of the freedom of religion constitutes the most legally appropriate response to the challenges of religious pluralism within multicultural societies, but at the same time it is worth examining to what extent the secular character of the State and its ensuing neutrality are sufficient to guarantee equal religious freedoms for everyone.[64] More specifically, the constant struggle between the acceptable limitation to one's positive liberty to practice and the other's negative liberty to remain spared from the religious practices of the others does not seem to find systematic and coherent answers within legal acts and before courts.

Linked to this balancing act is the question that concerns what Habermas characterizes as the "unleashing [of] religious voices in the political public sphere".[65] Is the expression of a plethora of potentially conflicting religious convictions necessary or even at all desired? From a strictly legal perspective, the answer that this study proposes is positive. Regarding education, in the US Supreme Court case of *Zorach* v. *Clauson* (1952),[66] Justice Douglas explained:

> When the state encourages religious instruction or cooperates with religious authorities by adjusting the schedule of public events to sectarian needs, it

62 Daniel Augenstein, 'The Contested Polity: Europe's Constitutional Identity Between Religious and Secular Values', University of Edinburg School of Law Working Paper Series, 2009/13 at 5.

63 Dorota A. Gozdecka, 'Religion and Legal Boundaries of Democracy in Europe: European Commitment to Democratic Principles', Dissertation, University of Helsinki, 2009, at 219, available at http://ethesis.helsinki.fi.

64 Juergen Habermas, 'Religion in the Public Sphere', Lecture at San Diego University, 2006 available at https://onlinelibrary.wiley.com/doi/abs/10.1111/j.1468-0378.2006.00241.x, at 6.

65 Habermas (2006) at 11.

66 343 U.S. 306 (1952).

follows the best of our traditions. For it then respects the religious nature of our people and accommodates the public service to their spiritual needs. To hold that it may not would be to find in the Constitution a requirement that the government show a callous indifference to religious groups. That would be preferring those who believe in no religion over those who do believe.

The argument was, nevertheless, made from the trajectory of the dominant religion of the time. Its essence about a State's non-indifference to religious groups, however, remains. Alongside the Habermasian argument that claims that it is necessary to allow such expressions because they constitute one of the key resources for the creation of identity, human rights law by virtue of the principles of equality and non-discrimination reaches similar theoretical conclusions.

The legal peculiarity of the right to religious freedom cannot and should not nevertheless be ignored: religion is after all a subjective mental activity, at times even irrational, that relies partly on non-scientific arguments. How then can courts and judicial bodies approach it (and protect it) through objective and scientific criteria? The prevailing tendency is to rely on the observation of the manifestations of religious belief in order to then adjudicate on what is worthy of legal protection within the scope of religious freedom. Indeed, there are two broad trends in international human rights protection of religious freedom that should be noted at this stage: first, protection of religious freedoms is gradually shifting from protection 'of' religion to protection 'from' religion. Second, and equally relevant in this case, there is an additional shift of the protection of religious freedom in itself to that of indirect protection of such freedom through the phenomena of its manifestation, registration and discrimination.[67]

The constitutional protection of the freedom of religion implies first and foremost that the secular State must remain neutral between the different religions. In a stricter educational context, this in turn may signify and justify the ban of religious symbols, such as the headscarf, from school. Such neutrality should not, however, be confused with discrimination between the Muslim headscarf and the Christian habit.[68] In other words, it should not allow for state neutrality to function within education as a means to privilege a national culture loaded for historical and socio-cultural reasons with Christian values. In the words of Modood, "radical political arrangements seem to suit and favor private kind of religions, but not those that require public action. It is surely a contradiction to require both that the state should be neutral about religions and that the state should require religions with public ambitions to give them up".[69]

Case law from various countries, including before pan-European fora, suggests precisely the opposite: discrimination against non-Christian denominations

67 For both trends see Malcolm Evans and Peter Petkoff, 'A Separation of Convenience? The Concept of Neutrality in the Jurisprudence of the European Court of Human Rights', *Religion, State and Society*, 36(3), September 2008, 205–223 at 216.
68 Augenstein (2009) at 16.
69 Tariq Modood, 'Anti-Essentialism, Multiculturalism and the "Recognition" of Religious Groups', *Journal of Political Philosophy*, 6, 1998, 378–399 at 393.

is constant, very often in the context of a classroom or regarding educational issues. The case of *Sahin* v. *Turkey*, which concerned the prohibition on students wearing headscarves or having beards while attending university classes and examinations underlined the manner in which Article 9 of the ECHR on freedom of religion can be distorted: the assertion of the need to preserve general public order and religious pluralism through the elimination and prohibition of a specific form of public manifestation of religious belief in state-run institutions in reality allowed for the possibility that the article of the Convention in question could be transformed into a tool of repression of religious liberty.[70] Or to put it more simply, as Lord Hoffman did in the UK case of *Begum* v. *Denbigh High School*,[71] "people sometimes have to suffer some inconvenience for their beliefs". The situation in *Begum* was similar in that it concerned a 14-year-old girl who had been excluded from school for wearing a jilbab in contravention of the school's uniform policy. The House of Lords concluded that there was no interference with the student's freedom of religion, as other schools that would allow her to wear the jilbab were available.

National legislation of European countries on the wearing of the headscarf offers a variety of schemes. Established burqa (face veil) bans at the time of writing exist in France, Denmark, Austria, Bulgaria, Belgium and the Netherlands.[72] In certain cases, such as Sweden or Finland, headscarves are allowed but not body covering garments. In several other countries, no regulation on this point exists precisely because the problem does not appear to arise for the moment.

The European Court of Human Rights has been given the opportunity on a number of occasions in recent years to pronounce itself on how it perceives its role and position of religion in the public sphere. More often than not, by virtue of Article 9 of the ECHR, the Court has adopted a form of 'decisional minimalism', consisting in finding no more than necessary in order to justify a certain outcome, while leaving as much as possible undecided with the assistance of the 'margin of appreciation' and 'proportionality tools'.[73] While an absolute right to religious freedom is difficult to imagine in the European legal space, the Court remains prepared to enforce what Danchin terms "liberal neutrality".

In that framework, let us consider the joint cases *Efstratiou* v. *Greece* and *Valsamis* v. *Greece*: in both cases, the Court found that the requirement of students to take part in school parades commemorating the outbreak of war between Greece and Italy in 1940 did not constitute an interference with the students' and their

---

70 For a similar point see Evans and Petkoff (2008) at 208.

71 HL 22 MAR 2006 (2006) UKHL 15, 1 AC100 (2006), 2 All ER 487.

72 Deutsche Welle, 'Where Are "Burqa Bans" in Europe?' 1 August 2019, available at www. dw.com/en/where-are-burqa-bans-in-europe/a-49843292.

73 The concept of decisional minimalism is borrowed from Cass R. Sunstein, *One Case at a Time: Judicial Minimalism on the Supreme Court*, Harvard University Press, 1999, 9–23. See, for example, *Kokkinakis v. Greece*, Appl. No. 14307/88, 260 ECtHR Ser. A.

parents' religious convictions as Jehovah's Witnesses.[74] The objective of achieving national unity outweighed the religious convictions of the students, with emphasis on the commemoration of national events as pacifist and public interest events. These cases represent precisely the type of neutrality prevalent in Europe. In an opposite direction, in *Folgero and others* v. *Norway*, the Court, striving towards pluralist education, required from the State to ensure that information of knowledge included in the curriculum be conveyed in an objective, critical and pluralistic manner.[75] In *Zengin* v. *Turkey*, the Court furthermore specified that a course on a specific (most often the dominant) religion cannot be compulsory.[76] Yet, in *Dahlab* v. *Switzerland*, the applicant, a teacher in primary school was forbidden to wear the headscarf, as the Court perceived a negative image of the veil by finding that:

> The applicant's pupils were aged between four and eight, an age at which children wonder about many things and are also more easily influenced than older pupils. In those circumstances, it cannot be denied outright that the wearing of a headscarf might have some kind of proselytizing effect, seeing that it appears to be imposed on women by a precept which is laid down in the Koran and which, as the Federal Court noted, is hard to square with the principle of gender equality. It therefore appears difficult to reconcile the wearing of an Islamic headscarf with the message of tolerance, respect for others and, above all, equality and non-discrimination that all teachers in a democratic society must convey to their pupils.[77]

In sum, ECtHR case law demonstrates the complexity of the balancing act that the legislators and/or adjudicators are called upon: on the one hand, the need to secure a minimum level of tolerance and peaceful co-existence between rival ways of life and, on the other hand, the assertion of universal rights as remedies and common ground for Western democracies.

5 The right to equality and non-discrimination in the context of religious diversity in public education

The notion of equality as connected to non-discrimination stems from the double recognition that all members of society (both those belonging to religious majorities and minorities) deserve equal recognition from the law; and that the

---

74 *Efstratiou v. Greece*, Appl. No. 24095/94, 24 Eur. Human Rights Report 294, 1997 and *Valsamis v. Greece*, Appl. No. 21787/93, 24 Eur. Human Rights Report 294, 1997.
75 *Folgero and Others v. Norway*, Appl. No. 15472/02, Judgment of 29 June 2007.
76 *Zengin v. Turkey*, Appl. No. 1448/04, Judgment of 9 October 2007.
77 *Dahlab v. Switzerland*, Appl. No. 42393/98, 10.

use of actionable and enforceable legal rights are the legal vehicles to protect social facts that differentiate individuals.[78]

Religious identity remains linked to economic determination and historical context, in similar patterns to class.[79] As a social construct, it has dynamic features that are time-specific, context-dependent and, as importantly, intertwined with other criteria such as gender, race, age or poverty affecting the type and degree of discrimination, wherever it occurs. There is, for instance, significant societal overlap between religious identity and ethnicity to the point of creating at times normative and legal overlaps, too.[80]

Also, any understanding of a normative entitlement to equality must assume at the very least that all actors engaged in an instance of conflict resolution between two competing 'rights' attach the same meaning to equality. More than that, equality as "the ignoring of difference between individuals for a particular purpose in a particular context, or the deliberate indifference to specified differences in the acknowledgement of the existence of difference"[81] is insufficient: the concept in itself is not only relational (i.e. it has to be viewed as a relationship and not a possession), it must also be accompanied by the necessary conditions conducive to the exercise of one's individual capacities, very similar to the spirit of the right to education. As such, laws, rules or normative statements that neglect the consideration of their impact on society are potentially discriminatory.

In general terms, there is little dispute that equality comes in various ideologically tainted shapes: from 'equality as rationality', where arbitrary behavior amounts to discrimination, subject to possible justifications for discrimination, to 'equality as fairness', where justifications are subjected to closer scrutiny (e.g. through indirect discrimination screening) and all the way to 'radical equality of opportunity', which focuses on institutional and structural barriers to equal rights[82] appearing almost unattainable.

The role of the State remains relevant in a human rights analysis of equality within religiously diverse frames with (again) a vast array of possible scenarios conceivable: states (and their governments) may choose to be hostile towards certain religious groups (e.g. by conceiving of them as 'security threats'); they may discourage on paper discrimination on the basis of religion but actually withdraw from any attempts to enforce non-discrimination, or, as it has become common, they may choose to link the majority religion with national identity at the cost of discriminating against smaller minority groups.[83]

Additionally, the consideration of the right to equality and non-discrimination when opposed to religious freedoms cannot ignore the growing importance that identity has acquired in the rise of racism and xenophobia, including when

---

78 Anne-Marie Mooney Cotter, *Heaven Forbid: An International Legal Analysis of Religious Discrimination*, Ashgate, 2009, at 3.
79 Cotter (2009) at 4.
80 See, for example, the case of the UK in Chapter 6 of this volume.
81 Cotter (2009) at 4.
82 Cotter (2009) at 7–8.
83 Cotter (2009) at 12–13.

connected with immigration. The link between discrimination, identity and immigration is more than obvious for xenophobic platforms. The increase of the influence of political parties and agendas that endorse arguments legitimizing hierarchical visions of representations, perceptions and treatments of value systems, often under labels of 'national preference' and particularly under conditions of economic stagnation, dictate a re-reading of equality and non-discrimination provisions within international human rights law. In that sense and with regard to religious freedom and equality, it has become crucial to interpret secularism in a way that does not lead to the legitimization of new forms of discrimination preventing some from full participation in public life because of their beliefs.[84]

Article 2 of the Universal Declaration of Human Rights states:

> 2 Everyone is entitled to all the rights and freedoms set forth in this Declaration, without distinction of any kind, such as race, color, sex, language, religion, political or other opinion, national or social origin, property, birth or other status.

It further adds, in Article 7 that:

> 7 All are equal before the law and are entitled without any discrimination to equal protection of the law. All are entitled to equal protection against any discrimination in violation of this Declaration and against any incitement to such discrimination.[85]

Indicatively and in an analogous vein, the African Charter on Human Rights and Peoples' Rights approaches equality in its Article 19 as follows by emphasizing the collective dimension of the principle:

> All peoples shall be equal; they shall enjoy the same respect and shall have the same rights. Nothing shall justify the domination of a people by another.

In the same text, Article 2 covers the prohibition of discrimination, including on the basis of religion:

> Every individual shall be entitled to the enjoyment of the rights and freedoms recognized and guaranteed in the present Charter without distinction of any kind such as race, ethnic color, sex, language, *religion*, political or

---

84 See United Nations, The Fight Against Racism, Racial Discrimination, Xenophobia and Related Intolerance and the Comprehensive Implementation of and Follow-Up to the Durban Declaration and Programme of Action, UN Doc. E/CN.4/2005/18.

85 An equivalent provision is available in Article 26 ICCPR that states:
  "26. All persons are equal before the law and are entitled without any discrimination to the equal protection of the law. In this respect, the law shall prohibit any discrimination and guarantee to all persons equal and effective protection against discrimination on any ground such as race, color, sex, language, religion, political or other opinion, national or social origin, property, birth or other status".

any other opinion, national and social origin, fortune, birth or any status [emphasis added].

This approach in international law towards non-discrimination translates to corresponding duties of states, including in relation to religion, outlined in Article 2 of the International Covenant of Civil and Political Rights (ICCPR), which stipulates:

> 2.1 Each State Party to the present Covenant undertakes to respect and to ensure to all individuals within its territory and subject to its jurisdiction the rights recognized in the present Covenant, without distinction of any kind, such as race, color, sex, language, *religion*, political or other opinion, national or social origin, property, birth or other status" [emphasis added].

Furthermore, the International Convention on the Elimination of All Forms of Racial Discrimination[86] covers non-discrimination in the context of older minorities who suffer discrimination on the basis of a combination of race and religious characteristics. The coverage of the Convention includes special measures destined to achieve adequate development. It states in its Article 5(d) (vii) the duty of states to implement:

> Other civil rights, in particular:
> (vii) The right to freedom of thought, conscience and religion;

Finally, the Convention on the Elimination of All Forms of Discrimination against Women[87] covers the right of all women against discrimination, including those who suffer several layers of discrimination, including on the basis of their faith, in reaching equality with men in public life when accessing nationality, education, employment, health and socio-economic benefits.

Particularly in the context of the right to education, non-discrimination is therefore a minimum core entitlement in human rights law.[88] Both the direct as well as the indirect forms of discrimination affect the potential for redressing social inequalities through education and conversely confirm the possibility that in many cases education may function as a mechanism that protects and advances the interests of those with access to power while maintaining the disempowerment of the disadvantaged.[89]

---

86 Adopted on 21 December 1965.
87 Adopted on 18 December 1979.
88 See Article 13 of the ICESCR as interpreted in the UN Committee on Economic, Social and Cultural Rights, General Comment No. 13: The Right to Education, UN Doc. E./C.12/1999/19, 1999, at paras. 31–37 that covers also the factors that may be conducive to discrimination such as geographical location, citizenship/immigration status, gender, age, ethnic origin in assessing access to equal educational opportunities.
89 Bourke Martignoni (2012) at 131.

4 Plural public education in Israel

For equal or different students?

"I'm not crazy. My reality is just different than yours".
Alice in Wonderland, Lewis Carroll

1 Legal pluralism in Israel: the context

The first case study on the 'empirical variations' of the right to religious freedom within public education focuses on Israel. The right is observed through a comparative frame of reference within legal pluralist jurisdictions. While there is one obvious level of constitutional analysis (and comparison with the ensuing case studies), the inquiry also carries the more ambitious and nuanced aim of offering a different perspective on how human rights may be understood, interpreted and applied by different categories of social actors, more particularly religious communities. The 'voice' of freedom of education and religion certainly belongs to governments, political parties and courts, but it should also be heard from religious communities, especially within divided social contexts.

Accounts of how religious diversity challenges public education, in Israel as well as elsewhere, involve scenarios of conflict. These conflicts appear to be multilateral, non-linear and often unpredictable in their components. They arise within a state-centered constitutional system, between a national and a supra-national entity, among the various layers of normative ordering within a state or even arise within one and the same cultural 'enclave'.

The analysis that follows is clearly not an anthropological one insofar as it attempts to move beyond observing the workings of legal pluralism: it emits concern, critique and frustration but at the same time also notes complexity, surprise and messiness when analyzing the normative content of complex human rights such as those connected to religion and education. The 'cage' imprisoning lawyers, caught in the process of legitimizing the diffusion of human rights as one self-sufficient 'culture' is clearly a matter of perspective: if we accept that the door to the cage is open, the process of observation may occur both from within but also from a greater distance, in the quest for better laws.

The relationship of the State to religion in Israel is both eclectic and ambiguous: while it can be claimed that the birth of the State of Israel was not entirely a religious project but more a reaction to the previous experiences of Judaism in diaspora, at the same time Judaism has been declared the national religion in the new State.[1] This implies that the relationship between law (understood here as legislation) and religion is often one of cause and effect. As a measure of comparison, the Israeli legal system has incorporated 14 state-recognized religious courts in an attempt to increase the State's authority (and control) but also for more practical reasons related to costs and religious strife avoidance.[2]

Despite, however, the Israeli state legal system having incorporated parts of the religious system in order to control it more efficiently, often at the cost of human rights compliance, non-state religious courts continue to exist and grow, signaling an uneasy type of deep legal pluralism. Israel's mixed secular-religious order hence is far from un-problematic despite a plural legal system incorporating religious law:[3] there is empirical evidence, for instance, that suggests that traditional pious Israelis are experiencing the need to establish and maintain a new category of non-state religious courts, despite the official absorption of religious norms into the state legal system, while the non-observant members of society decry the existing elements of legal plurality.[4]

A community-based court model, developing in Israel (particularly in private and commercial law) is evidence of a sustained need for religious adjudication, even for non-religious issues. For the purposes of the present analysis, recognizing and acting upon the need to install such tribunals, openly replacing State courts, and in addition to state rabbinical courts already having formal jurisdiction over family law cases, demonstrates how different efforts of opposing sectors in society may end up 'canceling' each other's effect on the development of pluralist legal systems.[5]

The implications of the work of these courts are even wider: there are consistent efforts from the founders of such courts to draw members of non-observant populations away from the state legal system.[6] For the ultra-Orthodox Jews,

---

1 Asher Maoz, 'The Application of Religious Law in a Multi-Religion Nation State: The Israeli Model', in R. Bottoni et al. (eds.), *Religious Rules, State Law, and Normative Pluralism—A Comparative Overview*, Springer, 2016, 209–227, at 209–210.

2 Yuksel Sezgin, 'A Political Account for Legal Confrontation between State and Society', *Studies in Law, Politics and Society*, 322, 2004, 199–233 at 213.

3 For example, Islamic Law in Israel is largely constituted by the decisions of the qadis, who are considered state officials and are paid as judges of state courts by the State (Sezgin (2004) at 214). The question of how legal pluralism has been used as an instrument of exclusion of Israeli Muslims is, however, a separate one and is also reflected in public education, as explained further in this chapter.

4 See in that respect Adam S. Hofri-Winogradow, 'A Plurality of Discontent: Legal Pluralism, Religious Adjudication and the State', *Journal of Law and Religion*, 26, 2010, 101–133 at 102, that demonstrates how 'unofficial' courts based on halachic principles have been created recently with the of adjudicating on private and criminal law disputes on the basis of religious law.

5 Hofri-Winogradow (2010) at 107. The movement of creation of such courts is noticeable since 2005 with fuller impetus but has existed since the late 1980s.

6 Hofri-Winogradow (2010) at 106.

there is consistent distrust (if not aversion) towards state adjudication.[7] It is also interesting to note that the need for such courts in Israeli is felt and is concentrated in Israel's poorer areas, within settlements in the occupied territories, where most of the observant populations are located and are staffed inter alia by heads of religious junior colleges for halachic studies (*Yeshivot Hesder*).[8]

This distrust is geared by the assumption that the state legal system in Israel operates as a 'standard-bearer for secularism'.[9] The growth of such courts nevertheless persists despite a Supreme Court finding in 2006 that private law and commercial cases are outside the scope of rabbinical jurisdiction.[10]

Turning to education, most modern education systems account for and have been shaped by the interaction between religion and the State. A classic horizontal depiction of the nexus between religion and education places at one end (legal) systems that at least nominally exclude all faith-specific subjects from the public curriculum (e.g. France, USA); in the middle, systems where elements of religious education are included and cover a variety of faiths (e.g. UK, South Africa); to systems that provide religious education for both majoritarian and minoritarian citizens-believers (e.g. Malaysia), and finally, those that enforce a state religion compulsory education based on a single mainstream faith (e.g. Iran).[11]

Israel is defined as a "Jewish and democratic State"[12] which signifies that a separation of State and religion does not exist. In the field of education, the role of religion in State affairs and the State's establishment of religion find an expression in the religious tracks of the public education system.[13] In practice, this ambiguous legal framework allows the state funding of religious institutions, particularly Orthodox-Jewish ones, which quite often enjoy equivalent and parallel political support from ultra-Orthodox parties in the Knesset. The combined efforts of the Ministry of Education with the Ministry of Religious Affairs actively subsidize a wide network of ultra-Orthodox (*Haredi*) educational activities.[14] Religious educational institutions (*Yeshivas*) enjoy thus a consistently high level of financial

---

7 Jews filing suit in state courts are considered in violation of the halachic prohibition on Jews adjudicating before state courts. [Cf. Hofri-Winogradow (2010) at 108.] To do so a Haredi plaintiff needs special permission from a Beth-Din.

8 Hofri-Winogradow (2010) at 112.

9 Hofri-Winogradow (2010) at 118.

10 HCJ 8638/03 *Amir v. Rabbinical Court of Appeals*, Jerusalem, 6 April 2006.

11 Corene de Wet, 'Religion in Education: An International Perspective', in Carl Wolhuter and Corene de Wet (eds.), *International Comparative Perspectives on Religion and Education*, Sun Press, Bloemfontein, 2014, 1–3.

12 Basic Law: Human Dignity and Freedom, §1(a), 1391 L.S.I. 150 (1992), "to protect human dignity and freedom in order to affix in a basic law the values of the state of Israel as a Jewish and democratic State".

13 *State Education Law*, 131 L.S.I. 137 (1953).

14 For more on this point, see Shimon Shetreet, 'State and Religion: Funding of Religious Institutions—The Case of Israel in Comparative Perspective', *Notre Dame Journal of Law, Ethics and Public Policy*, 13(2), 1999, 421–453 at 443.

backing, despite a duty of equal allowance towards all types of schools. The examples of the "Ashkenazi" and the "Sephardi Center of Fountain of Religious Education in Israel" are two ultra-Orthodox educational networks that have grown with the help of state funds.[15] These institutions offer education for lower or no fees, yet of a lower quality.

In the light of the analysis of the essential features of the role and position of religious diversity/freedom in public education in Israel, one recurring question emerges: to what extent does the system educate national subjects according to universal or particularistic values?[16] The issue becomes relevant when studying the effects of the clash between equality, the right to education and that to religious freedom.

In terms of a more socio-political reading of the role of the State in education, the shaping of citizens (and legal agents) belongs to the State, which continues to constitute a "structure of domination" (though a contested one) in line with Foucault's analysis.[17] One of the clearest projections of Israeli national ideology is that of a "nation by right of religion".[18] The aim of public education therefore continues to be that of deepening Jewish consciousness yet within a clear religious dimension,[19] with initially the intention also to close the social gap between Jews inside Israel.[20]

The immediate implication of this educational approach influences the connection between citizens and the polity: civic education suffers under the weight of religious training. Despite, therefore, a willingness to establish better conditions towards the exercise of rights, the deeper appreciation of the values of democracy and of democratic societies, the idea of civil society remains fuzzy in the educational system, even within the non-religious stream.[21] The "religious primordiality"[22] of the State and its education system predict an imbalance in favor of the right to religious freedom, against those of equality and the right to education.

Any account of the dynamics of religion in public education in Israel should also include the role of parents in shaping the educational content. The Ministry of

---

15 Shetreet (1999) at 443.
16 See, for example, Julia Resnik, 'Particularistic vs. Universalistic Content in the Israeli Education System', *Curriculum Inquiry*, 29(4), Winter 1999, 485–511.
17 Michel Foucault, *The Subject and Power in After Modernism*, New York: New York Museum of Contemporary Art, 1984, 417–432.
18 Resnik (1999) at 488.
19 Resnik (1999) at 492–493. The Jewish Consciousness Program (1958) stressed the new attitude towards religion: "the new generation will acknowledge the Jewish-religious way of life and will respect it", Director General's Circular 36/8, 20 March 1977, sec. 273. For a comprehensive account of the historical development of religious education in Israel, see Shmuel Shamal, ' "Cultural Shift": The Case of Religion Education in Israel', *British Journal of Sociology of Education*, 21(3), September 2000, 401–417.
20 Resnik (1999) at 494.
21 Resnik (1999) at 507.
22 Resnik (1999) at 507.

Education since the mid-1970s, has acknowledged that parents should have a significant role in the determination of the pedagogic environment of their schools.[23] Parents' organizations, as legal entities, initially received state funding and were actively involved in the design of educational programmes. Exercising their right to have their children educated according to their beliefs, parents reacted to a 1968 reform rejecting the placement of their children in integrated schools.

"Grey education" started developing by the mid-1980s, due to budget cuts towards schools, taking the form of parentally financed supplementary classes.[24] Inevitably, parents' control over educational content increased. This type of education subsists,[25] and, further to that, it enhances the gap in quality of education between social classes. Parents, as vital actors in the financial sustainability of schools, exercise pressure on school principals to shape educational goals according to their preferences, maintaining thus the gap between social groups of students.

Similar efforts in the 1990s to introduce a system of "controlled choice" whereby parents could only choose among a number of educational institutions by order of preference, in order to enhance socio-economic variety, failed, as principals validated parents' choices.[26] More recent civic education initiatives (i.e. *Being Citizens in Israel* 2000 textbook) showcase more openness towards an inclusive representation of Israeli society.[27] The lens has been adjusted, though not fully in line with the degree of social fragmentation in Israeli society. Administrative obstacles in the implementation of the new content have once more sensibly reduced its impact.[28]

2 The Normative justification of the close entanglement between religion and the State in education

The privileged position of religion in public life in Israel in combination with the strong standing of the Jewish Orthodox community are sourced from the "status quo agreement" between religious leaders and the secular Mapai party that formed a government after independence.[29] The content of the "status quo

---

23 Alexandra F. Leavy, 'The Failure of Education Policy in Israel: Politics vs Bureaucracy', *CUREJ Electronic Journal*, 2010, at 34, available at http://repository.upenn.edu/curej/115 (last accessed 21 June 2016). Parents can determine up to 25 per cent of material taught to students through "supplementary programmes" for official educational institutions.
24 Leavy (2010) at 35–36.
25 In 1994, 63 per cent of Israeli schools received private funding for such activities.
26 Leavy (2010) at 45.
27 Ami Pedahzur, 'The Paradox of Civic Education in Non-Liberal Democracies: The Case of Israel', *Journal of Education Policy*, 16(5), 2001, 413–430, at 426.
28 Pedahzur suggests a de facto reduced number of hours devoted to civic education or the lack of adjustment of teachers to the new materials to be some of the reasons for this mitigated effect. (Pedahzur (2001) at 426)
29 Mirjam Künkler and Hanna Lerner, 'A Private Matter? Religious Education and Democracy in Indonesia and Israel', *British Journal of Religious Education*, 2016, 1–29, at 7.

agreement" remains blurred, although it did initially translate into formal and informal regulations.[30]

The unofficial pact reached, at the origin of the steady role of religious communities in governance, included the following four guarantees:

(a) the Sabbath would constitute the official day of rest, with exceptions for the non-Jewish populations
(b) Kosher food would be observed in state-owned establishments
(c) the maintenance of jurisdictions of rabbinical courts over personal status matters
(d) a separate system of religious schools to be maintained.[31]

It transformed, thus, the exchange between religion and State to a "conversation about synagogue and state".[32] The partial establishment of Orthodox Judaism relies heavily on the privilege of all Jews in Israel being subjected to Orthodox Jewish religious personal laws. Correspondingly, other recognized religious communities are also subject to personal religious laws of their respective religions.

Concomitantly, in 1949, the Israeli government passed two resolutions providing for the education of Arabs in the new Jewish state. The first mandated free and compulsory education to both Arab and Jewish students, in identical terms. The second declared that Arabs would be taught in their own language.[33] At the difference of religious accommodations conceded to the Palestinian-Arab minority, which reflected a continuation of the Ottoman 'millet' system, Jewish religious accommodations became an integral part of the public sphere.[34] The main argument supporting the discrepancy in the treatment of the two communities, according to Maoz, claims that "(d)ivest Jewish culture and heritage from religious elements and one is left rather empty handed".[35]

Insistence on uniformity within the Israeli education system, especially in the early post-independence years, was indeed presented as a project aiming at the

---

30 For example, Kosher dietary observance in governmental institutions, exclusive Orthodox jurisdiction of marriage and divorce, exemptions of ultra-Orthodox students from the military service and an autonomous Orthodox education system.
31 See Amnon Rubinstein, 'State and Religion in Israel', *Journal of Contemporary History*, 4, 1967, 107, at 113.
32 Michael Karayanni, 'The "Other" Religion and State Conflict in Israel: On the Nature of Religious Accommodations for the Palestinian-Arab Minority', in Winfried Brugger and Michael Karayanni (eds.), *Religion in the Public Sphere: A Comparative Analysis of German, Israeli, American and International Law*, Berlin: Springer, 2007, 333–377, at 336.
33 Zvi Zameret, 'Fifty Years of Education in the State of Israel', Ministry of Foreign Affairs, 14 July 1998, available at www.mfa.gov.il/MFA/History/Modern+History/Israel+at+50/Fift y+Years+of+Education+in+the+State+of+Israel
34 Karayanni (2007) at 338.
35 Asher Maoz, 'State and Religion in Israel', in M. Mor (ed.), *International Perspectives on Church and State*, 1993, 239 et seq. at 243.

'general good' of the people, yet not all voices were provided with equal opportunities to be heard.[36]

Inequalities in the educational content between the two main ethnic tracks in the country appeared early on: Arabs were educated in Judaism and Israeli Jewish history, while not exposed to Palestinian history and culture. Hebrew has been required in Arab schools while Arabic is optional in Jewish schools. Efforts to include elements of Arab history, literature and culture were nevertheless made later on.[37]

One of the main targets of the Israeli education system has been, nevertheless, the closing of the gap of achievement observed among various communities within the country. To support this goal, the first two legislative acts on education, following the birth of the State of Israel, protected the right to education without discrimination on the basis of race, religion or gender (*Compulsory Education Act 1949*) and equal opportunities in accessing education regardless of political or other affiliation (*State Education Act 1953*). This legislative framework was heavily reliant on the principle of equity and included the intention to distribute the same curriculum, under the same conditions to all (e.g. same teacher-student ratio, same number of teaching days per school year and so on).[38] The practical discrepancies between school results in Hebrew as opposed to Arab schools led to subsequent five-year affirmative action plans in the 1990s with the aim to improve conditions, mainly in the Arab school sector.[39]

The 1953 State Education Act projected a centralized education system based on achievement, the principle of equality and liberty. Constitutionally, it resonated well the inception of the rights to equality and to education, by organizing public education through the uniform distribution of financial resources and by guaranteeing the choice for students and their parents of the stream of education best suited to their needs and beliefs. In practice, however, the Act accentuated disparities between ethnic and social classes, with the affluent communities

---

36 Pedahzur (2001) at 416. Pedahzur, in fact, classifies Israel as a 'non-liberal democracy', particularly inspired by Sammy Smooha's concept of "ethnic democracy", defined as a democratic system of government wherein rights are granted to all citizens although favored status is only given to the majority (Pedahzur (2001) at 417).

37 Muhammed Amaraa, Faisal Azaiza, Rachel Hertz-Lazarowitz and Aura Mor-Sommerfeld, 'A New Bilingual Education in the Conflict-Ridden Israeli Reality: Language Practices', *Language and Education*, 23(1), January 2009, at 18.

38 Nadir Altinok, 'The Hidden Crisis: Armed Conflict and Education', Paper commissioned for the Education for All Global Monitoring Report 2011, 2011/ED/EFA/MRT/PI/11, 2011 at 28.

39 Among positive changes between 1999 and 2001, the increase of enrollment rates of children between the ages of 14–17 was noticeable in the Arab sector by 26 per cent (compared to 6 per cent in the Hebrew sector). Cf Altinok (2011) at 28 for more on this point.

consistently securing enhanced access to resources for their schools.[40] Paragraph 2 of the Act is revealing in that respect:

> The goal of State Education is to establish a basic education in this State upon the values of Israeli culture and scientific achievements, on the love of the homeland and loyalty to the State and Nation of Israel.

In other words, education within Zionist citizenship required agreement, participation and identification with national projects. At the same time, the innovation (and achievement) of the Zionist approach to education was to legitimize secularization, with emphasis on the person's individual responsibility for his own actions.[41] Reforms in 1968 targeting social integration and the closing of gaps failed due to slow implementation and lack of political will.[42] As such, academic achievement remained correlated with ethnic background.

3 The design of educational religious pluralism: general features

Since 1975, the Israeli education system relies on a basic structure requiring six years of primary school (ages 6–12),[43] three years of junior high (ages 12–15) and three years of senior high (ages 15–17), following which students take the *bagrut*[44] and then join the Israeli Defense Forces (IDF) for compulsory military service.[45]

The basis for Israel's education system relies on a model of cultural pluralism, promoting the creation and preservation of religious/cultural pluralism based on cultural enclaves. The fundamental distinction within the Hebrew school systems foresees three sub-systems: (a) the secular state schools (*mamlachti*), (b) the religious state schools (*mamlachti dati*), and (c) the ultra-Orthodox schools, classified as independent schools and serving approximately 8–10 per

---

40 Leavy (2010) at 26.
41 Zehavit Gross, 'State-Religious Education in Israel: Between Tradition and Modernity', *Prospects*, 33(2), 2003, 149–164, at 159.
42 Leavy (2010) at 29–30.
43 Compulsory education in Israel begins at the age of 5.
44 Academic Secondary School Leaving Examination, resulting in a credit-system required for higher education.
45 Military service is compulsory for all Jews and Druzes but voluntary for Christians, Circassians and Muslims. It has a three-year duration for men and a two-year duration for women.

cent of the total Israeli population.[46] These schools are also benefiting from state funds.[47] A fourth segment of the system counts Arab schools (Christian, Druze or Islamic).[48]

Both state and state-religious schools are under the supervision of the Ministry of Education, Culture and Sport. The language of instruction in Jewish schools is Hebrew, while in Arab schools it is Arabic. Accordingly, a separate educational system is maintained for Arab students, although the possibility for Arab students to join the Jewish track exists.

In primary education, religious studies are part of the curriculum for all types of schools and, although teaching methods are determined by the schools themselves (teachers and principals) as well as local authorities, the content of the curriculum is laid down by the Ministry of Education. For secondary schools, there is more flexibility in the design and organization of the content of education than at the primary school level.[49] Within Israel's occupied territories (the Gaza Strip, the Golan Heights, the Sinai Peninsula and the West Bank), education is provided by combined public and private sponsorship.[50] The educational system in these areas is heavily influenced by the Egyptian and Jordanian systems. Only the Golan Heights follow the same curriculum as Arab schools in Israel. Finally,

46 Künkler and Lerner (2016) at 11 provide the following statistical breakdown of students based on 2012 figures: among 595,000 Jewish students in elementary schools, 55 per cent attended secular schools, 19 per cent religious state schools and 25 per cent ultra-Orthodox schools (Central Bureau of Statistics, 2012). More recent figures suggest that 39 per cent of students attend secular public schools (although 30 years ago the same schools enrolled 70 per cent of the elementary school population), 14 per cent of primary school students attend state religious schools, and Arabic-speaking schools enroll 25 per cent of the total student population (Cf. Laurence Wolff, 'Education in Israel: Divided Schools, Divided Society', 8 May 2017, available at www.momentmag.com/education-in-israel-divided-schools-divided-society).

47 The 2008 State Education Law as amended created a new category of State schools labeled 'combining State school'. This is a type of school that stresses in their curriculum Judaic studies and Jewish identity instruction. (Cf. Maoz (2016) at 221)

48 Article 1, 1953 State Education Act. According to the Act, public education has three streams: the national education track, serving the Jewish, Arab and Druze populations; the national-religious education track, serving religious Jews, and the national-incorporating education track, serving secular Jews who opt for programmes enhanced with intensive Jewish studies and emphasize Jewish identity.

49 There is a basic distinction between academic and vocational tracks at the secondary level. Grades 10–12 are not compulsory.

50 Following the 1994 Oslo Accords, Palestinians took over responsibility for their education system. Based on a centralized model, the curriculum, textbooks and regulations are sourced from the government. Education is provided in three types of schools: boys', girls' and co-educational ones, each representing roughly a third of the total number of schools. United Nations Relief and Work Agency serves children in refugee camps, an estimated 23 per cent of the total Palestinian student population. For more on these points, see Altinok (2011) at 15–16.

serving the ultra-Orthodox community,[51] ultra-Orthodox schools are a growing stream of non-public schools with distinct curricular design.

The Arab school system, catering to the educational needs of approximately 25 per cent of all school students in Israel,[52] is also supervised by the Ministry of Education. The curriculum in these schools is adapted to the religion of the student body (Muslim or Christian), and similarly schools in Druze or Circassian villages adopt the curriculum to the cultural needs of their respective student populations.[53]

The 1953 State Education Law provides specifically for non-Jewish schools to follow a differentiated curriculum that corresponds to 'their special conditions'.[54] The 1996 National Education Regulations established an Advisory Council on Arabic Education with the aim to promote equality in recognition of cultural specific needs.[55]

In terms of curricular content related to religion, in secular state schools the curriculum does not include religion classes, although Bible lessons (*Tanach*) are mandatory but organized from a literary perspective. Religious-state schools include religious studies together with general studies in their programmes.[56] These schools are governed by an autonomous division within the Ministry of Education, under the direction of the Council of Religious Education. Unlike the students of the ultra-Orthodox schools, graduates of religious schools may take the bagrut allowing them to apply to academic institutions for higher education.[57] The religious nature of the religious state schools is particularly pronounced as it has a pervasive Orthodox religious character in the provision of all educational services.[58]

51 Shulamit Almog and Lotem Perry-Hazan, 'Contesting Religious Authoriality: The Immanuel "Beis Yaakov" School Segregation Case', *The International Journal for the Semiotics of Law*, 26(1), 2012, 211–225, at 212. There are three main sub-groups in the Ultra-Orthodox Community: The Lithuanians, the Hasidim and the Sephardi. See also Gila Stopler, 'The Right to an Exclusively Religious Education—The Ultra Orthodox Community in Israel in Comparative Perspective', *Georgia Journal of International and Comparative Law*, 42, 2014, 743–796, at 748. Overall, 40 per cent of the Jewish population defines themselves as secular, 20 per cent as religious and 40 per cent as traditional (Shetreet (1999) at 452).
52 Künkler and Lerner (2016) at 10.
53 Künkler and Lerner (2016) at 10.
54 State Education Law, 5713–1953, 7 LSI 113 §4 (1952–1953).
55 National Education Regulation (Advisory Council on Arabic Education) 1996, Art. 5(1).
56 This category of schools is the only one defined by law (*State Education Law*, 5713–1953, (1952–2003)).
57 Künkler and Lerner (2016) at 10.
58 The 1953 State Education Law, in paragraph 18, allows the Council for Religious Education to ensure, for example, that all teachers and staff in religious state schools are religious themselves.

The final category of ultra-Orthodox or *Agudat* schools enjoy state recognition but are considered "non-official".[59] The main networks running these schools are the Independent Education Network and the Sephardic Centre of Religious Education in Israel (also known as 'The Fountain of Religious Education' – *Mayan Ha'hinuch Ha'torani*).[60] The level of supervision of the Ministry of Education on these schools is considerably lower, although the State supplies up to 75 per cent of their budget. It is relevant to stress, however, that schools associated with Agudat, Israel's Independent Education Network and Shas' Fountain of Religious Education enjoy full curricular autonomy as well as state funding. [61] Overall, ultra-Orthodox schools are exempt from a number of secular studies such as math, science, history, geography, English, and so on. As an indication of the type of education provided, after the age of 13, ultra-Orthodox (male) pupils are required to focus on religious studies alone, to the exemption of all other topics.

The way the ultra-Orthodox sub-system of public education is organized in Israel raises the question of the quality of education provided within it. The 1953 State Education Act provided for a 'core curriculum' requirement, but one has to wait until 2003 for a detailed programme of the mandatory 'core curriculum' for primary education and, until 2007, for one for the secondary education system.[62] In recent case law, the Supreme Court justified the need for a 'core curriculum' as an exercise in balancing the right of parents to educate their children in accordance with their beliefs and worldview with that of the State's duty to provide basic common educational values to all learners, preparing them for life and participation in society.[63]

The suggested practice emerging from the provision on the 'core curriculum'[64] requires fully funded schools (i.e. Hebrew secular schools, Hebrew religious-state schools and Arab schools) to teach the entire 'core curriculum'. The transfer of government funds to these schools is conditioned on the implementation of this

59 The legal basis for this ambiguous legal status is to be found in the *Compulsory Education Act*, 5709–1949, 3 LSI §1 (1948–1949) and is defined as the educational institutions 'which the Minister by declaration published in *Reshumot* (Official Gazette), has declared to be a recognized educational institution'. The decision for Agudat to opt out of the official education stream and obtain the status of 'recognized' schools was based on a willingness for autonomy, prioritizing cultural advancement on the basis of religion. [Cf. Shamal (2000) at 407.]

60 Founded by the Sephardic political party 'Sephardi Keepers of Torah', also known as Shas. *(Itahdut Sephardim Shomrei Torah)*.

61 In this respect, Künkler and Lerner (2016) at 12 note the difficulty to determine the level of state funding, hinting at an intentional lack of transparency (see in particular their footnote 35).

62 Basic (Core) Curriculum 1995 and Basic (Core) Curriculum 2007 respectively.

63 HCJ 4805/07 *The Center for Jewish Pluralism v. Ministry of Education* (2008).

64 The 'core curriculum' includes the subjects of the Bible, social studies, Hebrew, English, math, science, art and sports.

requirement. Additionally, in order to achieve recognition, a school must teach at least 75 per cent of the core curriculum as set by the Ministry of Education. A school that teaches that curriculum is consequently also eligible for 75 per cent of state funding given to public schools.[65]

The actual practice related to the implementation of the 'core curriculum' is nevertheless diverging from the initial intention of the lawmakers. There is evidence that ultra-Orthodox schools violate this condition, although comprehensive data is still lacking.[66] Case law such as *High Schools Teachers Union v. Minister of Education (2004)* or *Centre of Jewish Pluralism v. Ministry of Education (2008)* demonstrate that the scope of the 'core curriculum' is limited in these schools. The content of education provided in these establishments therefore merits a closer look: the actual content of the lessons, the textbooks used and the selection and training of educators are left to the autonomous control of these schools. There is also a discrepancy between the educational content in the programme designed for ultra-Orthodox girls and that for ultra-Orthodox boys: in the former case, greater weight is placed on general studies, considered inferior in the ultra-Orthodox society,[67] while in the latter, the weight of education revolves around religious texts alone. The political leverage exercised by ultra-Orthodox communities seeking to maintain (and expand) educational autonomy was sealed with the 2008 Unique Cultural Institutions Law, exempting state-funded secondary ultra-Orthodox schools for boys (grades 9–12) from 'core curriculum' entirely. The law was later challenged,[68] without success, with the Court arguing that the introduction of a core curriculum in ultra-Orthodox schools can only be achieved via gradual developments and not by legal means in the form of a court order, as this would be of limited efficiency.[69]

4 Constitutional pluralism and religious diversity

a. *The ambiguous principle of equality*

The canvas of public education in Israel has been painted with colors of aggressiveness and violence: between the secular and the religious, the older generations and the new immigrants, the Ashkenazi and the Mizrahi, the Jewish and the Arabs.[70] Social fragmentation takes the form of discontent arising from Israel's mixed secular cum-religious legal system. The level of this discontent is particularly visible in the ambiguous position accorded to the principle of equality.

For historical reasons and pre-state experiences of discrimination and persecution, Israel's Declaration of Independence placed some emphasis on the principle

65 Mandatory Study Act 5510–1949, SH No. 26, 287.
66 Cf. Künkler and Lerner (2016) at 13. See also the case law discussed later.
67 Künkler and Lerner (2016) at 14.
68 HCJ 3752/10 *Rubinstein v. The Knesset* (2014).
69 For more details on this see section 5 (b) of this chapter.
70 Pedahzur (2001) at 427.

of equality. While the Declaration states that Israel would be a "Jewish State", it was also declared to strive to "ensure complete equality of social and political rights to all its inhabitants irrespective of religion, race or sex; it will guarantee freedom of religion, conscience, language, education and culture".[71]

The principle of equality failed, nevertheless, to be endorsed within a formal constitutional text, due to resistance from religious political parties in the Knesset to confront the freedom of conscience with equality. Such a constitutional confrontation would involve the reconsideration (and reconfiguration) of the religious monopoly in family matters,[72] a privilege of which the religious actors and pious citizens were not prepared to let go.

Without a formal constitution or a bill of rights, the Israeli constitutional system relies on the 1992 *Basic Law: Freedom of Occupation* and the *1992 Basic Law: Human Dignity and Liberty* to regulate and address civil liberties. Together with decisions of the Israeli High Court, they form the sources of constitutional law. Judicial review is unclear within this framework: after 1992, and the passage of the two *Basic Laws*, the Court may, under circumstances, strike down laws violating individual rights.

A partial constitutional bill of rights, the *Basic Law: Human Dignity and Liberty*, introduced a projected remedy to the absence of constitutional force for the principle of equality through the recognition of the principle of human dignity. Human dignity (*kevod haadam*) was understood in the text as the superiority of human rights listed, not to be violated except by a law in accordance with the values of the State of Israel as a Jewish and democratic state.[73]

Specifically for education, there is no explicit right to education in the *Basic Laws*, yet the 1949 *Compulsory Education Act*, the 1953 *State Education Act* and the 2000 *Pupils' Rights Law* cover the right.[74] Both the 1949 and the 2000 Acts contain explicit non-discrimination provisions on the basis of ethnicity in the registration, admission or creation of separate classrooms within a school. Yet these prohibitions apply only to local authorities or the schools, not the central government.

In broader terms, the two major Basic Laws on *Freedom of Occupation* and on *Human Dignity and Liberty* intensified the debate on the relationship between

---

71 The Declaration of the Establishment of the State of Israel, Iyar 5, 5708, 14 May 1948, Official Gazette No. 1, at 1.

72 Frances Raday, 'Equality, Religion and Gender in Israel', *Jewish Women: A Comprehensive Historical Encyclopedia*, 1 March 2009, at 1, available at http://jwa.org/encyclopedia/article/equality-religion-and-gender-in-israel (last accessed 19 April 2016).

73 See indicatively the content of the 1951 Women's Equal Rights Law guaranteeing gender equality before the law, elevating it to a principle for interpretation for ambivalent legislation while subordinating it to halakhic rules on marriage and divorce on "prohibition and permission to marry and divorce" (Cf. Raday (2009) at 2). The rationale for the opposition in the Knesset was simply that the principle of equality (particularly for women) must be subjected to the principles and practice of Judaism.

74 The latter stipulates that: "every child and youth in the State of Israel has the right to an education according to all instructions of the law".

religion and state. The "Jewish" and "democratic" character of the State of Israel provoked the questioning of the compatibility between these two characteristics.[75] Indicatively, the constitutional marginalization of the Palestinian-Arab community inevitably resurfaced in both legal and public policy debates.[76] It was further intensified upon the observation of the gaps in the public accommodation and state funding of religious institutions between Jewish and Arab communities,[77] not exclusively attributed to the demographic preponderance of (Orthodox) Jews in Israel.[78]

In this respect, the issue of religious accommodations appears to operate on the basis of a variable geometry, to the extent that it creates a reversed type of multiculturalism, where autonomy becomes synonymous to the imposition of a patriarchal minority culture on the liberal majority.[79] As the more detailed outline of the patterns of discrimination will illustrate next, the right to education as connected to religious freedom, while having been recognized in an idiosyncratic constitutional form, is nevertheless implemented at the expense of the right to equality. The result is an asymmetric education in its contents and in its effects: it promotes a one-sided multicultural project "where Arab students are educated for control and Jewish students for ethnocentric rule".[80]

In response to such concerns, courts have, generally, actively interpreted (gender) equality as an essential component of the Israeli legal system, with a tacit reservation that in family law religious norms/values may pressure towards the restraint of the development of the principle. Yet, there seems to be an essential(ized) distinction made before state judicial fora between the balancing of equality and religion in the private sphere as opposed to the public one. In the former, the highest jurisdictions of the country have traditionally refused to consider equality in the context of divorce proceedings.[81] In the latter, a sophisticated

---

75 For an analysis on this point cf. Karayanni (2007) at 345–346, in particular his footnotes 49 and 51.

76 The Palestinian–Arab community in Israel has been described as "the most remote excluded community from the state's meta-narratives" in Gad Barzilai, *Communities and the Law, Politics and Cultures of Legal Identities*, University of Michigan Press, 2003, at 7, 42.

77 See indicatively cases HCJ, 240/98 *Adalah: The Legal Center for the Rights of the Arab Minority in Israel v. The Minister for Religious Affairs* (1999) 52(5) P.D. 167, 178; HCJ, 1113/99 *Adalah: The Legal Center for the Rights of the Arab Minority in Israel v. The Minister for Religious Affairs* (2000) 54(ii) P.D. 164; HCJ, 2422/98 *Adalah: The Legal Center for the Rights of the Arab Minority in Israel v. The Minister of Labor and Welfare* (not published). Cf. *The State of Israel, Implementation of the ICCPR: Combined Initial and First Periodic Report of the State of Israel* (1998) at 228.

78 Karayanni (2007) at 362.

79 Karayanni (2007) at 355.

80 Human Rights Watch (HRW), *Second Class: Discrimination Against Palestinian Arab Children in Israel's Schools*, 30 September 2001, available at www.hrw.org/reports/2001/israel2, at 92.

81 See indicatively *Plonit v. Plonit* (1997) 51(1) P.D. 198 where the High Court unanimously dismissed a case based on a ruling of the Grand Rabbinical Court refusing to oblige a husband, separated from his wife for more than six years, to give her a divorce.

web of balancing tools has been devised by the Supreme Court to decide on these clashes. In the *Poraz* case,[82] involving a challenge to the decision not to appoint women to the electoral board for the Tel Aviv municipal rabbi, the Court held that while "equality is an important principle but . . . a relative principle" (at 336), it was determinative in this case because there was no real barrier, in the form of a *halakhic* prohibition, to the functioning of a municipal rabbi, if women sat on the electoral board (at 337).

In the *Nevo* case, [83] on the issue of equal retirement age for women, the Supreme Court, per Justice Cheshin, described equality as

> The king of principles – the most elevated of principles above all others. . . . So it is in public law and so it is in each and every aspect of our lives in society. The principle of equality infiltrates every plant of the legal garden and constitutes an unseverable part of the genetic make-up of all the legal rules, each and every one. . . . The principle of equality is, in theory and practice, a father-principle or should we say a mother-principle.

Breaking away from the limits of formal equality, the Court has incorporated the notion of affirmative action and accommodation in order to build the concept of 'equal opportunity', obviously aiming at a 'socio-dynamic' type of equality.[84] For affirmative action, the Court has recognized the need to give preference to weaker groups in an attempt to correct past injustice and to promote equality of ability.[85]

Overall, the Supreme Court's approach towards the principle of accommodation requires a conciliation between the need for individuals to realize their potential, irrespective of their special characteristics, and the general goals of the continuation of society's existence.[86] In other words, a construct that rejects special treatment but also accepts complete blindness to discriminatory practices.

b The role of the State in Israel in the provision of religious services

In both constitutional and governance terms, the state-centered mode of education is in decline. New actors and organizations are increasingly taking more active parts and having discretion over educational processes on a global scale. Local schools, parents' associations, municipalities and regional councils are

---

82 Bagaz 953/87 *Poraz v. Lahat, Mayor of Tel Aviv et al.* (1988) 42(2) P.D. 309.
83 Bagaz 104/87 *Nevo v. The National Labour Court et al.* (22 October 1990).
84 Term borrowed from Raday (2009) at 6.
85 See indicatively the case IWN II (*IWN v. Minister of Labor* (1998) 52(3) P.D. 630), where the Supreme Court accepted that affirmative action was an integral part of the principle of equality.
86 Cf. *Miller v. Minister of Defense* (1995) 49(4) P.D. on the refusal of a female to enter the pilots' course of the Israel Air Force on grounds of her sex.

devising and shaping, together with the State, educational agendas. In Israel, this diversification of educational services becomes important for the purposes of this study in assessing the content of education from the angle of religious diversity.[87]

The essential question that arises with respect to state funding of religious schools in Israel is a recurring one. There is little disagreement that the public financing of religious/denominational schools is controversial. Given that the right to education affords the possibility for parents (and to some extent the communities to which these families belong) to educate their children according to their beliefs, the question becomes what kind of state-funded education should be available to them.[88] Assuming that in a liberal democracy the State must fund compulsory education, that public institutions and policies should not promote a particular conception of the "good life", and that public aid of such schools is constitutionally permissible, to what degree does it require state intervention in religious practices within such schools? Also, connected to this first question, does this intervention enhance or reduce religious freedom?[89]

Medina argues that in the Israeli context, the major concern behind State intervention is the facilitation of religious freedom by securing access to religious services.[90] He rejects the common argument that the extent of government support dictates also the extent and legitimacy of intervention. Further to that, State intervention may also be mandated in circumstances where there is a risk that a certain religious practice may cause harm to other interests (e.g. gender equality). The underlying threat present in State intervention remains, however, that government regulation may be perceived or interpreted as "biased, sectarian or aimed at secularization and promoting values of liberalism" and labeled as an act against the protection of religion.[91]

Affording the possibility for education according to one's beliefs and world vision, prima facie serves the purpose of the wider access to religious freedom. Closer consideration of the effects of Haredi education and the Arab Palestinian

87 Furthermore, the translation of curricular policies to classroom practice has to account for gaps in implementation. For more on this, see Aaron Benavot and Nura Resh, 'Educational Governance, School Autonomy, and Curriculum Implementation: A Comparative Study of Arab and Jewish Schools in Israel', *Journal of Curriculum Studies*, 35(2), 2003, 171–196, at 172. According to Benavot and Resh, current tools for overseeing implementation of educational policies include on-site inspection, mandatory achievement examinations, regulated teacher-training programmes and authorized lists of school textbooks. (Benavot and Resh (2003) at 173.)

88 Johan de Jong and Ger Snik, 'Why Should States Fund Denominational Schools?' *Journal of Philosophy of Education*, 36(4), 2002, 573–587.

89 Both questions have been pertinently analyzed and discussed, outside the context of education, in Barak Medina, 'Enhancing Freedom of Religion through Public Provision of Religious Services: The Israeli Experience', *Israeli Law Review*, 39(2), 2006, 127–157.

90 Medina (2006) at 130. Medina's primary field of application in this context is sourced from the case law surrounding the regulation of religious sites of worship.

91 Medina (2006) at 137.

sectors of education may, nevertheless, demonstrate a more nuanced conclusion that is likely to result to an infringement of either religious freedom or the right to education. In sum, the Israeli society remains deeply divided on religious issues: while freedom of religion is respected to some extent, freedom 'from' religion is paradoxically not as obvious.[92]

5 Educational diversification according to religious belonging

In the early days of Israeli statehood, educational affairs were tightly controlled by political authorities. The initial aims of State education in Israel were three-fold: first, to ensure between-school equality, as there were a variety of streams of education available, second, to strengthen the State's influence over the socialization of future citizens, through the medium of a unified national curriculum, and third, to contribute to the assimilation of new immigrants.[93] The official curriculum approach, in that respect, followed the 'melting pot' ideology combined with the goal of building a 'bottom-up' new Israeli-Jewish identity.[94] For the Arab component of the population, there was less clarity in educational goals, with more emphasis on controls over school practices and educational content. More recently, however, in the light of the decentralization of diffusion of educational policies, more school autonomy is allowed for.

The four sub-sectors of Israeli education (i.e. the Jewish state-secular, the Jewish state – religious, the Jewish independent (ultra-Orthodox) and the Arab one), have developed parallel educational narratives reflecting the religious identities of the communities that they have been serving.

a Arab sector education: patterns of discrimination against Israeli Palestinian Arab learners

From a legal anthropological perspective, it is worth noting that the separation of the Arab educational sector has been facilitated by the geographical distribution of the Arab populations in Israel. Israeli Arabs reside in distinct localities or within segregated neighborhoods in bigger cities.[95] At the same time, Arab sector schools have had less access to funds for their educational needs due to two major considerations: the first is based on the systematic discrimination over a period of time in budget allocations by the Ministry of Education.[96] The second is due to the limited additional sources of funding available to them, such as

92 Cf. I. England, 'Law and Religion in Israel', *American Journal of Comparative Law*, 3571, 1987, 196–203.
93 Benavot and Resh (2003) at 176.
94 Benavot and Resh (2003) at 178.
95 Benavot and Resh (2003) at 177.
96 See footnote 77 for an indicative list of case law.

resources from local councils, community institutions, private donors or non-profit organizations.[97]

Until the 1970s, the Arab sector lagged behind in curricular design, timetables and textbooks were identical to those used in Jewish schools, with the obvious exception of language instruction. Even within that element, however, there were asymmetries: Arab students, taught in Arab, were required to learn Hebrew as a second language, while Jewish students, taught in Hebrew, learned Arabic only as an elective second foreign language, after English.

More recently, the content of Arab education has undergone changes: there is at present, greater allowance for culturally diversified curricula, greater school autonomy in the implementation of curricula and more encouragement towards interdisciplinarity and less conventional subjects.[98] Still, the impact on the curricular content is characterized as 'conservative', in terms of practices and pedagogical philosophy.[99]

Overall features of education in the Arab sector present still today some differences with their Jewish counterpart: according to Benavot and Resh, curricula focus overwhelmingly on the compulsory subjects, with two-thirds of the instructional time devoted to five basic subjects.[100] As a result, Arab schools allocate less time to humanistic and social sciences subjects and often forgo completely aesthetic and social education, at the difference of Jewish schools, where a greater variety of subjects is taught.[101] This discrepancy is obviously also attributable to the gap in resources available between the two sectors.

In educational terms, the conflict between the Jewish and the Arabs in Israel represents an 'identity conflict':[102] it reflects a situation where "at least one of the sides denies the effects of the adversary's narrative regarding its national identity". [103] This conflictual background creates a corresponding mismatch in school curricula: while Hebrew-speaking students are taught courses in Judaism, Jewish and Israeli history, very few or no studies of Palestinian history/culture exist in Arab schools.[104] Teaching materials used in the numerically important religious streams of public education in Israel reveal complementary aspects of this kind of conflict: a 2013 comprehensive survey of textbooks used in Hebrew and Arab schools shows that 'dehumanizing and demonizing characterizations' are rare

---

97   Benavot and Resh (2003) at 177.
98   Benavot and Resh (2003) at 178.
99   Benavot and Resh (2003) at 179, 181. Quantitative research by Benavot and Resh makes the point that despite changes, Arab sector schools adhere more to conventional subjects, teach fewer subjects, and are less prepared to introduce less conventional ones or engage with special educational projects.
100 Benavot and Resh (2003) at 188.
101 Benavot and Resh (2003).
102 Muhammed Amara, Faisal Azaiza, Rachel Hertz-Lazarowitz and Aura Mor-Sommerfeld, 'A New Bilingual Education in the Conflict-Ridden Israeli Reality: Language Practices', *Language and Education*, 23(1), 2009, 15–35, at 16.
103 Amara et al. (2009) at 16.
104 Amara et al. (2009) at 18.

in both Hebrew and Arab schools.[105] Yet, both sides present 'unilateral national narratives' where the 'Other' is the 'enemy' without any instructive information of culture/religion. Particularly for ultra-Orthodox and Palestinian books (as opposed to Israeli State secular track books),[106] negative bias towards the religious 'Other' is pronounced.[107] In this respect, it should be noted that Palestinians assumed control of teaching materials in 1994 in connection to the Oslo Accords where they had committed to confidence-building measures, including through education.

Overall, the general picture of comparison between the content, type and features of education provided to Palestinian Arab children as opposed to Jewish children in Israel is one filled with inequalities, discrepancies and asymmetries. Palestinian Arab students are provided with public education by the State, which offers them schooling in larger classes, with fewer and less-trained teachers, often involving long-distance daily traveling to reach the nearest school, in facilities that may lack basic equipment.[108] Combined with stagnating curricula contents, Palestinian Arab children educated in under-resourced schools, from kindergarten to vocational training establishments, including special education, are statistically more likely to drop out of school. More macroscopically, the patterns of discrimination in this context appear cyclical and cumulative: poor quality education produces families with lower incomes, perpetuating the circle of disadvantage.[109]

The Israeli government in its 2001 report to the UN Committee on the Rights of the Child acknowledged:

> There is a great deal of variance in the resources allocated to the education in the Arab versus the Jewish sector. These discrepancies are reflected in various aspects of education in the Arab sector, such as physical infrastructure, the average number of students per class, the number of enrichment hours, the extent of support services, and the level of professional staff.[110]

The current perception of this type of educational pillarization is based on a continuing resistance from both ethnic groups concerned to opt for school integration. For Palestinian Arab Israeli citizens, school integration is synonymous to assimilation into the majority's education, at the expense of their own linguistic

---

105 Council of Religious Institutions of the Holy Land, 'Victims of Our Own Narratives? Portrayal of the "Other" in Israeli and Palestinian School Books', Study Report, February 2013, available at https://d7hj1xx5r7f3h.cloudfront.net/Israeli-Palestinian_School_Book_Study_Report-English.pdf [English translation].

106 Israeli State secular track books reflect since the late 1990s a more self-critical view, recognizing that some Palestinians were expelled from Israel and left their land, using the Arab term for Israel's 1948 War of Independence, *Naqba*, signifying the Catastrophy.

107 Council of Religious Institutions of the Holy Land (2013) at 46.

108 See HRW (2001).

109 HRW (2001) at 4.

110 Israel Periodic Report submitted to the Committee on the Rights of the Rights of the Child, 20 February 2001, CRC/C/8/Add.44., Para. 1155 at 295.

and cultural heritage.[111] At the same time, as school enrollment depends on residence, and even within 'mixed' cities such as Jaffa and Haifa, communities remain segregated and cross-community enrollment becomes unlikely.[112]

Of particular illustrative power in establishing the parameters and characteristics of discrimination in education is the case of the Bedouin communities, comprising an estimated 10 per cent of the country's total Palestinian Arab population.[113] These communities have been provided with even lower educational services by the State.

As already mentioned, the basic structure of the duty of the State to provide free education, under the 1949 Compulsory Education Act, allocates the duty to the Ministry of Education to develop curricula and educational standards, to supervise teachers and to construct school buildings. Local authorities have the duty to maintain these buildings and provide equipment and supplies, occasionally with the support from the Ministry. Particularly for funding issues, state education is supported by the central government and local authorities as well as private organizations and parents.

In fulfilling this duty, international law explicitly stipulates that education should be provided "without discrimination of any kind irrespective of the child's race, colour, sex, language, religion, political or other opinion, national ethnic or social origin, property, disability, birth or other status".[114]

More analytically, a number of systemic factors, as outlined next, demonstrate nevertheless a clear incompatibility between the legal guarantee to the right to education for all in international law and the lack of equality due to religious/ethnic belonging.

(i) Funding

The Ministry of Education distributes available funds to schools according to several factors: the largest part is destined to teachers' salaries and teacher training. A second kind is devoted to supplemental programmes (enrichment and remedial). For the latter type of funding, the Ministry has devised a system where resources are allocated according to need. Finally, the Ministry also supports school construction.[115]

NGO reporting, preceded by official government acknowledgment, has suggested that funding discrepancies between Arab Palestinian and Jewish schools are most visible in funding of supplemental programmes. The Israeli

---

111 HRW (2001) at 14.
112 HRW (2001) at 14.
113 HRW (2001) at 16.
114 UN Convention on the Rights of the Child, GA Res. 44/25 of 20 November 1989, Article 2(1).
115 HRW (2001) at 30.

government in its February 2001 Report to the UN Committee of the Rights of the Child stated:

> The gaps in government allocation are mainly a result of more limited allocations to enrichment and extracurricular activities such as libraries, programs for weaker students, cultural activities and councelling and support services.[116]

This particular discriminatory effect is largely due to the methods of assessment of 'need' used by the Ministry of Education: 'need' is measured according to indices such as priority area classification or the Ministry's own index of educational disadvantage.[117] For "priority area classification", the government enjoys discretion in classifying areas as "national priority areas".

By proportion, the Ministry has designated Jewish localities as priority areas much more extensively than Palestinian Arab localities. The latter are classified usually at a level that disqualifies them from education benefits.[118] The 'index of educational disadvantage (Nurture Index)', a main tool towards assessment of such needs, relies on two different standards for Arab and Jewish schools, ranking them separately. Instead of comparing them against a single common standard, Jewish schools are measured against other Jewish schools and similarly for Arab schools. The effect of this particular measuring tool is that Arab schools that would qualify for more resources if compared to Jewish schools receive less or no support because other Arab schools are in even worse condition.[119] Disparities are thus maintained as a result.[120] The 'Nurture Basket' was, nevertheless, initially devised to reduce education and academic gaps between population groups in Israel.

The Nurture Index is also complemented by the 'Prayer Time' Basket designed especially for Hebrew state-religious schools and schools with specialized Jewish studies in order to hold teacher-supervised prayers in the mornings.[121] Hebrew state-religious schools, benefiting from a higher Nurture Index, received additional unique baskets of funding (e.g. for separating boys and girls or for rabbi hours),

---

116 Israel Periodic Report (2001), Para. 1141 at 291.
117 HRW (2001) at 35.
118 HRW (2001) at 36.
119 HRW (2001) at 37. In the same 2001 Report to the UN Committee on the Rights of the Child, the Israeli government conceded that: "the distribution of hours and budgets, per schools is not equal in the two sectors, and does not take into consideration the existing gaps between the two sectors". (Israel Periodic Report (2001), Para. 1163 at 296.)
120 Nachum Blass, 'The Israeli Education System—State of the Nation Report 2018', Taub Center for Social Policy Studies in Israel, 2018, at 18 recommends a more subtle division of Nurture Index levels to remedy the situation.
121 Blass, 'The Israeli Education System' (2017) at 15.

while Arab, Bedouin and Druze sectors only received supplements in the context of five-year plans designed to reduce gaps.[122]

Similarly, regarding the Shahar Programmes, designed to assist academically weak students from low socio-economic backgrounds, preventing drop-outs, the records on the discrepancy between the average spent on Arab as opposed to Jewish pupils are striking.[123]

Parents also influence the general picture by participating in the funding of public education by virtue of the 1953 State Education Law that allows parent financing to increase regular teaching hours up to 25 per cent, if 75 per cent of parents in the school request so. Due to the divergences in socio-economic conditions between the two groups, Arab schools inevitably collect less money from parents.[124] Accordingly less resources become available towards the improvement of school infrastructures or the reduction of class sizes.

Although the Ministry of Education may contribute to such gaps arising, the requirement that matching funds be provided by parents and/or local authorities prevents any actual intervention, as Arab local authorities and families dispose of less resources.

In more recent terms, educational disparities between the Hebrew and Arab streams of education persist. A 2017 study highlights continuing severe educational discrimination, including through budget disparities – both per pupil and per class.[125] Funding decisions, with clear political and ideological implications, justify to a large extent the existing gaps. An implicit hierarchy is therefore de facto established, with Hebrew state-religious schools taking priority, followed by Hebrew state-secular schools and finally by Arab schools.[126]

(ii) Infrastructure and classroom shortages

In 2001, the Follow-Up Committee for Arab Education estimated that 2,500 additional classrooms were necessary for the Arab sector.[127] Classroom shortages carry multiple consequences: first, many classes in Arab schools are held in rented and often inadequate spaces.[128] Electricity or basic amenities may be lacking, with particularly harsh conditions in schools within spontaneous (unrecognized)

---

122 Nachum Blass and Haim Bleikh, 'The Determinants of School Budgets: Per Class and Per Students', Taub Center for Social Policy Studies in Israel, 2018, at 4.
123 HRW (2001) at 40, citing the Follow-up Committee on Arab Education states that in 1998 the average spent for these programmes was 18.75 USD per Arab pupil and 907 USD per Jewish pupil. The 1997 State Comptroller's Report also highlighted the issue.
124 HRW (2001) at 42.
125 Nachum Blass, 'The Academic Achievements of Arab Israeli Pupils', Policy Paper No. 04/2017, Taub Center for Social Policy Studies in Israel, at 4.
126 Blass and Bleikh (2018) at 22.
127 Blass and Bleikh (2018) at 47.
128 Blass and Bleikh (2018).

tribal settlements of Bedouins in the Negev. Second, classes in themselves may be overcrowded.[129]

At some levels of education, there are shortages of schools,[130] despite an international law requirement interpreted by the UN Committee on Economic, Social and Cultural Rights that schools be physically accessible (i.e. within safe physical reach, either by attendance at some reasonably convenient geographical location (e.g. neighborhood school) or via modern technology (e.g. access to a distance learning programme).[131]

A similar discrepancy in human resources is noted in the number of support staff available in Jewish and Arab schools (i.e. social workers, educational psychologists, speech therapists, and so on)[132] and in the level of experience between teachers in Jewish schools and those in Arab ones.[133] The gap between the quality of Arab and Hebrew teaching personnel appears, however, to be closing.[134]

Connected to these shortages, one may also add the inadequacy of teaching materials for the Arab sector schools. Materials, often translated from Hebrew, frequently produce culturally inadequate content, within a broad scarcity of available materials due to the absence of government resources devoted to this task.[135]

(iii) School Attendance

While the Arab sector shows an increase in school enrollment of girls,[136] one of the persisting obstacles in the provision of same opportunities for education to both ethnic/religious communities at issue is the rate of drop-outs. The Convention of the Rights of the Child places an obligation on the states to force measures to encourage regular attendance and the reduction of drop-out rates.

---

129 In 1998–99, the average pupils per class in Jewish schools was 26 students and 30 for Arab schools. In Bedouin schools (Negev), the number rose to 33 at the primary and 39 at the secondary level (HRW (2001) at 33).

130 For instance in the Bedouin 'unrecognized' villages, there is a severe shortage of compulsory kindergartens (HRW (2001) at 72), but the same also applies to impoverished Palestinian Arab communities (HRW (2001) at 67). The 1999 Law subsidizing preschool education has primarily benefited Jewish communities. The difference in preschool attendance rates between Jews and Arabs is striking (HRW (2001) at 69).

131 ICESCR, General Comment No. 13, Article 13: The Right to Education, adopted by the Committee on Economic, Social and Cultural Rights at the Twenty-First Session, E/C.12/1999/10, 8 December 1999), Article 13(2)—Accessibility (ii).

132 State of Israel, Ministry of Justice/Ministry of Foreign Affairs, Initial Periodic Report of the State of Israel Concerning the Implementation of the Convention of the Rights of the Child, 20 February 2001, at 309.

133 Arab teaching-training colleges received accreditation in the second half of the 1990s, and the Ministry of Education has been providing more in-service training to Jewish than to Palestinian Arab teachers, despite the prohibition of discrimination in "training for the teaching profession", as mandated by international law. (HRW (2001) at 63).

134 Blass (2017) at 9.

135 HRW (2001) at 88.

136 Blass (2017) at 13 reports an increase from 59 per cent in 1990 to 94.3 per cent in 2015.

As measures against drop-outs are less available to Arab Palestinian students, there is a considerable gap with their Jewish counterparts.[137] Similarly, in the context of matriculation examination (bagrut), Palestinian Arabs are more likely to fail, and even if successful, less likely to meet standards for university admittance.[138] In 2015, only 16 per cent of Arab Israelis between 25–35 years old had more than 13 years of schooling, as opposed to 72 per cent of their Jewish peers.[139] This is to suggest that the Arab learners' starting point in socio-economic terms is lower than that of the Jewish learners, particularly when also taking into account their socio-economic backgrounds.[140]

Finally, the gender dimension of school attendance shows that while Palestinian girls on average perform better than boys, they are less likely to reach high school, particularly girls from the Bedouin communities.[141] In many cases, it is the travel distance to get to the nearest school that penalizes their schooling.[142]

b Ultra-Orthodox education

In stark contradiction to the Arab Israeli education, Jewish ultra-Orthodox schooling enjoys unique privileges. Haredi society has been identified as a "society of scholars" but one that relies on the State in order to pursue its mission.[143] The socio-economic structure of ultra-Orthodox communities is directly related to the educational model prevalent in the schools dedicated to these communities. High fertility rates with low workforce participation are economically suffocating the ultra-Orthodox families that count among the poorest communities in Israel.[144] Due to the specificity of family structure among them, whereby men study the Torah and women have children, these families have grown heavily dependent on State benefits.[145] Interestingly, the employment dynamics within the same group were quite different at the time of the establishment of the Jewish

---

137 For the 1998–99 school year, 10.4 per cent of Jewish 17-year-olds dropped out compared to 31.7 per cent of Arab Palestinians, [CBS, Statistical Abstract of Israel, 2000, No. 51, Table 22.12].

138 Pass rates are 63 per cent for Jewish and 43.4 per cent for Arab Palestinians, while passing rates with admittance to university are 88.6 per cent for Jewish and 66.9 per cent for Arab Palestinians [Ministry of Education, Statistics of the Matriculation Examination (Bagrut), 2000 Report], at 5, 7, 45, available at www.netvision.net.il/bagrut/netunim2000.htm.

139 Blass (2017) at 15.

140 Blass (2017) at 30.

141 HRW (2001) at 25.

142 HRW (2001) at 25.

143 See the work of Menachem Friedman, The Haredi (1991) as quoted in Margit Cohn, 'Taking a Bus from Immanuel to Mea Shearim: The Role of Israel's High Court of Justice in Regulating Ethnic and Gender Discrimination in the *Haredi* Ultra-Orthodox Sector', 2012, at 4, available at http://ssrn.com/abstract=2176401.

144 According to 2010 figures of the National Insurance Institute, 65 per cent of the Haredi population suffered from poverty in comparison to 23.7 per cent of the entire Jewish population. [Cohn (2012) at 17].

145 Stopler (2014) at 749.

state: women's fertility rates were comparable to those of other Jewish women, while men quit religious studies to get jobs upon marriage.[146]

The category of ultra-Orthodox schools has increasingly developed a level of resistance to the mandatory school curriculum.[147] In 2012, the ultra-Orthodox education system spread to 25 per cent of primary and 23.3 per cent of secondary school students, within a broad background of a rapidly growing student population turning to these schools.[148] These schools reject the teaching of core subjects such as history, English or science. This rejection has led to Supreme Court decisions regarding the enforcement of core curriculum standards in state-funded ultra-Orthodox schools.[149]

(i) A Gendered Educational Philosophy

Education for girls in Haredi establishments is organized in a loaded social environment.[150] Clearly the right to education is not denied to these students, yet it comes in a context of gendered religious and cultural expectations emanating from their communities. Education and schooling for these girls represents a necessary stop prior to their final 'destination': marriage to a man who devotes

---

146 Stopler (2014) at 749.
147 Künkler and Lerner (2016) at 3.
148 Künkler and Lerner (2016) at 3. The authors claim that the percentage of students in religious state-funded schools has tripled in the last 20 years. Today, one in every four students in the Jewish educational system attends an ultra-Orthodox school. This is not surprising given that the average fertility rate of ultra-Orthodox women is at 7.7 children per woman, as opposed to 2.6 children per woman among the general Jewish population. (Data is from 2001 and is included in Hagai Levin, 'The National Economic Council—The Haredi Sector in Israel: Empowerment Through Workforce Integration', 10, 2009, as quoted in Stopler (2014) at 748.
149 See e.g. *High Schools Teachers Union v. Minister of Education* (2004); *Amnon Rubinstein v. The Knesset* (2012).
150 There are increasingly studies that claim that, in the Israeli case, student performance is influenced by the family's cultural environment. Within religious families, the prevailing reading environment affects students' reading habits [Yariv Feniger, Yossi Shavit and Hanna Ayalon, 'Religiosity, Reading and Educational Achievement Among Jewish Students in Israel', *International Journal of Jewish Education Research*, (7), 2014, 29–67 at 31]. De Graaf, De Graaf and Kraaykamp already in 2000 suggested that parental reading habits best predict students' school success. [N.D. De Graaf, P.M. De Graaf and G. Kraaykamp, 'Parental Cultural Capital and Educational Attainment in the Netherlands: A Refinement of the Cultural Capital Perspective', *Sociology of Education*, 73, 2000, 92–111]. As Judaism places cultural emphasis on books and reading, observant families provide an environment more conducive to studying, leading children from such families to better school results [Feniger et al. (2014) at 35]. Indicatively, students in the State religious sector were found to read more than students in the State sector. The percentages are 69 per cent against 43 per cent respectively. Cultural capital, thus, seems to be linked with Jewish religiosity, although scholarship cannot as of yet quantify the causal effects of school type and cultural/religious background on academic outcome [Feniger et al. (2014) at 47].

his life to the study of the Torah, having as many children as possible and the responsibility for managing their household.[151]

In the light of the growing necessity for these students to become the main breadwinners within their households, education is necessary in order to get employment, but not just any education. Their education is not the product of free choice: "a girl's education is meant, first and foremost, to serve the family rather than the girl's personal needs, or their wishes for self-fulfillment".[152]

Ultra-Orthodox education of boys is heavily sourced from religious studies, with few (if any) secular subjects taught. Contemporary ultra-Orthodox communities have idealized the goal of continuous study of the Torah, which has become the sole aim of their education.

From a formal legal standpoint, the requirements of both the right to freedom of religion and of education appear satisfied. In essence, nevertheless, the principle of equality is strikingly missing, as the aim of such education is primarily to serve the patriarchal order prevalent within the ultra-Orthodox community.

In terms of rights-consciousness, understood as "the process that enables people to define their aims, wishes, and difficulties in terms of rights", Almog and Perry-Hazan, in their work, identify two essential shortcomings, particularly for female members of these communities: first, these girls are not apt to reflect on and plan their personal growth, and second, they are unaware of their human rights entitlements and because of that fail to identify the constant violation of these rights.[153]

(ii) Content of Education

The curriculum for ultra-Orthodox girls contains both religious and secular subjects. Within religious studies, female students are not taught the Talmud.[154] Among secular subjects, they are taught linguistic skills, grammar, literature, history, geography, mathematics, English, science, music and art.[155] Following graduation from high school, and after two years of continuing studies, a common career path followed by ultra-Orthodox girls has been teaching.[156] Yet given the

---

151   Shulamit Almog and Lotem Perry-Hazan, 'The Ability to Claim and the Opportunity to Imagine: Rights Consciousness and the Education of ultra-Orthodox Girls', *Journal of Law and Education*, 40(2), 2011, 1–31, at 2.

152   Almog and Perry-Hazan (2011) at 3.

153   Almog and Perry-Hazan (2011) at 4.

154   The Talmud is instead the most significant subject matter for the education of ultra-Orthodox boys.

155   Almog and Perry-Hazan (2011) at 6.

156   Almog and Perry-Hazan (2011) at 6. In general, according to 2014 figures, the general rates for Haredi students to get admission to higher education programmes rose to 53 per cent but concerned mainly cases of exemptions to enroll without a bagrut to academic colleges and colleges of education but not universities that do not relax admission requirements. The opening of new Haredi colleges with lower admission requirements is also connected to this trend. With regards to female Haredi students, there are differentiations

saturation of the job market of ultra-Orthodox teachers, other career perspectives have begun to be considered by these girls.[157] The difference in content of school education between ultra-Orthodox girls and boys is clear: the latter focus only on religious texts after the end of their primary school education.[158]

Within a cultural setting of gender inequality, sourced from the ultra-Orthodox interpretation of the halacha (Jewish religious law), the rights to freedom of religion and freedom of education produce adverse effects of subordination and legal disempowerment. Ultra-orthodox girls and young women are not able to realize the full span of their legal entitlements despite receiving a (basic) education.[159] Their "rights consciousness" relies on human rights knowledge, lacking in this case.[160] Both gender and religious/cultural conventions operate as factors preventing the development of human rights education within these schools.

The paradox, within this segment of the ultra-Orthodox community, is characterized on one hand by the central position and recognition of the right to educate these girls according to their religious faith but at the same time by its outcome, which is "education for ignorance".[161] Utilizing the concept of 'honor' in this direction, the ultra-Orthodox communities require that the individual demonstrates honorable behavior, blocking any notions of personal autonomy and free choice.[162] The gender factor within public education in Haredi schools for girls is elevated to a guiding principle, relying on the undisputed and undisputable status of halakhic interpretation in order to deconstruct the essence of education for girls.

Some authors categorize this phenomenon as an expression of extreme multiculturalism that neglects the State's responsibility to maintain and promote human rights education.[163] Indeed, it is open to question whether acceptable

---

observed among the various streams of Haredim (i.e. Lithuanian, Sephardic, Hasidic and Chabad). High drop-out rates from these programmes have been connected to both lower admission requirements but also lower levels of perseverance, social pressure or lack of information. Social approval to pursue higher education studies is geared higher towards Haredi women in order for them to be able to become the family's wage earners. (See Eitan Regav, *The Challenge of Integrating Haredim into Academic Studies—The State of the Nation Report: Society, Economy and Policy*, Taub Center for Social and Policy Studies, 2016, 219–268).

157 Professional studies leading to computing careers, accounting, graphics, architecture and even fashion are also being considered (Cf. Almog and Perry-Hazan (2011) at 6).

158 This is legally validated by the 2008 Culturally Unique Educational Institutions Act, discussed elsewhere in this chapter.

159 For more on agency and legal (dis)empowerment within religion, cf. Topidi et al. (eds.), *Religion as Empowerment: Global Legal Perspectives*, Routledge, 2016.

160 Almog and Perry-Hazan (2011) at 15–16.

161 Tamar El-Or has described ultra-Orthodox female school graduates as "educated and ignorant" depicting well the prevalent paradox. (Cf. Tamar El-Or, *Educated and Ignorant: Ultra-Orthodox Jewish Women and Their World*, Boulder, CO: Lynne Rienner, 1993, 200).

162 Almog and Perry-Hazan (2011) at 20.

163 The prevailing international human rights standard guarantees four features of the right to education: (a) Availability of functioning educational institutions and programmes;

education is afforded to these female students in an environment where collective religious rights take precedence over individual ones.

(iii) Case law

The use of case law in this study represents a tool for qualitative analysis that extends beyond the observation of precedent, the study of normative statements and the interpretation of specific constitutional rights, such as the right to religious freedom, to equality or to education. Within a normative pluralist framework, a dialogical analysis of case law becomes useful: it allows for reflection on the complexity of decision-making, particularly if one notes also the post-decision dynamics of each case.[164]

It sheds light on the judicial and, to some degree, the societal perceptions on what is the normative consensus regarding the questions studied. Frances Raday points out that: "case law, whether constitutional or not, represents an amalgam of the priorities of petitioners . . . and the perceptions of judges based on their professional training and their individual perspectives".[165] In this sense, by carefully observing cases that reached courts in Israel and that pertain to the balancing of religious rights and the right to education, one may be able to locate the points of tension in this context, while getting a sense of the implications of the clashes between these fundamental rights. In both cases mentioned next, Court decisions mark the beginning of a process unique for each set of circumstances. Post-decision dynamics indicate the weakness of the intervention of the judiciary as an agent for social change.[166] Such cases are in many ways more than the sum of their parts, supporting the view that "[f]or the most part, Court decisions are tentative and reversible like other political events".[167]

- **The Immanuel "Beis Yaakov" School Segregation Case**[168]

In educational terms, many ultra-Orthodox Sephardic families (originating from North-African or Arabic countries) seem to prefer sending their children to ultra-Orthodox Ashkenazi (originating from Europe) schools, despite the existence of ultra-Orthodox Sephardic schools, established by Shas, the party representing

---

(b) Accessibility of educational institutions and programmes to everyone, without discrimination; (c) Acceptability of the form and substance of education; (d) Adaptability of education . . . to the needs of changing societies and communities and to . . . the needs of students within their diverse social and cultural settings'. [Cf. Chapter 3 of this book]

164 Cohn (2012) at 2.
165 Raday (2009) at 1.
166 A similar point is made by Cohn (2012) at 26 in relation to the same and additional cases.
167 Louis Fischer, 'The Curious Belief in Judicial Supremacy', *Suffolk University Law Review*, 25, 1991, 85, 87.
168 HCJ 1067/08 *Noar Kahalacha Association v. The Ministry of Education* (6 August 2009)

the latter in Israeli Parliament (Knesset).[169] The former schools are considered more prestigious by reference not to academic consideration but to the degree of piety and adherence to strict ultra-orthodoxy.[170] There is an established precedent of discrimination in these schools.[171] While ultra-Orthodox schools may select students according to religious affiliation, they many not apply selection criteria on the basis of ethnic origin and/or social status.

The Beis Yaakov ultra-Orthodox school for girls in Immanuel practiced since 2007 a policy of segregation between Ashkenazi Jews and Sephardic Jews in favor of the former.[172] Justice Arbel's concurring opinion in this case balanced equality and the right to denominational education as follows:

> A different treatment of equals, discrimination and segregation mean the adoption of an arbitrary double standard that has no justification. The segregation completely undermines interpersonal relations. The feeling of discrimination leads to the destruction of the fabric of human relationships.
>
> It is important to emphasize that the right of a community to denominational education on the basis of religious differences does not release it from the obligation of equality. . . . Although as a rule a certain sector of the population may impose demands on religious issues in order to realize purposes relating to religious education of the kind that it espouses, these requirements should not be confused with requirements that are based on ethnic backgrounds, nor should we be misled by the religious-ideological cloak which it is disguised.[173]

Thus, the Israeli Supreme Court considering this policy in 2009, declared it illegal.[174] The refusal of ultra-Orthodox parents to follow the judgement led the Court to order the imprisonment of these parents. The fathers were indeed imprisoned for ten days, following which, their release was announced after an

---

169 The social division between Ashkenazi and Sephardi communities has been of great concern in the process of creation and maintenance of the State of Israel. It has acquired a central role and remains maintained in Haredi society, with a clear preponderance of the Ashkenazi. [Cf. Cohn (2012) at 5].

170 Cohn (2012) at 11.

171 See, for example, AP (Jerusalem) 241/06 *Association for Civil Rights in Israel v. Ministry of Israel* (51 Report 2010, 931–986), the State Controller and Ombudsmen. There are quotas established for Sephardi girls to obtain admission that raise to a maximum of 30 per cent. The quota is the result of a rabbinical decree [Cf. Cohn (2012) at 11].

172 Ultra-Orthodox Sephardic Jews have a socio-historical background of systematic marginalization (Cf. Almog and Perry-Hazan (2012) at 213).

173 At para. 117 of the judgment.

174 The facts of the case relied on the de facto division of the school into a "Hasidic Track" and a "General Track" resulting in the creation of two segregated schools, with a wall separating them in the school itself and a class timetable that prevented contact between the girls attending the two sections. The Israeli Supreme Court found the "Hassidic Track" to be discriminatory.

agreement to perform a joint seminar the last three years of the school year was reached.[175] In the meanwhile, in late August 2010, the Ministry of Education accepted the request of some parents of students attending the "Hasidic Track" of the school to establish a new school that would not receive state funds but would uphold the essence of the discriminatory admission policy. The Israeli Supreme Court, closing the case, noted the danger in the Ministry's decision in upholding the segregationist approach of the school concerned.

The *Immanuel "Beis Yaakov"* case demonstrates and contains a set of constitutional trends with wider implications: First, in the Israeli context, it seems that fundamental rights and constitutional law have a limited role to play as a "generator of social change" within the ultra-Orthodox community.[176] Any changes in this setting and concerning this group seem to require internal agency, leaving a marginal role for state constitutional law to play.

Second, the assumption or acceptance of the 'secondary' or ancillary role of law leads us to reflect on the configuration between the right to religious freedom and other fundamental rights such as equality (and non-discrimination) or education. The clear and unambiguous precedence of the right to religious freedom comes at the cost of the observance of the right to equality. Further to that, it appears that religious freedom also comes at the expense of the right to education.

- **The Core Curriculum case law**

The conflict between religious educational autonomy and the perception of the role of the (liberal) democratic state is well illustrated in the series of the *Core Curriculum* cases.[177] The cases elucidated how ultra-Orthodox boys' education in publicly funded schools is missing essential elements of core education by not teaching comprehensively basic subjects such as math and English, citizenship lessons and the core democratic values of tolerance and equality. Instead, the focus remains on Torah studies. The cases relied on an argumentation whereby the aim of the Core Curriculum is to enable students to acquire basic knowledge and skills, as well as values allowing them to function independently in a pluralistic society. It is also designed to allow all students equal opportunities to develop their personality.[178]

The Court, in assessing the clash between parental autonomy to decide on the education of their children and the importance of a core curriculum in a divided country, such as Israel, found there to be a violation of the children's right to education.[179]

---

175 Almog and Perry-Hazan (2012) at 215.
176 Almog and Perry-Hazan (2012) at 223.
177 HCL 4805/07 *The Center for Jewish Pluralism—The Movement for Progressive Judaism in Israel v. Ministry of Education et al.* (unreported), available at http://elyon1.court.gov.il/files_eng/07/050/048/r28/07048050.r28.htm.
178 See in particular §31 of the judgement as per Procaccia J.
179 Ibid, at §55, 58

Despite the finding by the Supreme Court on the issue that the State should not continue to fund these schools on the basis of the arguments mentioned, the Israeli lawmakers passed a law labeled as *Unique Cultural Educational Institutions Act*,[180] allowing high schools for ultra-Orthodox boys (*Yeshivot Ketanot*) to continue receiving the equivalent of 60 per cent of the funding awarded to public schools irrespective of the content taught. The rationale of the Act ironically relied on liberal multicultural theory and democratic principles to justify it.

It is difficult to ignore in this particular instance the political power play behind the Act from the perspective of the blatant inequality and challenge that it creates for many categories of right-holders: the ultra-Orthodox students who will get an education without connection to the labor market, perpetuating the circle of poverty for many families, the non-Orthodox students who will have to 'share' state funding with schools that do not fulfill the same requirements as theirs, and finally, their parents as taxpayers who have to contribute towards a school system that applies blatant double standards, often allowing for the violation of fundamental rights and principles.[181]

6 Educational pluralism, autonomy and accommodation of religious identity in Israeli state-sponsored schools

Further to the four features of the right to education, as defined by the UN Committee on Economic, Social and Cultural Rights framed as "available, accessible, acceptable and adaptable", the Convention on the Rights of the Child (CRC) provides that education should promote "the development of respect for the child's parents, his or her own cultural identity, language and values, for the national values of the country in which the child is living, the country from which he or she may originate, and for civilizations different from his or her own".[182] By extension, Article 30 of the CRC ensures the same rights to children belonging to ethnic, religious or linguistic minorities "to enjoy his or her own culture, to profess and practice her or her own religion, or to use his or her own language".[183]

The implications of the right to "adaptable" education are wide and revolve around many layers of public policy. From school admission and allocation of funds to religious schools to cultural exemptions from schools or the content of

---

180 The Unique Cultural Educational Institutions Act, 5769–2008, §1. A "unique cultural educational institution" is defined in the Act as an educational institution which gives systemic education that originates from the way of life of the unique cultural group and is in accordance with the unique characteristics of the group. The only group to which the Act applies is the ultra-Orthodox communities.

181 Under the Minister of Education Naftali Bennett, at the time of writing, 85 per cent of the 18 million shekels allocated to support 'Jewish renewal' in secular schools has reached religious Zionist and ultra-Orthodox groups (See Wolff (2017)).

182 Art. 29(1)(c) of the Convention on the Rights of the Child, G.A. Res. 25 XLIV, 44 U.N. GAOR, Supp. No. 49, UN Doc. A/RES/44/25 (1989), also in 28 I.L.M. 1448 (1989).

183 Article 30 CRC.

curricula, there are many parameters that legislators and policy-makers need to plan and account for in execution of the right. At the ground level, educators ultimately shape, however, the final meaning and scope of the right to education.[184] This competition of agents to claim authority on what the right to education means and how it secures (or not) religious identity accentuates the centripetal tendencies, particularly in Israel.[185] The limitations of state law as a normative rule hence become particularly obvious: If we accept that "legal responsiveness depends on people with different identities, who narrate law differently, and differ as to what expectations it should fulfill",[186] any legal assessment of the religious diversity in public Israeli education must also account for the reframing of legal provisions as they travel from the Knesset to individual classrooms.

The observation of the interaction of law with socio-cultural norms appears, therefore, essential to study education law in a context of established plurality. Constitutional provisions and international human rights may guarantee through their wording a standard of legal protection (e.g. freedom of educational choice or equal opportunities), yet the different aspects of the right to education when confronted with religious values (sourced from religious freedom and human dignity in the case of Israel) may become alienated. The study of the process of (mutual) alienation makes the search for 'good' law meaningful. This would explain, for example, the resistance within ultra-Orthodox schools to apply government standards on education.

Stemming from one's interest to protect his/her identity, including his religious belief and way of life, Israel is called to address two sets of challenges: first, the Arab community, which continues to be excluded from the State's civil religion, and second, the ultra-Orthodox one due to its illiberal religious elements.[187]

While the State, according to the liberal point of view, should remain neutral on its citizens' religious beliefs and ways of life, open neutrality raises the standard of state intervention to assist and protect religious minorities, especially at times where illiberal practices are involved. For Israel, the special relationship of ultra-Orthodox communities with the State secures the State's support for a religion that is essentially illiberal, but the same state does not extend an equivalent level of involvement through support of other religious communities. Consequently, whether the accommodation towards the ultra-Orthodox

---

184 The content of policy thus depends on the methods, ideas and expertise of the implementing agents, (i.e. the teachers) (Lotem Perry-Hazan, 'From the Constitution to the Classroom: Educational Freedom in Antwerp's Ultra-Orthodox Jewish Schools', *Journal of School Choice*, 8, 2014, 475–502, at 3.)
185 Perry-Hazan (2014).
186 Gad Barzilai, 'Beyond Relativism: Where Is Political Power in Legal Pluralism', *Theoretical Inquiries in Law*, 9, 2008, 395–416, at 404.
187 Avishai Margalit and Moshe Halbertal, 'Liberalism and the Right to Culture', *Social Research*, 71(3), Social Research at Seventy, Fall 2004, 529–548, at 535.

communities' group-based entitlements is normatively acceptable remains a hotly contested matter.[188]

Intercultural encounters in Israel pose the seminal issue of equality. The latter, a central value within the law of the liberal state,[189] is confronted with a form of normative relativism that aims to 'defend' other standards that are culturally constituted.[190] Within ultra-Orthodox Jewish communities, tradition embodies the cultural standard applicable as it reflects the "ways . . . imperatives have been interpreted throughout the generations by Halakhic sages".[191] At the same time, tradition, as a binding force, implies a single concept of 'good life', against the plurality of the good within liberal societies.[192]

The right to education, as implemented within these communities, provokes inquiries as to whether there is sufficient 'harm' to dictate State intervention within illiberal religious groups.[193] Connected to this question stands also the question of whether and how the duty of the (multicultural) state is to hold diversity at its core, providing thus the framework for the peaceful co-existence of groups with diverse conceptions of the 'good life'.[194]

There is, therefore, a considerable degree of hermeneutic and physical 'violence' that is generated by the desire of the Orthodox Jewish establishment's wish to preserve religious patriarchal hegemony within religious schools.[195] This

---

188 See the seminal work of Will Kymlicka, *Mutlicultural Citizenship: A Liberal Theory of Minority Rights*, Oxford University Press, 1996, at 37 where the author claims that "liberal can and should endorse certain external protections, where they promote fairness between groups, but should reject internal restrictions which limit the right of group members to question and revise authorities and practices".

189 Charles Taylor in *Multiculturalism and the Politics of Recognition*, Amy Gutman (ed.), Princeton: Princeton University Press, 1992, at 62 warns against the neutrality of liberalism in itself: "[L]iberalism can't and shouldn't claim complete cultural neutrality. Liberalism is also a fighting creed".

190 Cf. Menachem Mautner, 'A Dialogue Between a Liberal and an Ultra-Orthodox on the Exclusion of Women from Torah Study', in S. Lavi and R. Provost (eds.), *Religious Revival in a Post-Multicultural Age*, 2013, at 18, available at https://ssrn.com/abstract=2169400.

191 Mautner (2013) at 30.

192 Mautner (2013) at 32.

193 Joseph Raz in *The Morality of Freedom*, Oxford University Press, 1986 on the question as to whether cultures of such communities should be tolerated, ultimately concedes: "[W]renching them out of their communities may well make it impossible for them to have any kind of normal rewarding life whatsoever because they have not built up any capacity for autonomy. Toleration is therefore the conclusion one must often reach". (at 424).

194 This discourse is linked to 'diversity liberals', opposed to 'imperial liberals' (such as early Raz himself) and was coined by Richard Shweder (R.A. Shweder, 'What About Female Genital Mutilation? And Why Understanding Culture Matters in the First Place', in R.A. Shweder, M. Minow and H.R. Markus (eds.), *Engaging Cultural: The Multicultural Challenge in Liberal Democracies*, New York: Russell Sage Foundation, 2002, at 235–236).

195 For a similar view, see Frances Raday, 'Claiming Equal Religious Personhood: Women of the Wall's Constitutional Saga', in Winfried Brugger and Michael Karayanni (eds.), *Religion in the Public Sphere in the Public Sphere: A Comparative Analysis of German, Israeli, American and International Law*, Vol. 190, Springer, 2007, 256–298, at 267.

level of 'violence' is maintained and framed as a perpetual conflict for cultural, religious and to some extent also political hegemony between secularist-libertarian elites and the ultra-Orthodox community, who represent a genuine type of 'enclave' community.[196] The expressions of this clash have shaped an independent political agenda for the ultra-Orthodox groups that has led to demonstrations against the driving of cars and public buses on the Sabbath, against proposals to draft ultra-Orthodox youth to army service or against the right of women to sit in religious councils or enjoy an equal share of matrimonial property in divorce proceedings.

The Israeli State over its short constitutional history has not hesitated to endorse this type of religious hegemony, although it may be claimed that this choice was guided by concerns rooted in political pragmatism rather than ideology.[197] Group discrimination permitted by the Israeli legal system remains, nevertheless, present in the religious jurisdiction over personal status.[198]

Apart from the commonly debated question as to how cultural dissent may be protected within ultra-Orthodox communities,[199] the right to autonomy that religious communities are awarded within the Israeli legal system seems to take precedence over universalistic values (and rights). Whether out of deep multiculturalist conviction, or political pragmatism, as already stated previously, individuals belonging to these communities are assumed to have provided their tacit consent to a set of normative commitments, including their right to be discriminating in some cases.

So, while cultural and religious ways of life carry an essential source of social cohesion, or "the glue that holds society together", constitutionally the case of religious diversity in public education in Israel highlights the continuing struggle between the right to equality and that of freedom of religion.

---

196 An 'enclave' is defined as "the typical structure of a community that chooses to disengage from mainstream society". For more on this point, see Yohai Hakak and Tamar Rapoport, 'Excellence or Equality in the Name of God? The Case of Ultra-Orthodox Enclave Education in Israel', *The Journal of Religion*, 92, April 2012, 251–276 at 256. The authors explain how Haredi education also serves the purpose to protect the community against possible defections of its members (at 257), in the light of instances of evasion of Haredi men into other areas of activity such as occupational training programmes and the labor market (at 261).

197 Raday (2007) at 269–270.

198 The maintenance of personal status law is a direct historical offshoot of the millet system practiced under the British Mandate prior to the genesis of the State of Israel. The pluralistic character of the system allowed the various communities (Jewish, Muslim and Christian) to have their own religious courts with exclusive jurisdiction over questions of personal status of members of their communities (in particular marriage and divorce.)

199 See in that respect the very interesting series of Israeli Supreme Court judgments on the Women of the Wall case law (Hoffman I-III) where the right of women to religious prayer was deconstructed without discussing the women's right to equality: HCJ 257/89 *Anat Hoffman v. Western Wall Commissioner* (1994) 48(2) P.D. 265; HCJ 3358/95 *Anat Hoffman v. The Prime Minister Office*, Tak-Al 2000 (2) 846; HCJ 4128/00 *Prime Minister Office v. Anat Hoffman* (2003) 57(3) P.D. 289.

Adverse consequences for the protection of the right to education can be observed as a result.

Several questions in this complex web of connections deserve clarification: first, with regards to education, what is the level of regulation and control of schools that provide religious as well as educational services, especially when funded partially or wholly by the State? In a famous passage from *Everson v. Board of Education*, Justice Jackson declared: "[i]f the state may aid . . . religious schools, it may therefore regulate them. Many groups have sought aid from tax funds to find that it carried political control with it".[200] In Israel, the extent of public involvement is not proportional to the level of regulation in ultra-Orthodox schools. One normative explanation for this may be that the Israeli state is not aiming for enforcing compliance with liberal norms but rather with facilitating the collective and individual exercise of freedom of religion.[201]

Martha Nussbaum's proposal for dealing with this dilemma posits that:

> The state and its agents may impose a substantial burden on religion only when it can show a compelling interest. But . . . protection of the central capabilities of citizens should always be understood to ground a compelling state interest.[202]

More critical voices of the intensive involvement of the State, such as that of Izhak Englard, argue that:

> [the] integration [of the established Orthodox Rabbinate into the State's organization], viewed by the Zionist religious parties as a positive manifestation of the State's identification with Judaism, has exacted a rather high price of lost independence vis-à-vis the government and a corresponding loss of moral stature.[203]

Seen from a distance, one may argue that despite the obvious religious diversity provided for in public education in Israel, the role and scope of education in the public space is and remains primarily to "provide an educational means to convert ideology into social objectives, and to facilitate individuals' needs".[204]

---

200 330 U.S. 1, 27 (1947) (Jackson J., dissenting).
201 For a similar point, see Barak Medina, 'Does the Establishment of Religion Justify Regulating Religious Activities? The Israeli Experience', in Winifred Brugger and Michael Karayanni (eds.), *Religion in the Public Sphere: A Comparative Analysis of German Israeli, American and International Law*, Max Planck Institut für auslandisches öffentliches Recht und Völkerrecht, Springer, 2007, 299–332 at 317.
202 Martha Nussbaum, *Women and Development: The Capabilities Approach*, Cambridge University Press, 2000, at 105.
203 As quoted in Medina (2007) at 330.
204 Yaacov Iram and Mirjam Schmida, *The Educational System of Israel*, Westport: Greenwood Press, 1988, at 113–114.

Clearly these goals are sustaining societal fragmentation rather than a qualitative enhancement of the exercise of religious freedom in consonance with equality and tolerance.

The educational system has also predictably avoided dealing with the topic and implications within education of Jewish-Arab relations.[205] The 1984 *Education for Jewish-Arab co-existence programme* was an indication of a more inclusive notion of statehood along the lines of religious pluralism. Yet it (also) failed.[206] Amendments to the 1953 Education Act in 2000 and 2003 introduced the right to adaptable education combining respect and training within one's own cultural identity, with an introduction to the language, culture and heritage of the Arab population in Israel.[207] The goals of the Act were shifted towards "getting to know the language, culture, history, heritage, and the unique tradition of the Arab population and to other population groups within the State of Israel and to acknowledge the equal rights of all citizens of Israel".[208] The amendments did not extend to a formal recognition of the group as a national minority. Also, given the structure and systemic specificities of the system, the legal framework depends on the form of implementation that teachers and school principals will give to these legal requirements.[209] For these reasons, the amendment ultimately has failed to produce notable changes in school curricula.

Thus, religious diversity in the form of curricular diversity, otherwise very explicit in the structure of the schools, remains incomplete. The various tracks available within the school system, based on religious identity, secure the exercise of the right to religious freedom as well as the right of parents to have their children educated according to their beliefs. Any reform, however, towards the introduction of more diverse-friendly content is hindered by this same school diversity: the decentralization of the administration of public education, combined with the variation in the curricular interpretation produce content asymmetries.[210] Variable curricular interpretations are particularly visible in Jewish

---

205 Leavy (2010) at 53.
206 Leavy (2010) at 57. The programme adopted a more comprehensive approach to Israeli citizenship, encouraging encounters between Arab and Jewish students, suggesting a revision of teaching materials resonating less prejudice and stereotypes and recommending the teaching of Arab history, language, literature and culture.
207 Article 2(1) and 2(11) of the 1953 State Education Law, as amended.
208 As quoted in Yossi Yonah, 'The Palestinian Minority in Israel: Where Common Core Curriculum in Education Meets Conflicting Narratives', *Intercultural Education*, 19(2), April 2008, at 106–107.
209 For a similar point see Lotem Perry-Hazan, Shulamit Almog and Nohad A'li, 'Applying International Human Rights Standards to National Curricula: Insights from Literature Education of Jewish and Arab High Schools', *Northwestern Interdisciplinary Law Review*, VI(1), 2013, 1–20 at 17.
210 These factors are highlighted in greater detail in Nura Resh and Aaron Benavot, 'Educational Governance, School Autonomy, and Curriculum Implementation: Diversity and Uniformity in Knowledge Offerings to Israeli Pupils', *Journal of Curriculum Studies*, 41(1), February 2009, 67–92.

studies, which in certain cases receive a disproportionate degree of emphasis at the expense of other core subjects.

Legislation in 2008 has furthered this asymmetric trend as it has loosened the Ministry of Education's control over curricular content in ultra-Orthodox schools. These latter may still receive funds without having the corresponding duty to implement proportionally the 'core curriculum'.[211] The law was challenged in *Amnon Rubinstein v. The Knesset (2012)* on the basis of the violation of the students' right to human dignity and liberty because of the limiting of education to religious studies at secondary ultra-Orthodox boys' schools. The Supreme Court rejected the claim.

While from the outset, one may claim that the organization of public education along religious lines promotes a multiculturalist, even pluralist, perception and implementation of the right to education, the same strict separation between religious schools and secular schools is rather conducive to social fragmentation.[212] The privileges of the ultra-Orthodox community in education, while a clear application of the right to religious freedom, come at the cost of a weaker enforcement of the right to education and, connected to that, a growing socioeconomic isolation of the groups concerned.

The balancing between a State's own universal principles with the reality of a multicultural population is awkward in the Israeli context: the educational system is the product of ideology combined with religion, whether one refers to the national conflict between Arabs and Jews or to the divide between religious and secular segments of society.[213] Education policies shift in opposing directions depending on the political parties, members of the Knesset, cabinet ministers and interests involved, in defiance of constitutional guarantees and the paramount

---

211 The level of funding raised to 60 per cent of the regular funds given to other schools implementing the Ministry's 'core curriculum' (Cf. Neta Sela, 'Yeshivas to Receive State Funds Without Teaching Basic Subjects', *Y Net News*, 24 July 2008, available at http://ynetnews.com/articles/0,7340,L-3572383,00.html.

212 A recent Pew Research Centre Survey confirms the deep divisions within Israeli society between Israeli Jews and the Arab minority but also among the religious subgroups of Israeli Jewry. The debate as to whether democratic principles or religious law should take priority demonstrates the division well. The vast majority of secular Jews (89 per cent) say democratic principles should take precedence over religious law while a similarly large share of ultra-Orthodox Jews (89 per cent) agree that religious law should take priority. In relation to education, a virtual totality of secular Jews (99 per cent) agree that giving their children a good general secular education is important to them while only 69 per cent of the ultra-Orthodox Jews say the same. As for the importance of giving children a good 'religious' education, the trend is reversed: nearly all Haredi respondents find it important and desirable, with only 54 per cent of the secular Jews viewing it as important. See Pew Research Center, 'Israel's Religiously Divided Society', 2016, available at www.pewforum.org/2016/03/08/israels-religiously-divided-society/ (last accessed 21 June 2016).

213 H.A. Alexander, 'Education in the Jewish State', in Ilan Gur-Ze'ev (ed.), *Conflicting Philosophies of Education in Israel/Palestine*, Dordrecht: Kluwer Academic Publishers, 2000, at 129.

principle of human dignity as understood in Israeli law.[214] The growth of sectoral polarization of Israeli society from the 1980s onwards is also responsible for the current shape of the educational landscape.[215]

7 Concluding remarks: education and democratic governance

The connection between education and democracy passes through the conceptualization of citizenship as a status serving the collective interest in contemporary democracies. It introduces future citizens into rights and duties and prepares them to be exposed to pluralistic values within society. In order to serve these goals, public education chose to become and remain secular in many cases, though not in Israel.

State regulation of religion within education includes, however, other paradigms, extending beyond the traditionally researched Western democracies with Christian-majority student populations and of secular-liberal character.[216] The case of Israel provokes a series of wider concerns: the country being constitutionally labeled as a 'Jewish and Democratic State',[217] as previously mentioned, it is worth inquiring to what extent 'Jewishness' reflects the religious dimension of the State, in which case this would qualify the country as a 'religious' state or whether 'Jewishness' assumes the character of an ethno-cultural attribute, in which case, it reflects another version of a secular state. [218] A careful observation of the educational system suggests a positioning of the Israeli state between a strictly secular state and a religious one.

In Article 2 of the 1953 State Education Act, the mission of national public education is described as being based on:

> the values of the Jewish culture and the achievements of science, on the love of the homeland and loyalty to the State and the Jewish people, on practice in agricultural work and handicraft, on *khalutzic* (pioneer) training, and on

---

214 Cf. Leavy (2010).
215 Leavy (2010) at 22 cites two examples demonstrating the wider trend: In the early 1980s, the Ministry of Education was controlled by the National Religious Party and gave preferential treatment to state religious schools in budget allocations and staffing decisions. In 1996, the same party controlled the Ministry of Education and withheld funding for the implementation of the Shenhar and Kremnitzer Commission Reports that were seeking to reform Judaic and civic studies.
216 For more on this point see Künkler and Lerner (2016) at 2.
217 On July 19th, 2018, the Israeli Knesset (Parliament) passed a new Basic Law stating that Israel is the Nation State of the Jewish people, excluding the prior mention to Israel's democratic character. The implications of this change are beyond symbolic and may affect minorities in the future. The new Law also maintains the omission of equality and downgrades the democratic character of the State.
218 Künkler and Lerner (2016) at 2.

striving for a society built on freedom, equality, tolerance, mutual assistance, and love of mankind.[219]

The implications of this constitutional choice are far from clear: the dilemma between state-supported religious education, founded on an established religion model, and a clear separation between religion and state may be answered in different modes. The Israeli constitutional scenario of state entanglement in religion has produced arguments claiming the excessive (mis)use of state funds in religious educational institutions.[220] Due to the low cost of Haredi education, these institutions enjoy a comparative advantage over other educational institutions within Israel drawing students at a fast speed towards a Haredi way of learning. Socially, this preference shapes students by limiting their choices in their later professional life.

There is also an observed antithesis in the position that branches of government take when balancing the right to religion as opposed to other fundamental rights, particularly equality and education. The judiciary tends to support a balanced protection of human and civil rights when conflicting with freedom to and from religion, while the legislative and the executive lower the guards of constitutional protection under pressure most likely emanating from political considerations and the radicalization over time of the groups concerned.[221] The growing disapproval of the choices of Israeli political leadership (and of secular society) indeed push a segment of the traditional Jews towards the adoption of a 'pseudo-Haredi' style of life, with increased submission to rabbis who take on additional roles.[222]

At the same time, there is a steady stream of ultra-Orthodox non-Zionist groups claiming political and societal agendas that go against the pluralist nature of Jews, democratic values or tolerance. The question of how 'traditional' Jews, defined as "middle of the road, moderate in matters of tradition . . . and supporting democracy"[223] position themselves within this clash remains an open issue worthy of further analysis.

The ultra-Orthodox community has developed steady access to political power with the aim of obtaining important budgets destined to finance community-related activities.[224] More than that, the political representatives of the community have served in key political positions, shaping thus a multitude of issues

---

219 As cited in Randolph Braham, *Israel: A Modern Education System*, Washington, DC: US Government Printing Office, 1966, at 35.
220 Shetreet (1999) at 422.
221 Shetreet (1999) at 439.
222 Hofri-Winogradow (2010) at 122.
223 Hofri-Winogradow (2010) at 449. On the disproportionate influence of Haredi political parties in the Israeli Parliament, cf. indicatively the results of the 2009 general elections: Central Elections Committee for the 18th Knesset, available at www.knesset.gov.il/elections18/heb/results/main_Results.aspx.
224 Stopler (2014) at 788.

affecting the broader Israeli society.[225] In that context, the process of introduction of the ultra-Orthodox agenda items in the public sphere is not restricted to education.[226]

It, nevertheless, provokes vigorous reactions whenever connected to the concepts of citizenship and the duties connected to it. Stopler suggests that members of ultra-Orthodox communities may indeed be acting as 'partial citizens', when exempting their schools from teaching their children basic skills or critical thinking.[227] The elements that render, however, the balance untenable, even within a multipluralist frame, are the degree of involvement of the ultra-Orthodox in political (and municipal) affairs and the heavy subsidization that they receive by the State in return.

The transformation of the members of these communities to a 'community of religious scholars' for its male members, combined with its isolation from the rest of the society has led to their ideological radicalization.[228] It is hard to dispute that educational autonomy has had an impact in this process that will only continue to grow.[229] In terms of empowerment, it is also clearly showcased how the ultra-Orthodox groups, and their leaders, far from powerless, have and maintain direct access to state power,[230] enforcing fully their ideology in the public space, favoring an education 'of ignorance'. The contrast with Arab Palestinian students is not so great in the impact of public education for both groups: it strongly differs, however, in that Israeli Palestinians are the recipients of an education to which they have not played any meaningful role in shaping.

225 Stopler (2014) at 788 states the positions of Minister of Interior, Minister of Housing, Deputy Minister of Health, Minister of Religious Services, President of the Parliamentary Committee on Finance and Mayor of Jerusalem.
226 Stopler (2014) mentions at 789 several examples of incidents demonstrating the clash between ultra-Orthodox religious ideology and liberal democratic values of the State.
227 Stopler (2014) at 790. The term 'partial citizens' is sourced from Jeff Spinner-Halev's work.
228 Stopler (2014) at 793.
229 See indicatively Yarden Skop, 'Forecast: Only 40 per cent of Israeli Students Will Attend Non-Religious Schools by 2019', *Ha'aretz Daily*, 7 August 2013, available at www.haaretz.com/news/national/premium-1.540130.
230 In the 18th Knesset, four of 34 ministers were Shas members; the party was also represented by a Deputy Minister in the Education Ministry. [Cf. Cohn (2012) at 6.]

5 Avoiding religion?

The question of religious identity conflicts in education in South Africa

"The hurrier I go, the behinder I get".

Alice in Wonderland, Lewis Carroll

1 Introduction: legal pluralism in South Africa[1]

South Africa is a county with unusual levels of plurality in its laws. Not only is it a mixed jurisdiction, incorporating elements of English and Dutch law, it has also recognized customary law officially, though not in entirely clear terms.[2] Yet beyond this narrow type of legal pluralism, labeled as 'state-law pluralism',[3] lies a more complex normative reality. At the same time, there is indeed tension between the "globalising legal and political order" of the country and its local socio-cultural one.[4] There is also a proliferation of religious institutions and organizations (e.g. rise in the profile of African Independent Churches) that use networks and procedures to reach wider audiences. This complex reality forms the challenging background for intense religious identity conflicts that are tainted by racial and cultural markers as a result of the country's past. This process is most evident in public education.

---

1 *Legal Pluralism* is understood here according to John Griffiths' definition as "normative heterogeneity attendant upon the fact that social action always takes place in a context of multiple, overlapping 'semi-autonomous social fields' [a] situation of legal pluralism . . . is one in which law and legal institution are not all subsumable within one 'system' but have their sources in the self-regulatory activities of all mutlifarious social fields present, activities which may support, complement, ignore or frustrate one another". [J. Griffiths, 'What Is Legal Pluralism', *Journal of Legal Pluralism*, 24, 1986, at 38–39]
2 C. Rautenbach and J.C. Bekker, *Introduction to Legal Pluralism in South Africa*, 4th ed., Durban: LexisNexis, 2014, at 5. Section 211 (3) of the South African Constitution provides that: "The courts must apply customary law when that law is applicable, subject to the Constitution and any legislation that specifically deals with customary law".
3 Rautenbach and Bekker (2014) at 5. Defined as the situation in which "at least two officially recognised legal systems run parallel and interact in limited, prescribed circumstances" (at 6).
4 Ebrahim Moosa, 'Tensions in Legal and Religious Values in the 1996 South African Constitution', in Mahmood Mamdani (ed.), *Beyond Rights Talk and Culture Talk*, Cape Town: David Philips Publishers, 2000, 121–135, at 122.

Historically, the recognition of customary law[5] has been a contested issue. Placed in the context of colonization, the question of recognition and application of customary laws can be traced back to the mid-19th century.[6] In historical retrospective, the recognition of customary law is not necessarily an 'innocent' liberal move: it occasionally has been used as a means of 're-tribalizing' the black population of the country at times where it sought to become more competitive.[7] In addition, the existence of other non-state laws (religious laws such as Muslim, Hindu and Jewish law) complicates the overall picture. The presence of these legal systems within South Africa has been labeled as a manifestation of 'deep legal pluralism'.

In the context of a more socially geared observation of law, it is worth adopting a perspective of a 'pluralist' legal lens: constitutionally, the South African Constitution makes provision for the recognition of other systems of family law and/or personal laws, yet the emphasis remains on state-law pluralism because recognition by the State is a precondition for 'existence' of those other systems of law.[8] Yet, in the absence of such recognition, South African courts have

---

5 Indigenous law and customary law are synonymous. The 1993 Interim Constitution speaks of indigenous law and the 1996 Constitution of customary law. 'Customary law' consists of both official customary law and living customary law and is the law applied by indigenous peoples. The most emblematic considerations of living customary law are included in *Bhe v. Magistrate, Khayelitsha (Commission for Gender Equality as Amicus Curiae)*; *Shibi v. Sithole*; *South African Human Rights Commission v. President of the Republic of South Africa* (2005) (1) BCLR 1 (CC); *Alexkor Ltd v. Richtersveld Community* (2003) (12) BCLR 1301 (CC). More recently in *Kievits Kroon Country Estate (Pty) Ltd v. Mmoledi and Others (LAC)* (unreported Case No. JA78/10, 24 July 2012), the Court found by a diversity of cultures, traditions and beliefs. "This being the case, there will always be instances where these diverse cultural and traditional beliefs and practices create challenges within our society. . . . It must be recognised that some of these cultural beliefs and practices are strongly held by those who subscribe [to] them and regard them as part of their lives. A paradigm shift is necessary by the state and also by the courts of the land; one must appreciate the kind of society we live in. Accommodating one another is nothing else but 'botho' or 'Ubuntu' which is part of our heritage as society" (As quoted in Pieter Coertzen, 'Religion and the Constitutional Experience of South Africa', in R. Bottoni et al. (eds.), *Religious Rules, State Law and Normative Pluralism—A Comparative Overview*, Springer, 2016, 343–355 at 349).

6 Tom W. Bennett, 'Law in the Face of Cultural Diversity: South Africa', in M-C. Foblets, J.F. Gaudreault-Des Biens and A. Duntes Renteln (eds.), *Cultural Diversity and the Law: State Responses from Around the World*, Bruxelles: Bruylant, 2010, 17–44, at 19. The application at that time was conditioned upon the indigenous law conforming to "general principles of humanity observed throughout the civilized world" (Bennett (2010) at 19.).

7 Bennett (2010) at 21 mentions the period of the 1920s where African populations were challenging the colonial white rule and the government decided to opt for the enactment of the Native Administration Act 38 of 1927, making customary law applicable nation-wide in a special system of courts where traditional leaders and native commissioners were sitting. These courts had only jurisdiction for blacks. Incidentally, the movement coincides with the beginnings of apartheid.

8 Section 15(3)(a) of the Constitution of the Republic of South Africa, 1996, provides as follows: "This section does not prevent legislation recognizing: (i) marriages concluded under any tradition, or a system of religious, personal or family law; or (ii) systems of personal and family law under any tradition, or adhered to by persons professing a particular religion, (b) Recognition in terms of paragraph (a) must be consistent with this section and the other provisions of the Constitution". To date, no such recognition has been given, though there is a Draft Bill on Muslim Marriages currently being considered in Parliament.

cautiously gone ahead and engaged with deeper forms of legal pluralism, especially in Islamic law.[9] The challenge for the courts in such cases remains, however, to have to deal with institutions that are not in line with Western values, which in part justified their reluctance to engage with such questions.[10] In general terms, religions have the freedom to make their own 'internal' rules, independent from those of the State, but must remain in consonance with the Charter of Rights of the 1996 Constitution (Chapter 2, section 36).[11]

The general picture of the different layers of normativity in the country leads to a number of initial observations: first, it is clear that customary law is persistently relevant and has the ability to adjust to changing political circumstances and arrangements. [12] There is a variety of fora that engage in the application of such law such as family councils, courts of ward heads or traditional courts that operate as dispute-settlement institutions. Second, it is gradually evident that official customary law is not entirely in tune with living customary law: in that respect State courts are taking notice of that discrepancy.[13]

The interim South African Constitution in 1993,[14] following the collapse of apartheid, in 1994 was an eagerly anticipated occasion to revise the legal order on many levels. Interestingly, the legal pluralist option was not favored as it was perceived as linked to the previous inegalitarian regime. Apartheid, ironically, was successful in maintaining cultural distinctions, albeit within inequalities in opportunities and wealth.

Resisting any calling towards the 'Africanization' of the new system to be created,[15] the role (and 'voice') of customary law was nevertheless not ignored. Traditional leaders were able to partake in the constitution-making process yet not with a cultural agenda. Their claim was more formulated in terms of continuing to have access to government and governance.[16] That claim was to some extent accommodated. Traditional courts were maintained but not for reasons

---

9 Rautenbach and Bekker (2014) at 7. The authors nevertheless also note a trend towards a "forced convergence of common law and customary law . . . into a unified law, within a framework of Western values" (Rautenbach and Bekker (2014) at 13). See also Christa Rautenbach, 'Deep Legal Pluralism in South Africa: Judicial Accommodation of Non-State Law', *The Journal of Legal Pluralism and Unofficial Law*, 42(60), 2010, 143–177.

10 Rautenbach and Bekker (2014) at 14.

11 See, for example, *Taylor v. Kurtstag* (2004) 4 ALL SA 317 (w); (2005) 1 SA 362 (w); (2005) 7 BCLR 705 (w), where the Constitutional Court considered the validity of a Beth Din decision to excommunicate a member, finding that the decision was valid under Jewish law, though invalid in terms of South African law, and was nevertheless upheld as binding to the member because there was no evidence of bias, unfairness and the right to fair administrative action was not infringed.

12 Rautenback and Bekker (2014) at 14.

13 See, for example, the case of *Mabena v. Letsoalo* (1998) (2) SA 1068 (T) that applied living Pedi law, finding that a woman could be the head of a family and receive *lobolo* (a bride price).

14 The Interim Constitution of the Republic of South Africa, Act 200 of 1993, into force on 27 April 1996.

15 Bennett (2010) at 24.

16 Bennett (2010) at 25 makes the same point.

of cultural diversity protection. The main argument was expedience in bringing affordable and culturally sensitive justice to rural populations.[17]

2 Equality and difference: constitutional contours and interpretation

From the point of view of diversity management, the new South African Constitution insisted on equality, with less gravitas on religion and culture, as a reaction to the painful past. This is also due to the treatment of religion and culture as a private matter, where the State had little or no interest in regulating the private sphere.[18] The key right towards the new constitutional goals was therefore equality.

Equality is guaranteed by Section 9 of the 1996 Constitution and includes three elements: first, under Section 9(1) the right to equality before the law, equal protection and benefit of the law; second, under Section 9(2) the possibility for the State to protect and advance previously disadvantaged groups; and Section 9(3) of the final Constitution prohibits unfair direct or indirect discrimination on many grounds, including race, gender, sex, pregnancy, age, disability, religion, conscience, belief, culture, language and birth by both the State as well as private individuals (Section 9(4)).[19]Additionally, the Promotion of Equality and Prevention of Unfair Discrimination Act 4 of 2000 created a network of Equality Courts around the country that are designed to provide a quick and effective way of resolving unfair discrimination disputes.[20]

In terms of education, equality implies the equal enjoyment of constitutional rights in the sense that all learners are entitled to receive a basic education. It also

---

17 Bennett (2010) at 31. These courts have been consistently criticized, however, for inadequate application of judicial standards as recognized by the Constitution.

18 Bennett (2010) at 30.

19 For specific categories of vulnerable groups, Article 9(2) of the Constitution also allows reverse discrimination as follows: "To promote the achievement of equality, legislative and other measures designed to protect or advance persons, or categories of persons, disadvantaged by unfair discrimination may be taken". Section 1 of the Promotion of Equality and Prevention of Unfair Discrimination Act 2000 reminds the prohibited grounds for discrimination as follows:

"(a) race, gender, sex, pregnancy, marital status, ethnic or social origin, color, sexual orientation, age, disability, religion, conscience, belief, culture, language and birth; or

(b) any other ground where discrimination [is] based on that ground:

    i   causes or perpetuates systemic disadvantage;
    ii   undermines human dignity; or
    iii adversely affects the equal enjoyment of a person's rights and freedoms in a serious manner that is comparable to discrimination on a ground in paragraph (a)".

20 Chris Mc Connachie, 'Equality and Unfair Discrimination in Education, Basic Education Rights Handbook—Education Rights in South Africa', in Faranaaz Veriava, Anso Thom and Tim Fish Hodgson (eds.), *Basic Education Rights Handbook: Education Rights in South Africa*, Braamfontein/Johannesburg: SECTION 27, 2017, at 93.

covers the accommodation of difference, including breaking down patterns of disadvantage.

For all other rights, equality is also subject to a general limitation clause under s.36 (1) of the 1996 Constitution that explicitly provides that: "[t]he rights in the Bill of Rights may be limited only in terms of law of general application to the extent that the limitation is reasonable in an open and democratic society based on human dignity, equality and freedom, taking into account all relevant factors". In *Hugo*, [21] the Court explained its position towards unfair discrimination as a violation of the principle of equality in a contextualized manner as follows:

> At the heart of the prohibition of unfair discrimination lies a recognition that the purpose of our new constitutional and democratic order is the establishment of a society in which all human beings will be accorded equal dignity and respect regardless of their membership of particular groups. The achievement of such a society in the context of our deeply inegalitarian past will not be easy, but that that is the goal of the Constitutional should not be forgotten or overlooked.[22]

To add a bit further that:

> To determine whether that impact was unfair it is necessary to look not only at the group who has been disadvantaged but at the nature of the power in terms of which the discrimination was effected and, also at the nature of the interests which have been affected by the discrimination.[23]

In legal interpretative terms, it is therefore essential to focus on the impact of discrimination on the alleged victim:[24] Does that create indirectly a constitutional

---

21 CCT 11/96 *President of the Republic of South Africa and Another v. Hugo* (1997) ZACC 4; BCLR 708; (1997) (4) SA 1 (18 April 1997). The court referred to the 1993 Constitution but it remains relevant for the equality provisions in the final 1996 Constitution.

22 CCT 11/96 *President of the Republic of South Africa and Another v. Hugo* (1997) ZACC 4; BCLR 708; (1997) (4) SA 1 (18 April 1997), at para. 41.

23 CCT 11/96 *President of the Republic of South Africa and Another v. Hugo* (1997) ZACC 4; BCLR 708; (1997) (4) SA 1 (18 April 1997), at para. 43.

24 Section 14 of the Promotion of Equality and Prevention of Unfair Discrimination Act 2000 provides guidelines for the assessment of fairness or unfairness as follows:

   14(1) It is not unfair discrimination to take measures designed to protect or advance persons or categories of persons disadvantages by unfair discrimination or the members of such groups or categories of persons.

   (2) In determining whether the respondent has proved that the discrimination is fair, the following must be taken into account:

   (a) the context;
   (b) the factors referred to in subsection (3);
   (c) whether the discrimination reasonably and justifiably differentiates between persons according to objectively determinable criteria, intrinsic to the activity concerned.

right to be treated differently under the South African Constitution? When assessing the constitutionally permitted level of differential treatment, the Supreme Court stated early on, realizing the challenge ahead that:

> It must be accepted that, in order to govern a modern country efficiently and to harmonise the interests of all its people for the common good, it is essential to regulate the affairs of its inhabitants extensively. It is impossible to do so without differentiation and without classifications which treat people differently and which impact on people differently.

Within the *Harksen* case, Sachs J, in his dissenting opinion, stressed further the necessity to evaluate "in a contextual manner how the legal underpinnings of social life reduce or enhance the self-worth of persons identified as belonging to such groups".[25]

He then went on to state further:

> The State . . . should not regulate in an arbitrary manner or manifest 'naked preferences' that serve no legitimate governmental purpose, for that would be inconsistent with the rule of law and the fundamental premises of the constitutional State.[26]

So, while there is no overt right to be different in the South African Constitution, it has been deducted from the existing provisions of the constitutional text. In *Christian Education*, Sachs J based a recognition of such right to difference through the combination of the constitutional requirement in the preamble of the text for a democratic and open society in an environment of tolerance and

---

(3) the factors referred to in subsection (2)(b) include the following:

    (a) whether the discrimination impairs or is likely to impair human dignity;
    (b) the impact or likely impact of the discrimination on the complainant;
    (c) the position of the complainant in society and whether he or she suffers from patterns of disadvantage or belongs to a group that suffers from patterns of disadvantage;
    (d) the nature and extent of the discrimination;
    (e) whether there are less restrictive and less disadvantageous means to achieve the purpose;
    (f) whether the discrimination has a legitimate purpose;
    (g) whether and to what extent the discrimination achieves its purpose;
    (h) whether there are less restrictive and less disadvantageous means to achieve the purpose;

        i   whether and to what extent the respondent has taken such steps as being reasonable in the circumstances to:
        ii address the disadvantage which arises from or is related to one or more of the prohibited grounds; or
        iii accommodate diversity.

25 CCT 9/97 *Harksen v. Lane No and Others* (1998) (1) SA 3000 (CC) at para. 125.
26 CCT 9/97 *Harksen v. Lane No and Others* (1998) (1) SA 3000 (CC), at para. 44.

cultural pluralism, combined with the protection of diversity which is an obligation of the State, and ss.31 and 18 of the 1996 Constitution guaranteeing cultural, religious and linguistic rights together with freedom of association.[27] The
Court concluded by affirming: "the right of people to be who they are without
being forced to subordinate themselves to the cultural and religious norms of
others, and highlight[s] the importance of individuals and communities being
able to enjoy what has been called the 'right to be different' ".[28]

In *Fourie*,[29] a similar conceptualization of the right to equality also implied the
right to be different. The Court again stated:

> Equality therefore does not imply a leveling or homogenization of behavior
> or extolling one form as supreme, and another as inferior, but an acknowl-
> edgement and acceptance of difference. At the very least, it affirms that dif-
> ference should not be the basis for exclusion, marginalization and stigma. At
> best, it celebrates the vitality that difference brings to any society.[30]

This sort of 'jurisprudence of difference' affirms and celebrates otherness beyond
mere tolerance.[31] It frames a new type of 'culture of justification' within a constitutional project that has been described in scholarship as 'transformative constitutionalism': it "connotes an enterprise of inducing large-scale social change
through non-violent political processes grounded in law . . . a transformation
vast enough to be inadequately captured by the phrase 'reform' in any traditional
sense of the word".[32]

27 *Christian Education South Africa v. Minister of Education* (2000) (10) BCLR 1051 (CC)
    (South Africa), at paras. 23–24. Section 18 of the 1996 Constitution stipulates: "Everyone
    has the right to freedom of association". Section 31 on Cultural, religious and Linguistic
    communities of the same text states: "(1) Persons belonging to a cultural, religious or lin-
    guistic community may not be denied the right, with other member[s] of that community
    (a) to enjoy their culture, practise their religion and use their language; (b) to form, join and
    maintain cultural, religious and linguistic associations and other organs of civil society; (2)
    The rights in subsection (1) may not be exercised in a manner inconsistent with any provi-
    sion of the Bill of Rights".
28 *Christian Education South Africa v. Minister of Education* (2000) (10) BCLR 1051 (CC)
    (South Africa), at para. 24.
29 (CCT 60/04) *Minister of Home Affairs and Another v. Fourie and Another* (2005) ZACC19;
    2006 (3) BCLR 355 (CC).
30 (CCT 60/04) *Minister of Home Affairs and Another v. Fourie and Another* (2005) ZACC19;
    2006 (3) BCLR 355 (CC), at para. 60.
31 The concept of 'jurisprudence of difference' reflects MI Young's politics of difference and
    relies on 'quality equality' described by Young as: "A goal of social justice . . . is social equal-
    ity. Equality refers not primarily to the distribution of social goods, though distributions are
    certainly entailed by social equality. It refers primarily to the full participation and inclusion
    of everyone in a society's major institutions, and the socially supported substantive oppor-
    tunity for all to develop and exercise their capacities and realise their choices". (Marion Iris
    Young, *Justice and the Politics of Difference*, Princeton University Press, 1990, at 173)
32 K. Klare, 'Legal Culture and Transformative Constitutionalism', *South African Journal on
    Human Rights*, 14, 1998, 146–188, at 150.

3 The right to religious freedom

Of equal importance to the study of religious diversity frameworks in public education is the consideration of the content of religious freedom within the South African constitutional framework. In Section 15 of the 1996 Constitution, the law-makers state that:

(1) Everyone has the right to freedom of conscience, religion, thought, belief and opinion.
(2) Religious observances may be conducted at state or state-aided institutions, provided that:

    (a) those observances follow rules made by the appropriate public authorities;
    (b) they are conducted on an equitable basis; and
    (c) attendance at them is free and voluntary.[33]

Sections 15(2) (a) and (b) of the 1996 Constitution specify how this right may become part of the public sphere (e.g. within schools). These qualifications have raised a number of objections on religious practices in public schools. The implications of section 15 (2)(a), (b) and (c) have been interpreted by proponents of more religion in schools to signify that s.15 prohibits 'unfair' discrimination, but not discrimination altogether. Second, and building on the unfair discrimination argument, separate programmes of religious instruction, according to the same line of argument, could serve better the purpose of the policy and finally relating to s. 15 (2) (c), the use of a 'conscience clause' could have been maintained in an attempt to retain Christian instruction and worship in schools. All these points were rejected by the new government policies advancing instead an education based on human dignity and equality, outside of any potentially divisive religious interests.[34]

The wider dynamic of the provision suggests that the right to religious freedom has two dimensions: as a belief, it appears to be absolute, yet as practice it is subjected to the limits of the 'reasonable and justifiable' (section 36(1) of the 1996 Constitution).[35] The South African Constitution does not include religiously motivated exemptions from laws of general application, although

---

33 Section 15(2) of the Constitution reflects a form of concession to the pre-1996 regime insofar as the inclusion of religious practices in state institutions represented an attempt to engage with religious but not the establishment of religion per se. (Cf. David Chidester, 'Religion Education and the Transformational State in South Africa', *Social Analysis*, 50(3), Winter 2006, 61–83, at 66.)
34 Chidester (2006) at 69–70.
35 Moosa (2000) at 129.

section 36 allows for the limitation of the rights in the Bill of Rights.[36] In other words, religion is a private concern and may be limited to the extent that it is not in consonance with (secular) constitutional values. Yet, the regulation of religious diversity in such a way does not match necessarily the diverse religious communities of the country.[37] Further to that, it subjects the exercise of religious freedom(s) to the 'language of rights', a 'rights-based' approach that remains ambivalent on the value and position of a religion as an autonomous normative discourse.[38]

Further to religious freedom, in Section 31 of the 1996 Constitution, the right to culture is guaranteed. The connection of this right to the study of religious diversity in South Africa's public schools is less straightforward insofar as it establishes a right of a religious community to practice religion with other members of the community. It matters, however, to the extent that it showcases how religion and culture become constitutionally fused. It also serves as a connecting link with the way that the right to religious freedom has a difficulty to acquire an independent and completely separate standing within the public education system.

All rights, including the ones just mentioned, have to be construed in context as stipulated in section 39 of the 1996 Constitution that stipulates:

(1) When interpreting the Bill of Rights, a court, tribunal or forum-

    (a) must promote the values that underlie an open and democratic society based on human dignity, equality and freedom;

    (b) must consider international law; and

    (c) may consider foreign law.

(2) When interpreting any legislation, and when developing the common law or customary law, every court, tribunal or forum must promote the spirit, purport and objects of the Bill of Rights.

(3) "The Bill of Rights does not deny the existence of any other rights or freedoms that are recognized or conferred by common law, customary law or legislation, to the extent that they are consistent with the Bill".

---

36 Section 36 of the 1996 Constitution reads: "(1) The rights may be limited only in terms of law of general application to the extent that the limitation is reasonable and justifiable in an open and democratic society based on human dignity, equality and freedom, taking into account all relevant factors, including. (a) the nature of the right; (b) the importance of the purpose of the limitation; (c) the nature and extent of the limitation; (d) the relation between limitation and its purpose; and (e) less restrictive means to achieve the purpose".

37 Moosa (2000) at 130.

38 Moosa (2000) at 134, noting that there is no equivalent consideration of the notion of duty in the Constitution.

In sum, from the perspective of the State, all religions merit equal treatment.[39] Yet there is a contrast between the treatment of customary law and the claims of the Muslim and Hindu communities to obtain a formal recognition of their laws. The former issue is treated as a cultural issue, while the latter is a religious one.[40] The distinction would have some significance in a constitutional setting with differential degrees of protection between the right to culture and that to religious freedom (in light of the difficulty to define both terms) but it is not as pronounced from the perspective of religious diversity frameworks in South African public education.

a Religion and the right to education in South Africa: accommodating difference in schools?

Defining religion, from any disciplinary perspective, is a perilous intellectual exercise. From the point of view of law and State management, the definition of religion matters for the conferral of legal recognition, tax exemptions or even the constraining of forms of religious life when they come into conflict with state law.[41] From a more sociological perspective, it can be useful to consider religion as a form of Foucaultian 'biopower',[42] that sourced from the State's demands for control and conformity regulates the more gendered, sexual or emotionally intrinsic dimensions and expressions of religion towards 'a polity of society' and away from one 'of sovereignty'.

For South Africa, a very common trajectory is to perceive religion as an instrument of colonial containment;[43] put simply, a 'system for keeping people in place'. As such, the failure of the secularization thesis for the social sciences did not change much in South Africa. Similar to other post-colonial spaces, the country has not witnessed a significant decrease in its number of believers.[44] Quite to the

---

39 *Ryland v. Edros* (1997) (2) SA 690 (C); *Daniels v. Campbell No and Others* (2004) (5) SA 331 (CC).

40 For a detailed discussion of the difficulty to reconcile customary law with constitutional principles see C. Rautenbach, F. Jansen van Rensburg and G. Pienaar, 'Culture (and Religion) in Constitutional Adjudication', *PER/PELJ*, 6(1), 2003, available at https://journals.assaf. org.za/per/issue/view/331.

41 David Chidester, 'Religious Fundamentalism in South Africa', *Scriptura*, 99, 2008, 350–367, at 360.

42 The term was coined in the last chapter of Michel Foucault's, *The Will to Knowledge: History of Sexuality, 1976*, Vol. 1, R. Hurley (trans.), London: Penguin Books, 1998. The author speaks of "[a] power that exerts a positive influence on life, that endeavours to administer, optimize, and multiply it, subjecting it to precise controls and comprehensive regulations" [at 137]. This type of power is opposed to 'juridico-discursive' versions of power being repressive and negative [at 82].

43 Chidester (2008) at 351.

44 Despite a clear majority of Christian believers in the country, what is nevertheless noticeable is the fragmentation of Christian denominations into smaller apostolic and charismatic groups [Cf. Ivon Chipkin and Annie Leatt, 'Religion and Revival in Post-Apartheid South Africa', *Focus: The Journal of the Helen Suzman Society*, 62, August 2011, 39–46, at 42].

contrary, it remains a deeply religious country: religious in Christianity, within African customary traditions, Islam, Hinduism and Judaism, among the many minority religious groups.[45]

As already mentioned, apartheid maintained these religious differences, but it did more: it accentuated and essentialized them. Both the former National Party and opposition movements relied on religion to stage their claims.[46] Christianity came to represent apartheid's 'political theology of race', which had a lasting imprint on education. Christian national education became a model of education that was hard to completely remove post-apartheid. Constitutionally, however, religious identity has been projected since 1994 through the lens of equality and state neutrality. The lawmakers took account of the ambivalent nature of religion as a tool of exclusion but also inclusion. They opted for an approach that invested in religion as an instrument of nation-building. To be more precise, they adopted a co-operative model of state-religion relations in order to mobilize the resources of many religions in the national interest.[47] This approach, however, did not reflect or acknowledge any dimension of the social meanings of religious practice.

The concept of religious freedom in s.15 of the 1996 Constitution does not prevent the State from recognizing or supporting religion, yet it requires the State to do so equally for all religions. The South African Constitutional Court has repeatedly used the approach to the concept endorsed in *R. v, Big M Drug Mart Ltd* [1985 (18) DLR 132] of the Canadian Supreme Court, whereby it is defined as the right to entertain such religious beliefs as a person chooses, the right to declare religious beliefs openly and without fear of hindrance or reprisal and the right to manifest religious beliefs by worship and practice or by teaching and dissemination. Essentially, freedom of religion implies an absence of coercion or restraint.[48] Read together with s.9 on equality, s.15 carries both a free exercise and an equal treatment component. The onus to prove that there has been constraint or coercion rests with the person alleging the violation.[49] In *S v Lawrence*, the Constitutional Court formulated the right to religious freedom as "the right to entertain such religious beliefs as a person chooses, the right to declare religious beliefs openly and without fear of hindrance or reprisal, and the right

---

45 According to Coertzen, 79.8 per cent of the population declare to follow a form of Christianity, of which African Independent Churches have a membership of 40.8 per cent of the total Christian population. The second biggest faith is the African Traditional Religion. (Cf. Coertzen (2016) at 344). See also Willem J. Schoeman, 'South African Religious Demography: The 2013 General Household Survey', *HTS Theologiese Studies/Theological Studies*, 73(2), 2017, at 3837.

46 Chipkin and Leatt (2011) at 41.

47 Chidester (2008) at 352.

48 See indicatively *S v. Lawrence, S v. Negal, S v. Solberg* (4) SA 1176 (CC) at 1208F–1209A; *Prince v. President of the Cape of Good Hope and Others* (2002) (2) SA 794 (CC) at 247 [38] at 812; and *Christian Education South Africa v. Minister of Education* (2000) (10) BCLR 1051 (CC). Both the individual and collective dimensions of the right are emphasized in some of these decisions.

49 Rautenbach et al. (2003) at 11.

to manifest belief by worship and practice or by teaching and dissemination",[50] echoing Canadian case law.

In cases of conflict between freedom of religion with other rights, the Constitutional Court has declared that a nuanced and context-sensitive balancing of rights is mandated, on the basis of proportionality,[51] without implying that a different level of scrutiny might be used.[52] There is, therefore, no constitutionally warranted right to be exempted from laws of the land on the basis of one's beliefs, as already mentioned.[53] Justice Sachs has, however, stated in that respect in the *Christian Education* case that: "the State, should, wherever reasonably possible, seek to avoid putting believers to extremely painful and intensely burdensome choices of either being true to their faith or else respectful of the law".[54]

Section 10 of South African Schools Act imposes a constitutionally acceptable limitation to the right of parents' free exercise of religious beliefs.[55] According to Justice Sachs, a statute that bars parents from authorizing schools to administer corporal punishment does not impose a constitutionally untenable limitation on the parents' right. From the perspective of the child, whose perspective is missing altogether in the case at issue, one may conclude that the position of the Court vis-à-vis the protection of otherness is one that restrains the 'Other' when measured against constitutional values and norms.

The *Pillay* case provided another notable instance of conflict between the rights to religion/culture and equality in a school environment. The Court found that voluntary religious/cultural practices may entitle learners to exemptions from school uniform regulations, subject to reasonable limitations.[56] Langa CJ compared the situation of the learner at issue wishing to wear a nose-stud for cultural and religious reasons with those learners whose sincere religious beliefs were not compromised by school regulations.[57] Conversely, an interpretation of this argument can lead to the conclusion that a Western dress code may be open to

---

50 *S v. Lawrence; S v. Negal; S.v. Solberg* (1997) (10) BCLR 1348 (CC) [100]–[102]; [116]–[118].

51 *Nkosi v. Bührmann* (2002) (6) BCLR 574 (SCA) at 578.

52 *Christian Education South Africa v. Minister of Education* (2000) (10) BCLR 1051 (CC).

53 *Christian Education South Africa v. Minister of Education* (2000) (10) BCLR 1051 (CC), per Sachs J, at 779.

54 *Christian Education South Africa v. Minister of Education* (2000) (10) BCLR 1051 (CC), per Sachs J, at 779.

55 Section 10 of the South African Schools Act 84 of 1996 states: Prohibition of corporal punishment (1) No person may administer corporal punishment at a school to a learner; (2) Any person who contravenes subsection (1) is guilty of an offence and liable on conviction to a sentence which could be imposed for assault.

56 The contrast should be noted with *Antonie v. Governing Body Settlers High School* (2002) (4) SA378 (C) that treated a case of a learner wearing dreadlocks as a result of her Rastafarian beliefs and was expelled from her school for violation of the school's code of conduct. The Cape High Court decided the case on the basis of its administrative unfairness as the school board had not justified the learner's serious misconduct.

57 CCT 51/06 *MEC for Education: Kwazulu-Natal and Others v. Pillay* (2007) SA 474 (CC), at para. 44.

challenge with regards to its alleged 'neutrality'. Additionally, the Court chose to extend protection not only to mandatory, but also voluntary practices, conducive to higher levels of exercise of individual autonomy. In this sense, the right to be different covers also the right to express one's religious beliefs in the following way:

> The protection of voluntary as well as obligatory practices also conforms to the Constitution's commitment to affirming diversity. It is a commitment that is totally in accord with this nation's decisive break from its history of intolerance and exclusion. Differentiating between mandatory and voluntary practices does not celebrate or affirm diversity, it simply permits it. That falls short of our constitutional project which not only affirms diversity but promotes and celebrates it. We cannot celebrate diversity by permitting it only when no other option remains.[58]

The effects of *Pillay* in relation to school uniform rules were also clarified through the prism of reasonable accommodation:

> It does not abolish school uniforms; it only requires that, as a general rule, schools make exemptions for sincerely held religious and cultural beliefs and practices. There should be no blanket distinction between religion and culture. There may be specific schools or specific practices where there is a real possibility of disruption if an exemption is granted. Or, a practice may be so insignificant to the person concerned that it does not require a departure from the ordinary uniform. The position may also be different in private schools, although even in those institutions, discrimination is impermissible. Those cases all raise different concerns and may justify refusing exemption. However, a mere desire to preserve uniformity, absent real evidence that permitting the practice will threaten academic standards or discipline, will not.[59]

In fact, the acceptance of the notion of reasonable accommodation rendered discrimination against the student unfair. The Court explained the concept as follows:

> At its core is the notion that sometimes the community, whether it is the state, an employer or a school, must take positive measures and possibly incur additional hardship or expense in order to allow all people to participate and enjoy all their rights equally. It ensures that we do not relegate people to the margins of society because they do not or cannot conform to certain social norms.[60]

---

58 CCT 51/06 *MEC for Education: Kwazulu-Natal and Others v. Pillay* (2007) SA 474 (CC), at para. 65.
59 CCT 51/06 *MEC for Education: Kwazulu-Natal and Others v. Pillay* (2007) SA 474 (CC), at para. 114.
60 CCT 51/06 *MEC for Education: Kwazulu-Natal and Others v. Pillay* (2007) SA 474 (CC), at para. 73.

Such bold assertions in *Pillay* have not found application beyond issues of dress code infringements as manifestations of a sincerely held belief. Where dress is concerned, the State (or other related authority) needs to meet a high standard justifying the failure to accord the exemption precisely because of the constitutional commitment to diversity and tolerance. This does not automatically transform difference into an unqualified legal concept stricto sensu. It represents above all a policy statement that works against the essentialization of religious identity.

Apart from dress codes and visible religious symbols worn by learners, the issue of head styles, as connected to religion, has been raised. Rastafarian learners on a number of occasions in the early 2000s[61] have been prevented from attending schools on the grounds of uniform policies, prohibiting dreadlocks. More recently, a concerned group of parents under the organization *Organisasie vir Godsdienste – Onderrig en Demokrasie* (OGOD) approached the High Court in 2015 to challenge the Christian ethos and practices in their children's schools.[62] While the interim and the 1996 Constitution provide for the possibility of religious observances to be upheld, they remain silent about religious instruction in state and state-aided schools.[63] It is hence still disputed whether it is up to the national government to dense rules about religious observances in schools or rather the school governing bodies, given the decentralized form of organization in educational matters.

b Religion with(out) culture

The *Pillay* case is also connected to a separate debate that is particularly pertinent in the South African context: the relation of religion to culture. Amoah and Bennett claim that there is a clear hierarchical relationship between religion and culture in the South African context,[64] with traditional religions receiving less than equal treatment due to their "arrested" development and their distance from Western values.[65]

The 1996 Constitution, in fact, uses the term 'culture' in various ways.[66] The most relevant here is culture approached as "a modality that identifies and binds

---

61 See Tim Fish Hodgson, 'Religion and Culture in Public Education in South Africa', in Faranaaz Veriava, Anso Thom and Tim Fish Hodgson (eds.), *Basic Education Rights Handbook—Education Rights in South Africa*, Braamfontein/Johannesburg: SECTION 27, 2017, 185–203, at 196.
62 The schools in question required learners to attend compulsory Bible study classes (Cf. Hodgson (2017) at 198).
63 *Wittmann v. Deutscher Schulverein Pretoria and Others* (1998) (4) SA 423.
64 Jewel Amoah and Tom Bennett, 'The Freedoms of Religion and Culture Under the South African Constitution: Do Traditional African Religions Enjoy Equal Treatment? *African Human Rights Journal*, 8, 2008, 357–375, at 358.
65 M. Mutua, 'Limitations on Religious Rights: Problematising Religious Freedom in the African Context', *Buffalo Human Rights Law Review*, 5, 1999, 75–105, at 96–97.
66 For the various uses of 'culture' see Rautenbach et al. (2003), 2–20, at 4–5.

a specific group of people".[67] In some way, religion education policy formed a cultural project that aimed to create the conditions conducive to respect for the many religious cultures of South Africa. The policy is also closely related and resonating the notion of *Ubuntu*, an all-encompassing concept of humanness that relies on human solidarity because humans are only humans through their interaction with other humans.[68]

Within *Pillay*, religion and culture as grounds for discrimination are not entirely merged: "religion is ordinarily concerned with personal faith and belief, while culture generally relates to traditions and beliefs developed by a community",[69] the possibility, however, for overlap is distinctly present. The Court in the same case noted that "[c]ultural convictions or practices may be strongly held and as important to those who hold them as religious beliefs are to those more inclined to find meaning in a higher power than in a community of people".[70] It is therefore worth observing that in South Africa's case, the separation between culture and religion is not constitutionally warranted, neither is it deemed a priority, as the overarching normative goal is to guarantee equality on the basis of the various identity markers of each individual.

4 The right to education

South Africa is one of the few countries in the world that guarantee socio-economic rights in its constitution. In January 2015, however, when the country ratified the International Covenant on Economic, Social and Cultural Rights, it introduced a declaration that it would only take progressive steps to realize the right to education, in contradiction to the unqualified nature of the right under the 1996 Constitution.[71]

The nature and extent of the State's obligation to provide education was outlined in *Madzodzo v Minister of Basic Education*, where the High Court held in paragraph 20 that:

> [t]he State's obligation to provide a basic education as guaranteed by the Constitution is not confined to making places available to schools. It necessarily requires the provision of a range of educational resources: schools, classrooms, teachers, teaching materials, and appropriate facilities for learners.

---

67 Rautenbach et al. (2003) at 5. The other two uses of the term identified by the authors are "a specific tradition based on ethnics" and a "collective term for aesthetic expression".
68 Chidester (2006) at 72.
69 CCT 51/06 *MEC for Education: Kwazulu-Natal and Others v. Pillay* (2007) SA 474 (CC), at para. 47.
70 CCT 51/06 *MEC for Education: Kwazulu-Natal and Others v. Pillay* (2007) SA 474 (CC), at para. 53. In fact, evidence suggested that the nose-stud practice was not mandatory of either religion or cultural practices.
71 Section 29(1) of the 1996 Constitution declares: "Everyone has the right (a) to a basic education, including adult basic education and (b) to further education, which the state, through reasonable measures, must make progressively available and accessible".

The 1996 South African Constitution covers the right to education in its section 29. It covers the right to basic education, to adult basic education (section 29 (1) (a)) and to further education (section 29 (1)(b)). The right to basic education remains unqualified, while further education is subject to reasonable measures and a progressive realization. It should be noted that the right to education does not include cultural rights. Subject to equity, practicability and the need to redress the past experiences of racial discrimination, everyone has the right to receive education in the official language(s) of his/her choice in public education institutions. Groups also have the right, at their own expense, to establish independent educational institutions provided that they do not discriminate on the grounds of race.

The legal framework on education is characteristic of a decentralized nature: it allows considerable autonomy to provinces for the management of education.[72] The main statutory tool to instill equality into education has been the 1996 South African Schools Act (SASA). The Act required all schools to create democratically elected school governing bodies (SGB). At the same time, it mandated the creation of Codes of Conduct for learners, according to section 8 of SASA.[73] Guidelines for Codes of Conduct were also devised to assist in the process. Such Guidelines stressed the importance of advancing learners' fundamental rights, including religion and culture, in the framework of the Constitution.[74] School Governing bodies were required to supplement official funds with additional funding, including through fees policies. The overall legislative framework created a complex scheme of joint governance for schools that at times was subjected to conflicting interpretations.[75]

This version of the law failed, however, to foster equality in that it created de facto 'categories' of public schools according to socio-economic criteria between those who could afford to pay some fees and those who could not.[76] In recognition of that failure, the Act was amended in 1998, exempting parents

---

72 Ibid, at 74. The national minister of education has direct responsibility for higher education but limited discretion over schools.

73 The Code must be approved by the SGB, after having consulted with learners of the school, their parents, educators and only then becomes enforceable, in line with the democratic principles of the Constitution, in particular the principles of human dignity, equality and freedom.

74 Section 3.2 of the Guidelines for Codes of Conduct on fundamental rights and section 4.3 on holding others' beliefs and cultural observances in high regard. Similar Guidelines were also established on uniforms in order to support SGB in their efforts to establish dress codes for learners that are respectful of their constitutional rights.

75 See indicatively Clive Roos, 'Public School Governance in South Africa', *The Journal of the Helen Suzman Foundation*, 56, 2010, 57–61.

76 According to the South Africa Reconciliation Barometer and its Living Standards Measure, South Africans perceive class as the biggest division in society: 27.9 per cent see class as the biggest dividing line, while 14.6 per cent see race [Cf. UNICEF/Learning for Peace, *Investment in Equity and Peacebuilding: South Africa Case Study-FHI 360*, Washington: Education Policy and Data Center, 2016, at 32]

from paying school fees through waivers calculated on the basis of each family's total income.[77] Further to that amendment, the Amended National Norms and Standards for School Funding was passed in 2006, eliminating school fees for schools in the poorest areas. The effects of these adjustments into the levels of equity in the education system have not, however, been successful in reversing school resource legacies and low levels of local resource mobilizations.[78]

More broadly, the practice of (indirect) forms of discrimination persists: there are incidents of active aversion to integration in schools. In fact, there is growing awareness of the ways that schools may function as institutions that reproduce racial hierarchies.[79] White parents have either left public education entirely or enrolled their children in former Model C schools (former white schools) with the expectation that they would provide for better education.[80] Similarly, the language of instruction has also been used as an indirect medium of exclusion of poor or less-achieving students,[81] given that black learners usually cannot speak Afrikaans.

On a more practical level, section 8 of the SASA requires the School Governing Body to adopt a Code of Conduct for learners following consultation with parents, educators and learners. Once adopted, the Code is binding on those partaking in the process of education in the specific school. For religious diversity purposes, s.7 of the SASA allows religious observances to be conducted in public schools, subject to the rules issued by the School Governing Body. Similarly, according to section 20(1)(c) of the same Act, the broader mission of the School Governing Body is to develop a mission statement that reflects the value system underpinning their religion, taking into account the s.7 obligation of equal treatment.[82]

The question of religious dress at schools has attracted attention both by the policy-makers and subsequently also within case law, as already discussed. The Guidelines on School Uniforms are underpinned by the understanding that

---

77 As a result of the amendment, it has been calculated that public expenditure in 2005 is devoted by 57 per cent of the national school allocation to the poorest 40 per cent of students [Cf. UNICEF/Learning for Peace (2016) at 16].

78 UNICEF/Learning for Peace (2016) at 20, 28. Ex-Model C schools still enjoy more resources and smaller class sizes, suggesting a restratification along socio-economic lines of the student population.

79 See indicatively, Chana Teeger, 'Ruptures in the Rainbow Nation: How Desegregated South African Schools Deal with Interpersonal and Structural Racism', *Sociology of Education*, 88(3), 2015, 226–243, at 226–227.

80 UNICEF Learning for Peace (2016) at 33.

81 UNICEF Learning for Peace (2016) at 34. The requirement of students to know Afrikaans is a way to exclude black students, who are usually taught in English.

82 In fact, the Guidelines for Consideration of School Governing Bodies when adopting a Code of Conduct state the need for schools to focus on a positive discipline, within a culture of reconciliation, teaching, learning and mutual respect and the establishment of a culture of tolerance and peace in all schools [Cf. Department of Education, 1998, sections 1.4, 1.5 and 2.3]

section 15 of the 1996 Constitution taken together with section 9 (3) prohibit the State from discriminating against any religious groups imposing a combined right of free exercise and equal treatment.[83] Wearing something different at school, however, is limited by the need not to disrupt education or impede on the fundamental rights of others.[84] Thus, sections 29(1), (2) and (3) of the Guidelines on School Uniforms stipulate:

(1) A school uniform policy or dress code should take into account religious and cultural diversity. . . . Measures should be included to accommodate learners whose religious beliefs are compromised by a uniform requirement.

(2) If wearing a particular attire . . . is part of the religious practice of learners or an obligation, schools should not, in terms of the Constitution, prohibit the wearing of such items. Male learners requesting to keep a beard as part of a religious practice may be required. . . (to) produce a letter . . . substantiating the validity of the request. The same . . . is applicable to those who wish to wear a particular attire.

(3) A uniform policy may . . . prohibit items that undermine the integrity of the uniform . . . such [as] a T-shirt that bears a vulgar message or covers or replaces the type of shirt required by the uniform.

Case law pertaining to the right to religious freedom suggests the use of three techniques when deciding where to draw the line of the right: the identification of the sincerity of the claimant's belief, the proof expected by the claimant that the prohibited practice is central to the religion practiced and the interpretation of the practice in contextual terms in order to determine if the Constitution covers its protection.[85] In *Pillay*, for example, the Constitutional Court considered the practical effect that allowing the student to wear the nose-stud would have at the school level, the importance of the issue at hand and the complexity, among other factors to demonstrate the need to apply reasonable accommodation as a tool for resolution of similar conflicts. More specifically, the Court insisted on the requirement to include in school uniform rules procedures for the granting of religious/cultural exemptions, noted the failure of the school to treat differently students in different situations arising out of their different culture/religion and ultimately deplored the perpetuation of existing structures of discrimination as they arose from the specific case at hand.[86] From a broader policy perspective the focus in this context remains in striking the right balance between freedom

---

83　This duty carries also a horizontal application between individual persons according to *Taylor v. Kurtstag* (2005) 1 SA 362 (W) at para. 45.

84　Section 3 of the Guidelines on Uniforms, echoing s.16(2) of the SA Constitution that finds that not all types of expression are constitutionally protected.

85　E. de Waal, R. Mestry and C.J. Russo, 'Religious and Cultural Dress at School: A Comparative Perspective', *PER/PELJ*, 6(14), 2001, 62–95, at 70.

86　CCT 51/06 *MEC for Education: Kwazulu-Natal and Others v. Pillay* (2007) SA 474 (CC) paras. 5, 15, 37 and 17.

of religion and safe and orderly learning environments at public schools, not neglecting the possibility that in some cases religious dress may be less the result of agency and more that of coercion. In all contexts, the voice of learners should, however, also be heard.

5 The special case of independent schools in South Africa

Born out of the concern of working-class and lower middle-class parents over the quality and moral underpinnings of public education, a rapidly rising number of low- and middle-fee income independent schools have been created in South Africa.[87] Religious independent schools are struggling to reconcile the need to respond to a specific market demand while uploading the constitutional principles of equality and non-discrimination.[88]

While the percentage of learners attending such schools remains small,[89] their expansion is rapid.[90] Furthermore, since South Africa's state school system includes a fee policy, with 60 per cent of learners attending no-fee schools, the educational landscape includes inherently unequal public schools. In this light, and given that independent schools may receive state subsidies, provided they fulfill a number of criteria,[91] they enter into direct competition with public schools.

The religious ethos of some of these schools is largely overshadowed by the wish (and concern) of parents to send their children to superior quality schools with better educational programming and infrastructure. Similar to the public ones, independent schools are of varying levels of quality and contribute towards the maintenance of a highly stratified society in South Africa.

While Section 29(3) of the 1996 Constitution provides that private parties have the right to establish their own educational institutions at their own expense,[92] these schools must also abide by the non-discrimination principle contained in the Constitution, in particular in Section 15 of the Constitution. Admission tests or the charging of fees are permitted, but unlawful discrimination covering both state policies and actions that discriminate both directly

---

87 Shaun Franklin, 'Education Rights in Independent Schools', in Faranaaz Veriava, Anso Thom and Tim Fish Hodgson (eds.), *Basic Education Handbook—Education Rights in South Africa*, 2017, 353–371, at 354.
88 Franklin (2017) at 360.
89 In 2015, 4.5 per cent among an approximate total number of 12.8 million learners between Grade R and Grade 12 attend such schools (Franklin (2017) at 356).
90 Attendance between 2002 and 2015 has doubled (Franklin (2017) at 356).
91 These generally concern charging limited tuition fees, submitting to greater state oversight and adhering to performance standards (Franklin (2017) at 355).
92 In *Gauteng Provincial Legislative in re Gauteng School education Bill* of 1995, the Constitutional Court confirmed the right to establish independent schools in order to preserve cultural or religious beliefs and practices.

and indirectly against learners on the basis of race are not permitted.[93] It is not permitted for state-subsidized schools to favor certain religions over others in both admission or curriculum content or mandating participation in religious instruction or prayer.

From the perspective of the State, however, the picture is more nuanced: as the per learner cost within such schools is considerably lower for the State, compared to public schools, the cost efficiency argument becomes more prominent, in a policy area that is already characterized by extreme inequalities.[94] State subsidies are only awarded if independent schools serve explicit social purposes. The risk present, as also in other countries, is nevertheless that the number of unregistered independent schools (even without subsidies) may spiral out of control absent regulation from the State,[95] with all the implications that this carries in terms of the quality of education offered.

6 The South African approach to religious diversity in education

a A historical account: the legacies of apartheid

In colonial terms, the instruction and indoctrination according to a specific system of faith was not a neutral project: in South Africa, the propagation of missionary schools by the English had the aim of anglicizing Africans (and Afrikaners) towards future subservience.[96] Employing religion for political gain in that sense is not novel.

Pre-1994, the 1953 Bantu Education Act established education systems along racial lines.[97] There is, in fact, a record of 19 different educational departments according to race and geography, all guided by the ideology of Christian National Education. The designated aim for black South African students was to become

---

93 See, for example, the 1998 High Court judgment in *Wittmann v. Deutscher Schulverein*, Pretoria and Others where the Court held that a Christian German independent school could expel a learner who refused to attend religious instruction classes and school prayers on the basis of a notion of consent to abide by school rules and the possibility to attend school elsewhere. 1996 (3) SA 165; 1996 ZACC 4.

94 Franklin (2017) at 365.

95 Franklin (2017) at 364 gives the example of the Western Cape in South Africa where the Education Department closed a number of unregistered schools.

96 Andrew E. van Zyl, 'A Historical-Educational Investigation into the Decision to Remove Religious Education from Public Schools in South Africa', *Mediterranean Journal of Social Sciences*, 5(20), September 2014, 1613–1622, at 1616. Van Zyl quotes Sir George Gray, the governor of the Cape (1841–1845) as having declared that: "We [the British] should try to make [the blacks] a part of ourselves, with a common faith and common interests, useful servants, contributors to our revenue" (van Zyl (2014) at 1616).

97 As a result of this law, missionary education covering more than 90 per cent of blacks' schooling was transferred to the Department of Native Affairs division, known as Bantu Education. (Cf. van Zyl (2014) at 1619).

menial labor, based on a four-year training programme. Later, the *Christian Education Policy Act* 1967 implemented a single-tradition approach, openly discriminating against non-Christian students. All schools were required to have a Christian character, with compulsory religious instruction. More specifically, the Christian Education policy emphasized mother-tongue instruction, separate identity and development of each nation as God-given and the active parental involvement and control of and in education.[98] For colored or black education, the same principles applied conditioned by the exclusion of white financial liability for that stream of education. During the last years of apartheid, the white South African students attended Model C schools, which represented elite education establishments with a number of facilities.[99]

It would be, nevertheless, inaccurate to claim that Christian Education policy and apartheid in broader terms had a 'uniform' interpretative meaning. The ideological basis of 'separate-ness' varies and drew for Christian Nationalists from German 'volksnationalism' and the projecting of a nation as a collective endeavor, from metaphysical idealism that claimed that differences between groups had a spiritual basis, from psychological and physical variances between the groups, from political theology and theologized politics putting forward the argument that God willed nations to maintain their distinct identities, cultural incompatibility (a familiar argument in Europe at present) or even from biological justification for maintaining the biological traits of nations.[100]

Financially, investment in white education was 4.5 times higher than black education.[101] The legacy of the Model C school systems did not disappear with the dismantlement of apartheid, as these schools remained better equipped than those in rural or poorer areas.

Similar to the Israeli case, South Africa's ethnic groups are regionally segregated in the post-apartheid era, with groups clustered in particular provinces as a result of forced migration under apartheid.[102] Consequently, ethnic diversity in schools is empirically limited precisely because communities are homogenous on the local level. Another reason for their homogeneity, closely linked to the apartheid ideology, concerned how areas were developed along racial lines (i.e. white areas, black areas, Indian areas and colored areas). Schools established within those areas had learners coming from them almost exclusively. Today, those

---

98 van Zyl (2014) at 1617.

99 In 1992, the State announced that all white schools would be given Model C status. The provision establishing those schools was revoked by the 1996 South African Schools Act. These schools adopted an 'assimilationist' model of education with little sense of cultural awareness of the learners' backgrounds.

100 S. Dubow, *Afrikaner Nationalism, Apartheid and the Conceptualisation of "race"*, University of Witwaterstand/African Studies Institute, 1991.

101 UNICEF/Learning for Peace (2016) at 6.

102 Admissions to schools in South Africa are based on students' residence. Students are allowed to enroll in any school in their province, but those residing withing a 5-kilometer radius are given priority in admission.

divides remain because individuals do not move as easily and therefore schools' demography still reflects these trends.[103]

Post-apartheid, the main trajectories of policy-making in education are relying on the concepts of equity and social cohesion. The underlying consideration remains to find ways to reduce past inequalities through education. Education policy research suggests, however, that inequalities persist in South Africa's education system along the same racial lines, despite substantial ethnic, cultural and religious heterogeneity.[104] Efforts towards progressive, equity-driven policies regulating school funding since 2006 have, however, reduced the gaps in access to education, especially for the poorest students.[105] The effects of the same policies are more questionable, though, towards the formation of a common national identity.[106]

In line with the constitutional primordiality of the principle of equality, education policies have developed a particular concern for horizontal equality, equity and social cohesion.[107] These three concepts are consistently operationalized to the detriment of religious identity. The National Strategy on Social Cohesion (DAC, 2012) found that societies achieve cohesion when "inequalities, exclusions, and disparities" are "reduced or eliminated in a planned and sustained manner". In the area of education, the reduction of inequalities in education was projected to gradually eliminate inequalities in the labor market, political participation or health outcomes, echoing the understanding of the right to education as a gateway right. Indirectly, reinstalling social cohesion was also seen as beneficial towards the remaking of the nation.[108] The role of religious diversity is not accounted for explicitly in this context.

b Religion in education in contemporary South Africa

The cornerstones of post-1994 education in South Africa have been 'equal opportunities, democratization, desegregation and decentralization'.[109] The policy of

---

103 Point raised to me by Professor Christa Rautenbach.

104 UNICEF/Learning for Peace (2016) at 2.

105 These policies are the no-fee policy and the school nutrition programme encouraging more regular attendance for financially weaker students (UNICEF/Learning for Peace (2016) at 2).

106 UNICEF/Learning for Peace (2016) at 3.

107 In this context, social cohesion may be approached as a product of low levels of inequality and marginalization, positive social bonds and an inclusive national identity [Cf. F. Stewart, 'Why Horizontal Inequalities are Important for a Shared Society', *Development*, 57(1), 2014, 46–54]. Equity is "the correction of a historical imbalance of inequality in access to a public or private good", such as education [Cf. UNICEF/Learning for Peace (2016) at 10]. Horizontal inequality described the inequality between identity-based groups, defined by ethnicity, religion, language, race or cultural characteristics [UNICEF/Learning for Peace (2016) at 10].

108 UNICEF/Learning for Peace (2016) at 12.

109 Erika Mariane Serfontein, 'Education and Religion in South Africa: Policy Analysis and Assessment Against International Law', *Journal of Law and Criminal Justice*, 2(1), March 2014, 117–136, at 123.

education has been clearly premised on the link between classroom teaching as a means of nation-building and economic improvement.

When faced with the need to redefine the approach to religious diversity within education, the South African polity opted for an approach of multi-religion education that would teach students about religion and rejected both the option of eliminating religion from the school curriculum as well as the option of establishing parallel programmes in religious instruction as a reaction to the experiences of apartheid.[110] One of the implications of this policy choice is the multi-leveled conceptualization of diversity: according to the Department of Education, diversity has many layers. It may include race, class, gender, religion, culture, or talents, lifestyles, levels of physical and mental ability and languages.[111] Religious diversity also has been framed within the process for the quest of social justice relying on the "redistribution of resources and wealth and the politics of recognition".[112] The social justice agenda is particularly relevant in assessing the levels of (dis)continuity of obstacles in accessing education by reason of race, culture, language or class.

Given the insistence on an approach that would fully embrace human rights principles,[113] the present challenge in multicultural South African schools has become to balance the often-competing rights of equality, education and religious freedom. The first indication of the conceptual underpinnings of such a policy was revealed in the 2001 *Manifesto on Values, Education and Democracy*, where the Department of Education announced its intentions and set the primary educational objective of forming "learner[s] that should be able to demonstrate an active commitment to constitutional rights and social responsibilities and show sensitivity to diverse cultures and belief systems". To do so, the Manifesto encouraged schools to expose learners to the diversity of religions.

South Africa's National Policy on Religion and Education was subsequently fully unveiled in 2003.[114] It defined teaching and learning about religion, religions, and religious diversity as "Religion Education", clearly departing from the religious agenda on Christian Education of the apartheid regime.[115] The context of the policy was the attempt to deal with past fragmentation of South African society while celebrating diversities as a unifying national resource. The policy

---

110 Chidester (2006) at 66.
111 Wayne Alexander, 'Dealing with Diversity in the Classroom: Teachers Perspectives', PhD Thesis, Faculty of Education and Social Sciences/Cape Peninsula University of Technology, 2009, at 3 [in file with the author].
112 N. Fraser and A. Honneth, *Redistribution or Recognition? A Political-Philosophical Exchange*, London and New York: Verso, 2003, at 58.
113 See, for example, Article 26 (2) of the UDHR that requires education "to promote understanding, tolerance and friendship among all nations, racial or religious groups".
114 Department of Education, 'South Africa National Policy on Religion and Education', Government Gazette No. 25459, Vol. 459, 12 September 2003.
115 Christian Education was promoted by the apartheid regime relying on Christian indoctrination, pervading every subject. Cf. David Chidester, 'Unity in Diversity: Religion Education and Public Pedagogy in South Africa', *Numen*, 55, 2008, 272–299, at 273.

also connected well with the broader approach on the relationship between the State and religion: separation in principle but with avenues for cooperation in practice.[116] It was also entirely integrated in the "Values in Education Initiative" that sought to identify and develop a number of values such as equity, tolerance, accountability and social honor as antidotes to racist and sexist educational schemes of the past.

The aim of Religion Education was to promote multi-religious education in a non-confessional frame, as part of a civic duty to promote rights and responsibilities: a project for the development of values, attitudes and skills, preparing students to co-exist in a multi-religious society.[117] The emphasis in designing the new policy was primarily placed on educational outcomes and wider social benefits connected to these outcomes.

The 'division of labor' within that framework was clear: the policy distinguished between religious and educational aims assigning religious instruction to the family, the home and the religious community, and teaching and learning 'about' religion(s) to schools.[118] In other words, the policy was not based on religious interests but relied instead on core constitutional and citizenship values, particularly those that guarantee freedom for religious expression and freedom from religious coercion.[119] Religion in Education reflected also the concern to create the conditions for cultural rebirth and promotion of values while preserving the country's heritage.

In quantitative terms, although Religion Education accounts for a very small percentage of the overall curriculum, equal to approximately 0.5 per cent,[120] it has been the focus of disproportionate (to its size) controversy. Conflict arose between the general culture of human rights that the 1996 Constitution promoted and religiously motivated collective rights claims of specific communities. Within that frame, the South African state seems engaged in a permanent struggle between being a constitutional and cultural state at the same time.[121]

More specifically, conservative Christian elements of South African society, particularly the African Christian Democratic Party along with other groups

---

116 Chidester (2008) at 279.
117 Raj Mestry, 'The Constitutional Right to Freedom of Religion in South African Primary Schools', *Australia and New Zealand Journal of Law and Education*, 12(2), 2007, 57–68, at 61–62.
118 Chidester (2006) at 62.
119 David Chidester, 'Religion Education in South Africa: Teaching and Learning About Religion, Religions and Religious Diversity', in Lena Larsen and Ingvill T. Plesner (eds.), *Teaching for Tolerance and Freedom of Religion or Belief: Report from the Preparatory Seminar Held in Oslo*, 7–9 December 2002, at 2, available at http://folk.uio.no/leirvik/Oslo Coalition/DavidChidester.htm.
120 Chidester (2008) at 275.
121 Chidester (2006) at 63.

identified as "Concerned Christians",[122] saw in this new policy a parody on "non-religiosity", imposing on students a new religion of secular humanism. The objection was at its strongest when connected to the argument that the majority of South Africans are Christians, and religion education should reflect that.[123] The new policy, in sum, violated, in their view, their human and constitutional rights to freedom of religion.[124] Further to that, insistence on 'non-racial rainbowism' and African renaissance cultural claims were also criticized for creating a uniformity in which differences and conflicts were frozen within an 'artificial imagery for creating consensus'.[125] The alternative vision on the character of religion education proposed was suggesting learning processes that engage more directly into learning from, with and through religion.[126]

The crucial challenge for the policy to move forward seems to be in finding ways to think about the multiplicity of religious identities and the negotiation of the differences that arise. In doing so, the State seems to be operating within a process of transformation from apartheid to a democratic dispensation, which adds complexity to the balancing exercise. In some sense, the exercise of modern State power entails a certain degree of 'legitimated violence' in the Weberian sense: the coercive power, the compelling legitimacy and the control over territorial sovereignty in our case take the shape of a (disputed and often contested) discourse towards a transformation of an oppressive, formerly racist state to one that claims some power in advancing human rights and engaging with diversity. To serve that aim (and respond to the critique), the 2003 National Policy on Religion and Education in section 26 proposes to create the necessary space and conditions for the learners to understand both themselves and others in a spirit of empathy, with the help of critical reflection.

---

122 The campaign drew together different organizations such as the Pestalozzi Trust (a Christian organization for home schooling), the Frontline Fellowship (a Christian organization for evangelizing Africa) and the African Christian Democratic Party. The arguments used were in their way advocating a type of religious apartheid but among others, advocating the proposal that Christian education was a good and sufficient basis for dealing with religious diversity. For more on this, see also David Chidester, 'Religion Education in South Africa', in M. de Souza et al. (eds.), *International Handbook of the Religious, Moral and Spiritual Dimensions in Education*, Springer, 2009, 433–448, at 438 et seq.

123 Mestry (2007) at 62.

124 Chidester (2008) at 358 explains how Christian conservative groups argued that teaching and learning about religions was promoting a religious worldview akin to New Age religion due to their emphasis on relativism, situational ethics and equality for all religions. Chidester argues further that through such argumentation there is a clear link to be established with right-wing Christian organizations in the United States. A wider debate on authenticity of religion is also recurring as a result of such conflicts but remains largely outside the scope of this study.

125 Chidester (2008) at 291.

126 Chidester (2002) at 7.

c Desegregation: a determining framing factor

An essential factor in shaping education policy towards religious diversity in the South African context is desegregation. Desegregation policies in South Africa are highly complex and politicized processes. They entail the official abolition of the separation of races in the public domain (including in schools by opening admission to all). At the difference of Israel, where the corresponding policy was framed within a Zionist nation-building process, in South Africa nation-building relied on desegregation as a guiding principle within a vast area of policy reforms.[127]

Religion, within desegregation, occupies a distinct position: beyond its contribution to end apartheid, it has also adopted the role of 'facilitator' in the process of national reconciliation.[128]

The great heterogeneity of the student population along with the radical reorientation of education policy perspectives and legislation have imposed a considerable burden on educators in the implementation of this new approach. Opening, thus, schools to all races (and religions) does not, ipso facto, guarantee mutual understanding. The otherwise impressive legal and policy architecture on religious diversity within education needed to be projected against the broader aim of desegregation in order to translate commitments into practice.[129]

A less explored, but pertinently relevant, factor in the realization of desegregation is the decentralized nature of the implementation of education policies. Soudien and Sayed have explored the link between decentralization and the implementation of education policies to highlight the risk of persisting exclusionary trends: SASA 1996 has been designed under an arrangement that devolves authority and governance to schools (through SGB) providing an indirect but clear means to preserve previous privileges.[130] While decentralization is an instrument of democracy, it also allows for the possibility that it may be transformed into a project of maintenance of the status quo ante. In their preliminary empirical research, Soudien and Sayed found that indeed the way that decentralization was implemented did little to change the dynamics of past segregation: it

---

127　It should be noted, however, that a number of factors that extend beyond the legal freedom to choose a school complicate the exercise of the right to educational choice. These can be high school fees, transportation costs, language/skills barriers, lack of information about schools and even social costs associated with school attendance outside a learner's community. [Cf. Meredith Startz, 'Income, School fees and Racial Desegregation in Post-Apartheid South Africa: Evidence from Cape Town Public Secondary Schools', CSSR Working Paper No. 287, December 2010].

128　Moosa (2000) at 123. There is a broader picture to consider here: the religious sector in South Africa has envisaged a political role post-apartheid (Moosa (2000) at 125).

129　For a similar point, see C. Meier and C. Hartell, 'Handling Cultural Diversity in Education in South Africa', *SA-eDUC Journal*, 6(2), November 2009, 180–192, at 180.

130　C. Soudien and Y. Sayed, 'A New Racial State? Exclusion and Inclusion in Education Policy and Practice in South Africa', *Perspectives in Education*, 22(4), 2004, 101–115.

provided racially and economically defined communities with the means to pre-serve their advantage.[131] In other words, not only was desegregation not moving forward, but religious diversity and diversity per se were also not an integral part of the curriculum, despite the legal and policy changes.[132] These observations clearly accentuate the role of SGB as focal points "dictating the pace, content and direction of change".[133] Ultimately, schools may invoke race, without naming it, and develop new practices and discourses against integration. These may take the form of informal practices that, for example, aim at the maintenance of 'stand-ards' that are presented as non-negotiable to 'outsiders' wishing to join in or to the streaming of students on the basis of language (withholding a consideration of race and class in reality).[134]

The 'movement' of learners among schools suggests that schools have, nev-ertheless, been relatively successful in making schools more 'mixed' but there are clear indications of under-achievement on the level of social integration of students.[135]

7 Effects of religious diversity policy in education: governance implications

Racism in the social sphere persists in South Africa. Among others, the 2009 Ministerial Report of Craig Soudien on "Transformation and social cohesion and elimination of discrimination in public higher education institutions" claims that tensions arising from diversity have not been eased. The recurring argument of the myth of the 'homogenous' concept of a nation seems to be largely blamed for relying on an 'imagined community'.

The question of common values resurfaces: is it really possible to arrive at social consensus on which values are essential? Public pedagogy is once more demonized for creating the fiction of uniformity within difference, an artificial creation to mask disagreement. The Manifesto's assumption that Religion Edu-cation would instill in learners a broader sense of values, operating for the benefit

---

131 Soudien and Sayed.
132 Meier and Hartell (2009) at 184.
133 Meier and Hartell (2009) at 184.
134 Meier and Hartell (2009) at 185. Standards concern students as much as teachers, who may be prevented from appointment.
135 Around 25 per cent of black learners have shifted from the former township schools to other schools since 1996, but only 7 per cent are in formerly 'white' schools. More Indian and colored learners have moved to the same schools. White learners at a vast majority (86 per cent) remain in former 'white' schools, but some have moved to independent or private schools. [Cf. L. Chisholm, 'The State of South African Schools', in J. Daniel, R. Southall and J. Lutchman, (eds.), *State of the Nation: South Africa, 2004–2005*, Cape Town: HSRC Press, 2005, 210–226, at 216]. The implications of the 'white flight' of students to neigh-boring white schools leaves formerly 'white schools' to become poor black schools. [Meier and Hartell (2009) at 186.]

of society as a whole, has not materialized in that respect.[136] The South African state is struggling to convince that freedom 'of' religion is not synonymous with freedom 'from' religion, precisely because studying religion from a neutral perspective is not in itself a neutral, value-free act.[137] Connected to this point, it is also evident from the South African case how contextual factors affect the implementation of diversity management policies. The issue of power is particularly evident in the present case as an inhibiting factor towards the achievement of a plural type of public education. Social power as embedded in traditions of teaching is not completely neutralized through the recognition and celebration of differences: teaching appears to perpetuate patterns of domination for the benefit of certain groups. In fact, culture (and religion) is not simply about rituals, dress, food and holidays of specific groups. In contexts such as the South African one, it overlaps with status, positionality and hierarchy within society.[138] This is why the social justice framework is part of the policy objectives within education in South Africa. If, as Young claims, social justice requires the establishment of the conditions conducive to the promotion of self-determination and self-development of all members of society, oppression and domination are the main obstacles towards the aim of genuine agency. If education is conceived as a means towards the same agency, religion and culture more broadly, necessary for self-development, cannot flourish in conditions of marginalization, powerlessness, cultural imperialism and violence.[139]

Religion Education may have been designed as Citizenship Education and training in religious literacy, but it is persistently described nevertheless as a 'utopian discourse'.[140] Recent research suggests that religious diversity in the classroom is not a reality: Ferguson and Roux claim that the South African educational landscape is marked instead by mono-religious experiences, training and resources.[141] According to UNICEF, the only schools that have experienced some degree of integration are those designated for white learners during apartheid.[142] The same report notes that: "the attempt of schools to facilitate positive social

136 Marilyn Naidoo, 'Engaging Difference in Values Education in South African Schools', *Alternation*, Special Edition, 10, 2013, 54–75, at 58.
137 Naidoo (2013) at 58.
138 Alexander (2009) at 47.
139 I.M. Young, *Inclusion and Democracy*, Oxford: Oxford University Press, 2000.
140 Naidoo (2013) at 61.
141 R. Ferguson and C. Roux, 'Teaching and Learning About Religions in Schools: Responses from a Participation Action Research Project', *Journal for the Study of Religion*, 17(2), 2003, 6–23; C. Roux, 'Religion in Education: Who Is Responsible?' *Alternation*, Special Edition, 3, 2009, 3–30.
142 UNICEF/Learning for Peace (2016) at 37–38. This is contested in the 2001 data from the National Education Management Information System (EMIS) that may be interpreted as suggesting that there has been more integration of African learners into previously Indian and colored schools than in white schools. (Cf. Alexander (2009) at 29).

relations between students from diverse backgrounds is undermined by limited school integration that is largely a result of the racial and ethnic homogeneity of surrounding communities".[143] At the same time, the greatest resistance to religion education has been observed in former Model C Afrikaans schools and Xhosa-speaking schools.[144]

'Assimilationist' trends, whereby learners are expected to adapt to the existing character of the school, including curricula designed for a different learner population, have not disappeared either.[145] Educators classically claiming to 'see children and not color', ignoring the cultural and religious dimension of their pupils, fail ultimately to engage with the meaningful encouragement of diversity. In that sense, 'white' is still perceived as the norm insofar as it entails a treatment of learners as same, ignoring the unequal relations of power in their backgrounds. Further to that, good academic results are used as the only method of assessment in the performance of these schools, allowing them to get away with discriminatory behavior.[146]

In other instances, the religious and cultural 'baggage' of students is partly introduced into the learning experience by including aspects of the non-dominant cultures into the daily curriculum. This 'contributionist' type of educational approach is not in itself sufficient in overcoming segregation.[147] A third alternative, labeled as 'education for national reconciliation', proposed by Cross and Mkwanazi-Twala, argues that multicultural education does not necessarily correct the social and cultural imbalance in South African society.[148] At the opposite of a use of education towards disempowerment of certain segments of society, they propose one that redresses that painful legacy, away from a stereotypical (and ineffective) model of multicultural education. Schools can be used as sites for social and curriculum reconstruction.[149]

---

143 Alexander (2009) at 39.
144 Ferguson and Roux (2003) at 275.
145 Meier and Hartell (2009) at 181. In this context, all learners, regardless of race, ethnicity or class level, should assimilate into the dominant (white in this case) culture based on Eurocentricism and related economic power assumptions.
146 Alexander (2009) at 187.
147 Payne (2009) at 182. The focus here is on teaching students about the contributions made by each cultural group. Authors note with regards to this approach that: "[t] he problem is not that schools start here, but that they often stop here: what schools need to do instead is to move more quickly and steadily transform the entire curriculum".
148 M. Cross and Z. Mkwanazi-Twala, 'The Dialectic of Unity and Diversity in Education: Its Implications for a National Curriculum in South Africa', in M. Cross, Z. Mkwanazi-Twala and G. Klein, *Dealing with Diversity in South African Education*, Cape Town: Juta, 1998, 3–34. This model attempts to redress the legacy of a racist and oppressive values education system and reconciles unity and diversity, amending existing imbalances in society likely to hinder the process of South Africa's nation-building.
149 Alexander (2009) at 35.

A second major set of implications that arise out of the policy on Religion Education concern teachers. The socio-political context of diversity is best accounted from within:

> [e]ducation [that] becomes a form of action that joins the language of critique and possibility. It represents, finally, the need for a passionate commitment by educators to make the pedagogical more political, that is, to make critical reflection and action fundamental parts of a social project that not only engages forms of oppression but develops a deep and abiding faith in the struggle to humanize life itself.[150]

The design of the policy implies the assumption that teachers will deliver the projected multi-religious approach without difficulties. Put differently, it relies on teachers to act as "street-level bureaucrats",[151] endorsing a level of active agency from the bottom. This is particularly so given that the new curriculum expects teachers to act as 'curriculum developers'. In reality, however, teachers have received little training in that respect and continue to teach from a largely mono-religious perspective, which is their own.[152] Religious illiteracy is widespread among teachers, too. This is because most teachers have received a mono-religious experience in education in religion themselves, and this fact influences their capacity to moderate and transmit diversity through religion education.[153]

From its introduction, the religion education policy is struggling to train, motivate and enable teachers to moderate religious diversity programmes in their classrooms, without necessarily sharing a common understanding of diversity. Within that struggle, teachers ultimately address diversity primarily through forms of multicultural education[154] and strictly within an individual approach.[155] The focus, at best, is placed on the acknowledgment of differences between cultural and religious groups. Yet, it is questionable whether emphasis on multiculturalism will reverse the legacy of segregation. In other words, educational requirements towards desegregation call for a deeper understanding

---

150 H.A. Giroud, *Schooling and the Struggle for Public Life: Critical Pedagogy in the Modern Age*, Minneapolis: University of Minnesota, 1988, at 160.

151 M. Lipsky, *Street-Level Bureaucracy: Dilemmas of the Individual in Public Services*, New York: Russel Sage Foundation, 1980 as quoted in Alexander (2009) at 71.

152 The guide on Values and Human Rights in the Curriculum (Department of Education, 2005, Pretoria, Government Printer) provided further information, interpretation and examples, but divergence in the implementation persisted. (Cf. Naidoo (2013) for more on this point, at 60)

153 Zahraa McDonald, 'The Classroom, an Inadequate Mechanism for Advancing Diversity via Religion Education in the South African Context', *Journal for the Study of Religion*, 28(2), 2015, 202–219, at 214.

154 Payne (2009) at 130.

155 There is a noticeable recurring lack of school approach on diversity, coupled with absence of strategic guidance. See Payne (2009) at 139.

of religions, not as threats but as opportunities for enrichment.[156] Culture and religion cannot be restricted to symbolic factors. They involve other elements that range from interaction patterns to concepts of time and space, to processes of formal and informal education.[157] This is even more so in the context of the South African public education system, where it is increasingly difficult to draw clear lines between the racial, the economic or the religious and the cultural. Poverty, for instance, is inherently connected to education and affects the learning process in manifold ways.[158] This is why race and religion are not regarded as determining factors, for example, in the learning process in former black schools, while poverty is.[159] For strict education purposes, the primary concern of teachers remains language, as a barrier for instruction.[160] Still race explicitly dominates the educational landscape. In the words of a (colored) teacher at a white school:

> Strangely, when I think of diversity I think of colour, especially given that I had taught for 23 years in the township and now at a former model C school, I see the difference between black and white and also experience it. Although I did not enter the school with such a mindset, I now just feel how people think and see how they refer to other races. I'm telling you racism, stereotyping and prejudice is still rife. There is many a coloured school that is doing much better than we are.[161]

Critical multiculturalist approaches to education would criticize the outcome described earlier as one that does not allow learners to become reflective about social stratifications that keep them underprivileged.[162] Instead, it reduces normative openings for equal opportunity to learn and succeed in one's professional arena of choice precisely because students are taught to ignore differences. Payne adds to that in his work: "It would appear that to attend a former model C school and succeed requires the ability to speak English or Afrikaans, espouse Christian values, enjoy rugby and hockey, adopt certain values, adopt the ways of learning or feel excluded".[163]

Where is the gap then? One suggestion is that religious identity as a process through which values can be sourced has not been fully operationalized.[164]

---

156 Payne (2009) at 131.
157 Payne (2009), quoting the work of A.L. Kroeber and T. Parsons, 'The Concept of Culture and of Social System', *American Sociological Review*, 23, 1958, 583.
158 For more on this point, see E. Landsberg, *Addressing Barriers to Learning: A South African Perspective*, Pretoria: Van Schaik Publishers, 2005.
159 Payne (2009) at 215.
160 Payne (2009) at 160.
161 The quote is drawn from Payne's (2009) empirical research on education, at 166.
162 See the work of R. Moletsane, 'Beyond Desegregation: Multicultural Education in South African Schools', *Perspectives in Education*, 18(2), 1999, 31–42 in this respect.
163 Payne (2009) at 250.
164 Naidoo (2013) at 63.

Recognition of learners' value systems, experiences and cultural norms facilitate the learning process and, as such, must be supported by schools. Texts, rituals and symbols can produce elements of citizenship in the sense that they can be used to express citizen identity in practical, instead of rhetorical, terms. By looking more closely at how religious identity is connected to other forms of social difference, the learning experience in public schools may come closer to the stated ideals of law and policy in South Africa on diversity in education. To return to Young, individuals have to live together in interdependence, where each has an impact on the condition of the lives of others.[165]

The Manifesto establishes the connection between diversity and religion education clearly: learners will be offered the possibility 'to explore diversity of religions that impel society, and the morality and values that underpin them' through religion education, in order to enhance democracy in society, not to promote religion.[166] Given that religion is present, active (and heavily contested) in the public sphere, the mission of providing religious literacy to future citizens is particularly relevant for nation-building in South Africa. The main challenge, thus, for Religion Education is to include religious plurality in the practice by avoiding the pitfall of relegating religion completely to the private sphere. In this context, it is difficult to ignore the fact that the policy at issue appears to have the effect of serving the interest of the State while weakening that of religious communities who wish to exercise their religious freedom. Concretely, this can mean that individual learners may have to challenge the SGB in order to obtain the possibility to exercise their religious freedom, usually from the position of a minority. Processes such as that just described disorientate the aim of education within a broader Social Justice agenda.

Education is not a neutral force: it is the product of a particular socio-economic political system.[167] A Social Justice agenda is expected to include issues such as poverty, race, social environment, health, status and class within the broader aim of a fairer redistribution of resources.[168] Applied to education, the same agenda requires the redistribution of educational goods. The current educational policy is still searching for efficient ways to re-energize the process towards social justice, on new cultural and religious bases. A Social Justice agenda is conceptualized as being transformative in the South African context: diversity consciousness relies

---

165 I.M. Young, 'Communication and the Other: Beyond Deliberative Democracy', in S. Benhabib (ed.), *Democracy and Difference Contesting the Boundaries of the Political*, Princeton: Princeton University Press, 1996, 120–137, at 126.

166 Department of Education (2003) at 3. The same document states at 7: "In the interest of advancing informed respect for diversity, educational institutions have a responsibility for promoting multi-religious knowledge, understanding, and appreciation of religions in South Africa and the world".

167 This is a view that is linked to the critical theory of the education framework. Cf. Payne (2009) at 192.

168 The Department of Education in 2003 identified social transformation in education as aimed at ensuring that the educational imbalances of the past are redressed, and the equal educational opportunities are provided for all sectors of the population.

on the link between the past and the present, giving insight on the current state of affairs. The policy begs, however, for more: it requires the realization that the added value of education in post-apartheid South Africa lies in the deeper exploration and reflection of what Chisholm labeled the "education of politics and the politics of education".[169]

Today's South African classrooms show, to some extent, remains of values and attitudes of the pre-colonial apartheid and rural worlds.[170] At the same time, the diversity and hybridity of identities of learners pose insistently the question of how these children 'ought' to be educated for their country and for the world. In parallel to the development of a sense of identity through socialization,[171] where culture and religion are transmitted at home, the school represents an additional social system where the expectation is that individual learners will be evaluated on the basis of objective, or at least standardized, criteria. It is becoming clearer, however, that a learner's ascribed characteristics (e.g. socio-economic status, race, religion, place of residence) are likely to largely influence the learner's access to and quality of education.[172]

In educational terms, the balance between the African dimension of education and tools towards universal knowledge has not been reached, mainly because classrooms fail to function as 'communities of inquiry',[173] where children "take each other's views seriously and collectively arrive at understandings if not solutions. . . . they come to recognize their interconnectedness with others – an ancient African value".[174] Ubuntu, translated in educational values, leans towards an outcome-based education (OBE) where "all learn and succeed, we are all human and therefore equal".[175] Yet, this type of equality appears unworkable, probably even untenable.

The denial of the learners' religious and cultural capital, when combined with globalization, profoundly affect the content and quality of education. As explored earlier, the filters of the curriculum between its theoretical outline and practical application in the classroom entail the active role of teachers who influence greatly the final outcome in accordance with their own preferences, experiences or knowledge in ways that ultimately may perpetuate de facto discrimination on

---

169 L. Chisholm, 'Education Policy in South Africa', Speech Presented to the South African Society of Education, Soweto, 6 February 1993.
170 Rinelle Evans and Ailie Cleghorn, *Complex Classroom Encounters: A South African Perspective*, Sense Publishers, 2012, at 17, 26. The most common features observed are concern with control from the education ministry top-down, importance attached to obedience and discouragement of independent thought.
171 Evans and Cleghorn (2012) at 19 define socialization as "the process through which a person takes on the ways of thinking, seeing, believing and doing that prevail in the social world he or she was born into".
172 Evans and Cleghorn (2012) at 20.
173 Evans and Cleghorn (2012) at 27.
174 Evans and Cleghorn (2012) at 27.
175 Evans and Cleghorn (2012) at 29.

the basis of gender, race, religion, ethnic, linguistic or social class and towards learning opportunities.[176]

Similarly, parents exercise more and more actively their power to choose where to send their children to school, indirectly affecting the values on which the whole education system is based. The typical illustration in this context is the fast-growing corporate involvement in education and how this is likely to foster further inequality of opportunity.[177]

Ultimately, public education in a diverse social context such as the South African one is fulfilling its aims when it achieves a plural type of literacies (cognitive, social, cultural, including religious ones) if it is to direct learners towards skillful navigation in superdiverse societies. Placing the rights of every learner at the center of such a process is the most efficient way towards "the best way to be human".[178]

While the end of apartheid has certainly altered the terms of the discussion on access to education in South Africa, it is clear that a shift is in operation: the key factor of race has given its place to socio-economic status as a ground for inequality.[179] Yet the overlap is clear: black South Africans, due to historic educational disadvantage, remain those most affected at present due to lack of adequate education.

The historically strong presence of churches in education,[180] as also reflected in the Afrikaner educational concept of Christian National Education (CNE) brought no separation between the church and the school. According to CNE, formal schooling was structured to maintain and enhance the role of Afrikaners to lead society in South Africa in accordance with Calvinist theology. At the same time, the control of the black schools was taken away from missionary bodies and placed under the control of the State by virtue of the Bantu Education Act for the period between 1954 to the end of apartheid in 1994.

The implication of the 1953 Act in educational terms sets the background for the chronic disadvantage of the black population that wished to seek more socio-economic mobility.[181] Despite an opening of the white state schools to all races as of 1990, but given that these schools represented only 13 per cent of the

---

176 Evans and Cleghorn (2012) at 106.
177 Evans and Cleghorn (2012) at 107.
178 K. Egan, *Getting It Wrong from the Beginning: Our Progressive Inheritance from Herbert Spencer*, John Dewey and Jean Piaget (eds.), Yale University Press, 2002, at 182.
179 Christopher B. Meek and Joshua Y. Meek, 'The History and Devolution of Education in South Africa', in D.B. Holsinger and W.J. Jacob (eds.), *Inequality in Education: Comparative and International Perspectives*, Comparative Education Research Centre, 2009, 506–537, at 506.
180 Meek and Meek (2009) at 509 show that the arrival of the British in South Africa accentuated the number of mission schools, and prior to the 1953 Bantu Education Act, 5,000 out of 7,000 schools in South Africa serving the black population were owned and run by various churches.
181 Meek and Meek (2009) at 517–518 illustrate the impact of these policies between 1904–2001 on the educational attainment of blacks.

total number of schools,[182] the traditional segregated picture of education did not change significantly. To this also contributed the economic stagnation of the country in the post-apartheid years.

In human capital theory terms, where the link between education and the economic growth of a country is correlated,[183] the consequences for the majority learners' population become easier to understand. For South Africa, it is clear that religious identity within public schools has much wider implications than the celebration of diversity.

182 Meek and Meek (2009) at 521.
183 Meek and Meek (2009) at 531.

6 From tradition to modernity and back

Religious diversity in English schools as a test-case for multicultural societies

> "*Who in the world am I? Ah, that's the great puzzle*".
> *Alice in Wonderland*, Lewis Carroll

1 Introduction: multiculturalism, legal pluralism and conflict

Within every multicultural society, there is conflict; conflict on territory, on recognition, on resources, on reputation or respectability. Ethno-religious identity is the epicenter of many such conflicts that present themselves in the form of an "us v. them" clash, more often than not on 'culturalized' or 'religionalized' terms.

In Britain, immigration has been the source of such great ethno-religious diversity. The current state of the debate has moved here, too, however, beyond the boundaries of the relationship between religion and the State, economic considerations or the question of race. In fact, some argue we are in the post-race era, and the State is seen struggling to address religious and cultural identity[1] in order to find ways for individuals to 'live together' in increasingly diverse societies. The development of human rights in liberal societies, together with the Western understanding of the notions of human dignity and personal autonomy (or agency in other disciplines) should in theory pose no obstacle for us to accept that 'everybody is ethnic'.[2] Yet, they do.

One of the challenges for contemporary British (and not only) society is to find ways to strike a balance between assimilation and cultural diversity. The debate is certainly not new, yet the quest for the limits of 'acceptable' behavior is ongoing. Public schools have become relevant in this wider debate because they represent common space for all regardless of ethnic, religious or other identity and provoke the question of how this common space should be shared.

Similar to the other cases in the present study, the principle of equality is vital in this process and includes the (not only) legal question of special exemptions

---

1 Werner Menski, 'Immigration and Multiculturalism in Britain: New Issues in Research and Policy', *KIAPS: Bulletin of Asian-Pacific Studies*, X, 2002, 43–66, at 43.
2 Menski (2002) at 44.

and privileges aimed at protecting, among others, religious and cultural practices of minorities within the realm of publicly funded education. International human rights law, to some extent, has provided solid ground for the equality concern. Identical treatment, however, regardless of religious difference, may not constitute the most suitable solution in such a case. Connected to the equality argument are, also, the wider socio-economic dimensions of integration and advancement for these same minorities. Schools reflect those dimensions, as will be explained next.

To this complex scenario, a further point of contention has been added more recently: the concern that the active promotion of separate ethnic and religious identities may ultimately lead to disruptions of social cohesion, due to the alleged failures of multiculturalism.[3] In this context, multiculturalism is understood as a "broad set of mutually reinforcing approaches or methodologies concerning the incorporation and participation of immigrants and ethnic minorities and their modes of cultural/religious difference".[4] The preoccupation remains: reports, for example, about independent 'faith schools' presenting a 'radicalization risk' surface regularly, fueling the debate on many levels.[5]

The face of legal pluralism in Britain complicates the parameters of religious freedom exercise: in essence, the UK remains a State that has never been a nation-state and that currently fits best under the Habermasian label of "post-nation state", requiring rules of contestation of religious rights and values within education that reflect its multicommunal character. There are, for instance, religious alternative dispute resolution bodies in the UK that provide community-based services for Jews, Muslims and Catholics. For Muslims, for example, there is great variety of such fora with different degrees of recognition. These fora have become more important due to the demographic change as a result of immigration,

---

3 All of these points are recurring in socio-legal scholarship. See, for example, the less recent, yet still valid, analysis in Sebastian Poulter, 'Muslim Headscarves in School: Contrasting Legal Approaches in England and France', *Oxford Journal of Legal Studies*, 17(1), 1997, 43–74, at 47.

4 The definition is one of many possible ones for a term that is notoriously difficult to define and belongs to Steven Vertovec and Susanne Wessendorf, 'Introduction: Assessing the Backlash Against Multiculturalism in Europe', in Steven Vertovec and Susanne Wessendorf (eds.), *The Multiculturalism Backlash: European Discourses, Policies and Practices*, Routledge, 2010, at 4.

5 See indicatively Richard Adams and Aisha Gani, ' "Radicalisation risk" at Six Muslim Schools in London, *The Guardian*, 21 November 2014. The report included references to both Muslim schools and the Church of England schools. Prior to that, the 'Trojan Horse' affair in Birmingham in 2014, concerning an alleged plot to take control of a number of schools in the city with the intention to install a narrow Islamist curriculum, concerned 21 non-faith maintained schools or academies lead to the conclusion that while there was no evidence of terrorism or radicalization in the schools concerned, there had been "co-ordinated, deliberate and sustained" attempts "by a number of associated individuals to introduce an intolerant and aggressive Islamic ethos" into these schools (Cf. OFSTED Letter to Secretary of State regarding 21 Birmingham schools as reported on in www.theguardian.com/education/2014/jun/2014/trojan-horse-schools-wilshaw-ofsted-gove.)

although their decisions, with the exception of those emanating from the courts of the Church of England, are not part of the law of England and Wales. Their scope of decision-making extends to marriage, divorce other family disputes as well as inheritance, particularly for the Muslim and Jewish sects.[6] By virtue of the Arbitration Act 1996, parties may, by written agreement, request a religious tribunal to act as arbitrator, specifying the terms of the procedure and accepting the decision as binding. Both the London Beth Din as well as the Muslim Arbitration Tribunal may be called upon to function as arbitrators for civil disputes. In this case, decisions are enforceable in state courts.[7]

In this context, an often used and widely explored area of empirical demonstration of the application of legal pluralism in the country's legal system is family law. Although not strictly related to education, the enactment of the Divorce (Religious Marriages) Act of 2002 has signaled the possibility that a religious dissolution of a marriage may be recognized by English courts, provided it occurs prior to the pronouncement of a civil divorce. Such legal developments give shape to the operation of 'parallel' legal systems. Particularly for Islamic law, the system remains normatively effective but not officially recognized. It purports to selectively endorse aspects of Islamic law while at the same time adapting them to the British social reality.[8] One obvious repercussion of this symbiotic relationship has been the adaptation, reinterpretation and at times reconceptualization of Islamic law. This process can hardly be isolated from the historical-legal experience of statutory legal pluralism under the British Empire (especially in India). At the same time, as a phenomenon with transnational features, it attempts to give a "post-modern answer to legal modernity".[9]

Within such a context, and as multiculturalism has been finding itself under 'attack', the contribution of faith communities in public life, including in education, has been supported by successive governments in Britain.[10] This was often because they were taking on the role of providers of public services, such as education. Almost in parallel, the discourse on minorities has also been changing: it

---

6 For the Jewish faith, the London Beth Din issues religious divorces (Get) but a finalization of a divorce requires also the decree absolute from a family court. Muslim shari'a councils also operate in the same area and offer mediation and counseling for married couples, issue Islamic divorces (talaq and khula) together with other civil services (e.g. insurance, loans). Such decisions are not enforceable in UK state courts, but that does not prevent parties from abiding to them (Cf. Commission on Religion and Belief in British Public Life, 'Living with Difference: Community, Diversity and the Common Good', Report of the Commission on Religion and Belief in British Public Life, The Woolf Institute, 2015, at 74).

7 For more on the forms of these fora see Maleiha Malik, *Minority Legal Orders in the UK: Minorities, Pluralism and the Law*, London: The British Academy, 2012.

8 Andrea Büchler, *Islamic Law in Europe? Legal Pluralism and its Limits in European Family Laws*, Ashgate, 2011, at 17.

9 Büchler (2011) at 17.

10 Christopher McCrudden, 'Multiculturalism, Freedom of Religion, Equality and the British Constitution: The JFS Case Considered', *International Journal of Constitutional LAW (I-CON)*, 2011, at 3.

is rapidly moving from its 'racial' basis (including a later phase of 'ethnicity') to a prominent 'religious' phase.[11] The case of 'faith schools', developed further later in this chapter, illustrates well both points. As Grillo points out:

> Yet despite questioning multiculturalism, government policy has assigned an important role to 'faith communities' as channels for representation, consultation and dialogue in the major conurbations. There has emerged a faith-based multiculturalism, evident in the favouring of "faith schools", and measures making religious hatred . . . a crime. This faith-based multiculturalism is in accord with both government policy, based on communitarian theories, and claims by minorities increasingly defining themselves in religious terms.[12]

In that sense, and as McCrudden has also noted, criticism of multiculturalism is now connected with the role of religion in public space.[13]

Within education, the analysis of the framework to accommodate religious diversity in the public school system asks for an examination not only of the legal framework, but also of the structure of schooling in Britain, the content of the curriculum, the question on the ethos promoted in schools, school dress and religious symbols policy within schools, as well as the role and expectations of teachers in managing religious education programmes.

Constitutionally, the role of the established church in England – the Anglican Church of England – is still linked to the workings of the State in Britain, although regressively so. It remains distinguished from other religious traditions and groups but at the same time enjoys a degree of self-rule.[14] Patterns of religiosity and non-faith in the country are, however, gaining in complexity, especially within the historically dominant faith, Christianity. Within England, of particular interest to this study,[15] but also across the UK, there is scientific debate as to whether 'Christian' signifies more and more identification with a race rather

---

11 McCrudden (2011) at 3.
12 Ralph Grillo, 'British and Others: From "race" to "faith"', in Steven Vertovec and Susanne Wessedorf (eds.), *The Multiculturalism Backlash: European Discourses, Policies and Practices*, Routledge, 2010, 57–58.
13 McCrudden (2011) at 5.
14 For an overview of the historical background of the role and position of the Anglican Church, see Paul Weller, 'Religions and Governance in the United Kingdom: Religious Diversity, Established Religion, and Emergent Alternatives', in P. Bramadat and M. Koenig (eds.), *International Migration and the Governance of Religious Diversity*, McGill–Queen's University Press, 2009, 161–194, at 163 et seq.
15 England is the focus of this case study primarily as a result of the fact that within its territory one finds the largest concentration of individuals from minority religious traditions, in particular London, which, with the exception of Sikhs located in the West Midlands, is characterized by a pronounced religious diversity (see Weller (2009) at 169–170). Further, religious diversity remains an urban phenomenon, particularly most evident in Liverpool, London and Cardiff (Wales).

than a religion.[16] In fact, "believing without belonging" and "belonging without believing" are two concurrent trends that blur the picture of Christian religiosity in Britain, suggesting fragmented forms of faith.[17]

The parallel growth of Muslims, as the second largest religious minority in the UK, rooted in migration between the 1950s and 1970s of significant numbers of South Asian Muslims but also in the more recent waves of African Muslim immigration, adds another layer of contested identitarian claims. The material advantage of the British case, at the difference of minorities in other European countries, is that minority religious group members for the most part, enjoy citizenship status in the UK, establishing a stronger base towards equality claims.[18] For these groups, religion continues to matter.[19]

Despite, therefore, declining religiosity among Christian believers, the State through its successive governments has shown keen interest and enthusiasm to maintain the link between religious organizations and schools. The place of religion in education, nevertheless, has become unsurprisingly contested: based on numerical criteria, in England, a growth of state-maintained schools with a religious ethos ('faith schools') was observed under the New Labour and recent Coalition governments. The implications of this growth are double and contradictory: on the one hand, it is argued that such schools provide higher standards of educational attainment and moral education while on the other they are critiqued for applying socially selective criteria, ultimately favoring middle-class children.[20] Inevitably, a string of questions on the role and nature of religious education, as an expression and embodiment of religious freedom, within pluralistic societies are posed.

Such debates are premised on established arguments of schools as 'authors of the dialogic space' which have an essential role to play in structuring communication across religious lines, not only within the strict confines of a religious education lesson, but well beyond, shaping discourses beyond the school.[21] This exchange happens, however, regardless of whether the Anglican Church enjoys established church status.[22] The dialogue remains 'trapped' between considerations of religious groups as 'bearers of social capital' and the same groups

---

16 Weller (2009) at 168.
17 Weller (2009) at 169.
18 Weller (2009) at 179.
19 Weller (2009) quotes the 2000 Home Office Citizenship Survey that notes that for British Asians religion ranks second in importance in their lives while for the general UK population it ranks ninth (Weller (2009) at 180.)
20 For a survey of literature on both strands, see Nigel Fancourt, 'The Classification and Framing of Religious Dialogues in Two English Schools', *British Journal of Religious Education*, 38(3), 2016, 325–340, at 325.
21 Fancourt (2016) at 337.
22 The point made indirectly here is that having an established church is no longer relevant to ensure a space for religion in public life, as Modood argued in 1997.

as sources of radicalization and extremism, particularly for the Muslim groups, threatening integration.[23]

2 Education and faith in curricular development in the UK

The history of education and the related legislative framework is organized with variation between England and Wales, Scotland and Northern Ireland. English state schools were first founded in 1870 as 'Board Schools', creating the dichotomy between state and church schools, later integrated in the Local Education Authority system in 1902. The founding of minority Catholic, Jewish, Methodist and Quaker schools in the late 19th century was connected to the need to address poverty, educational inequalities, enhance socio-economic mobility and to cater to some extent to successive waves of immigration (e.g. Irish immigration between 1847 and 1906).[24]

The first Jewish school dates back to 1732, and today there are Jewish schools in Manchester, Liverpool, Birmingham and northeast and northwest London.[25] Independent Muslim schools emerged much later, from the 1950s onwards, and their growth has accelerated since the 1990s. Since 2001 their growth is supported further in the maintained sector through the government's support of the Association of Muslim Schools (AMS). Finally, the first state-maintained Hindu school was created in September 2008 in west London, while the first state-funded Sikh school opened in 1999 in Hillingdon, London.

An analysis of the features of religious rights in education in Britain presupposes an understanding of the country as both a "community of communities" but also a "community of individuals" striving for recognition and protection of their individuality through overlapping identities.[26] It also relies on the acceptance that, as with other policy areas, legislation and public policies have limits in bringing about real changes in attitudes of people towards difference,[27] particularly when faced with claims that shift between a liberal and a more communitarian approach.

---

23 Weller (2009) at 183. The conflicting considerations are evident in the *2001 Denham Report on Cohesive Communities*, the *2001 Cantle Report on Community Cohesion* and the *Parekh 2001 Report on the Future of Multi-Ethnic Britain*.

24 Elizabeth Oldfield, Liane Hartnett and Emma Bailey, 'More than an Educated Guess: Assessing Evidence on Faith Schools', Theos Report, 2013, at 17, available at www.theosthinktank.co.uk/cmsfiles/archive/files/More%20than%20an%20educated%20guess.pdf (last accessed 25 September 2019).

25 Sara Scott and Di McNeish, *Leadership and Faith Schools: Issues and Challenges*, Nottingham: National Centre for School Leadership, 2012, at 4.

26 Bhikhu Parekh, 'The Future of Multi-Ethnic Britain: Reporting on a Report', *The Round Table*, 90(362), 2010, 691–700, at 695.

27 Parekh (2010) at 692.

The governance of religion in Britain is also set against a background of the mid-20th century, as mentioned. The implications of this process lead to a fuller appreciation of the country's internal plurality, which needs to be reflected within a shared educational system.[28] Within this context, Bhikhu Parekh is right to caution, however, against the complicating factor of "shifting" boundaries of such communities. He points out that "(u)nlike nations, communities are porous, open, loosely structured and capable of both containing and joining an ever-widening circle of communities".[29] Accordingly, the need to build that system with an eye for a "constantly evolving body of values" should not come as a surprise. In such conditions, human rights appear narrow and offer a "simplistic language", when attempting to resolve the perennial conflict between the quest for equality (through the combat of discrimination) and the larger, more complex issue of (re)defining British identity.[30]

Having an established church in Britain, the historical presence and legal character of the faith have paved the way for the penetration of culture and religious institutions in the State system, guaranteeing a certain degree of public space for religion.[31] This indirect "legitimization" of religious claims has also resulted in the transformation of non-majoritarian religious groups into valuable social partners for the secular institutions of the country, which acknowledge diversity, while paradoxically relying heavily on integration strategies and the discourse of shared values of "Britishness".[32]

a Religion in education: the legal framework

The aim of religious education in English schools is to foster knowledge and understanding of Christianity as well as of other main religions present in British society while helping pupils to form their personal views and develop critical thinking on religious matters. A priori, this approach to religious education seems unproblematic, yet the threat of religious education as a form of indoctrination remains real.[33] Syllabi for religious education are drafted at the local level through designated committees comprising teachers' representatives, the Church of England, other denominations' representatives and local politicians.

The Education Act 1944 acknowledged the historic involvement of the churches in public education but affirmed the need to find more appropriate

---

28 The 2001 Decennial Census for England, Wales and Scotland as well as Northern Ireland produced Christian, Muslim, Hindu, Sikh, then Jewish, Buddhist, Jain, Baha'i and Zoroastrian as the largest groups of respondents, in this order of size (cf. Weller (2009) at 168–169).

29 Parekh (2010) at 695.

30 Parekh (2010) at 697.

31 Weller (2009) at 179.

32 Weller (2009) at 183.

33 Robert Jackson and Kevin O'Grady, 'Religions and Education in England: Social Plurality', *Civil Religion and Religious Education Pedagogy*, 2007, 181–202, at 182.

solutions, particularly in the context of the post-war reconstruction of Britain. The compromise was found in the classification of voluntary church schools in two separate categories: the first, 'aided' schools, were allowed to maintain their independence from the State, while the second, 'controlled schools', were less independent, without, nevertheless, completely abandoning their church-related character. In this way, Christian churches managed to maintain a certain role for religion in modern schools.

In practice, the division meant that the churches were responsible for 'aided' schools' expenditures, the right to appoint the majority of governors and the headteacher as well as to provide denominational religious instruction and worship. For 'controlled' schools, the major difference lied in the churches' non-involvement in financial matters. The 1944 Act also introduced, for fully state-funded schools, the use of Agreed Syllabuses for Religious Instruction (ASRS), which gradually included teaching materials on religions other than Christianity from the 1970s onwards.[34] Section 25 of the 1944 Act dealt specifically with religious education comprising both 'religious instruction' (now renamed religious education) as well as 'collective worship'. On collective worship, the Act stipulated:

> The school day in every county school and in every voluntary school shall begin with collective worship on the part of all pupils in attendance at the school, and the arrangements made therefore shall provide for a single act of worship attended by all such pupils unless, in the opinion of the local education authority or, in the case of a voluntary school, of the managers or governors thereof, the school premises are such as to make it impracticable to assemble them for that purpose.

Section 25(4) of the same Act gave parents the right to withdraw their children from religious worship attendance.

The Act also created provision for the Standing Advisory Councils on Religious Education as bodies competent to determine the syllabus, methods of teaching and training for teachers on religious education. The aim of these councils was primarily to reflect local religion and beliefs. Overall, the basic structure of the 1944 Act has remained unaltered, despite the important changes in the educational landscape, as testimony of the difficult bargaining process over the control of church schools.[35]

---

34 Jackson and O'Grady (2007) at 183. The 1998 Education Reform Act sealed this process by requiring that any new Agreed Syllabus locally 'shall reflect the fact that religious traditions in Great Britain are in the main Christian, whilst taking account of the teaching practices of the other principal religions represented in Great Britain' (section 8.3 of the Act).

35 Charles Clarke and Linda Woodhead, 'A New Settlement: Religion and Belief in Schools', Westminster Faith Debates Report, 2015, at 11, available at http://faithdebates.org.uk/wp-content/uploads/2015/06/A-New-Settlement-for-Religion-and-Belief-in-schools.pdf (last accessed 25 September 2019).

The 1988 Education Reform Act devised the national curriculum (section 2 of the Act) and emphasized the role of religion in all schools by stipulating in its first clause that spiritual education is one of the main purposes of schooling.[36] As such, all head teachers were required to conduct daily worship, and religious education remained compulsory within the curriculum, though not part of the centrally prescribed national curriculum. Specifically, for collective worship, section 7 of the Act stated that it shall be "wholly or mainly of a broadly Christian character reflecting the broader traditions of Christian belief without being distinctive of any particular Christian denomination.

Religious education within the basic curriculum should also "reflect the fact that the religious traditions in Great Britain are in the main Christian while taking account of the teaching and practices of the other principal religions represented in Great Britain".[37] It also stipulated that voluntary-aided schools, like all other state-maintained schools, have to follow the national curriculum, teaching religious education and organizing collective worship according to the religious tradition which they represent. For non-'faith schools', the class is expected to be inclusive and balanced in its content.[38] Voluntary-aided 'faith schools', academies and trust schools enjoy more discretion in shaping the content of the curriculum.

More importantly, the 1988 Act reorganized the categories of schools as they are at present, introducing the concept of schools of 'religious character'. In 1992, the Education (Schools) Act established the Office for Standards in Education (Ofsted) as part of a national system of inspection of school life. According to the Act, Ofsted is responsible to inspect religious education in all state schools.[39] The 1998 School Standards and Framework Act also introduced the schools' organization committees, deciding inter alia about the creation of new faith-based schools and shifting the task from the central government to the local communities in that respect. The Education Act 2006 abolished these same committees, replacing them with local authorities who will have the power to open, close or change the status of schools, subject to referral to a Schools' Adjudicator in case of objections.

b Types of schools

All children in England between the ages of 5–16 are entitled to a free place at a State school. In most cases, State schools have to follow the national curriculum. The following types of schools are available:

- **Community schools** are controlled by the local councils and not affected by religious groups. For these schools, the local authority is responsible to

---

36 The Act introduced the national curriculum, with compulsory and core subjects, in which religious education was not included.

37 Section 8 of the 1988 Education Reform Act.

38 Jodie Reed, 'Religion Renewed? The Right Path for English Schools', *Public Policy Research*, 2006, 252–257, at 256.

39 The system of inspection for independent schools was broadened in 2008 by the Education and Skills Act.

organize the employment of staff, it also owns the land where the schools are located and sets admission criteria if the school has more applicants than the places available. They are not of direct relevance to this study as they do not carry a pronounced religious element in their policies and operation, with the exception of the considerations on the content and religious education and its teaching.

According to the Schools Standards and Framework Act 1998, beyond state schools, there are several other categories of schools, such as:

- **Foundation schools** and **voluntary schools** enjoy more discretion in their programmes. These schools are run by their governing body, which decides on the employment of staff, the admission criteria, and which usually owns the land and buildings of the school. These schools can be either 'voluntary-aided' in which case the governing body (or charitable foundation) appoints the majority of governors; or 'voluntary-controlled', in which case the governing body appoints a minority of governors.

  'Voluntary-aided' schools are mainly schools of religious character. They operate under similar conditions to the foundation schools. These schools may apply religious criteria in filling the places and may also apply religious criteria for appointing members of staff if there is a genuine occupational requirement. Religious education in these schools follows the school's trust deeds.

  'Voluntary-controlled' schools are run by the local authority but are otherwise similar to voluntary-aided ones. The land and buildings are often owned by a religious organization, and they can reserve up to a fifth of their teaching posts as religious posts. They follow the locally agreed syllabus.
- **Academies** are run by a governing body and are publicly funded schools independent from the local council and follow a differentiated curriculum. These schools are independently managed and are set up by businesses or faith groups in partnership with the Department of Education and local authorities. The partners fund together the land and buildings, with the government contributing to the running costs for their operation. Some academies are new free schools, while some were previously maintained schools that 'converted'. Finally, a third category of academies are schools that were underperforming and that with the help of businesses, universities or faith bodies, are set up anew as schools. All three categories of academies may be 'faith schools'.
- **Grammar schools** are run by councils, a foundation body or a trust, select pupils on academic ability and often require them to pass an exam prior to entry.
- **Private or independent schools** charge fees to attend and do not receive funding from the government. They are not obliged to follow the national curriculum and are regularly inspected by the Ofsted.[40] These schools offer

---

40 The inspection regime for independent schools has been gradually tightened between 1998 and 2014.

education that is a radical alternative to the 'secular' programmes of state-maintained schools. There are currently around 2,400 independent schools in England, of which 1,000 follow a Church of England ethos, and around 140 Muslim independent schools, affiliated with the Association of Muslim schools.[41]

3 Religion and equality

The notion of equality has been legally protected primarily through the Race Relations Act 1976, which rendered discrimination on racial grounds in education and employment unlawful. The Act, however, protected only groups that were both religious minorities as well as considered as individual races, leaving outside of its scope of protection, for example, Muslims, Catholics or Methodists.[42]

The current legal framework in the UK unambiguously recognizes religious freedoms by virtue of the ECHR as reflected in the Human Rights Act 1998. Yet, when courts are faced with the question of the exercise of religious rights through manifestations such as, for example, the wearing of religious symbols in the classroom by a religious minority member, they have difficulties in implementing and enforcing the content of the right to religious freedom. They tend to take a restrictive stance with regards to the manifestation of religious belief through symbols. Relatively recently, case law has placed emphasis on claims emanating from the Muslim religious minority, particularly on the wearing of the headscarf, despite the absence of national rules on school uniforms.[43]

The expansion of the principle of equality and its quasi-constitutional standing is linked to religion through the prohibition of discrimination on grounds of religion and belief. The 2010 Equality Act,[44] through the prohibition of all discrimination, including on grounds of religion and belief, acts as a complimentary facet to the HRA 1998. Religion and belief are defined very broadly in the Equality Act and include religions and philosophical beliefs, as well as lack of religion or belief. The prohibited acts are

---

41 Clarke and Woodhead (2015) at 19.
42 The Race Relations Act 1976 prohibited discrimination on racial grounds in employment and education but extended its protection scope only to those groups that were both a distinct religious group as well as an individual race. Consequently, only groups such as the Sikhs and Jews were covered.
43 Schools are permitted to have their own policies on uniforms "sensitive to the needs of different cultures, races and religions" (Department for Education and Skills, School Uniform Guidances, June 2004).
44 On 1 October 2010, the Equality Act 2010 replaced all existing equality legislation (the Race Relations Act, the Disability Discrimination Act as well as the Sex Discrimination Act).

those of direct[45] and indirect[46] discrimination, harassment[47] and victimization in the areas of employment, education, goods and services and premises. The 2010 Act introduced a further innovation in establishing a public sector equality duty (PSED) requiring all public bodies to have due regard to the elimination of discrimination, harassment or victimization, to act towards the advancement of equality of opportunity between persons sharing one of the protected characteristics (in this case religious belief) with those who do not share it and to foster good relations between persons who share a relevant characteristic and those who do not. Concretely, the PSED can be translated as the duty of the public sector to have "due regard" for the equality implications of its decisions on protected characteristics, with the accompanying obligation to publish information on how they are complying with the duty and set equality objectives.[48] For the advancement of equality of opportunity, schools have thus to take concrete steps to meet the needs of those having a particular characteristic and include information as to how these concrete steps have been implemented. Finally, regarding the advancement and fostering of good relations between groups, curricular activity demonstrating the cultivation of tolerance and understanding between religions and cultures should also be demonstrated.

For schools, the Equality Act implies that they cannot unlawfully discriminate against pupils on the basis of inter alia religion or belief, although the exceptions for certain schools in relation to the content of the curriculum, collective worship and admission to schools of religious character continue to apply. The maintenance of these exceptions is justified by the wish to allow schools to conduct themselves in a way that is compatible with their respective religious ethos but do not allow them, by the same token, to discriminate on any other protected characteristics (e.g. refusal to admit a child because he/she is gay).[49]

---

45 Defined as when one person treats another less favorably because of a protected characteristic than they would treat other people (Department for Education, 'Equality Act Departmental Advice', 2014, at 9), even within the same religion (e.g. between Orthodox and Reform Jews, between Shia and Sunni Muslims).

46 Defined as when a "provision, criterion or practice" is of general application but has the effect of putting people with a particular characteristic at a disadvantage when compared to others without that characteristic (Department for Education, 'Equality Act Departmental Advice' (2014) at 9).

47 Defined in the Act as "unwanted conduct, related to a relevant protected characteristic, which has the purpose or effect of violating a person's dignity or creating an intimidating, hostile, degrading, humiliating or offensive environment for that person".

48 Department for Education, 'The Equality Act 2010 and Schools', May 2014, at 32.

49 Department for Education, 'The Equality Act 2010 and Schools' (2014) at 13. The sensitive issue of views on sexual activity or orientation grounded on religious beliefs for certain schools is also addressed, and the interpretation of the Act allows schools to continue holding them provided that delivery of such views are not harassing and berating and also taking into account that teachers, when expressing such views, exercise influence on pupils (Department for Education, 'The Equality Act 2010 and Schools' (2014) at 22–23).

While the content of curriculum may vary for schools of religious character, the delivery of the curriculum must be organized without discrimination.[50] In all remaining cases, the Act makes it unlawful to discriminate in relation to admission, in the way that education is provided, when giving access to pupils to any benefit, facility or service or by excluding a pupil or subjecting him/her to any other detriment.[51]

Overall, the 'legacy' of multiculturalism infused the application of the principle of equality with considerations revolving around recognition, voice and participation of groups, but it is now moving in the direction of advancing notions of human dignity as a criterion of its application.[52] In observing its use in litigation related to religious freedom in public education, this transition signifies that greater emphasis ought to be placed on the individual's self-identity and less on group disadvantage, including economic disadvantages of marginalized groups. In practice, equality is used less to protect ethnic minority groups and individuals and more to limit the activities of these groups and individuals when seen to be in conflict with the rights and values of others.[53] The use is connected with the role and position of religion in the public space and implies an internal hierarchy in conditions of clash between freedom 'from' discrimination that trumps when measured against the right 'to' religious freedom. This balancing outcome seems to stand even against the traditional position of courts to leave out of consideration the internal organization of religions.

In the case of *R (on behalf of Begum) v. Denbigh High School Governors*,[54] the learner, Ms Begum, invoked her right to wear a jilbab (garment covering the majority of the body, including arms and legs) instead of a less strict religious dress that the school's policy had allowed female students to wear (the *shalwar kameeze*) as part of the school uniform policy.[55] Upon Shabina Begum's refusal to comply with the school's uniform policy, the school authorities prevented her from entering the school premises. The learner and her family challenged this decision, which made its way to the House of Lords.[56] The Court found in favor of the school authorities. Interestingly, three of the judges sitting did not think that there was a sufficient link with Article 9 ECHR on freedom of

---

50 The DfE Equality Act 2010 departmental advice contains some examples to illustrate the differences on this point (Department for Education, 'The Equality Act 2010 and Schools' (2014) at 14).

51 Department for Education, 'The Equality Act 2010 and Schools' (2014) at 7.

52 McCrudden (2011) at 7–8.

53 McCrudden (2011) at 8.

54 (2004) EWHC 1389 Admin.

55 The school had provided three alternatives catering to the needs of Muslim students, one of which was the shalmar kameeze.

56 For an overview of the procedural evolution on the case at first instance and on appeal see Amy Jackson, 'A Critical Legal Pluralist Analysis of the Begum Case', Osgoode Hall Law School Research Paper Series, Research Paper No. 46/2010.

religion, and used the "specific situation" rule.[57] This argument on its own merit reduces de facto the possibility for claimants to invoke Article 9 in similar circumstances and at the same time transforms it into a tool for the restriction of religious liberties.

The common ground for all judges in this specific case was the fact that wearing certain religious clothing in school can disturb the peace and social balance if not subjected to certain limits. Begum's claim, therefore, represented an obstacle to social balance in the school. As such, the limitation under Article 9(2) ECHR would have been applicable in any case. As for the alleged violation of Article 2 of the First Protocol, also claimed by the learner, according to the Court, the interruption of her education was due to her unwillingness to observe the school's uniform policy. Ultimately, the broader implication of *Begum* has been to uphold the autonomy of schools in deciding their uniform policies.

In the same context, more problematic was the use of the argument within the House of Lords' majority decision related to the "impossibility test". Sourced from the *Jewish Liturgical Association Cha'are Shalom v. Tsedek* decision against France,[58] holding that

> there would be interference with the freedom to manifest one's religion only if the illegality of performing ritual slaughter made it impossible for ultra-Orthodox Jews to eat meat from animals slaughtered in accordance with the religious prescriptions they considered applicable.

The Court found by analogy that *Begum* could attend another school more in line with her beliefs. This last argument is questionable insofar as education is a statutory duty of the State and not comparable to a contractual choice as in the ECtHR decision against France.

In terms of Begum's positionality in this debate, it is worth noting that as an adolescent it cannot be presumed that her choices are the product of a fully developed individual autonomy. At the same time, her clothing was assessed against the majority interpretation of her subjective religious beliefs, not against her own individualized one. In *R (on the application of Williamson) v. Secretary of State for Education and Employment*, the House of Lords had, however, clearly stated

---

57 The content of this rule stipulates that there is no interference with the right to manifest one's religious belief where an individual has voluntarily accepted a role that does not accommodate that practice or observance and there are other means open to observe the religion without undue hardship or inconvenience. Cf. ECtHR, *Kalac v. Turkey*, Appl. No. 20704/92, 1997 stating that "Article 9 [does] not protect every act motivated or inspired by a religion or belief . . . in exercising his freedom to manifest his religion, an individual may need to take his specific situation into account" (at para. 27).

58 *Jewish Liturgical Association Cha'are Shalom Ve Tsedek v. France*, Appl. No. 2742/95, 2000.

that it is the subjective belief that must be protected by the right to freedom of religion.[59]

Following *Begum*, the related question of wearing of a niqab (a veil that covers the face and head, leaving only the eyes exposed) was raised before the British courts.[60] A 12-year old Muslim student, basing her claim on the fact that her three sisters had been allowed to wear this veil in the same school, challenged the school board's decision to deny her the same right.

The High Court, in finding for the school, replicated the House of Lords findings in *Begum* by arguing that the plaintiff's freedom of religion remained protected because she maintained the option of changing schools if she chose to. Yet the question still stood: regardless of the presence of an alternative, was the school's decision permissible and above all justifiable under the ECHR? The common argument between this case and *Begum* stems from the fact that the use of religious clothing should not become an obstacle for student integration, in which case its use can be legitimately restricted. The court's conclusion may indeed be justifiable by educational and security concerns, but it reminds us of the repeated attempts of courts to 'align' religious beliefs with "mainstream Muslim opinion" by excluding all religious practices that escape the 'average' practice of a given faith system. This attempt also runs contrary to the exclusion of "discretion on the part of the State to determine whether religious beliefs or the means used to express such beliefs are legitimate".[61] Finally, what is worth repeating is that the judge of this case also found the applicant's right not violated in its substance, as she retained the right to transfer to a school where her claim would have been accommodated.[62]

A third case, this time concerning a teaching assistant wishing to completely cover her face while teaching, asked the same question.[63] Her request was also

---

59 *R (on the Application of Williamson) v. Secretary of State for Education and Employment* (2005) UKHL 15; (2005) 2 A.C. 246 at 22. In *Saggers v. British Railways Road* (1977) IRLR 266, the Employment Appeal Tribunal had earlier on held that the belief which is considered is that which is held by the person at issue, rather than the established body of creed or dogma appertaining to the individual and the groups to which he/she belongs [at 267].

60 *R (on the Application of X) v. Headteachers and Governors of Y School* (2007) EWHC (Admin) 298.

61 *Manoussakis and Others v. Greece*, Appl. No. 18748/91, 1996, at para. 47.

62 The Muslim cases can be contrasted with *R* (on the application of *Watkins-Singh) v. Aberdare Girls' High School Governors* (2008) EWHC 1865 (Admin). The case concerned whether a school was allowed to prevent a Sikh girl from wearing a kara (bangle of great religious significance), and the applicant was successful as the claim was based on the Race Relations Act 1976 prohibiting discrimination on the basis of race, not Article 9.

63 *Azmi v. Kirklees Metropolitan Council* (2007) UKEAT, Appl. No. 0009/97/MAA (25). In previous case law, *Ahmad v. Inner London Education Authority* (1978) 1 All ER 574, courts had found that in a case involving a dispute between a Muslim teacher requesting time to attend Friday prayers and the local education authority, that there was need "not for a policy of the blind eye but for one of understanding. The system must be made flexible to accommodate their beliefs and their observances. Otherwise they will suffer discrimination" (at 583).

denied by school authorities, on the basis that, without visual contact, her teaching would be severely undermined. The Employment Tribunal did not support the plaintiff's claim that she was the victim of religious discrimination, as she failed to prove that she had been treated less favorably than non-Muslim teachers. The Tribunal identified as the relevant comparator in her case a person, not of the Muslim religion, who covered her face for some reason. It, therefore, concluded that Ms Azmi was refused the permission to wear her veil on objective criteria because it constituted a barrier to the learning process and her ability to communicate with students. Likewise, there was no ground to find indirect discrimination, as the school's actions were proportionate and guided by the public interest. The Employment Appeals Tribunal found as much.

All three cases suggest a common stance: there is clear interference on behalf of courts and the State into the strictly personal decision of manifesting one's religious liberty. More disturbing, however, is the contrast between cases involving Muslim students and cases such as the one involving, in July 2008, the exclusion by Aberdare Girls School in South Wales of a Sikh pupil for refusing to take off her religious bangle. The High Court overturned the school's decision because "in this case there is clear evidence it was not a piece of jewelry but to Sarika was, and remains, one of the defining focal symbols of being Sikh". The claim was successful because it was based on the Race Relations Act 1976 rather than Article 9 ECHR. Muslim women have not-so-far enjoyed similar legislative protection. The Court even pointed out that there is "an enormous difference" between this case involving a "very small" bangle and the rulings allowing schools to ban the niqab or jilbab.

In a sense, *Begum* made clear that the question of the wearing of the veil is resolved once and for all, as following the case as a precedent in the UK context, no interference with the claimant's right under Article 9(1) ECHR is to be found, and even if there were one, it would be found justifiable under 9(2).[64] However, regarding the wearing of religious symbols covering parts of their body, Muslim women in the UK (and elsewhere) consider it part of their identity, a spiritual and an essentially personal choice. Insisting on the issue of religious identity through its manifestation is genuinely limiting the broader scope of the right to equality as connected to the right to work and the right to be educated for groups that are vulnerable to marginalization of their economic, social and cultural rights.[65]

---

64 R *(on the Application of X) v. Headteachers and Governors of Y School* (2007) EWHC (Admin) 298, at 100.

65 Many European Muslims, especially women, are victims of discrimination in employment, housing or education, inevitably leading to social exclusion (cf. Manisuli Ssenyonjo, 'The Islamic Veil and Freedom of Religion, the Right to Education and Work: A Survey of Recent International and National Cases', *Chinese Journal of International Law*, 6(3), 2007, 653–710, at 656–657).

4 The special case of 'faith schools' in Britain

'Faith schools' in England make up one-third of all state-maintained schools, as previously mentioned.[66] The majority of these schools belong to Christian denominations, with an official estimate of 50 schools being non-Christian. In general, there are two broad categories of such schools, as already discussed: 'voluntary-aided' ones that are funded up to 90 per cent by the State, with the rest of their budget coming from religious bodies to which they are affiliated, and 'voluntary-controlled', whose governing bodies have control over admissions and teaching content. For all schools, however, there is an obligation to incorporate the national curriculum. A third category of schools are 'independent' schools that do not receive state funding and may determine their own curriculum while meeting the Independent School Standards.[67]

The official designation of 'faith schools' is "schools with a religious character", which indicates that some of these schools have moved away from confessional education towards more inclusive education from a diversity of religious backgrounds. Yet the creation of separate faith community schools originated primarily as an expression of the need to maintain a separate cultural life.[68] As such, these schools retained freedom over religious education, while non-'faith schools' in accordance with the 1988 Education Act were required to teach about the plurality of religions in Britain.

The historical background in Britain surrounding the Church of England's role as a traditional provider of education justifies in the first place the popularity of such schools. The establishment of Jewish and later Muslim schools confirmed, however, the realities of religious identity-based schooling on the basis of ethnic separatism.[69]

For the Jewish faith, The Future of Jewish Schools 2008 Report of the Commission on Jewish Education distinguished two categories of schools: a mainstream group of highly observant, progressive and pluralist schools and a strictly Orthodox Hasidic group of schools focusing mainly on Jewish studies (independent

---

66 Rob Berkeley, 'The Runnymede Trust', 11, 2008, available at www.runnymedetrust.org/uploads/publications/pdfs/RightToDivide-2008.pdf/. The number refers to England only as it is where the vast majority of these schools are located.

67 The Education (Independent School Standards) Regulations, 2010, S.I. 2010/1997, Sched. 1, pt. 1. The type of education that should be given is described as follows: "gives pupils experience in linguistic, mathematical, scientific, technological, human and social, physical and aesthetic and creative education" and ensures "adequate preparation of pupils for the opportunities, responsibilities and experiences of adult life". The same schools must "provide pupils with a broad knowledge of public institutions and services in England; [and] assist pupils to acquire an appreciation of and respect for their own and other cultures in a way that promotes tolerance and harmony between different cultural traditions" (at pt. 2).

68 Julia Ipgrave, 'Identity and Inter Religious Understanding in Jewish Schools in England', *British Journal of Religious Education*, 38(1), 2016, 47–63, at 49.

69 Ipgrave (2016) at 49.

schools) or combining secular and Jewish studies education (state-maintained and independent).[70]

For Muslim Independent Schools, educating an estimated 1 per cent of the 500,000 Muslim children in British schools, there is a choice made in terms of the content of education: they either follow the national curriculum, using the existing textbooks, or, if more conservative, eliminate aspects of the curriculum considered un-Islamic, such as music, dance or arts. What these schools share is an educational approach relying on Islamic instruction, dress codes and communal prayers as well as observance of the Islamic calendar.

Overall, the development of 'academy' schools, among which a number of 'faith schools' are included, after 2000 has allowed for local curriculum determination with the implication that such schools enjoy a wider margin, outside state control, in deciding what to teach.[71]

In parallel, religious education in State schools in England has been steadily marginalized and merged with thematic learning connected to ethics, citizenship and cohesion.[72] This has led to a corresponding downgrading of religious education as a tool towards forming citizens who can recognize and engage with difference. Educational policy is at the same time pushing for contradictory policy aims, insisting on extremism, migration and welfare,[73] without any emphasis on the lived religion as a society issue. Whether as a means to achieve cohesion in society (a distinctly political aim) or a way to engage with religious difference successfully (a more practical skill),[74] religious literacy is a missing element that is nevertheless necessary as both an instrument for citizenship but also one for co-existence.

Alongside recognized 'faith schools', there is a growing concern over unregistered 'faith schools', based on religious faith, the number of which is "far higher than is currently known",[75] dispensing education with emphasis on Islamic and Jewish religious study mainly in unsafe conditions for their pupils. The content of such education is characterized as "misogynistic, homophobic, anti-Semitic" in classrooms segregated by gender on the basis of religious grounds.[76]

---

70 Ipgrave (2016) at 50.

71 Adam Dinham and Martha Shaw, 'Religious Literacy Through Religious Education: The Future of Teaching and Learning About Religion and Belief', *Religions*, 8, 2017, 119, available at www.mdpi.com/2077-1444/8/7/119, at 3 note that this has led to a situation where a growing number of schools are not required to follow the Agreed Syllabuses.

72 Dinham and Shaw (2017) at 3.

73 Dinham and Shaw (2017) at 8.

74 Dinham and Shaw (2017) at 11 contest in part the first aim of cohesion insofar as they see the risk that such an approach would enhance an individualistic understanding about religions failing to address the width and richness of lived religion, which in reality may look nothing like the divisive, violent or oppressive perception of it.

75 Peter Walker, 'OFSTED Targets "growing threat" of Unregistered Schools', *The Guardian*, 11 December 2015.

76 Walker (2015).

5 The question of citizenship education in a post-multicultural setting

In educational terms, developments in minority religious education have stemmed from the realization in the 1980s of the new pluralism reigning within British classrooms calling for differentiated responses to the educational needs of the various groups. Both the Rampton Report of 1981 and the Swann Report of 1985 noted the educational discrimination within schools and the broader communities. At the time, the multicultural response prevailed:

> The role of education should be: To broaden the horizons of all pupils to a greater understanding and appreciation of the diversity of value systems and life styles now present in our society whilst also enabling and assisting ethnic minority communities to maintain what they regard as essential elements of their cultural identities.
>
> [Swann Report, 1985, at 5]

The policy concerned primarily minorities from the Indian subcontinent: Hindus, Muslims, Sikhs and other faiths and their religious needs. Religion, in that context, was considered a defining element for a community's survival and a point of vulnerability in the face of racism and discrimination.[77] The symbolic shift in 'faith schools' from being an expression of a minority's vulnerability with the ensuing obligation of the majority to accommodate and protect, to that of a threat to British values as a result of their separateness, reached its peak later within the 2001 Cantle report that required all state-funded schools by law to "promote community cohesion". According to the Department of Education, 'community cohesion' is defined as:

> working towards a society in which there is a common vision and sense of belonging by all communities; a society in which the diversity of people's backgrounds and circumstances is appreciated and valued.
>
> [DCSF 2007][78]

In 2002 and 2007, a new citizenship curriculum was therefore introduced with the aim "to actively promote . . . social cohesion". It was made compulsory for all state-funded schools. At the same time, however, there is preliminary evidence that the role of 'faith schools' may be shifting from the narrower aim of perceived

---

77 See the Swann Report, *Education for All: Report of the Committee of Enquiry into the Education of Children from Ethnic Minority Groups*, London: Her Majesty's Stationery Office, 1985 in particular 202 and 466 as quoted in Ipgrave (2016) at 48.

78 DCSF, *Faith in the System*, London: DCSF, 2007.

indoctrination of students to academic excellence within a culturally supportive environment towards better preparation to access the job market.[79]

The 2010 coalition government introduced the notion of 'Big Society' to fill the policy void, but the debate related to the events of the 2001 riots and the 2005 London bombings have questioned intensively and without interruption the role of 'faith schools' as obstacles to the integration of young minority people. New curricular requirements expect 'faith schools' to demonstrate how they positively contribute to society. In particular, the 2007 Department of Education Faith in the System report stressed this point as follows:

> The government and faith school providers believe that: all schools – whether they have a religious character or not – play a key role in providing a safe and harmonious environment for all in society, thereby fostering understanding, integration and cohesion.
>
> [DCSF, 2007, at 1]

The underlying concern in these schools has become how they respond to religious 'otherness'. The case of Jewish schools and the failed opening of their admission policy to include non-Jewish pupils is illustrative: parents have threatened or have proceeded to withdraw their children from Jewish schools if/when non-Jewish students are accepted.[80] Similarly, teachers expressed concern about having to take account of non-Jewish perspectives while maintaining the essence of the Jewish cultural and religious content intact. Naturally, delivery of education in 'faith schools' is a matter of interpretation as well as perspective, with many possible nuances.[81]

There is also widespread questioning of the use and utility of the practice of collective worship within maintained schools. Recent governmental non-statutory

---

79 Inga Niehaus, 'Emancipation or Diengagement? Islamic Schools in Britain and the Netherlands', in Aurora Alvarez Venguer et al. (eds.), *Islam in Education in European Countries*, Muenster: Waxmann, 2009, 113–130, at 125.

80 Ipgrave (2016) at 53.

81 Ipgrave (2016) at 54. In that respect, the research of Mary Parker-Jenkins, mentioned in Ipgrave (2016) at 53–54, has classified the types of schools engagement with 'Otherness' as follows:

  (1) Meaningful engagement: significant interaction through ongoing sustained projects;
  (2) Sustained engagement: strong evidence of different forms such as knowledge of interaction with other faiths and the wider community;
  (3) Temporary engagement: perhaps due to one teacher or member of the community but which is not sustained once they have left the school;
  (4) Tokenistic engagement: a one-off event or trip;
  (5) Superficial engagement: a veneer, weak and of no consequence or significance;
  (6) No engagement: in terms of curriculum, ethos, contact with others within and beyond the school community [M. Parker-Jenkins, *Terms of Engagement: Muslim and Jewish School Communities, Cultural Sustainability and Maintenance*, Derby: University of Derby, 2008, unpublished paper].

guidance on the issue in December 2014 maintains that: "[a]ll state schools are also required to make provision for a daily act of collective worship".[82] In practice, however, there is evidence to suggest that 76 per cent of secondary schools were failing to meet this requirement and that only 28 per cent of pupils attended daily worship at school.[83]

6 Religious literacy and religious education policy outcomes

The educational landscape in Britain is affected by significant shifts towards greater religious diversity and at the same time a higher proportion of religiously unaffiliated individuals.[84] Due to a parallel decline in traditional faiths, in particular, Christianity in the UK, the influence of Christian religious authorities is also seen to diminish, with the possibility that more disorganized forms of religious authority may grow. Part of the overall fragmentation of the religious landscape is also due to the influence of conservative, also labeled 'fundamentalist' elements of religion, which is on the rise.[85]

In general terms, religious education courses are perceived by English learners as a 'safe forum' to observe and learn more about diversity.[86] There is nevertheless a crucial underlying (and artificial) dichotomy that often operates in teaching religion in public schools in England: while religion of the 'Other' from both the learner and teacher bodies evokes respect, culture is treated less favorably and is often challenged, as if the two categories are fixed and entirely distinct.

The dominant approaches in teaching religion, from an educational perspective, propose to 'learn about religions', emphasizing the need to include a broad range of religions, as well as to 'learn from religion' as a means to enable reflection and critical thinking about fundamental religious questions and the respect of other beliefs, including of non-belief.[87] These approaches largely constitute the current mainstream targets for religious education.[88] Essentially, the prevailing model of religious education aims to inform pupils about religious diversity and encourages them to relate to these different systems of faith towards their own personal development. There is the question as to how this aim can be

---

82 www.gov.uk/government/publications/national-curriculum-in-england-framework-for-key-stages-1-to-4/the-national-curriculum-in-england-framework-for-key-stages-1-to-4.
83 Both figures as quoted in Clarke and Woodhead (2015) at 21.
84 Clarke and Woodhead (2015) at 16.
85 Clarke and Woodhead (2015) at 16.
86 Nigel Fancourt, ' "The Safe Forum": Difference, Dialogue and Conflict', in J. Ipgrave, R. Jackson and K. O'Grady (eds.), *Religious Education Research Through a Community of Practice*, Münster: Waxmann, 2009, 201–215.
87 In that respect, see the seminal work of Michael Grimmit, *Religious Education and Human Development*, Great Wakering: McCrimmons, 1987, as well as R. Jackson's, *Religious Education: An Interpretive Approach*, London: Hodder & Stoughton, 1997.
88 Qualifications and Curriculum Authority, *Religious Education: The Non-Statutory National Framework*, London: QCA, 2004.

achieved within state-funded 'faith schools' where there is the intention to combine religious formation, understood as education within a particular religious tradition, with religious education, conceived as the need for children to understand the importance of religion in the contemporary setting.

According to Clarke and Woodhead, religious formation within 'faith schools' should be conditioned on allowing room for the exercise of agency and criticism by learners and on abstaining from ignoring or distorting other forms of religion or belief.[89] Research and expertise in education studies emphasize that religious education should achieve the dual aim of allowing students to form views and experiences through the curriculum, while at the same time privileging the multi-faith aspects of education in this area, going beyond surface description of religious phenomena and connecting students with a more empathetic awareness of themselves (the "who am I" question).[90] As importantly, religious literacy,[91] lacking in modern multicultural societies, remains another crucial target of religious education, enabling pupils to participate in "liberal agendas of respect and tolerance", and enhancing the levels of their agency in their own education and development of values and beliefs.[92] In briefer and simpler terms, the delivery of religious education should ideally be based on a dialogical exchange between the learners and the materials, in an obvious attempt to halt rampant 'cultural racism' as (dis)connected with and from multiculturalism and citizenship.

a The place of religious education in the national curriculum

As school structures are continuing to grow more diverse in England, and as the national curriculum for schools was the subject of an extensive review between January 2011 and July 2013,[93] the need for a revised curriculum on religious education is present.[94] This need is accentuated by the duty of teachers with

---

89 Clarke and Woodhead (2015) at 34.

90 Jackson and O'Grady (2007) at 194.

91 The notion of religious literacy is difficult to define. There are, however, indicators to approach it. These are the following: major religious traditions share a number of similarities but also some significant differences. Within each religious tradition, there is inherent plurality as they also exist and evolve within specific cultural, historical and political contexts. For some people, belonging or not to a religion is connected to their cultural heritage and sense of identity. The practice of religion is tri-dimensional and covers affiliation and identity, practice and doctrine/ideas. The fact, however, that someones believes is not necessarily in consonance with what he/she believes. Finally, religious concepts and teaching may still be relevant for secular governments and as such merit their presence in the public sphere. All of these points are spelled out in more detail in the Commission on Religion and Belief in British Public Life (2015) at 26–27.

92 Jackson and O'Grady (2007) at 195.

93 Religious education was not part of the review as it is not a national curriculum subject.

94 See in this respect the proposal of the Religious Education Council of England and Wales, 'A Curriculum Framework for Religious Education in England', October 2013.

responsibility for religious education to be subject to assessment since September 2014 on pupil progress and their own performance.

Combined with Ofsted's recurring concerns about the uneven quality of learning and teaching of religious education across the country, there has been debate about the direction of any forthcoming changes. A 2013 Ofsted report highlighted the superficial nature of pupils' knowledge and understanding of the topic, leading to low levels of religious literacy of pupils and low-quality curricula.[95] It further insisted on the persisting weaknesses in the teachers' understanding of the subject (due among others to limited access to training), which, combined with fragmented curriculum planning and ineffective monitoring, gave religious education the impression of an "over-structured and bureaucratic lesson . . . with insufficient stress on promoting effective learning".[96]

The sense of confusion about the purpose and aims of religious education is noted and accentuated by the apparently incompatible goals of extending and deepening pupils' ability to understand religion and belief as opposed to the wider goal of using the subject as an opportunity for personal development.[97] Several factors have contributed towards the decline of the content and delivery of the subject, among which the report notes the reduction in teacher training places for religious education, the reduction in local government spending as well as the loss of publicly funded national support for curriculum development work in the subject.[98] The expansion of the academies' programme also had an impact as a growing number of schools have moved outside local authority control and are no longer required to follow the locally agreed syllabus.[99]

In light of these shortcomings, the Religious Education Council has proposed main axes of intervention on curriculum aims focused on knowing a range of religions, expressing ideas about them and developing the necessary skills to be able to engage with them.[100] These proposals, however, barely disguised the broader issue of concern, which is whether religious education should remain locally determined in accordance with the current legal framework or whether a nationally established religious education curriculum would be more

---

95 OFSTED, 'Religious Education: Realising the Potential', No. 130068, October 2013, at 8. The quality was low in almost two-thirds of the primary schools visited. (OFSTED (2013) at 12) Similar weaknesses were noted in Ofsted's 2010 report on the same topic, suggesting a continuous trend. Types of schools surveyed included academies, community and voluntary-controlled schools but not voluntary-aided with a religious character, which are under separate inspection arrangements for religious education.

96 OFSTED (2013) at 10.

97 OFSTED (2013) at 14–15.

98 OFSTED (2013) at 19–20.

99 OFSTED (2013) at 21.

100 Religious Education Council of England and Wales (2013) at 1–12. The key areas of enquiry include briefs, teachings, sources of wisdom and authority; ways of living; ways of expressing meaning; questions of identity, diversity and belonging; questions of meaning, purpose and truth and questions of values and commitments (Religious Education Council of England and Wales (2013) at 27).

effective.[101] Local authorities are beginning to acknowledge these tensions and could be moving towards a redefinition of their role as facilitators, instead of that of maintaining authorities.[102] At the same time, schools are more and more involved in partnerships of various kinds, forming a new 'middle tier' category of schools.[103] These new formations are setting the foundations for a 'new school improvement market', with a vast variety of consultants, companies and the local authorities themselves competing to sell services to these schools.[104] The call for a national religious education curriculum is further emphasized by the lack of specific curriculum requirements for independent schools.[105]

b Teachers' Agency in delivering religious diversity in education

The declining number of practicing Christian believers among teachers was already a policy concern in the mid-1980s.[106] It has been consistently connected with the risk that teachers' commitment and belief in the need for church schools may reduce, leading at to a gradual loss of their religious distinctiveness as institutions.[107]

A separate yet connected issue relates to the profile of teachers teaching religious education. The correlation between personal religiosity and professional performance and judgment within these schools is crucial in contributing to the success of religious education, as well as academic excellence. There is, at times, objective difficulty for teachers to maintain impartiality when teaching religious education, particularly in a social context of parallel secularization and

---

101 This is a recurring point made by both the 2010 and 2013 Ofsted reports. For the 2013 Ofsted report, see at 22. There are 174 locally agreed syllabi in local authorities in England and Wales and several thousand in academy schools, which are the majority of secondary schools in England (Cf. Commission on Religion and Belief in British Public Life (2015) at 34).

102 N. Parish, A. Baxter and L. Sandals, 'Action Research into the Evolving Role of the Local Authority in Education', 2012, available at https://assets.publishing.service.gov.uk/government/uploads/system/uploads/attachment_data/file/184055/DFE-RR224.pdf.

103 Scott and McNeish (2012) at 21 identify various types of federations, including cross-phase, performance, size, faith federations of relevance for schools of religious character (report available under www.bristol.ac.uk/media-library/sites/cubec/migrated/documents/leadershipandfaithschools.pdf (last accessed 25 September 2019)).

104 Scott and McNeish (2012) at 21.

105 The government issued guidance in November 2013, updated in November 2014 on 'Improving the Spiritual, Moral, Social and Cultural Development on Pupils: Departmental Advice for Independent Schools, Academies and Free Schools'. (For the later version see: www.gov.uk/government/uploads/system/uploads/attachment_data/file/380396/Improving_the_spiritual_moral_social_and_cultural_SMSC_development_of_pupils_supplementary_information.pdf)

106 See, for example, L.J. Francis, *Partnership in Rural Education: Church Schools and Teacher Attitudes*, London: Collins, 1986.

107 See C. Wilcox and L.J. Francis, 'Church of England Schools and Teacher Attitudes: Personal Commitment or Professional Judgement?' in L.J. Francis, W.K. Kay and W.S. Campbell (eds.), *Research in Religious Education*, Leominster: Gracewing, 1996, 311–333.

pluralization.[108] The standard of neutrality required, however, does not seem to necessitate from teachers the disguise of their own religious beliefs (if any) but instead their use (together with those of their pupils) in the context of a herme-neutical comparison towards a better understanding of religious diversity.[109] At present, there is no consistency in the results of existing research on the nexus between the two,[110] and there is little empirical knowledge of the situation in the newer independent schools, particularly those of non-Christian faith.

What is clearer is the lack of subject knowledge and confidence of teachers to achieve goals that incidentally are not clear to them, as well as the limited time and resources towards the teachers' professional development in the subject.[111] A 2010 Ofsted report amply highlights how, in addition to more resources, the emphasis on local arrangements for the oversight of religious education are no longer sufficient. The local determination of the religious education curriculum requires reconsideration towards higher quality and more consistency in this area of education.

Particularly for voluntary-aided schools, the law permits, as already mentioned, by virtue of Section 60 of the School Standards and Framework Act 1998, to give preference in appointment, remuneration and/or promotion to teachers whose religious opinions are in accordance with religious ethos of the schools at issue, or who attend religious worship in accordance with the school's tenets or even who are willing to provide religious education in the same schools, again in line with its ethos. The sharp contrast with the spirit of the 2010 Equality Act is evident, although faith bodies argue that personal conviction in these cases operates as a genuine occupational requirement. The clash between the freedom of religion and the principle of equality is resolved in favor of the former in this case.

c Religious freedom as manifestation: religious symbols and school uniforms

Religious symbol claims in schools are often related to school uniforms. Decisions on school uniform policy belong to the governing body of each school. This duty flows from section 88 of the Education and Inspections Act 2006 as well as the Education (Independent School Standards) (England) Regulations 2010, placed

---

108 For the educational perspective of this question, see Robert Jackson and Judith Evering-ton, 'Teaching Inclusive Religious Education Impartially: An English Perspective', *British Journal of Religious Education*, 39, 2017, 7–24.

109 Jackson and Everington (2017).

110 Leslie J. Francis and Mandy Robbins, 'Teachers at Faith Schools in England and Wales: State of Research', *Theo-Web*, 9(H.1), 2010, 141–159, at 151 et seq. A relative excep-tion in this respect concerns the selection of headteachers whose religious commitment is shown to influence educational practice within both 'faith schools' and schools without any religious character (Francis and Robbins (2010) at 15–16).

111 See OFSTED Report, Transforming Religious Education, 2010 based on evidence in 94 primary and 89 secondary schools in England.

in the context of school policies promoting good behavior and discipline. The Equality Act 2010 does not affect the existing framework with regards to school uniforms, although schools must have regard to the HRA 1998, avoiding blanket uniform policies.

In making these decisions, the governing body is advised to take into account the views of parents and learners and, as importantly, consider carefully reasonable requests to vary the policy, inter alia to meet the needs of any individual pupil towards accommodating his/her religious beliefs.[112] In balancing such requests with the general interest of the school policy on uniforms, the school may restrict an individual's right to manifest her/his religion but subject to a good reason for doing so (e.g. promotion of cohesion and good order, genuine health, safety or security considerations). Adjacent to this consideration is the legal requirement of the school not to discriminate either directly or indirectly. For cases of indirect discrimination, this would involve measures or requirements that, although equally applicable to all, seem in their effects to place certain pupils at a disadvantage. Such measures require a proportionality assessment in achieving their reasonable objectives and to be reasonable enough to allow for exceptions.[113]

According to the Race Relations Act 1976, sections 1, 3 and 17, pupils may not be lawfully refused admission to schools or sent home for a breach of the school rules about uniform if he/she is complying with ethnic rules about dress. In that sense, it has already been established that Sikh boys may wear turbans at school[114] and Asian girls may wear shalwar trousers. Regarding religious symbols, English schools have developed a policy of accommodation towards such symbols, with rare exceptions.[115] It is thus not unusual for Muslim girls, for example, to be allowed to wear the hijab or for Sikh boys to wear a topknot or a turban. Yet, like in the rest of the European continent, there is mounting intensity against the dangers of multiculturalism. Culture and religion have become potential sources of social division, pushing to the defensive a number of politicians and even some past prime ministers.[116]

d 'Faith schools' as a test-ground of religious diversity education

'Faith schools' or schools of 'religious character' represent a controversial category of schools in England. They are organized similarly to other State schools

---

112 Department for Education, 'School Uniform: Guidance for Governing Bodies, School Leaders, School Staff and Local Authorities', September 2013, at 4.
113 Department for Education (2013) at 6.
114 *Mandla v. Dowell Lee* (1983) 2 AC 548.
115 See the case of *Begum v. Denbigh High*, analyzed earlier in this chapter.
116 In this respect, see the speech of Tony Blair on 8 December 2006, as then Prime Minister stating: "multicultural Britain was never supposed to be a celebration of division; but of diversity. . . . We must respect both our right to differ and the duty to express any difference in a way fully consistent with the values that bind us together". (www.number10.gov.uk/output/Page10563.asp, as quoted in Jackson and O'Grady (2007) at 191).

and follow the national curriculum except for religious studies, where they enjoy discretion to formulate content about their own faith. One side of the debate argues that such schools are "a very good use of social capital", serving the poorest parts of the country, while the other side reminds that these schools run at public expense, prioritizing evangelization over public service.[117]

In 2012, 35 per cent of state-maintained schools had a religious character, with almost 70 per cent among them being Church of England and 30 per cent being Roman Catholic.[118] In 2001, the then government pledged 42 million pounds to the support of state-funded voluntary-aided schools, which are allowed to select students on the basis of religious beliefs and practice.[119] The expansion of 'faith schools'[120] is justified by a variety of factors: the argument that such schools are 'good schools' through both their sense of mission and also their academic record is widespread.[121] It is also partially explained by the 'equity of choice' argument that claims that schools run by organizations other than Christian ones will satisfy the 'demand' for cultural education for wider audiences. Whether, however, this type of projected variety of schools' offer is a realistic one is a separate matter: reasonable geographical distance of such schools and concerns of headmasters about possible alienation of the quality and character of education remain relevant considerations. Along these more practical concerns, the broader debate as to whether the expansion of 'faith schools' will lead to further separation between the various groups in British society reflects unambiguously the findings of the 2001 Cantle Report. Attached to this is the claim that schools with strong values are not conducive to the same degree to create the kind of values relevant for plural societies.[122]

So, despite the declining religiosity of younger generations in Britain,[123] 'faith schools' are growing in numbers.[124] Trapped in the Janus-faced profile of such schools as highly successful academic institutions but also as sources of education that may clash with British values, there is open questioning of their quality. Yet, not all 'faith schools' are alike; there is no clear understanding (or explanation)

---

117 BBC, 'Archbishop of Canterbury Defends Faith Schools', 4 May 2014, available at www. bbc.com/news/uk-27273053 (last accessed 25 September 2019).

118 As quoted in Scott and McNeish (2012) at 6.

119 Reed (2006) at 252.

120 See in that respect the 2005 DfES Schools White Paper introducing trust schools on a not-for profit basis, with faith organizations seeking involvement in such ventures.

121 Reed (2006) at 253.

122 Reed (2006) at 255.

123 Recent research based on the Social Attitudes Survey, indicates that 71 per cent of young people are not religious. [Cf. James Williams, 'How Better Education Has Built a More Secular Britain', *The Conversation*, 13 September 2017, available at http://theconversa tion.com/how-better-education-has-built-a-more-secular-britain-83656]

124 Olivia Rudgard, 'Don't Let Faith Schools Take in more Pupils on the Basis of Religion, Leaders Warn', *The Telegraph*, 5 March 2018, available at https://telegraph.co.uk/ news/2018/03/05/dont-let-faith-schools-take-pupils-basis-religion-leaders-warn

of 'fundamental British values' and the situation of such schools operating in the independent sector (i.e. without state funding) is largely unchartered.

In more extreme scenarios, Ofsted has identified a number of independent Islamic and Christian schools that were judged inadequate, among other grounds also for their failure to prepare students for life in modern Britain.[125] According to the Education Act 2011, Ofsted, in their evaluations, must consider "the spiritual, moral, social and cultural development of pupils at the school" (part 21 of the Act), but the additional layer of challenging extremism more recently has been added to the checklist of the inspecting body.[126] Ofsted's current equality objectives for 2016–2020 arising from the Equality Act 2010 place emphasis on the assessment of equality of opportunity and on how gaps between different groups of pupils, including those with protected characteristics such as religion, are being narrowed in order to respond to equal opportunities concerns. [127]

The academic value of 'faith schools' is another issue for disagreement: 'faith schools' are consistently favored by the government as symbols of choice and diversity in the education system. Their high academic and market demand among parents is theoretically justified less on their educational programmes and methods and more because they are attended by pupils issued from families that have different preferences and attitudes towards education. The impact of the modalities of their selection processes may, however, be affecting the type of students accepted in a completely different direction.[128]

Of particular relevance for the study of the clash between the right to religious freedom and equality are exemptions on the admission regulations of 'faith schools'. Schools designated by the Secretary of State for Education under section 69(3) of the School Standards and Framework Act 1998 as having a religious character ('faith schools') are exempted by Schedule 11 to the Equality Act 2010 from the requirement in section 85 of the Equality Act not to discriminate on the grounds of religion with regards to their admission policy. As such, these schools may prioritize applicants on the basis of faith, provided that 50 per cent of places are allocated to pupils in fulfilling the said faith criteria and 50 per cent are reserved for students across the local community without reference to faith. This exception

125 Richard Adams, 'OFSTED Finds Serious Failings at Private Faith Schools', *The Guardian*, 24 November 2015. See also the letter of Ofsted's Chief Inspector Michael Wilshaw to the Secretary of State for Education and Minister for Women Equalities Nicky Morgan on 27 April 2016 reporting incidents of segregation in independent 'faith schools'.

126 Scott and McNeish (2012) at 22.

127 OFSTED, 'OFSTED'S Equality Objectives 2016–2020', No. 160019, April 2016, at 2.

128 Stephen Gibbons and Olmo Silva, 'Faith Primary Schools: Better Schools or Better Pupils?' *Centre Piece*, Summer 2007, 24–25. More recent analysis by the Education Policy Institute confirms that academic excellence may be due to the fact that 'faith schools' take on a lower proportion of poor and disadvantaged pupils (Cf. Rachel Pells, 'Faith Schools Academically "No Better" than Any Others, Major New Report Suggests', *The Independent Online*, 2 December 2016). A 2013 survey by YouGov in 2013 also found that the most important reasons for choosing 'faith schools' are, in order of preference, the school's academic standards, location, discipline, and ethical values (Cf. Clarke and Woodhead (2015) at 52)

is based on the argument that such schools represent an 'alternative educational system', initially conceived and implemented for a Catholic target group.[129]

According to the Church of England, these schools fulfill a double mission: first, they respond to the Church's traditional mission of serving the nation through education at the local level, and second, they provide a distinctive Anglican education for those wanting it.[130] Current circumstances have extended the same possibility to Jewish and Muslim voluntary-aided schools.

More analytically, voluntary-aided schools enjoy, according to para. 1.10 of the School Admissions Code (SAC),[131] in force since 1 February 2012, the discretion to determine the criteria most suitable towards admission of students, in light of local circumstances.[132] Particularly for schools with a religious character, paragraph 1.38 requires admission authorities of such schools to "have regard to" guidance provided by the relevant faith body for each school when establishing faith-based criteria. Such faith-based criteria in 'faith schools' apply in conditions of oversubscription when there are more applicant pupils than places available. Guidance from faith bodies, while persuasive, may be departed from by admission authorities for good reasons.[133] Such criteria, according to paragraph 1.8 of SAC must be "reasonable, clear, objective, procedurally fair" and easily understandable by parents as to their fulfillment (paragraph 1.37). Concretely, guidance often relates to deciding how "membership and practice of faith is to be demonstrated"[134] and has been the focal point of contestation for many 'faith schools'.[135]

---

129 Francis and Robbins (2010) at 146.
130 See the Durham Report (1970) on this matter.
131 The aim of the Schools Admissions Code is to monitor the allocation of places in maintained schools and academies according to the stipulations of the legislation.
132 Paragraph 1.10 stipulates: "It is for admission authorities to decide which criteria would be most suitable to the school according to the local circumstances". The Code, however, stipulates that in drawing the criteria, admission authorities must ensure that these are:

(a) clear and easily understood
(b) objective and based on known facts
(c) procedurally fair and equitable for all groups of children
(d) enabling the parents' preferences for the schools of their choice to be met to the maximum extent possible
(e) providing easy access for parents or carers to admission information
(f) compliant with all relevant legislation, including on equal opportunities.

Failure to comply entails a breach in statutory duties and may result in an objection made to the school's adjudicator.
133 Cf. *London Oratory Case* (2015) EWHC 1012 (Admin.), in particular para. 90 of Cobb J's Judgement.
134 At paragraph 1.38 of the Schools Admission Act.
135 See indicatively Office of the Schools Adjudicator (OSA) Determination ADA 3117 *Surrey County Council v. The Governing Body of St Ignatius Roman Catholic Primary School, Sunbury-on-Thames, Middlesex,* 2 November 2016, on the Certificate of Catholic Practice, requiring priests in the designated diocese to award such certificates to interested families; Determination ADA 2796 *The Fair Admissions Campaign v. The Academy Trust for Nishkam High School, Birmingham,* 11 February 2015, on the admission requirement to a Sikh academy free school that "the child is nurtured in the faith through home or Gurdwara education" (at para. 34).

The interpretation of the SAC treats such questions as the means to determine whether a school place should be offered and not as a religious question stricto sensu, implying a formal administrative interpretation of the religious admission requirement and implicitly attempting to limit the influence of faith bodies in selecting pupils. Related admission criteria are usually considered those assessing the family's active involvement with the church,[136] the child's attendance at church/temple or evidence of baptism,[137] again to be defined by the school's admission authority. In such cases, the controversy arises through the requirement that individual priests are called to make the decision as to whether a child and his/her family are actively involved with the Church with the possibility that this may lead to variations and inconsistencies in the absence of clear criteria of assessment.[138]

These criteria are not the object of controversy exclusively within Christian schools.[139] In one of the Muslim schools, for example, the school's admission arrangement assessed applicants through the score attained on a form evaluating their level of religious commitment,[140] adding that "all applicants are expected to give their committed, unreserved and positive support to the moral code, principles and character and aims of the school". Such requirement was declared impermissible by the Office of Schools Adjudicator. In other cases, within the same faith, the issue arose as to whether faith could be assessed through the Imams' capacity to attest to beliefs held by individuals and the following of the Islamic code of dress as an objective criterion,[141] or through the "verbal assessment" of the practicing of the Islamic faith criterion by applicant pupils.[142] In a Jewish context, certificates of suitability for admission in terms of the Jewish faith criterion have also been an issue of contention, particularly

---

136 This is particularly relevant for the Christian faith. See indicatively, OSA Determination ADA 3243, *The London Borough of Bexley v. The Governing Body of Christ Church of England Primary School, Shooters Hill, Royal Borough of Greenwich*, 31 October 2016.

137 See indicatively OSA Determination ADA 3250, *A Member of the Public v. The Governing Body of St Ursula's Covent School Greenwich*, 29 November 2016, at paras. 18, 29. See also OSA Determination ADA 2776 *The Fair Admission Campaign v. The Governing Body of the Manchester Mesivta School*, 1 October 2014, contesting inter alia the requirement of attendance of both parents in daily worship (para. 17) and the definition of "Orthodox Jewish".

138 ADA 3243, at para. 39 of the determination. Discussions with priests may also be construed as interviews, prohibited by para. 1.9m of SAC (Cf. OSA, Determination ADA 3080 *Surrey County Council v. The Governing Body of Our Lady of the Rosary Roman Catholic Primary School, Staines*, 2 November 2016, at paras. 67–68)

139 Faith-based admission arrangements are reported to be the most common reason for complaints to the Office of School Adjudicator. (Cf. Eleanor Busby, 'Faith Schools: Complaints Over Admission Rise as Number of Selective Religious Schools Set to Increase', *The Independent*, 26 February 2018)

140 OSA Determination ADA 2136 *Local Government Ombudsman v. Islamia Primary School, Brent*, 11 February 2011, in particular paras. 12, 15.

141 OSA Determination ADA 2582 *The Academy Trust of Al-Madinah Academy Derby*, 5 August 2014, in paras. 16 et seq.

142 OSA Determination VAR 0575 *The Governing Body of the Al-Hijrah School*, 21 March 2012, at para. 41.

when it is unclear how "children of applicants . . . support and reinforce at home the Torah values".[143]

The wider legal problem of conflict between the principle of non-discrimination and freedom of religion finds perfect illustration in the area of admission criteria, although it remains unresolved. The case of *JFS* demonstrates this complex normative entanglement: The facts at issue concerned the admission policy of the Jewish Free School and the extent to which these were discriminatory on the basis of race/ethnic origin because they favored those who were 'Jewish'. The case was not fought on the basis of religious discrimination because the Equality Act allowed an exception for 'faith schools'. Instead, it was based on the Race Relations Act 1976 (still applicable at the time) and in particular section 3 defining "racial grounds" as "colour, race, nationality or ethnic or national origin". Once the case reached the Supreme Court, the majority of the judges held that there was indeed discrimination against the applicant on the basis of his ethnic origin. Ethnic origin and ethnicity were approached by the Court in their broad sociological or anthropological dimensions, similar to the *Mandla* case, and not as confined to strictly biological criteria.[144] In fact, the applicant was refused a place in the school due to the fact that he lacked a matrilineal Orthodox Jewish antecedent, which was the school's admission requirement. McCrudden, in his analysis of the case, reminds us of the underlying normative philosophy of the Race Relations Act 1976 that treated individuals in their autonomy and individuality and not as members of a group,[145] in order to confirm the contradictory messages between the 1976 Act and the 2010 one, essentially due to the exemptions afforded to 'faith schools' in setting their admission criteria. This inconsistency leads to further reflection and inevitable comparison with the outcome in *Begum*, where the content of freedom of religion proved insufficient to protect the pupil because she had the alternative to go to another school (the requirement of no alternative missing in race discrimination). The fusion of ethnicity with religion stands confusingly confirmed in *JFS*.

In some of the cases, in order to determine whether a child will be offered a place in a given faith school, admission authorities may also ask for supplementary information (paragraph 2.4. of the SAC). Such requests, however, may

---

143 OSA Determination ADA 2577 *A Member of the Public v. The Board of Directors for the Independent Jewish Day School*, at para. 27 et seq.

144 McCrudden (2011) at 13–14. See *Mandla v. Dowell Lee* (1983) 2 AC 548, where the House of Lords accepted that ethnic origin is wider than the concept of race and carries at the very least two essential characteristics: a long shared history that distinguishes the group from other groups and a cultural tradition that includes family and social customs and manners, associated with religious observances. Other relevant characteristics considered were common languages, a common geographical origin, a common religion different from that of neighboring groups or the general community and being a minority or an oppressed group within a larger community.

145 McCrudden (2011) at 17.

only seek information that is directly relevant to determine the oversubscription criteria.[146]

In sum, retaining faith-related admission criteria is not without risks: there is some evidence of abuse in fair admission policies, by Catholic schools, for example, with a high-profile judgment issued in July 2014.[147] The practice of the schools concerned responded to the need of children from families that regularly worship to secure a spot in schools of their religious choice, yet at the same time there is the broader policy picture to consider: the same practice encourages families to attend church for the sole purpose of securing a place in one of these schools, especially if these schools hold high academic credentials. In that sense, the connection between 'faith schools' and greater academic achievement remains consistently influential in policy formulation.[148] It also indirectly produces other discriminating effects such as limiting choices for children whose families have no faith practice, or those without their own worshipping community to enhance their possibilities of placement.[149] It fosters segregation of children according to religious heritage, which in practice and in effect is often along ethnic and socio-economic status lines.[150] Whether 'faith schools' perpetuate, however, socio-economic divides remains contested.[151] Current research has not identified as of yet a deliberate policy of socio-economic discrimination in 'faith schools', but the evidence of indirect sorting of students is being continuously questioned. Possible avenues, in that respect, include, for example, the empirical observation of how supplementary information forms (SIFs) assist schools in gathering information about the socio-economic status of applicant families leading to selection or how religious families from

---

146 According to para. 2.4 of the SAC, they may not ask for personal details (e.g. maiden names, criminal convictions, marital or financial status), the first language of parents/child, details about parents'/child's disabilities or medical conditions, parents to agree to support the ethos of the school in a practical way or for both parents to sign the form or for the child to complete it.

147 www.gov.uk/government/uploads/system/attachment_data/file/330614/ADA2410_The_London_Oratory_School.pdf

148 Oldfield et al. (2013) at 38. The reality claims, however, only a small advantage in achievement between pupils of faith and non-faith state-maintained schools and in any case is linked to selection criteria not content of curriculum (Oldfield et al. (2013) at 39–40). For an opposite view, see Scott and McNeish (2012) at 11.

149 Similar points are made in Clarke and Woodhead (2015) at 56–57.

150 Commission on Religion and Belief in British Public Life (2015) at 34. See also the critique of Accord, the National Secular Society and the British Humanist Association that oppose the expansion of 'faith schools' on the basis of their effects of undermining social cohesion.

151 See, for example, evidence from the Catholic Education Service that claims that DfE figures show that 18.6 per cent of pupils at the Catholic primary schools live in the 10 per cent most deprived areas of England, compared with the national average of 14.3 per cent, as quoted in Oldfield et al. (2013) at 32.

immigrant or lower socio-economic backgrounds may be penalized by the existing admission criteria of 'faith schools'.[152]

What is clearer is that school choice may in practice come at the cost of a more limited implementation of the right to education, though initially designed to enhance it: given that popular schools are oversubscribed, it is not children and their parents that select schools but rather schools that select children.[153] There is, nevertheless, contradicting emerging quantitative evidence that supports the argument that the intake of 'faith schools' is in fact ethnically diverse and in any case no less successful than in the rest of the education system.[154]

The May government was considering the relaxation of admission regulations of such schools in the selection of pupils[155] in order to allow for new Catholic schools to open in England. The Catholic Education Service supports the move of lifting the cap based on its internal normative commitment to not turn away Catholics within its framed duty to educate them. [156] It was also argued that this would respond to the persistent need to make minority schools more diverse but was also based on the great demand for such schools from parents, due to their academic results. The 50 per cent cap on religious selection for these schools[157] was introduced in an attempt to improve integration and inclusion, privileging conditions of learning over academic results. The prevailing political compromise at the time of writing proposes the maintenance of the 50 per cent cap in exchange for support to local authorities for the creation of a new category of voluntary-aided schools that can be fully selective on the grounds of religion.[158]

Education is not a neutral activity when it happens in a context of one predominant form of spirituality or ethos. This ethos will necessarily have an impact on the final delivery. More concrete prospects for the assessment of the nature of such influence could come in the form of the development of partnerships between 'faith schools', their faith communities and beyond but also in the consideration of their contribution to social cohesion through the taking on of a

---

152 For the latter case, church attendance for these social categories is more difficult because they are new to the country, need to work in several jobs or have more difficulties to navigate the complex application processes for schools that may often be oversubscribed. See Oldfield et al. (2013) at 35.

153 Oldfield et al. (2013) at 33.

154 Oldfield et al. (2013) at 23–24.

155 The current requirement expects religious free schools to reserve at least half of their places to local children, regardless of faith, which is likely to be lifted. See BBC, 'Theresa May to Relax Faith Schools Admissions Rules', 9 September 2016.

156 There is an interesting paradox at play here: existing Catholic schools that are able to allocate all places on the grounds of faith appear to be ethnically diverse, educating more than 300,000 non-Catholics, including 27,000 Muslims [Cf. Rudgard (2018)]

157 According to a 2012 study by the Organisation for Economic Co-operation and Development, the UK and Ireland were among a small group of states allowing religious selection at state schools.

158 BBC, 'Grammar Schools and Faith Schools Get Green Light to Expand', 11 May 2018, available at www.bbc.com/news/education-44067719

community leadership role.[159] The difficulty, at present, is to connect from the policy perspective ethos with outcome, given in particular that there is more than one theoretical approach to define and quantify ethos.[160]

In more general terms and, as mentioned, precisely because individualized circumstances matter, 'faith schools' cannot be treated as a homogenous block of uniform schools. The mediatization and at times misrepresentation of such schools masks a nascent area of research, currently carrying more questions than answers. Their contribution to community cohesion is carefully acknowledged[161] but ultimately depends on their broader vision of education. Their role can, therefore, only be assessed against clear conceptions of secularism, equality and moral/ ethical standards,[162] bearing in mind the challenges of reconciling the distinctive character of such schools when competing with "the secular, market-dominated curriculum; a performance-based pedagogic regime, and a system of evaluation and accountability dominated by visible and measurable outcomes".[163] Aware of the declining religiosity of their membership, Church of England and Catholic schools, but also Jewish ones, have unsurprisingly began to consider more inclusive and diverse practices in admission, shifting away from their historic models of providing education for their own community members.[164]

7 Concluding remarks: the ambiguous role of religious belief in English public education

It is a given that within the last 25 years the face of religion and religiosity in the UK has changed considerably: traditional forms of religious authority and practice have given way to less uniformity and an increasingly diverse span of religious and non-religious commitments.[165] At the same time, religion- and belief-based organizations have been called to develop a network of social services in response to austerity and cuts in public services.[166] Their sustained social action, often through innovative models, indicates their growing role within the public space. This role is conditioned by a complicated relationship of mutual criticism with the State and its agencies. Just like it has been the case historically in education,

---

159 Scott and McNeish (2012) at 11.
160 Oldfield et al. (2013) at 44. See also the work of Trevor Cooling, 'Doing God in Education' (Theos, 2010) that combines this point with the observation that ethos is shaped also by the personal background of teachers and their own values.
161 Oldfield et al. (2013) at 48.
162 See also in that respect Scott and McNeish's (2012) analysis on 'distinctiveness' and how this is shaped according to headteachers' personal attitudes towards religion, at 12.
163 As quoted in Scott and McNeish (2012) at 13.
164 See, for example, the Guidance on admissions to Church of England schools issued by the Archibishops' Council (2011) or the Jewish Leadership Councils of 2008 and 2011 that considered the strategic issues of increasing diversity in admissions, subject to parents' reactions that it would threaten the content of education provided.
165 Clarke and Woodhead (2015) at 6.
166 Commission on Religion and Belief in British Public Life (2015) at 64.

religious and faith communities are now (re)claiming a partnership with the State in the provision of services.[167]

The recent case of gender segregation in 'faith schools' is telling: when faced with the question of gender segregation within religious schools on the basis of a claim of discrimination, the Court of Appeal found that a mixed-gender Islamic school was guilty of sex discrimination for segregating girls and boys from year five.[168] The school in question was a voluntary-aided Islamic faith school in Birmingham. The appellants' main argument relied on the observation that the policy of segregation left learners 'unprepared for life in modern Britain'. It clearly reverted to the broader issue of British values and indirectly referred to the comparison of the standard of education received comparatively by boys and girls in the school in question. In the first instance, the High Court had raised the argument that parents, by sending their children to the specific school, were in principle supportive of the policy in question. The Court of Appeal, however, stressed that segregation caused prejudice to both boys and girls equally, as they were both denied the opportunity to interact with the opposite sex. Learners were subjected, in the Court's opinion, to a "detriment" understood as the inability to mix socially and interact with pupils of the opposite sex. To reach this conclusion, the Court identified each individual learner as the relevant comparator – instead of each gender group as previously held on first instance – subjected to less favorable treatment in order to trigger the application of the Equality Act 2010.

The findings of the Court in this case have implications for the approximately 20 mixed-sex 'faith schools' in England that are believed to apply gender segregation rules.[169] Beyond that and while the uncertainty on the exact number of schools applying this policy is an indication of the regulatory complexities surrounding faith education in Britain, the next phase of the debate involved exchanges between a Jewish Orthodox school and the Department for Education that proposed the solution of splitting schools that practice segregation in two, in order to avoid a violation of the Equality Act 2010.[170]

In legal and policy terms, two practical issues remain thus pending: first, the splitting of a faith school practicing segregation does not offer a solution that addresses concerns of integration, unless the school otherwise promotes

167 Commission on Religion and Belief in British Public Life (2015) at 66.
168 *HM Chief Inspector of Education, Children's Services and Skills v. The Interim Executive Board of Al-Hijrah Schools and Ors* (2017) EWCA Civ 1426.
169 Louise Rea, 'Gender Segregation—Faith-Based Organisation Update', Spring 2018, 7–8, at 7, available at http://bateswells.co.uk/wp-content/uploads/2019/06/faith-basedup date-spring18-pdf (last accessed 25 September 2019).
170 Harriet Agerholm, 'Government Allows Faith Schools to Split in Two to Avoid Gender Segregation Law', *The Independent*, 11 November 2017, available at www.independent. co.uk/news/education/education-news/government-faith-school-split-hasmonean-high-al-hijrah-two-boys-girls-gender-segregation-law-jewish-a8042386.html (last accessed 25 September 2019).

interaction between girls and boys. Second, the case exemplifies the parameters of the ongoing debate on the role of religious belief in public education in modern Britain.

The essential concern with 'faith schools', however, still lies with the content of what is being taught in their programmes:[171] whether mixed-sex or single-sex, the criterion of assessment is to be found in their curricula. The gender dimension of the issue was stressed in the Court's assessment through Lady Justice Gloster's arguments on the reasons why gender segregation was more detrimental for girls. She argued that girls in the school in question were subjected to a practical detriment based on the likelihood that the gender segregation policy would reinforce misogynist attitudes as showcased from references to books in the library of the school. Further to that, it subjected girls to "excessive harm" because it "risks endorsing and perpetuating stereotypes about girls and women that are still pervasive in society and which are widely recognized as detrimental and unduly limiting".[172]

Against this evolving background, the reality in English schools fits perfectly a multicultural scenario but of a special kind: "the teachers are still mainly white, but many of the pupils are now brown or black, come from all kinds of cultural backgrounds, and have as mother tongue speakers an amazing fluency in many languages that other people are struggling to study".[173] The question then becomes how the law, the school system and the religious organizations involved in it take into account this kind of diversity. As importantly, it also becomes an issue of devising policy and law that understands what are clearly the pluralizing effects of globalization.[174] To borrow a quote from Yasmin Alibhai-Brown's text, *After Multiculturalism*, "one of the things that multiculturalism has done is to problematize some of the traditional political ideologies leaving unresolved the two major issues of our times – difference and equality".[175]

Current discourses insist on 'British values', almost as a defense mechanism, to indicate the prevailing anxiety as to whether religious and ethnic communities are able and willing to promote the 'common good'. The government has made the teaching of British values an important part of the framework of spiritual, moral, social and cultural development in British schools.[176] Further to that,

---

171 Rea (2018) at 8.
172 *HM Chief Inspector of Education, Children's Services and Skills v. The Interim Executive Board of Al-Hijrah School* (2017) EWCA Civ 1426 (OFSTED v. Al-Hijrah).
173 Menski (2002) at 46.
174 Expression borrowed from Menski (2002) at 47.
175 Stuart Hall, 'Interview National Portrait', *BBC*, Radio 4, 2 November 1999, as quoted in Yasmin Alibhai-Brown, 'After Multiculturalism', *The Political Quarterly*, 2001, 47–56, at 48.
176 These values are democracy, the rule of law, individual liberty and the mutual respect and tolerance of those of different faiths and beliefs. See Department for Education, 'Promoting Fundamental British Values as part of SMSC in Schools: Departmental Advice for Maintained Schools', London, 2014, available at www.gov.uk/government/uploads/sys tem/uploads/attachment_data/file/380595/SMSC_Guidance_Maintained_Schools.pdf

there is a growing range of areas where the initial settlement between the Church and the State as, for example, expressed in the 1944 Education Act, no longer corresponds to the current realities: some of its aspects are more "honoured in the breach than the observance".[177] The act of collective worship is clearly one such example, followed by the quality of religious education or the admissions policies based on the religious observance of families, commonly the object of dishonesty.[178]

In the meantime, anthropological research particularly has highlighted how religious and cultural minorities in Britain have literally reconfigured the environment in their own terms in a way to be able to navigate skillfully between two (or more) cultures.[179] So the question is becoming whether English schools enhance education for all towards this "skillful navigation"[180] by providing learners with the tools to co-exist and understand each other. Measured against this standard, religious diversity education in British schools has not explored its full potential. But are we then prepared to face the scenario where religious minorities, in response to systematic discrimination, resort to the same effective self-organization in education that they have utilized to organize their lives and businesses in Britain? The school framework would allow that in particular through the category of independent schools, and it seems to be already happening with the blessings of successive governments. For Islamic schools, which are at the center of the heated debate, Lawson found that these can be "a vigorous and idealistic response by the Muslim communities to address the social issues of our time and that such schools are frequently . . . more committed to finding solutions than perhaps many in the state sector", despite being presently comparatively poorly resourced.[181]

The analysis of case law such as the *Begum* case shows an additional aspect of legal regulation that both law- and policy-makers usually ignore: law "does not regulate communication channels neutrally, but directs them in accordance with dominant cultural understandings".[182] In that capacity, law may ultimately disempower by avoiding the questions of individual autonomy and human dignity and by ignoring the implications of the normative plurality in the regulation of religious diversity in schools: the conflicts arising within the self-regulation spaces of state schools on uniform policies, the role of Ofsted School Inspections and their interpretation of state law in both statutory and non-statutory contexts, or even the role of faith organizations in 'certifying' true faith and authentic interpretations of religious identity showcase the level of the challenges.

---

177 Clarke and Woodhead (2015) at 7.
178 Clarke and Woodhead (2015) at 7.
179 Roger Ballard (ed.), *Desh Pardesh: The South Asian Presence in Britain*, London: Hurst & Co, 1994 at 8.
180 Ballard (1994).
181 I. Lawson, *Leading Islamic Schools in the UK: A Challenge for Us All*, Nottingham: National College for School Leadership, 2005.
182 Roger Cotterrell, 'The Struggle for Law: Some Dilemmas of Cultural Legality', *International Journal of Law in Context*, 4(4), 2009, 373–384, at 381.

And yet what pupils learning to co-exist need is precisely to understand how to represent themselves in religiously diverse environments and not how to be represented by school authorities, religious authorities or learned judges.[183] Empowerment, not fear, can be sourced by the constantly changing demographics provided that the promotion of religious diversity through education catches up with the rhythm of evolution of British society. This kind of empowerment requires more than secular liberalist approaches, based solely on individual rights and freedoms, because such schemes leave less and less room for individuals to believe and belong.[184]

183 John Mikhail, 'Dilemmas of Cultural Legality: A Comment on Roger Cotterrell's "the Struggle for Law" and a Criticism of the House of Lords' Opinions in Begum', *International Journal of Law in Context*, 4(4), 2009, 385–393, at 392.
184 Alibhai-Brown (2001) at 51.

7   Negotiating religious identity in public classrooms

1 Introduction: the efficiency of legal pluralism as a frame in religiously diverse education: power, agency and the law

The legal challenge in regulating and promoting religious diversity in public education across very different countries has one common basis: it presupposes the development and subsequent use of mechanisms that while engaging with legal, political and religious systems, recognize a base of broadly shared values. These values allow for negotiation to take place when conflicts arise.

In terms of equality, this requires "the ethical and political space which sets out the terms of reference for the recognition of people's equal moral worth, their active agency and what is required for their autonomy and development".[1] This egalitarian trajectory does not deny local realities or a range of different values, nor does it question the value of the universalistic principles of freedom of religion, non-discrimination or the right to education. Instead, it deals with the more empirical dimensions of assumption and use of power to defend religious identity within and through education.

The use of legal pluralism, combined with comparative legal methodology, both from a global(izing) perspective and with the intention to protect difference, have been used to demonstrate how law is not the prerogative of the State and its institutions in public schools. This is, of course, not a novel statement. What is less widespread is the examination of how non-state actors – in our case, teachers, parents, religious organizations – compete, coordinate or clash with the liberal state.[2] The focus, therefore, is shifting from the State to the lived reality of religiously alert individuals and communities asserting their religious identity in publicly funded schools, as the three case studies have shown. Actor-oriented approaches to the study of normative conflicts in public education reveal additional dimensions to the disputes for the legal

---

1 David Held, 'Cosmopolitanism: Ideals and Realities', 49, 2010 as quoted in Paul Schiff Berman, 'Global Legal Pluralism as a Normative Project', *UC Irvine Law Review*, 8, 2018, 149–182, at 150.
2 This trajectory is emphasized also in Berman (2018) at 154.

discipline: they help understand better the use of available legal frameworks, the symbolic but also real power dimensions as to who decides how religious diversity is taught (or not) in public schools, or the role of institutions in plural legal situations.

Within the framework of the competition as to who has the right to make and enforce rules in a given space, it emerges that legal pluralism as an approach is therefore inherently about normative conflict and the scope for conflict resolution. Law matters insofar as it has been perceived as "the main medium of social and institutional change"[3] within States, although to maintain its unified character has today become largely fiction.[4] With the State no longer being recognized as the exclusive 'creator' of law, new kinds of conflict on which norms must prevail in each case arise. They do so, as shown previously, both in situations where state law recognizes as its part norms developed outside its own context (e.g. personal and family law provisions in Israel) as well as when non-state normative orderings are rivals to state law (e.g. customary law in South Africa to a certain extent).[5]

With an established connection to 'governance', understood here as the ways that and conditions under which law is produced, legal pluralism is insightful on the journey of State norms relevant to the protection of religious diversity in education: from their creation to their application, through the mediation of 'street level bureaucrats', such as teachers or parents, norms are at times interpreted differently from the 'official' guidelines.[6]

A second type of fiction, in this respect, is to be found in the assumption that State and non-state law remain completely separate entities.[7] Indeed, a more constructive, in terms of contextualization, reading of how legal pluralism affects law (and vice versa) would be to accept their interactions as 'relational'. The State and societal actors use polycentric normative systems to accommodate the claims of sub-state groups, gain political support, reduce/escalate the risk of religious conflict or extend the rule of law into previously 'unregulated' areas.[8] These interactions among actors and the State shed light on the state of 'legal

---

3 Yüksel Sezgin, 'A Political Account for Legal Confrontation Between State and Society: The Case of Israeli Legal Pluralism', *Studies in Law, Politics and Society*, 32, 2004, 199–235, at 201.

4 Sezgin (2004) at 203 argues on this point that "legal pluralism is the fact while legal centralism is a myth" restating the 1986 position of John Griffiths.

5 In the context of the present analysis, legal pluralism is viewed in the form of the recognition of one legal system by the State (i.e. another legal system) and is labeled 'normative legal pluralism' [Cf. Keebet von Benda-Beckmann and Bertram Turner, 'Legal Pluralism, Social Theory and the State', *Journal of Legal Pluralism and Unofficial Law*, 2019, 255–274 at 264, doi:10.1080/07329113.2018.1532674]

6 von Benda-Beckmann and Turner (2019) at 260–261.

7 For a categorization of the interactions between the two, see J. Starr, 'Folk Law in Official Courts in Turkey', in A. Allott and G.R. Woodman (eds.), *People's Law and State Law*, Foris Publications, 1985, 123–141.

8 Sezgin (2004) at 208–210.

consciousness'[9] of actors. They also highlight the changes that the assumptions and uses about and of law are producing in the area of education. On the one side, there is a supra-national legal framework that pushes national legislators towards a given content for norms such as religious freedom, education or equality and, on the other, a vast variety of 'voices' that advocate diverse legal and policy positions on the role of religious identity in education. In some cases, it is clear that the intended plurality of norms is able to empower specific interests, to the point of 'forcing' the State to recognize them.[10]

This type of empowerment poses great challenges to state-centric analyses of law, but, at the same time, in some sense it pushes forward the celebration of diversity, of flexible and elastic identities and of multiplicity.[11] So, are we all fundamentally the 'same' or are we rather unambiguously 'different' and should we expect that 'difference' to be defended? In other words, how do and should legal and governance systems respond to the described plurality of religious identities in public schools?

Managing without elimination could be a preliminary response to these difficult questions, with the usual (but again difficult to define) caveat that certain practices may be considered worthy of being "killed off", even within a pluralist framework if they are deemed 'intolerable'.[12]

Approaches to religious education within state schools accordingly vary:[13] it is quite common that they are rooted in the history and socio-economic development of each state. Among the states surveyed in this study, teaching on religions can be confessional or non-confessional, obligatory or optional and with or without alternative options. In other cases, not covered here, such as the French model,[14] religious education is entirely channeled through the teaching of historical religious facts and is thus integrated in other subjects.

Regardless of the approach chosen, it is becoming harder to contest that the relevance of educating learners about religious diversity with multicultural

---

9 The term is here approached as "the various sets of assumptions, ideas about justice, conceptions of global strategy, and beliefs about morality". [Cf. Berman (2018) at 155].

10 Consider the examples of the claims of the Haredi communities in Israel towards exceptions in their stream of education or the movement for the proliferation of schools with a religious ethos in England analyzed in Chapters 3 and 5, respectively.

11 Berman (2018) at 156.

12 On the 'violence' of judicial interpretations and judges as 'jurispathic' entities for elimination competing normative assertions, see Robert M. Cover, 'The Supreme Court 1982 Term—Foreword: Norms and Narrative', *Harvard Law Review*, 97(4), 1983, 53. See also William Twining (ed.), *Human Rights, Southern Voices-Francis Deng, Abdullahi An-Na'im, Yash Ghori and Upendra Baxi*, Cambridge University Press, 2012.

13 The most common ones are non-confessional religious education, optional confessional religious education, compulsory religious education with opt-outs or teaching of religious facts (*fait religieux*) integrated in other subjects. (Cf. Luce Pépin, *Teaching About Religions in European School Systems: Policy Issues and Trends*, NEF Initiative on Religion and Democracy in Europe, 2009, at 19).

14 Based on Régis Debray's 2002 Report to the French Minister of Education distinguishing between *laïcité d'incompetence* and *laïcité d'intelligence*.

schools is becoming the norm.[15] There is a constant that explains the evolution of public school teaching: changes in state-religion relations directly affect relations between schools and religion.[16] But the constitutional framework does not operate in isolation either: for different reasons in each case, as the three cases have shown here, very often the pressure towards educational efficiency and quality push State school policy-makers to place emphasis on civic and intercultural education policies at the expense of teaching about religions.[17] These policies aim to privilege citizenship aspects over religious identity ones.[18]

Yet, the traditional religions in all three cases occupy the most important positions within public education systems and enjoy access to both financial and public opinion privileges. The examples of Israel and England share an interesting commonality in this respect: while there is an openness to religious diversity (through separate tracks of education or types of schools), there has been an impressive growth in the number of private 'faith schools', provoking heated debates and criticism. At the same time, parental choice of such schools appears less and less determined by its religious ethos and more and more dictated by other priorities such as academic reputation (e.g. Catholic schools in England) or financial concerns (e.g. Haredi schools in Israel), among many others. Opposition is, nevertheless, growing on the use of certain admission criteria by faith independent schools,[19] as well as by the de facto segregation that they may cause either on religious or socio-economic grounds. Whether designed to foster the acquisition of knowledge or to encourage learners to include their life experience of religion, teacher training on religious diversity management remains a persisting concern in all cases examined. The focus of such training is on non-biased teaching of religions.[20] This entails the critical examination of sources and documents as well as the consideration of a variety of interpretations of the same fact.[21] Teaching about religions also often strikes politically sensitive cords, whether on the basis of historical and national identity reasons or for fear of fundamentalism and extremism.

15 See, for example, the Final Declaration of the 22nd Session of the Permanent Conference of European Ministers of Education of 4–5 May 2007 in Istanbul that stipulates "regardless of the religious education system that exists in a particular country, children must receive tuition that takes account of religious and philosophical diversity as part of their intercultural education", at para. 23.
16 Pépin (2009) at 13.
17 Pépin (2009) at 18.
18 The example of South Africa is perhaps a system where a strong preference for shared citizenship is expressed (cf. Chapter 5 in this volume).
19 Here the typical illustration would be 'academies' in England, publicly funded types of independent schools in the form of public-private partnerships (Cf. Pépin (2009) at 39–40).
20 The OSCE's Toledo Guiding Principles declare: "Teacher-training should ensure that educators' personal, religious or non-religious commitments do not create bias in their teaching about different religions and philosophies".
21 Pépin (2009) at 45.

2   Religious diversity as a conflict regulating factor: testing the limits of the social magic of law[22]

The role of religion in contemporary societies is plural: it may factor as a strategy towards conflict resolution, but at the same time it can also function as an obstacle to it, as discussed in the previous case studies. Within social environments on a global scale that are gradually growing used to (not without contestation) more visibility of religion in the public sphere, public education is an area where the reconfiguration of religious identities is to be expected: the State, communities, (new) religious movements and actors, as well as individuals, are creating patterns for believing and belonging.

As all three case studies have shown, the limits of the Western state-centric understanding of the interaction between human rights and religious norms demand a 'new methodology' that addresses to a larger extent the expanding presence of religions, including as a result of global immigration.[23] Legal pluralism, a common feature with different nuances in all three cases, replaces a narrower juridical approach insofar as it has allowed the observation of relations among communities, power and authority. It has also functioned as an enabling factor to proceed with the comparative analysis among the three cases, not neglecting the exchange among legal cultures of communities within multicultural societies.

As a note of caution, or perhaps a conceptual barrier towards deeper analysis, in some instances, religion is seen to operate as a 'culturalized' element of identity, relying on a group dynamic to resist change (e.g. in Israel) or simply is treated as a taboo in the name of cultural pluralism (e.g. in South Africa and in a different way in the UK). In education, as much as in other fields of social interaction, religious pluralism explicitly connects to and uses multiculturalism as a normative frame. This linkage is problematic insofar as it invites the reification of religious identity and the illusion of homogeneity,[24] which in public classrooms is shown to be far from the reality.

The use of religion and religious identity in this study thus serves a dual purpose: first, to highlight existing inequalities in and through education between the different ethnic groups, but second, also to stress its potential use as a pathway to address these inequalities. Its use is also largely dependent on the State's approach to multiculturalism: from 'conservative', where the State does little beyond observing how minority cultures are expected to accept the beliefs and practices of the majority in order to reach a certain level of social stability, to more 'liberal' or even 'radical forms', where the State becomes a regulator, targeting the construction of a consensus around common principles, or even in some cases, advocating a transformative agenda to accommodate difference.

---

22 Pierre Bourdieu, *Language and Symbolic Power*, Harvard University Press, 1992.
23 José Casanova, 'Public Religions Revisited', in Hent de Vries (ed.), *Religion: Beyond the Concept*, Fordham University Press, 2008, 101–119.
24 Susanne Baer, 'A Closer Look at Law: Human Rights as Multi-Level Sites of Struggles Over Multi-Dimensional Equality', *Utrecht Law Review*, 6(2), 2010, 56–76, in particular 59.

It has also emerged from the case studies that the conflicts among the three main rights of interest (i.e. the right to religious freedom, to education and to non-discrimination) are rarely resolved before judicial 'fora' without resorting to policy. This observation, in many ways, points to the 'manipulability' of legal rights that are by necessity reduced to balancing tests.[25] How the balancing happens then depends on the practical context and often in connection to non-rights based arguments, according to the level of harm produced by the various potential resolution of the conflict.

There are, therefore, two broad directions for further inquiry as they have emerged from the three case studies in this study. The first is based on the observation that the individual learner in a public school classroom, when it comes to his/her religious identity within a multicultural social setting, is interdependent and relying on various networks of social solidarity.[26] This is particularly so from the perspective of migration and migration studies: for the new nomad or, as Martin labels these groups, the 'internal proletariat', religion is of social, political and legal significance. Minority status of a religious and ethnic group in diaspora tends often to reinforce religious identification.[27] Breaking the limits of territoriality while creating new types of transnational religious communities, diasporic religion has the tendency to strengthen the link between religion and ethnicity,[28] often against human rights discourses (or through them whenever the group acts in its own collective defense).[29] This dynamic movement is inevitably reflected in different patterns within public education (e.g. Islamic 'faith schools' in the UK, former Model C schools in South Africa or ultra-Orthodox Jewish schools operating on public funds in Israel).

The second direction stresses how religion is a heavily politicized identity marker with power implications ignoring the claimed dichotomy that politics is rational while religion is not.[30] This is visible in the role that religion has played in the birth of nations (e.g. in Israel) or in their return to democracy (e.g. in South Africa).[31] Depending therefore on its role, as either a 'benign midwife' or as a 'malign fairy', its vitality is accordingly shaped in relational terms.[32]

Its massive political significance and (as a result) the renewed appreciation of religion in the public sphere[33] connect free exercise of religious freedoms,

---

25 Duncan Kennedy, 'The Critique of Rights in Critical Legal Studies', in W. Brown and J. Halley (eds.), *Left Legalism/Left Critique*, Duke University Press, 2002, 179–227, at 198, 210.

26 David Martin, *Religion and Power: No Logos Without Mythos*, Ashgate, 2014, at 3.

27 Martin (2014) at 91 using the examples of Jews, Muslims in Europe and Chinese in South East Asia. Already very strongly argued in Ballard's (1994).

28 Martin (2014) at 92.

29 Martin (2014) at 94.

30 Martin (2014) at 5.

31 Martin (2014) at 17 draws an interesting parallel between religion, nationalism and political ideology in their use of the main concepts of charisma, martyrdom, commemoration, purification, and boundaries between insiders and outsiders.

32 Martin (2014) at 99. He gives the examples of Poland and Ireland in this context.

33 See José Casanova, *Public Religions in the Modern World*, University of Chicago Press, 1994.

including within public classrooms, with access to public space. In this respect, sociology reminds us of the deep embeddedness of religion with the secular in European Christian discourse, but it seems that the same observation is made in post-colonial studies that consider the power dimension within their own secularization debates.[34]

It should also be recalled from the observation of religious diversity normative struggles in public education, as depicted also in national and supra-national case law, that religion is not definable and delimited.[35] When it becomes so, it acquires specific (and expected) characteristics, which, depending on their use and design, can either connect it to the origins of war and violence or function as 'social glue' in solidarity.[36] In that sense, religious identity is often 'othered' in an attempt to locate the problem in multicultural education elsewhere, occasionally in 'orientalized' terms that assume the unlabeled standards of the West as established and beyond debate. Connected to this last point, it has hopefully emerged from the preceding analysis of three very different national systems of public education that State neutrality (or secularism) is an ideological concept that often hides the complex ways in which the State may actually privilege the education and belief systems of some while disadvantaging that of others.[37]

At the same time, and arguing from the level of the individual learner in public education, the assertion of religious identity at school essentially boils down to an exercise of choice: the ability to choose to have an individualized form of faith or to be part of a community beyond the State. This choice is again very pronounced within diasporic religions, where adherence tends to be more conscious.[38] This same choice is connected also to autonomy, within a human rights framework, keeping in mind the link between religious concepts and human rights.

The politicization of religion in public education is also affected by the (not so) new type of agency that religious organizations are embracing in education: through competition with the State as the 'legitimate' provider of education or, at best, in cooperation with it, religious bodies act as agents of change and modification.[39] Particularly for minorities whose interests may not be well protected and/or understood by the mainstream, these actors may play a powerful social and economic role through the creation of culture, of public morality, of economic activity through providing jobs, and as such become able to influence the gravitas of non-discrimination laws and equality to the point of even discrediting

---

34 See the seminal work of Talal Asad, *Formations of the Secular: Christianity, Islam, Modernity*, Stanford University Press, 2003 but also Martin (2014).
35 Martin (2014) at 45.
36 Martin (2014) at 47.
37 Baer (2010) at 68.
38 Martin (2014) at 81.
39 This role is parallel to that of churches as NGOs (e.g. in Africa). See Martin (2014) at 107 and 112–113.

them.[40] In some instances, these bodies are even able to build an entire (alternative) social environment that includes schools but also banks, hospitals and other services to cater to the needs of their believers.[41] They thus become 'systems of power' in their own right.[42]

On many levels though, the patterns of religious diversity frameworks in public education reflect the degree of homogeneity/pluralism of a State's identification of a nation with faith. This identification is increasingly challenged by the developing patterns of transnational religious pluralism emerging from diasporic religious communities,[43] as noted. As immigration and integration discourses continue to challenge the contours of *res publica*, public education systems, including in the cases of states with historical religious diversity (e.g. South Africa and to a certain extent Israel) find it harder to 'divorce' the pursuit of religious diversity from political, identity or other 'culture wars'.

To the extent however that law-making on religious freedoms and non-discrimination is perceived as a way to 'teach people moral lessons',[44] diversity ends being ignored in favor of a fictitious 'common culture' which encourages and maintains the lived reality of discrimination.

As such, the role of national education systems remains most commonly the reproduction and transmission of this 'common culture' but not in terms that seek to understand, explain or reflect on the fact that citizens are more and more religiously diverse. As case law explored within the case studies emphasized, constitutionally recognized human rights are heavily balanced with their competing rights (e.g. the classical religious freedom vs equality paradigm) while being in constant need of contextualization. They risk becoming (unintentionally) communitarian in their application,[45] despite their design as individualized entitlements. Empirical investigations, at the level of legal analysis, reveal that universal norms, such as equality and religious freedom or education continue to be constructed on the basis of specific historically rooted communities.[46]

Two separate points deserve a closer look in the frame of religious diversity as a factor towards the regulation of normative conflicts: the first highlights how religious education can be perceived as a common public good in order to ease a number of tensions. The second relates to the more reflective connection between religious education and equality as it emerges in religiously plural settings and operating as an important variable towards normative conflict resolution.

---

40 Carolyn Evans and Beth Gaze, 'Between Religious Freedom and Equality: Complexity and Context', *Harvard ILJ Online*, 49, 21 April 2008, 40–49 at 45.
41 Martin (2014) at 108 and 112–113, explores the example of Pentecostal churches in Africa or Evangelical Christians in South Korea.
42 Martin (2014) at 142.
43 Martin (2014) at 170–171.
44 Howard Adelman, 'Rights and the Hijab: Rationality and Discourse in the Public Sphere', *Human Rights and Human Welfare*, 8, 2008, 43–77, at 49.
45 Adelman (2008) at 55.
46 Adelman (2008) at 70. See also evidence in Chapters 4–6 of this study.

a Religious education as a public good

The examination of modern terms of religiosity validates a wider trend towards subjective and privatized forms of religion.[47] Creating one's own patterns of religious ideas and symbols, paying less attention to external sources of religious authority or, put simply, 'believing without belonging', as suggested in the case of England, invites reflection on the role of state and non-state actors in managing religions (at times for their own benefit). Public education does not escape this consideration.

In many cases, as Beckford suggests, 'fuzzy fidelity' can be more connected to commercial forces and less to the free choice of individuals.[48] Interestingly, the success of 'faith schools' seems to be guided by an analogous logic, at least in part.[49] Religious groups, operating as 'social enterprises' and defined as "profit-seeking businesses that aim to invest their profits for the benefit of society",[50] are active in the area of education driven by moral/religious motives. In that sense, Habermas's notion of the public sphere as a space of rational debate on religion no longer exclusively controlled by the State (or the economy) can now be subjected to qualification, including within public education.

Yet, the State continues to play a role: it interferes with civil society although it is also affected by transnational and global forces that shape the face and actions of the so-called 'public religions'.[51] In some cases, the level of competition and conflict among public religions pushes the State to forge partnerships and co-operate with them.[52] For education, this means that faith organizations are encouraged to position themselves as "agents or mediators of government policies".[53] In those scenarios, the State opts for selective and strategic partnerships that are usually labeled as community cohesion initiatives. This explains in many instances legal and policy choices within public education.

The risks in this approach to religious diversity management remain that competition among religious groups for resources may become fierce and produce additional conflicts among them,[54] not to mention that in fact faith groups may in some cases maintain ethnic and religious divisions against the more vulnerable

---

47 See indicatively James A. Beckford, 'The Return of Public Religion? A Critical Assessment of a Popular Claim', *Nordic Journal of Religion and Society*, 23(2), 2010, 121–136 at 123.

48 Beckford (2010) cites the examples of Tai Chi, aromatherapy, reiki or Kabbalah as potential examples of this trend.

49 See, for example, Chapter 6 in this volume on the success of 'faith schools' in England, provoking phenomena of fake religiosity in order to secure places in such popular schools.

50 Beckford (2010) at 132.

51 Beckford (2010) at 125.

52 The trend is particularly obvious in public education in the UK, with a long-standing cooperation of the State with faith organizations (e.g. New Labour's 'faith sector' policy). It is also quite present in Israel for a select number of religious communities.

53 Beckford (2010) at 129.

54 Beckford (2010) at 131.

groups of society.[55] The path of the clear separation of States from religion seems thus questionable. Modernity, therefore, perhaps lies in accepting that States have a role to play in shaping public religions, not abstaining from them.[56]

In parallel and beyond the legal discipline, current education scholarship has registered the growing support for engagement with religion in public schools,[57] even in negatively secular legislative contexts. While the introduction of religion remains feared as a potential source of conflict, its exclusion has now become quasi-impossible as it represents a primary source of values that learners from different backgrounds bring to the classroom.

From a diversity management and governance perspective, the utility of including religion in the public space, including education, is triple:[58] first, it is conducive to the sharing of experiences with those with whom school as a social space is shared; second, religion often operates as a guideline to explain social processes; and third, it plays a significant role in the evolution of social change.

The three preceding case studies are not, however, unanimous with regard to the need for the presence of religion in public education from a public policy and constitutional perspective, with South Africa opting for a relegation of religious identity to the private sphere. All three, however, share the anxiety of striking a balance on how best to integrate (and negotiate whenever needed) the diversity of religious beliefs and values of their learners. Negotiating religious pluralism in public schools is thus clearly the aim, especially since religious diversity is an empirical fact that public education cannot ignore. This is, as noted, because learners bring their religious identity into the classroom in ways that affect their learning capacities as well as their levels of engagement with knowledge, potentially rendering otherwise valid legislative and policy frameworks inoperative.

At the same time, the marginalization of religious groups (often minorities) has indirectly reinforced the processes of corporatizing of religious organizations.[59] This is again mostly visible in the growth of 'faith schools' across the globe as an indication of how religious actors are striving towards autonomy in the provision of services towards their members.

Echoing these concerns and with a clear preference for dialogic pedagogies, education scholarship proposes cross-cultural sensitivity training that reflects more closely society's political pluralism. Dialogic religious literacy is precisely associated with learning to understand others at the level of values, mission and

---

55 Beckford (2010) at 131.
56 Beckford (2010) at 133.
57 See, for example, Sardar M. Anwarudding and Rubén A. Gaztambide-Fernandez, 'Religious Pluralism in School Curriculum: A Dangerous Idea or a Necessity?' *Curriculum Inquiry*, 45(2), 2015, 147–153.
58 M. Dillon, 'The Sociology of Religion in Late Modernity', in M. Dillon (ed.), *Handbook of the Sociology of Religion*, Cambridge University Press, 2003, 3–15
59 Anwarudding and Gaztambide-Fernandez (2015) at 150.

vision through points of connection and overlap,[60] without underestimating the normative conflicts arising between faith and society's changing conditions. The need for such dialogue is more intensely felt in contexts where religious communities have had or are still experiencing conflict. This dialogue is premised, however, on the link between religious identity (as connected with ethnicity and cultural heritage) and citizenship: all public schools, including faith-based schools, that are supported by the State, carry the duty to encourage students and their families to value positively religious difference while allowing the development of a sense of identity in all students.

In order to stress and achieve a conceptualization of religious education as a public good, capable of operating as an agent of transformation towards social cohesion, religious perspectives within education have to be managed by teachers who are tasked to provide education about religious values and their civic and ethical dimensions towards co-existence within difference. Legal frameworks, as has been shown, have limited impact within this process, unless courses about religion and the overall presence of indicators of religious identity are managed within a critical framework that encourages the (reasonable) right to religious difference.

b (In)equality in and through education

Religious pluralism in the 21st century appears inevitable: massive migration connected to a globalized market economy, easy access to information on religions and, as importantly, the transnational character of migrants who maintain religious and social connections to their communities of origin and create the conditions for plural religions shape the new normative environment. Sociology of law has considered the question of how to determine who will prevail when a conflict, sourced from normative pluralities, emerges: social status, prestige and cultural intimacy with those making decisions usually dictate the outcome.[61] Public education has diachronically been a useful tool to analyze and explore comparatively the socio-legal arrangements that protect both individual religious freedom but also equality in its personal and group dimension, as connected to both belief and non-belief.

Inequality in education is inextricably linked to inequality in the production of human capital. Currently, there is considerable scientific exploration of the connection between educational attainment and full equality.[62] This kind of

---

60 Cf. C. Baker, 'Blurred Encounters? Religious Literacy, Spiritual Capital and Language', in A. Dinholm, R. Furbey and V. Lowndes (eds.), *Faith in the Public Realm*, Bristol: Policy Press, 2009, 105–122 at 105.

61 James T. Richardson, 'Religious Diversity, Social Control, and Legal Pluralism: A Socio-Legal Analysis', in G. Giordan and E. Pace (eds.), *Religious Pluralism*, Springer, 2014, 31–47, at 39, discussing the work of Donald Black.

62 See the Gini index or Gini coefficient, which measures precisely the gap between the actual distribution of education attainment and full equality. (Cf. James Jacob and Donald B. Holsinger, 'Inequality in Education: A Critical Analysis', in Donald B. Holsinger and James Jacob (eds.), *Inequality in Education: Comparative and International Perspectives*, Comparative Education Research Centre, 2009, 1–33, at 2.

empirical exploration on the impact of equality in education includes an understanding of the notion of equality beyond the letter (and interpretation) of the law, extending to its social justice ramifications in terms of fairness, justness and impartiality.[63]

If the distribution of education matters towards economic growth,[64] "individuals should have equal opportunities to pursue a life of their choosing and be spared from extreme deprivation in outcomes".[65] It is often the case, as discussed in earlier parts of this study, that existing educational institutions, policies and legal frameworks are designed in ways that maintain and perpetuate existing inequalities in and through education, with clear repercussions on people's capabilities to shape their lives. So, how education is distributed matters towards the future distribution of educational attainment and, of course, income, since the right to education is a 'gateway' right. With public resources devoted to education, it is of crucial importance to offer equality of opportunity to a more religiously and ethnically diverse population.[66]

In this sense, the role of religion as an identity marker needs to be perhaps reframed: Habermas's 'post-secularity', understood as the project of opening the public space to the various secular and religious actors for exchange, tells us half of the story. The other half, as demonstrated in the case studies of this volume, incites us to reflect on how public space is affected by the interests, discourses and ultimately preferences of the most powerful religious social groups to the detriment of the less powerful ones.[67] This process starts in and with education.

In other words, normative statements on equality, neutrality or education are conditioned by certain religious groups within public education (but also beyond) that shape what equality signifies in everyday terms. The legal arrangements of religious pluralism are therefore clearly insufficient, without the contribution of social and political actors to give us a sense of how they are supported and implemented (or not) both within public schools but also in the workplace and other similar social spaces.

63 Jacob and Holsinger (2009) at 4.
64 Vinod Thomas and Wang Yan make that point in V. Thomas and W. Yan, 'Distribution of Opportunities Key to Development', in Donald B. Holsinger and James Jacob (eds.), *Inequality in Education: Comparative and International Perspectives*, Comparative Education Research Centre, 2009, 34–58.
65 World Bank, *World Development Report 2006: Equity and Development*, Oxford University Press, at 2.
66 Donald B. Holsinger and James Jacob, 'Education Inequality and Academic Achievement', in James Jacob and Donald B. Holsinger (eds.), *Inequality in Education: Comparative and International Perspectives*, Comparative Education Research Centre, 2009, 558–567, at 564. The authors assume at 565 that public education spending is biased towards the rich, based on political decision-making.
67 Siniša Zrinšèak, 'Re-thinking Religious Diversity: Diversities and Governance of Diversities in Post-Societies', in G. Giordan and E. Pace (eds.), *Religious Pluralism*, Springer, 2014, 115–131, at 129.

3 The management of religious disputes within education in plural societies: methods, conditions and challenges

Accepting in this analysis that secularism should not necessarily be anti-theistic,[68] the survey of the three distinct arrangements of religious diversity in public education as presented in the case studies reveals the following main approaches to conflict resolution: first, there is a clearly discerned rights-based approach, where individuals resort to the judicial resolution of conflicts that allegedly infringe on their constitutional liberties. This trend is noticeable in the case law in South Africa, where the apex court has developed very sophisticated reasoning on the notion of equality and diversity. Through this approach, what is essentially targeted is the relationship between the State and a certain individual and/or group.[69]

In terms of the method of religious conflict management in schools, the case studies also show, despite the variety of legal cultures examined, a common emphasis on a rights-based approach as the primary tool of entitlement and claims, though with mixed outcomes. There is, at present, little allowing one to diagnose any consideration of a culture based on responsibilities of individuals and/or communities, especially if one focuses on the official constitutional discourse. As a matter of fact, religious communities are developing skills in utilizing this type of discourse based on rights' entitlements in effective ways both formally and informally.[70]

In that respect, it is worth highlighting how there is a close alignment observed between the notions of 'race' and 'religious identity'. This in part explains why the concept of (and right to) equality emerges prominently in legal discourse on religious diversity in education. In such conditions, it could be argued that we are witnessing a process whereby religion is indeed becoming the 'new' race. The limits of this option are nevertheless demonstrated in the case of Israel and the recent jurisprudence on the correlation of the requirement to teach the national core curriculum in ultra-Orthodox 'faith schools' that receive state funding.

Second, there is an alternative option, as evidenced in the English case, where schools as social spaces of religious diversity have been equipped with a set of

---

68 Li-Ann Thio, 'Relational Constitutionalism and the Management of Religious Disputes: The Singapore "Secularism with a Soul" Model', *Oxford Journal of Law and Religion*, 1(2), 2012, 446–469 at 447.

69 Thio (2012) at 447.

70 There is a wider trend towards the use of rights-based assessment to reflect on the situation of religious minorities in public education. In the field of education, the development of 'rights-based indicators' signals the attempt to assess the conformity of education with human rights standards by taking into account both what happens inside classrooms but also outside of them (e.g. infrastructure, learning materials, methodology, children's socio-cultural characteristics, opportunities for stakeholders' participation). Cf. The Right to Education Project, 'Beyond Statistics: Measuring Education as a Human Right', London, 9 July 2010, at 1.

'soft' law tools combined with 'hard' law benchmarks in order to ease potential inter-religious group tensions. The school uniform policy is one such example demonstrating a tendency towards a relational approach to school diversity management. This version of school diversity policies as practiced in the UK is nuanced when compared, for example, to more developed forms of relational constitutional practices emphasizing 'racial and religious harmony' in Asian contexts.[71] An approach similar to that in the UK is largely based on broad general guidelines combined with the expectation of the internalization by all learners of a number of commonly agreed upon social norms. This process is aptly implemented in the drawing of a list of values that British schools are expected to promote throughout their teaching programmes. Such a process presupposes, however, a vision of religious identity but also of religion more broadly as a 'positive factor' and a generator of 'social capital'.

Coming back to the role of the State in managing religious disputes/conflicts within public education, it is clear that for all three cases studied there is a consistent tendency to avoid coercive legal norms (with the exception of cases perceived as 'intolerable'). This means that States and public officials are consciously avoiding telling people and communities 'how to practice their religion'.[72] This withdrawal is, however, motivated by different intentions: in the case of Israel, we are witnessing an institutionalized pillarization of the education system that was initially conceived as a tool towards cultural and religious autonomy but in the cases of the Arab Israelis and the ultra-Orthodox Jews potentially constitutes negative and positive discrimination, respectively. For South Africa, the withdrawal of the State from the management of religious diversity in the public space is based on the (contested) assumption that religious identity is a private matter, while for the UK, the role of the State in managing religious diversity in the public school system is sourced from policies of multiculturalism that rely on the realization of the plurality of British society, coupled with the underlying concern of 'not wanting to offend' the variety of religious communities present and active in British society in order to avoid intensifying conflicts and tension.

Without neglecting the role of religion in the construction not only of personal but also of national identity, the dimension of the values transmitted through the education system is as crucial. Both cases covered in previous chapters here, as well as broader scholarship findings, suggest that school choice may be determinant in that respect, especially when parents have the potential to exercise choice/discretion when selecting a school for their children.[73] The right of parents to select a school in accordance with their religious and philosophical beliefs

---

71 See Thio (2012), characteristically for the example of Singapore that adopts a view of diversity management based not on rights or punishment, susceptible to alienating communities, but instead on informal regulation and reconciliation techniques discreetly but entirely coordinated by the State.

72 Expression borrowed from Thio (2012) at 463.

73 See, for example, Gabriela Pusztai, 'Schools and Communities of Norm-Awareness', *Religions*, 2, 2011, 372–388.

for their children is legally and empirically established and comes with certain assumptions: a basic distinction (yet one with nuances) between denominational schools and secular public schools is located in the degree of autonomy cultivated to learners. On one side, religious schools are perceived as establishments that encourage to a lesser degree individual emancipation while non-religious education, on the other, supports further the moral autonomy of children.[74] In simpler terms, choosing religious schools reflects more the dimension of the right to education that corresponds to the parents' exercise of choice, while choosing a public school stresses a learning process that ideally aims for more autonomy in the choice of values, restricting to a greater degree the influence of other culturally dominant factors in a child's development.

The problem with such a binary classification of schools is, however, that there is little in terms of uniformity among religious actors (i.e. faith communities, including religious schools) on the ways to practice one's faith, creating different variations of religiosity, as was also discussed in the case studies.[75] Attached to the process of school choice, as connected to the exercise of religious freedom, is also the issue of quality of education. In the examination of 'faith schools' in the English context, it emerged that some of these schools were particularly coveted, even beyond the communities to which they were catering to spiritually, due to their academic results. Inversely, in the Israeli case, it was noted how Haredi schools were gradually attracting higher numbers of students due to the low-cost education offered in exchange at times for lower standards of education. Both aspects lead us to question the extent to which denominational or 'faith schools' help students address any potential socio-economic disadvantage but also to what degree they train learners as future citizens according to certain values that connect their respective religious communities with their school communities.[76]

Three distinct areas have emerged as determining variables from the comparative analysis between Israel, South Africa and England in religious diversity management and policy formulation in public schools: the role of context is shaping religious diversity patterns in education, the new role (and expectation) from the State when undertaking its 'regulatory' mission of managing religious diversity in schools, and finally, the types of challenges that lie ahead in this same area.

a The role of context in promoting religious diversity in education

The experience of the cyclical movement of multiculturalist policies in the UK, but also elsewhere in the world, showcases the dynamics of a growing trend

---

74 Pusztai (2011) at 378.
75 See indicatively the case of the UK in Chapter 6. Pusztai (2011) argues, for example, that in general terms individual autonomy appears to be on the increase among religious groups' educational values.
76 Pusztai (2011) at 380–381.

towards 'aggressive majoritarianism'.[77] To be clear, following 9/11, government policy in the UK embraced the view that the promotion of minority cultures (even without any corresponding firm commitment to de facto equality) led to the further fragmentation among communities, moving against social cohesion. Combined with calls for integration and security, this 'observation' was translated in education, for instance, into guidance on school uniforms, emphasizing the security/integration dimension, most prominently with respect to Muslim religious symbols.[78] The argument was also pursued through the way that the ethno-religious composition of schools has prevented social mixing.[79] In this sense, it is probably premature, looking also at the remainder of the case studies in this discussion, to argue convincingly that public education systems, with the help of legal frameworks, have entered into a 'post-racial' frame, understood as the 'end of racism',[80] especially to the extent that race and religion become conflated.

At the same time, "central government policy is left to teachers, head teachers and local authorities to interpret and act on; for teachers and administrators often with limited training in diversity and equality this may prove challenging".[81] A teacher's personal convictions, perceptions, interpretation and experiences greatly influence the content and degree of normative force and balancing of the rights to education, equality and religious freedom in the school.

A third element that has emerged is the expansion of 'faith schools'. Largely due to religious community mobilizations, as has been shown for all three cases, where religious communities are developing successful strategies to satisfy their claims, these schools are contested, particularly when representing a minority religion. The standard arguments in favor of such schools claim that they stand as the implementation of the collective dimension of the right to religious freedom for learners and their parents who wish to educate them in accordance with their religious beliefs. Opponents voice their concern over the effects of such education, with the support of public funds in a number of cases, on the risk for further segregation of society and respond to the human rights-based claim by counterclaiming that learners should retain the right to choose their own beliefs, as autonomous legal agents with 'faith schools' practically eliminate that possibility.[82] The interesting paradox, however, in this case is that the potentially

---

77 See Katy Sian, Ian Law and Salman Sayyid, 'Debates on Difference and Integration in Education: Monitoring Extremism in the UK—Muslims in School', TOLERACE Project, Leeds: CERS, University of Leeds, 2011.

78 Sian et al. (2011) at 5.

79 As noted in Chapter 6, income/wealth, housing market factors as well as parents' preferences affect the composition of public schools as well as 'faith schools'.

80 Term borrowed from Sian et al. (2011) at 8.

81 H. Mirza, *Multicultural Education in England, International Alliance of Leading Education Institutes (IALEI)*, London: Institute of Education, University of London, 2010, at 21–23.

82 Sian et al. (2011) at 17.

detrimental effects of 'faith schools' are usually raised for minority religions only (e.g. Muslim schools in the UK).[83]

b Religious pluralism and the new role of the State

Religious pluralism terminologically suggests a normative dimension in the protection of difference.[84] According to Beckford, religious pluralism is a polysemic term that can signify an empirical form of diversity in religious terms but also a value judgment on the positive value of religious diversity, a framework of public policy/law or even a relational context of interaction between individuals and groups.[85]

For the purposes of this study, religious pluralism has been approached as "a powerful ideal meant to resolve the question of how to get along in a conflict-ridden world",[86] with emphasis on how the State finds itself in "competition among private interests, in which it brokers, bargains and manages conflicts".[87]

In the context of the regulatory level of religious difference in public education, one should stress how religion follows modernity by transforming its agenda through a constant negotiation between its dogmatic principles with the socio-cultural contexts prevailing in each case.[88]

As the global trends in religiosity, however, also show, the implications of this negotiation are pushing learners as believers towards the individualization of their beliefs. What the three case studies stress is that the agency of religious actors de facto is the one shaping the terms of this negotiation on the basis of the needs of the individuals-believers.[89] This process becomes particularly evident in diasporic religious communities whose presence, as already mentioned, has transnational features.

---

83 Mirza (2010) at 16 notes for the British context: "The consideration of faith schools and their role in fostering community cohesion is not necessarily conceived as a concern of the majority Christian schools; rather it appears to be subsumed within the overall discussion of violent extremism and integration of BME groups within a system of British core values". This is although Muslim 'faith schools' represent a small percentage of the total number of 'faith schools' in the UK.

84 See the distinction between religious pluralism, on its normative regulation, and religious diversity, with a descriptive connotation in Giuseppe Giordan, 'Introduction: Pluralism as Legitimization of Diversity', in G. Giordan and E. Pace (eds.), *Religious Pluralism*, Springer, 2014, 1–12 at 1.

85 James A. Beckford, 'Re-thinking Religious Pluralism', in G. Giordan and E. Pace (eds.), *Religious Pluralism*, Springer, 2014, 15–29 at 16.

86 Courtney Bender and Pamela E. Klasses (eds.), *After Pluralism: Reimagining Religious Engagement*, Columbia University Press, 2010, at 1.

87 Yuri Kazepov and Angela Genova, 'From Government Fragmentation to Local Governance: Welfare Reforms and Lost Opportunities in Italy', in Paul Henman and Menno Fenger (eds.), *Administering Welfare Reform*, Policy Press, 2006, 233–255, at 249.

88 Giordan (2014) at 3.

89 For a similar conclusion see Giordan (2014) at 5–6.

Legal pluralism becomes, therefore, reflected within public education through individualized belief that often escapes the religious institutional aspects of faith. The role of the State in such a context, when faced with increasingly diverse demands towards the practice of one's faith, is to combine the general interests of the community in its broadness with the interest of religious minorities or individual believers.[90] It is worth observing, however, that religion has become both the object and the subject of regulation,[91] and this is evident in public schools in the way that actors, such as parents, teachers or religious communities 'respond' to the State's regulatory attempts.[92] Against this complexity, where religious pluralism is "the normal state of affairs",[93] there is evidently not a single mode to regulate religious diversity, especially when geographical, cultural and community boundaries are porous.

The omni-present risk remains that pluralism may be tainted with arbitrarily relative normative standards, especially when religious beliefs are treated as absolute 'truths' only for those believing them, in a society that is striving to treat all religions as of equal value.[94]

One approach prominent in a different way in both the case of Israel and England, suggests that "to enhance the role of voluntary associations does not result in a diminution of the authority of the State; it merely relocates it".[95] This relocation, however, is heavily qualified by other overlapping factors that include the intense juridification of equality and non-discrimination vis-à-vis belief, the rising volume of labor migration between countries of significant 'cultural distance' and the complex globalizing and glocalizing processes taking place within religious groups.[96] Conceived as a study on the limits of 'pluralization',[97] this analysis has aimed to show how contexts shape, manage and ultimately control the expression of religious beliefs in public education in different cases.

90 Giordan (2014) at 8.
91 Cf. James A. Beckford and James T. Richardson, 'Religion and Regulation', in James A. Beckford and N. Jay Demerth III (eds.), *The Sage Handbook of the Sociology of Religion*, Sage, 2007, 396–418.
92 Examples of this duality from this study can be found in that way in which ultra-Orthodox Jewish communities have shaped the content of education in Haredi schools or in how South African teachers have diluted the contests of religious diversity management approaches in public education or even in how 'faith schools' have expanded in the UK as a result of the joint efforts of parents and religious organizations.
93 Nancy T. Ammerman, 'The Challenges of Pluralism: Locating Religion in a World of Diversity', *Social Compass*, 57(2), 2010, 154–167.
94 This argument is also made in Beckford (2014) at 18.
95 David Runciman, *Pluralism and the Personality of the State*, Cambridge University Press, 1997, at 264.
96 Beckford (2014) at 23.
97 Defined as the "process of testing the limits of acceptable or reasonable forms of diversity". [Cf. William E. Connolly, *The Ethos of Pluralization*, University of Minnesota Press, 1995].

c The challenges of education systems in protecting religious difference

Contemporary education systems are increasingly under pressure to provide education that meets the requirements of economic competitiveness while contributing to social cohesion.[98] Economic imperatives affect religious education insofar as they dictate a certain vision of education towards its marketization and commodification.

In broader terms, it is difficult to contest that public education systems in general, and religious education in particular, are currently struggling to balance internal factors to each country with globalization forces and their impact. The class divide between elites and the masses is maintained not only on the level of the cultivation of human capital towards competitiveness in the job market but also in terms of expectations out of education systems: the demand for moral-religious training within school is growing among a considerable number of Christian, Muslim and Jewish groups.[99] What emerges, however, in that respect, is that there is not always clarity on the distinction between morals and values education with religious education as educative goals.[100]

Depending on the national context, and also on the degree of religious homogeneity, education systems are correspondingly varying in their pursuit of religious diversity. The constitutional relationship between the State and religion(s) is also important, which in a number of cases influences the historic role of the church in educational matters.[101]

Yet the influence of globalization is persistently present: whether in purely economic terms – as a project that touches on the restructuring of economies, the migration of the labor force or the strife towards effectiveness in the job market – or in more comparative terms as a project where systems 'borrow' educational features from each other that are connected to international normative expectations, such as human rights, children's rights or minority rights.[102] Aware of both trends, the global discourse on human rights has been particularly explicit in stressing the need for a culturally adapted form of education as a tool for both economic success and social cohesion.[103]

While the class dimension seems to play an important role in the access to and provision of education,[104] the demand for religious and multicultural education

98 Hager Daun, 'Religious Education and Islam in Europe', in D.B. Holsinger and W.J. Jacob (eds.), *Inequality in Education: Comparative and International Perspectives*, Comparative Education Centre, 2009, 348–368 at 348.
99 Daun (2009) at 348.
100 Daun (2009) at 349.
101 The English example discussed in Chapter 6 is indicative here.
102 Daun (2009) at 352.
103 See Chapter 2 of this book.
104 Daun (2009) at 353 claims that there is a clear division in Europe, for example, where the elite demands secular-oriented education while the lower classes and minorities see education as a moral-religious training project.

is growing.[105] The expansion of Muslim 'faith schools', in particular for instance, illustrates the expression of the perceived lack by parents of morals and values education and/or discrimination and racism experienced in state schools as well as a lack of multicultural and multi-religious training.[106]

Despite the variety of approaches to teach religion, that range from education 'in' religion (in decline), to educating 'about' religion or learning 'from' religion, it has been observed that the contents of education are largely regulated in the form of core curriculum frameworks. This does not mean, however, that this framework of 'core' knowledge is uniformly or consistently taught, even within the same public educational system. The same applies for teachers' agency that due to its individuality determines also how core curricula are implemented.

The availability of private (i.e. non-state) religious schools is also a crucial variable in the assessment of religious diversity in public school systems: according to Daun,[107] private religious education is shaped in relation to a series of factors such as whether compulsory education is allowed to take place in non-approved private schools, whether private schools are subsidized/controlled/inspected, whether these schools are under the obligation to teach the core curriculum, whether students obtain a valid certification upon completion of their study programme and, finally, whether religion is even part of the curriculum. In such a context, the issue of State subsidies remains particularly controversial, especially when the State gives financial support without a corresponding duty to control the content of education provided.[108] In general terms, however, subsidies vary and, in many cases, cover teachers' salaries, school premises offered rent-free, or lump sum payments per student.[109]

And what about social cohesion? Is social cohesion threatened by religion being taught in public schools? On one side, religious education is based on the need to develop further one's confidence in one's religious identity, while reminding that contact with children of different cultural and religious backgrounds is not enough to eradicate prejudice. To push the argument further, the State and its educational system having failed to combat racism and encourage societal cohesion, appear to indirectly incite parents to turn to alternative types of schooling.

On the other side, however, is the argument that religion in public schools is redundant by virtue of secularization. By extension, the claim that 'faith schools' create and maintain artificially closed spaces is recurring. Yet both elements may

---

105 Both the cases of Israel and England clearly show this trend.
106 Daun (2009) at 354. This can be contrasted with parents who privilege human capital preferences over religious preferences but still choose 'faith schools' due to their academic excellence and results.
107 Daun (2009) at 356.
108 See Chapter 4 on ultra-Orthodox Jewish schools in Israel and state funding as an example.
109 Daun (2009) at 357.

also counter the marginalization experiences for a number of religious minority groups in the broader society. Ultimately, to the extent that discrimination may be connected to under-achievement in State schools,[110] it is still debatable whether exposure to a single religious identity is sufficient to give a coherent vision of the world with reasonable anti-discrimination impact.[111]

110 A. Pilkington, 'Racism in Schools and Ethnic Differentials in Educational Achievement: A Brief Comment on a Recent Debate', *British Journal of Sociology of Education*, 20(3), 1999, 411–417.
111 The cases of privileging of single-sex religious schools for one's education principally because they are single-sex on the basis of a perceived religious/cultural requirement, irrespectively of the quality of education provided is a point of contention. Shah and Iqbal (2011, at 764) in the case of girls-only Muslim schools in the UK posit that a vast array of considerations dictate that choice of education such as "cultural determinants, social manipulations, gender discrimination, economic priorities, religious interpretations and simple pragmatics, to vested interests, and many others".

8 Legal empowerment through religious diversity in schools

1 Religion in education: a shifting agenda

Current aims of the role and position of religious education in public schools at the global scale are still lingering between transmitting or instructing a specific religious system of faith and responding to the challenges of globalization and super-diversity in more holistic terms. The example of the recent *Guidelines for Teaching about Religion* developed by the American Academy of Religion is telling:

> enhancing literacy about religion . . . can enrich civic dimensions of education and promote respect for diversity, peaceful coexistence, and cooperative endeavors in local, national and global arenas.[1]

In other words, the constitutionally declared secular States are presently realizing the need to move beyond the mere acknowledgement of the relevance of religion to more pro-active attempts to control and/or at least influence prevalent discourses on religions as they are connected to religious diversity management.[2] This process is spearheaded considerably by the presence of religious institutions as actors within and outside the education system. For education, this translates into attempts to influence and even control in some cases how beliefs and traditions are taught (e.g. through textbooks) with the broader intention to construct positive imagery of certain faiths.[3]

The path from a "laïcité of ignorance" to a "laïcité of intelligence",[4] if not religious literacy, relies on three essential requirements: first, the need for

---

1 National Endowment for the Humanities, Religious Worlds of New York; Teaching the Everyday Life of American Religious Diversity, available at www.religiousworldsnyc.org as quoted in A. Barb, 'Governing Religious Diversity in a (Post)Secular Age: Teaching About Religion in French and American Public Schools', *Theo-Web*, 16(2), 2017, 204–222 at 209.
2 Barb (2017) at 210.
3 Barb (2017) at 215.
4 Both terms belong to Régis Debray, *L'Enseignement du fait religieux dans l'école publique*, Paris: Report to the Minister for National Education, 2002.

learners to engage with their own religious heritage, second, a better understanding of religious identity politics and, finally, the preparation to live in diverse societies.[5]

Post 9/11, Habermasian post-secular consciousness seems to be connected at present explicitly with religious literacy as a civic skill designed to build 'global citizens' able to comprehend and negotiate differences. The English and South African case studies analyzed in previous chapters are moving towards a more pluralistic model of religious education with growing comparative and non-devotional elements in the study of religion and religious ethics. This move towards religious culture and ethics training is not, however, without obstacles, essentially because it cannot be value-free and thus will be contested, at least by some.

a Education as development: globalizing and transnational dimensions

Education remains a dominant variable in the determination of both individual but also collective economic growth. The general tendency at present is for states to embrace the internationalization of both education theory and education systems, understanding that globalization and educational reform are interrelated.[6] Transnational funding (e.g. through the World Bank) has been distributed within that spirit, although not without criticism.[7]

This movement has been 'translated' into a corresponding "astonishing processes of global alignment"[8] among education systems that follow a pattern characterized by: "a standardized model of schooling that is strongly institutionalized, with funding and control exercised by the state, organized in terms of levels and courses of study and end-of-stage examination . . . and with government regulations of teaching and learning through syllabi, examinations, etc."[9] These processes of 'global alignment' do not account for national contexts, parental preferences or teachers' agency.

In an opposite direction, hybridity, however, among the types of schools but also among the discourses used within them, as the cases of Israel, South Africa and the UK revealed, suggest a corresponding plurality in the functions and approaches that these schools undertake towards religious diversity promotion.

---

5 Barb (2017) at 207.
6 John Trevitt Scott and Ann Cheryl Armstrong, 'Faith-Based Schools and the Public Good: Purposes and Perspectives', Paper presented at the AARE Annual Conference, Melbourne, 2010, 1–13, at 4.
7 Scott and Armstrong (2010) at 4.
8 J. Schriewer, 'Worldsystem and Interrelationship Networks: The Internationalization of Education and the Role of Comparative Inquiry', in T.S. Popkewitz (ed.), *Educational Knowledge: Changing Relationships Between State, Civil Society, and the Educational Community*, State University of New York Press, 2000, 305–343 at 313.
9 Scott and Armstrong (2010) at 4.

Depending on how each school positions itself vis-à-vis itself, the wider community or particular faith communities, it may choose to prioritize different tasks: fostering expressions of personal beliefs, shaping identities as they emerge through the commitments of each community and the individuals who belong to it, creating social bonds and networks, forming moral discourses, promoting civic engagement and political participation and providing social services, collaborating with or replacing the State.[10] The two parallel yet apparently contradictory processes of the local and the international understandings of the role of education are not, however, mutually exclusive but are instead parts of a synthetic transnational, more globalized comprehension of religious diversity management within societies characterized by multiple modernities.

This transnational layer of normativity for the purposes of the present analysis means first, the need to account for non-state laws (particularly religious norms) in education as connected to the expansion of religions through immigration,[11] and second, a diversified understanding of the role and agency of religious organizations in shaping religion within education both directly (i.e. jointly with the State) or indirectly (i.e. for example, within independent religious educational establishments).

An overarching element from the case studies is the relevance of emerging religious diversity agendas in schools for purposes of social cohesion. In all three cases examined, public schools face, to varying degrees, segregation, due among others to factors such as residence, the public/private divide, ethnicity, social class, access rules and parents' preferences. While it has not been the aim here to provide a hierarchy among these factors, it is worth wondering whether it is religious belonging that perpetuates educational segregation or rather other factors such as the exercise of parental choice as influenced by socio-economic criteria.[12] What should rather have been retained as the predominant criterion of assessment is the content and level of the learners' religious diversity training.[13]

b 'Faith schools': religious communities' agency in action

A pertinent example of how religious freedom is exercised through public education is to be found in the expansion of 'faith schools'. Schools with a distinct religious ethos flourish,[14] reflecting the willingness of religious communities to educate their children according to their religious beliefs, with the support of international human rights law.[15]

---

10 Scott and Armstrong (2010) at 5.
11 On this point see William Twinning 'Normative and Legal Pluralism: A Global Perspective', *Duke Journal of Comparative and International Law*, 2010, 473–518, at 506.
12 Scott and Armstrong (2010) at 7
13 Scott and Armstrong (2010) at 7.
14 See the cases of Israel and the UK as discussed in Chapters 4 and 6.
15 See Chapter 3 for more on this point.

'Faith schools' are increasing their share of the educational market, as previously noted.[16] The reasons and rationale behind the increase are largely attributed to academic standards and quality of teaching but also to the values upheld by each respective school.[17] Their increase is also not completely detached from a personalized approach of learners to religious education which is individualistic, with the notable exception, however, of learners coming from conservative religious backgrounds where religion is adopted in its entirety.

Miedema identifies three types of religious (denominational) schools: the 'segregated' ones that cultivate an absolute and homogenous kind of belief combined with a missionary message; the 'programme' ones, where it belongs to the discretion of the teachers to define the religious position of the school through an educationally justifiable programme; and finally, the 'encounter' schools, where the school is more open to religions, including when recruiting teachers and learners not adhering to the specific faith to which the school belongs.[18]

Parekh summarized well a number of advantages of this type of education by finding that 'faith schools' "instill a distinct set of moral and cultural sensibilities, increase the available range of educational options, add to the variety of collective life by producing citizens with different characters and perspectives on life, respect the wishes of parents, prevent the State from acquiring a monopoly of education and exercising total control over its content".[19] The reverse arguments link 'faith schools' with concerns over "social segregation, reported 'parallel lives' between different ethnic and faith groups, violent terrorism carried out in the name of religion, and ongoing discussion about the proper relationship between religion and the state",[20] with clear implications for increased social conflict and division.

Ultimately, the terms of the debate on 'faith schools' pose real questions on the role of the State, on the aims of faith education, on the nature and distinction between education and indoctrination and, more broadly, on their compatibility

---

16 Apart from the cases mentioned in this book, see, for instance, the case of Australia as discussed in Philip Hughes, 'The Future of Religious Education in the Context of Postmodernity', in M. de Souza et al. (eds.), *International Handbook of the Religious, Moral and Spiritual Dimensions in Education*, 349–362, Springer, 2009.

17 Hughes (2009) at 351.

18 Siebren Miedema, 'Education for Religious Citizenship: Religious Education as Identity Formation', in M. de Souza et al. (eds.), *International Handbook of the Religious, Moral and Spiritual Dimensions in Education*, Springer, 2009, 967–976 at 971–972.

19 Bhikhu Parekh, *Rethinking Multiculturalism, Cultural Diversity and Political Theory*, Macmillan, 2000, at 333.

20 R. Berkeley and S. Vij, 'Right to Divide? Faith Schools and Community Cohesion', *The Runnymede Trust*, London, 2008, 176, at 3. See also Will Kymlicka, 'Education for Citizenship', in M. Halstead and McLaughlin (eds.), *Education in Morality*, Routledge, 1999, 79–102 at 88, arguing that learners in 'faith schools' miss the opportunity to co-exist with those of different cultures and religions to their own.

with liberal values. [21] At the center of this debate one finds the questioning of the need and realistic potential for education towards 'good liberal' citizenry, linked to autonomy. Autonomy is understood here as 'self-knowledge, independence of thought, self-sufficiency, as responsibility for one's own actions, individual freedom and the worth of the individual as an individual'.[22] This type of consideration is typically, however, one premised on the Western state-focused approach to education. It can be contrasted with the end of education in Islam, for example, which is to produce a 'good man', not a 'good citizen'.

But how can the expansion of these schools then be explained in diverse geographical settings? The success of 'faith schools' is the result of multiple factors, including institutional goals and ethos, historical context, status of the school, as well as selection processes. Research on the reasons leading to the establishment of such schools, in particular the recent and very controversial wave of Muslim schools' creation in Europe,[23] suggests that these schools provide a culturally safe and familiar environment for their learners, especially when operating on the basis of minority faiths, and aim to improve the academic achievement and performance of their pupils.[24] From the perspective of parents who choose to send their children to such schools, the motivation is similar and multi-layered: concerns over academic results, over differing or even clashing values with the dominant state education approach, or over discrimination or issues of identity and belonging. Based on claims of equality of opportunities in and through education combined with the wish to exercise the right to identity and religious freedom, the normative connection with culturally relevant education is hard to miss.

---

21 The division between education and indoctrination is difficult to establish, as the aim of education is to inform and introduce a child into the beliefs and doctrines of his/her social environment. [Cf. R. Ameen and N. Hassan, 'Are Faith Schools Educationally Defensible?' *Teacher Education*, 3(1), 2013, 11–17, at 13.] Indoctrination, however, is based on a structured, hierarchical relation between 'teacher' and 'learner' resulting in a closed-minded belief. [Cf. R.M. Taylor, 'Indoctrination: A Renewed Threat to Autonomy in Today's Educational Environment', Stanford University, 2012, available at www.philosophy-of-education. org/uploads/papers/Taylor.pdf]. The setting and planning of the curriculum remains in principle within the competence of the State. In the European context, for example, Article 2 of Protocol 1 does not prevent states from including knowledge of a religious kind in their programmes of education. Parents may not object to such integration in the school curriculum on the basis that all teaching would be potentially indoctrinating. The State retains the obligation, however, to impart information in an objective, critical and pluralistic manner and not disrespect parents' religious and philosophical convictions. [Cf. Regina Valutyte and Dovilé Gailute, 'The Exercise of Religious Freedom in Educational Institutions in the Light of ECtHR Jurisprudence', *Wroclaw Review of Law, Administration and Economics*, 2(2), 2012, 45–62, at 47–48.

22 Ameen and Hassan (2013).

23 C. Hewer, 'Schools for Muslims', *Oxford Review of Education*, 27(4), 2001, 515–527.

24 For the UK, see indicatively also the policy of the New Labour Governments (1997–2010) that facilitated the creation of Muslim state schools in the interest of higher levels of academic achievement.

One of the most controversial aspects of faith school education concerns sex-segregation in these schools: single-sex schooling is a growing trend[25] and is often a conscious, religiously inspired choice. Along with this trend, however, a growing number of questions on this type of schooling have emerged. Does single-sex education affect learners' achievements? Do single-sex religious schools make a difference in attitude and/or attainment of learners? There is presently no firm evidence that single-sex schooling impacts directly on educational attainment.[26] Nor is there, incidentally, a clear causal link between attendance of religious schools and learners' degree of autonomy in thinking capabilities.

Overall, 'faith schools' appear to be sought after by parents as establishments of academic excellence as much as, in certain contexts, protection mechanisms of religious identity and against discrimination.[27] The complex balancing acts that individuals as learners, parents and educators are called to make between ethnic, religious and mainstream worldviews and ideologies justify the crucial dimensions of religious education in public schooling. At the same time, there is already a process underway where young religious individuals are encouraged to adjust their 'take' on religious self-identification, putting aside traditional affiliation in favor of positionality in civil society terms[28] and more selective approaches to belief. In that sense, the expectation from believers to adopt more critical approaches towards their own faith may indeed be moving the debate towards the replacement of multiculturalism with a social cohesion approach.[29]

Regardless of the specific national context, all of the different types of 'faith schools' carry a dual connection: one to the religious community to which they belong and one towards a wider system of education. Depending on their degree of affiliation with the community in question, oversight from religious authorities varies, as the three case studies explored show. The type of teachers and learners, along with the kind of school governance, the content of education and the school's values will be affected by this side of the connection. At the same time,

25 In the UK, 'faith schools' in the independent school sector amount for 20.9 per cent of the total number of schools and are becoming a more common arrangement for children between 7–11 years old. [Cf. Independent School Council, 'ISC Census 2013', available at www.isc.co.uk]

26 S. Shah and C. Conchar, 'Why Single-Sex Schools? Discourses of Culture/Faith and Achievement', *Cambridge Journal of Education*, 39(2), 2009, 191–204 at 199. See also A. Smithers and P. Robinson, *Co-education and Single-Sex Schooling-Revisited*, Brunel University, 1997, at 46–47.

27 Ansari in 2004 finds that schooling is "a major area of struggle for equality of opportunity and assertion of identity". [Cf. H. Ansari, *The Infidel Within: Muslims in Britain Since 1800*, London: C. Hurst and Co., 2004, at 298.]

28 For an example in the UK, see P. Thomas and P. Sanderson, 'Unwilling Citizens? Muslim Young People and National Identity', *Sociology*, 45(6), 2011, 1028–1044; or for an example in Central and Eastern Europe, see also K. Topidi, 'Religious Freedom, National Identity, and the Polish Catholic Church: Converging Visions of Nation and God', *Religions*, 10, 2019, 293, available at www.mdpi.com/2077-1444/10/5/293.

29 N. Meer and T. Modood, 'The Multicultural State We're in: Muslims, "Multiculture" and the "Civic Re-balancing" of British Multiculturalism', *Political Studies*, 57, 2009, 473–497.

as part of a broader school system, these schools are also expected to subscribe to regulations, principles and values that govern the state system to the extent that they are mostly supported financially by the State. Constraints on staff qualifications, curriculum, educational and professional standards or equal opportunities are linked to this other side of the connection.[30]

2 Religious diversity in education within an empowerment frame

Based on Martha Nussbaum's conceptualization of 'human capabilities' as an approach to establish a threshold of social justice,[31] it becomes relevant to explore if and how religious diversity in education can contribute towards empowerment of learners. As exposed in previous chapters, pluralism and respect for difference are explicitly articulated in the legal frameworks studied. Yet, according to Nussbaum's capabilities frame, this is not sufficient: legal empowerment requires the material and institutional resources for right-holders to voice claims.[32] The right to education being a 'gateway' right towards further access to various other rights and liberties amplifies the relevance of this frame: the degree to which individual learners (and their families) are able to access their right to religious freedom in the public school system constitutes in itself a distinct political, social and legal project. Any socio-legal frame has to account also for differences due to natural endowment or power structures towards giving learners as believers a real choice in education.

The duty of the State to provide education therefore has a potentially strong impact in shaping capabilities to exercise rights, both during education years but also beyond. The relevance of education both for economic growth as well as political functioning is crucial towards empowerment.[33]

While interpretations of the rights to education and religion may differ on the understanding of their nature (individual vs. collective rights), on their function (constraints to state behavior or action-oriented) or on their ultimate aim (achieve well-being, realize goals, access resources), an empowerment agenda requires public policy to focus on all actors, including institutions that affect one's capability to access the rights at stake.[34] Public policy choices are highly contextual. In order to promote equality, however, it remains crucial for

---

30 For more on this point, see John Sullivan, 'Faith Schools: A Culture Within a Culture in a Changing World', in M. de Souza et al. (eds.), *International Handbook of the Religious, Moral and Spiritual Dimensions in Education*, Springer, 2009, 937–947, in particular 938–939.

31 Accepting at the same time that any notion of full capability equality is less realistic (M. Nussbaum, *Women and Human Development: The Capabilities Approach*, The Seeley Lectures, Cambridge: Cambridge University Press, 2000, at 12).

32 Nussbaum (2000) at 54.

33 Nussbaum (2000) at 90.

34 Nussbaum (2000) at 246.

learners to have options understood as possibilities to obtain culturally relevant education. In that respect, education not only functions as a source of skills and possibilities but also as a source of 'images of worth'[35] that also leads to empowerment.

The importance of this dual dimension for empowerment cannot be underestimated for religious minorities. Gary Becker, in his 1992 Nobel address, argued that "the beliefs of employers, teachers, and other influential groups that minority members are less productive can be self-fulfilling"[36] in the sense that vulnerable groups can and do internalize their second-class status in ways that force them to maintain this status. In addition, tradition and cultural settings often interfere with preference for basic liberties.[37] In fulfillment of the right to equality, if not of a right to difference, States therefore have a compelling interest to provide education that is conducive to active citizenship.[38] This cannot, nevertheless, justify unlimited interference with the parents' liberty to pursue education for their children according to their religious beliefs.

And yet, this does not preclude from a human rights perspective the right to live a traditional hierarchical life to the extent that alternative choices are also available. But because religious groups and practices are human phenomena,[39] and because religion should represent a matter of choice, the protection of religious belief occupies a firm position in the moral education of learners,[40] as a 'central vehicle of cultural continuity'.[41] It is also legally framed as the object of (limited) State protection[42] on the basis of autonomy and human dignity,[43] so as to avoid harm to others.

---

35 Expression borrowed from Nussbaum (2000) at 288.
36 Among vulnerable groups Becker includes blacks, women, religious groups, immigrants. (Cf. Gary Becker, 'The Economic Way of Looking at Behavior', in Ramon Febrero and Pedro Schwartz (eds.), *The Essence of Becker*, Hoover Institution Press, 1995, 633–658, at 634.
37 Nussbaum (2000) at 115.
38 See, for example, in *Wisconsin v. Yoder* (1972) 406 U.S. 205 the finding of the US Supreme Court that the State needs to have a "compelling interest" in preparing "citizens to participate effectively and intelligently in our open political system". Conversely, see the analysis on Israel in Chapter 4 of this book, in particular on the educational content of ultra-Orthodox schools.
39 Nussbaum (2000) at 238.
40 Nussbaum (2000) at 179.
41 Nussbaum (2000) at 180.
42 Nussbaum unambiguously finds that "no State can allow its citizenship to search for the ultimate meaning of life in any way they wish, especially when it involves harm to others". [Cf. Nussbaum (2000) at 180.]
43 Jacques Maritain expressed this point as follows: "There is real and genuine tolerance only when a man is firmly and absolutely convinced of a truth, or of what he holds to be a truth, and when he at the same time recognizes the right of those who deny this truth to exist, and to contradict him . . . not because they are free from truth but because they seek truth in their own way, and because he respects in them human nature and human dignity". Cf. Jacques Maritain, 'Truth and Human Fellowship', in *On the Uses of Philosophy: Three Essays*, Princeton University Press, 1961, at 24, as quoted in Nussbaum (2000) at 181.

In other words, learners should be enabled (in conjunction with their parents) to choose a way of life and learn in accordance with it. This choice should be coordinated with each learner's individual capabilities, irrespective of the fact that religious communities function on a relational and collective basis.[44] Any choice should therefore be tested at the individual level to confirm that it is consonant with the person's will (vis-à-vis its degree of voluntariness) and as such empowering to them.[45] This approach to legal empowerment on the basis of religious freedom exercise comes, however, at times at the cost of inequality in fact: inequality between religions seems almost inevitable when learners, for example, make exemption claims and are successful.

Ultimately, harmonizing religious pluralities in public education systems remains an essentially political process: the recognition of religious differences in the name of access to education and empowerment can produce consequences that are not necessarily desirable for all to the same degree. International human rights standards permit distinctions to be made on the basis of religion and culture. For those distinctions that constitute 'harmful practices',[46] however, with discriminatory effects,[47] reform or removal is recommended. An intersectional dimension of conflicts of rights, where rights ought to be 'balanced' adds a different, more complex dimension: in scenarios of conflict of rights, often connected to contexts of plural legal orders, international human rights law advises their 'enjoyment in totality',[48] in indivisible terms in order to avoid the fragmentation of one's identity. As seen, nevertheless, in the preceding chapters on the individual national contexts, this indivisibility rarely is applied on the ground.

So how does one then assess claims to religious difference articulated in human rights terms? Empirically, this can only happen in contextual terms focusing on the impact of one's choice.[49]

---

44 Nussbaum (2000) at 188.
45 The learner's (child's) age of consent is a grey zone in international human rights law. See Chapter 3 for more on this point.
46 The term is a carefully nuanced condemnation of discriminatory practices connected to certain aspects of culture and/or religion and appears, for example, in the Protocol to the African Charter on Human and People's Rights on the Rights of Women in Africa.
47 For examples see International Council on Human Rights (ICHR), *When Legal Worlds Overlap: Human Rights, State and Non-State Law*, 2009, available at http://www.ichrp.org/files/reports/50/135_report_en.pdf.
48 See, for example, the Human Rights Council General Comment No. 28 on Equality of Rights Between Men and Women (at para. 2). Most debates in this specific frame relate to the clash between religion/ethnicity and gender.
49 This point echoes the work of Karima Bennoune, 'Secularism and Human Rights: A Contextual Analysis of Headscarves, Religious Expression and Women's Equality Under International Law', *Columbia Journal of Transnational Law*, 45(2), 2007 at 393, 396. In connection to Muslim veiling, she puts forward the following factors of assessment: impact of the veil on other women (and girls) in the same environment; coercion; gender discrimination; violence against women related to the specific situation; motivations behind any imposed restriction; religious discrimination and Islamophobia; alternatives to restriction; the human rights consequences of both the restriction and non-restriction; the degree of consultation with the impacted communities.

a Religious identity-building as empowerment

One of the main aims of education is for learners to develop the capacity to reflect on their own identity.[50] Within that process, diversity is not antithetical to identity, given the multiple identities of children sitting in contemporary public classrooms. In terms of religion and religious education, this identity-building process connects well with multi-faith religious education based on a 'conversational' mode of religious education.[51] It also echoes the need for 'interaction in diversity'[52] as a means to reach autonomous and responsible interpretation, agency and ultimately empowerment, based on respect for the 'Other'.

Aiming for the flourishment of the *homo interagens*,[53] religious identity becomes in such a context interpretation, enabling both teachers and learners to overcome stereotypes while thinking critically about religion, culture or race/ethnicity. The aim for societal harmony within such an approach is hard to ignore.[54] It brings to the surface the question of how the State should be perceived by learners in order to enhance such an outcome: within religious education, the State should be critically conceived as "something less than the ultimate arbiter of justice and the seat of ultimate loyalty", yet something "more than a temporary instrument that is blocking human unity".[55] In such a frame, teachers of religion have to bypass considerable obstacles: that of interpreting religion in a pluralistic context and that of forging a shared understanding of religion when there is none. [56] At the same time, to implement an interpretative approach in their teaching of religion, a number of essential components are also required:[57] first, the maximum levels of freedom of belief should be pursued for all actors involved (teachers, learners, parents, the State/local authority, religious organizations). Connected to this first element is a second requirement for tolerance, understood as the recognition and acceptance of those whose beliefs are different, even incompatible with

50 Wilna A.J. Meijer, 'Plural Selves and Living Traditions: A Hermeneutical View of Identity and Diversity, Tradition and Historicity', in M. de Souza et al. (eds.), *International Handbook of the Religious, Moral and Spiritual Dimensions in Education*, Springer, 2009, 321–332, at 322.

51 Meijer (2009) at 322.

52 Expression borrowed from Meijer (2009) at 325.

53 Expression borrowed from Meijer (2009) at 325.

54 See, for example, Eleanor Nesbitt, 'Ethnography, Religion and Intercultural Education', in M. de Souza et al. (eds.), *International Handbook of the Religious, Moral and Spiritual Dimensions in Education*, Springer, 2009, 387–398, at 387.

55 Gabriel Moran, 'Religious Education and the Nation-State', in M. de Souza et al. (eds.), *International Handbook of the Religious, Moral and Spiritual Dimensions in Education*, Springer, 2009, 41–50, at 42.

56 Andrew Wright, 'Critical Realism as a Tool for the Interpretation of Cultural Diversity in Liberal Religious Education', in M. de Souza et al. (eds.), *International Handbook of the Religious, Moral and Spiritual Dimensions in Education*, Springer, 2009, 333–347, at 333.

57 The list of elements is taken form Wright (2009) at 334–335. Wright mentions also a fourth element: the pursuit of truth and truthful living.

one's own. It is this recognition of difference that lays the foundation for a third component, which is the presence of reasoned debate and interaction.

In terms of educational aims, religious education or teaching about religion[58] in public schools towards empowerment can target three principal objectives: a better understanding of religious culture or access to cultural heritage (in the case of teaching about religion), the development of an education of tolerance and the acquisition of an understanding of the contemporary highly diverse world.[59] If "faith is no longer socially given, but must be individually achieved",[60] a further adjusted aim of religious education becomes the need to foster 'multiple cultural competence'.[61] The adjustment required is to make space for a better understanding of how local, national and global religious and cultural networks have claimed a share of the space that learners occupy in society.[62]

Equivalent processes have already been described in educational studies for a longer period. The education discipline has confirmed since the 1980s that in religious education the current focus is shifting towards teaching world religions.[63] The implication of this agenda is that religious plurality as a teaching principle is moving to the mainstream but also that secularity and non-belief are gradually losing their predominance. These evolutions are in contrast to the one happening in the legal discipline, where the protection of belief and non-belief are still considered through the prism of secularity and state neutrality, at least from a human rights perspective.

From an empowerment perspective, the aim of religious education, similar to education in general, is to enhance conscious participation in the process of identity construction.[64] To do so, methodological pluralism in providing such education cannot be excluded but rather needs to be encouraged. A rights-based approach to religious freedom in education dictates the entitlement of parents

---

58 According to Estivalezes, 'teaching about' religion suggests an academic approach to religion that relies only on knowledge that can be observed (e.g. Buddhism arrived in Japan in the 19th century). It considers religion part of culture but reduces it to expressions of religion in architecture, art, rites or social gatherings without consideration of its symbolic/spiritual dimensions (Cf. Mireille Estivalezes, 'Teaching About Religion at School in France', in M. de Souza et al. (eds.), *International Handbook of the Religious, Moral and Spiritual Dimensions in Education*, Springer, 2009, 475–486, at 475.

59 Estivalezes (2009) at 479–480.

60 P. Berger, B. Berger and H. Kellner, *The Homeless Mind: Modernisation and Consciousness*, Vintage Books, 1973, at 81.

61 Robert Jackson and Eleanor Nesbitt, *Hindu Children in Britain*, Trentham Books, 1993.

62 For a concrete example, see Sissel Ostberg, 'Islamic Nurture and Identity Management: The Lifeworld of Muslim Children and Young People in Norway', in M. de Souza et al. (eds.), *International Handbook of the Religious, Moral and Spiritual Dimensions in Education*, Springer, 2009, 501–512.

63 Geier Skeie, 'Plurality and Pluralism in Religious Education', in M. de Souza et al. (eds.), *International Handbook of the Religious, Moral and Spiritual Dimensions in Education*, Springer, 2009, 307–319, at 308. See also Chapter 6 in this book.

64 Skeie (2009) at 316.

to bring up their children according to their religious beliefs. But, as was shown, this entitlement can be misused by fundamentalist religious groups to assert and attempt to impose their vision of the 'good life' in a polity or social context. It can also be used by political actors to mask discrimination on the basis of race/ethnicity.[65] Religious education, therefore, often becomes a decisive tool to influence politics. A counterweight to this danger can be the enhancement of the role of (religious) educators, who, through the provision of scientifically-based knowledge and careful methodological interventions, can (re)launch the workings of the empowerment processes within modern pluralist societies.

With pluralism thus acquiring a normative dimension,[66] as a value to be pursued, it becomes less clear how its pursuit can be neatly divided between education (at school) and private life (in the family).[67] Learning being both a social and a cognitive process,[68] it has to rely on the inevitability of religious diversity, using education for learners to learn to co-exist and cultivate rational and critical thinking.[69] Yet if traditional religious bases of authority are continuously challenged, accepting that religion as identity is individualized and privatized probably reflects only a Western-centric view of the issue. The Global South in its own variations reveals also the parallel collective dimension of religion in education.

Particularly for religious minorities, and in reaction to secularist approaches to religion, a trend has been developing where by virtue of religious individualization, particularly in constitutionally declared secular States, religious identity is also (if not primarily) formed informally and transmitted at home and in strictly religious education contexts (e.g. mosques), not public schools. The privatization of religious education (through religious weekend schools, private home classes or attendance at 'faith schools') confirms the expansion of religious identity outside the secular public school context. This dimension also needs to be taken into account by both the State as well as by educators and policy-makers. Additionally, to the different options of religious education currently on offer, one can also add how, by socialization at school and through the use of the media and the digital world, religious identity is further transformed. This transformation is not necessarily happening in the direction of cultural clashes but more as a challenge to the development of 'multiple cultural competence'.[70] Formal schooling, as a result, risks becoming less relevant, to the extent that it does not acknowledge and participate in the process of religious identity formation through these additional channels.

---

65 Both points made in Skeie (2009) at 317.
66 A distinction can be made with 'plurality' noting merely the presence of diversity of religion in a given space (Cf. Skeie (2009) at 308–309).
67 Skeie (2009) at 309.
68 Skeie (2009) at 309.
69 This corresponds to Skeie's 'rationalist' attitude to socio-cultural plurality. See Skeie (2009) at 310–311.
70 Ostberg (2009) at 510.

b Religious education and citizenship – plurality as opportunity

The overview of the patterns of religious diversity management in Israel, South Africa and England confirm that it is both individual and broader institutional choices that shape outcomes in religious diversity promotion within public schools.

Schools 'choose' learners just as parents 'choose' schools, resulting in more (or less) ethnically mixed schools. The implementation of religious diversity frameworks in schools both within the public as well as the private sectors of education demonstrates how parents, teachers, communities and religious organizations shape education along ethno-religious communitarian terms.[71]

For religious minority groups, the challenges of affirmation of religious identity operate on two levels: first, when their religious identity is perceived as a 'negative' difference through stigma, prejudice, exclusion and/or discrimination; and second, on the level of their own sense of religious identity, which constantly evolves.[72] These two broad sets of parameters constitute key entry points for religious diversity management in public education.

What about national identity? A pluralized conception of national identity, in terms of 'rethinking the national story', in the direction of readjusting one's vision of what is the whole in which difference is to be integrated,[73] could be another starting point in reviewing the role of religious identity in public schools. The South African example represents one such attempt to 'rebuild the nation' under the umbrella concept of diversity. A priori an inclusive concept, diversity as State policy remained incomplete as a result of the element of religious (and cultural) difference being left outside the public sphere. Similarly, in the UK context, the process of rethinking 'Britishness' has been mitigated by majoritarian claims and immigration fears (with Brexit being a troubling illustration).

At the same time, at the global level, there is a tendency within public education systems to marginalize religious education, replacing it with teaching that focuses on citizenship, cohesion and culture or ethics.[74] The underlying assumption (yet again) in such a shift is that religion is a purely private matter (e.g. as in South Africa). The contemporary features of public faith in relation to citizenship seem paradoxical: on the one hand, faith communities and their members adopt an active approach to citizenship through volunteering, social action and

---

71 Tariq Modood, 'Multiculturalism and Integration: Struggling with Confusion', EUI RSCAS Accept Pluralism, 2011, at 2, available at www.coe.int/t/dg4/cultureheritage/mars/source/resources/references/others/38%20-%20Multiculturalisme%20and%20Integration%20-%20Modood%202011.pdf.
72 Modood (2011) at 5.
73 Modood (2011) at 10.
74 Adam Dinham, 'Public Religion in an Age of Ambivalence: Recovering Religious Literacy After a Century of Secularism', in Lori G. Beaman and Leo Van Arragon (eds.), *Issues in Religion and Education: Whose Religion?* Leiden: Koninklijke Brill, 2015, 17–33, at 17.

participation in community governance.[75] The public presence of faith groups signals a transfer of state duties, in particular welfare and education, to non-state actors,[76] at times where belief, at least in a European context, is much less formal. On the other hand, religion is perceived as a cause of division and conflict within government policies, including in public education.

Quite commonly, public schools choose to approach religious diversity as a requirement to primarily escape litigation.[77] The implication of such an approach restricts the conception of equality to a compliance factor, without accounting for broader social justice and intersectional human rights concerns. In parallel, the other recurring dimension of public education in relation to religious education insists on replacing religion with citizenship, values or culture education.[78] The Canadian, Australian and, in some cases, the continental European public education systems promote explicitly an understanding of religious diversity that aims to connect across difference in response to growing religious diversity.[79] The underlying aim is to produce citizens who are tolerant. Yet more than tolerance is required to encourage informed engagement in society: future citizens need to appreciate the rich variety of lived religion, as identity, (contested) tradition and even daily experience. The current state of socio-legal scholarship is lacking the necessary tools to fully reflect on this kind of education: little in terms of up-to-date data, teaching that avoids engagement with one's own prejudice and an assumption of religion as 'a thing of the past' are a few of the obstacles.[80]

Yet religious education can fulfill an essential social function that impacts the creation of solid ground towards the recognition of the 'right to be different': it connects across difference.[81] The skills required to engage with ideas and concepts different to those one holds render religious education also potentially useful towards the cultivation of tolerant citizenship, although more than understanding differences is needed to create the conditions for tolerance and respect to flourish.[82] So, if more than understanding religions is called for, the contents of religious education programmes should focus on teaching learners to engage with prejudice, including their own. They should also focus on real, lived experienced characteristics of religions as an integral part of education as well as an essential component of one's identity.[83]

---

75 Adam Dinham and Stephen H. Jones, 'Religion, Public Policy and the Academy: Brokering Public Faith in a Context of Ambivalence?' *Journal of Contemporary Religion*, 27(2), 2012, 185–201, at 186.
76 Dinham (2015) 8–23, at 7 discussed the spheres of activity that faith groups have captured.
77 Dinham and Jones (2012) at 193 argue this for higher education institutions in Britain, yet the case studies of the UK and South Africa in this book also point in this direction for primary and secondary education.
78 Dinham (2015).
79 Dinham (2015) at 17.
80 Dinham (2015) at 18.
81 Dinham (2015) at 17.
82 Dinham (2015) at 17.
83 Dinham (2015) at 18.

To reach the ambitious goals of accepting that a right to difference exists in both social and legal terms, it is essential to acquire religious literacy. According to Dinham and Shaw, "literacy in religion is about an understanding of the grammars, rules, vocabularies and narratives underpinning religions and beliefs".[84] Among the cases surveyed within previous chapters, it has emerged that not only is religious literacy required towards democratic citizenship within multicultural societies, but also it is a quality in public education that is in fact lacking.

As the religious landscape is rapidly changing on a global scale, and with it the content of our beliefs, too,[85] teaching about religion is currently not reflecting the evolution of the real world. The role of the public school is crucial in this debate, when designed to serve an integrative function in society by educating the future citizens.[86] Its mission in multicultural settings has moved beyond the creation of a national identity as its sole purpose, although a number of public education systems still place disproportionate emphasis on this task.[87] With religion occupying an increasing proportion of the public domain, in direct connection with Casanova's "deprivitization" theory,[88] schools are called to address the concern of preparing learners for the encounter with the religious and cultural 'Other'. The task is certainly complex, not least because postmodern religiosity is diffuse and, in the Global North, unambiguously individual-centered.[89]

Assuming, therefore, that public schools function as "mediating institutions"[90] in the production of religious, cultural and ultimately social meaning, religious literacy and education "can free students from a fixation on patterns of mere conventional ritual behaviour . . . and from stigmatizing the cultural and religious ideas, habits and practices of others".[91] Active and dynamic citizenship presupposes more than 'neutral', descriptive information of religious worldviews.[92] This

---

84 Adam Dinham and Martha Shaw, 'Religious Literacy Through Religious Education: The Future of Teaching and Learning About Religion and Belief', *Religions*, 8, 2017, 119, at 1.
85 Dinham and Shaw (2017) at 2.
86 Siebren Miedema, 'Educating for Religious Citizenship: Religious Education as Identity Formation', in M. de Souza et al. (eds.), *International Handbook of the Religious, Moral and Spiritual Dimensions in Education*, Springer, 2009, 967–976, at 968.
87 Topidi (2019).
88 See, for example, Jose Casanova, 'Public Religions Revisited', Keynote Speech at the International Conference "Religion Revisited—Women's Rights and the Political Instrumentalisation of Religion" ', Heinrich-Böll-Foundation and United Nations Research Institute for Social Development (UNRISD), 5–6 June 2009, Berlin, available at www.gwi-boell.de/sites/default/files/assets/gwi-boell.de/images/downloads/Religion_Revisited_Keynote_Casanova_June2009.pdf
89 Miedema (2009) at 970.
90 Term borrowed from Miedema (2009) at 973.
91 Miedema (2009) at 973.
92 This is translated as the need to combine educational approaches based both on 'learning about religion' and 'learning from religion'. Cf. Clive Erricker, 'Religious Education and Spiritual Development: Pedagogical Insufficiency and Possibility', in M. de Souza et al. (eds.), *International Handbook of the Religious, Moral and Spiritual Dimensions in Education*, Springer, 2009, 697–715, at 699.

is especially relevant for both individual as well as group identity formation processes, which inherently require negotiation with the perspective of 'Others'.

As far as the connection between democracy and religion is concerned, there is a growing movement that claims that religion can act as a supporting element to democracy in its quest for legitimacy.[93] With the central value in democracies now becoming pluralism – instead of tolerance – religion becomes by extension a tool for personal growth that can be mobilized in the educational process, including within State schools. In other words, if we accept that religion is relativized in the direction of legitimizing other beliefs, then it becomes conceivable to claim that belief also becomes more democratic.[94]

In the same direction, citizenship education must also extend to conflict education and conflict management training in order to address the conflicts of legitimacies and norms,[95] whenever they occur both in public classrooms but also later in the learners' lives, in line with a broader deliberative conception of democracy. In such a frame, citizenship education, constructed through religious education, can aim, according to Ouellet, to contribute to the cultivation of the following crucial values: the preservation of cultural diversity; the adaptation of institutions to diversity in all of its forms; social cohesion in a context of pluralist values; the critical participation in society and in democratic deliberations; equality and equity; solidarity with oppressed groups; and the preservation of biological diversity and sustainable development.[96]

In that light, religious education becomes more educational rather than religious, opening new pathways to reach the public space.[97] More than that, it claims the function to cultivate cosmopolitan identity in learners who will face in a globalized world "economic realities, social processes, technological and media innovations, and cultural flows that traverse national boundaries".[98]

Especially when adopting methodological reflexivity in religious education, learners can acquire their own agency as they undertake dialogues between them, between them and their teachers or even between them and the materials studied. This type of agency leads us back to the connections of religion with power. Against a learning environment that is often characterized by competing equalities, religions ultimately become both 'possession' and 'process' in education:

---

93 See, for example, Fernand Ouellet, 'Religious Education and Citizenship in Postmodern Societies', in M. de Souza et al. (eds.), *International Handbook of the Religious, Moral and Spiritual Dimensions in Education*, Springer, 2009, 363–374, at 367.
94 Ouellet (2009) at 368.
95 See the work in this respect of F. Galichet, 'L'education a la citoyennete', *Anthropos*, 1998, at 144 who advocates for a 'conflict pedagogy'.
96 Ouellet (2009) at 371.
97 Anne Looney, 'Religious Education in the Public Space: Challenges and Contestations', in M. de Souza et al. (eds.), *International Handbook of the Religious, Moral and Spiritual Dimensions in Education*, Springer, 2009, 949–966, at 950.
98 M.M. Suarez-Orozco and D.B. Qin-Hilliard, 'Globalisation: Culture and Education in the new millennium', in Suarez-Orozco and Qin-Hilliard (eds.), *Globalisation, Culture and Education in the New Millennium*, University of California Press, 2004, 1–31, at 5.

they bring to the fore cultural resources while encouraging the exploration of the individual dimension within the system of faith in itself. This kind of interpretive approach, as described in educational terms by Robert Jackson,[99] also requires comparison and contrast between the learner's own beliefs together with those of the 'Other' system she/he is studying.

The role and expectation from teachers within this process is not to have a given religious background but rather a positive attitude towards religious difference. This positive attitude can then be translated into a 'bridging' skill when comparing and contrasting one's own concepts with those of other religious experiences.[100] Awareness of beliefs and values contained in the religious experiences of learners increases the impact of teaching in a variety of directions including in citizenship and intercultural education. Towards this aim, it is not unreasonable to find that teachers are "potentially the single most important asset in the achievement of a democratically just learning society".[101] Not only for the implementation of any state religious diversity policy in public education, but well beyond that, teachers are asked to balance the need for a standardized system under pressure of requirements for accountability and measurable performance.

There is therefore a growing gap between the actual religious landscape of our societies and the one imagined by lawmakers, policy-makers and educators.[102] Setting aside, therefore, the quest for neutrality or state secularity as impossible tasks, the public visibility of faith begs a higher level of religious literacy. In many ways, the public sphere is shared between secularism, as a normative position, and a renewed kind of assertive religion. Constant change and fluidity have become the norm,[103] as spearheaded by globalization and transnationalization. The question that is posed as a next logical step in interdisciplinary terms is whether the intense presence of religion is only filling the void left by the State or whether it reflects more an autonomous phenomenon changing the public sphere in its own right.[104]

Faced with a process of de-formalization of religion,[105] the discourse within education on the cultivation of values, as a 'proxy' for religion,[106] points at a

---

99 Among others, see, for example, Robert Jackson, 'Understanding Religious Diversity in a Plural World: The Interpretive Approach', in M. de Souza et al. (eds.), *International Handbook of the Religious, Moral and Spiritual Dimensions in Education*, Springer, 2009, 399–414. Jackson identifies three aspects of reflexivity applicable to religious education: 'edification' (the review of the understanding of one's own way of life), the constructive critique of materials studied and the involvement in the review of the methods of study (Jackson (2009) at 403).

100 Jackson (2009) at 411.

101 Christopher Day, *A Passion for Teaching*, Routledge, 2004, at 9.

102 Dinham (2015) at 9.

103 Christopher Baker and Adam Dinham, 'New Interdisciplinary Spaces of Religions and Beliefs in Contemporary Though and Practice: An Analysis', *Religions*, 8, 2017, at 2.

104 Baker and Dinham (2017) at 5.

105 Baker and Dinham (2017) at 11.

106 Term borrowed from Baker and Dinham (2017) at 11.

misleading discussion on the ground (e.g. within education systems) on equality as a secular human rights principle (and idea), omitting its religious roots and its social embeddedness.[107]

3 Concluding remarks

It is clear from the analysis of the preceding case studies that in an area such as public education, it makes little practical sense to ignore the State, particularly given the fact that it is the primary duty bearer in relation to the right to education. The duty extends to protect and take action when a violation of the right occurs but also to prevent violations from occurring. Yet what is also emerging at the same time is how the local struggles for rights enforcement have appropriated not only the language of rights but also universal general human rights principles, often against the State and its interests. [108] This blurs the line between State and non-state legal orders and exposes the interaction between the two to power considerations.

For the cases examined here, it is also evident that recognition or incorporation of a non-state legal order is more a political than a legal act. While it may be connected to the principle of equality, paradoxically it asks for the recognition or acknowledgement of something that is not universally accepted.[109] Within education, the quest for religious difference cannot be absolute, but neither should be the tendency to advance de facto and de jure the majority religion/culture.

The right to education, freedom of religion and the principle of equality are highly dependent on how actors both in the Global North and the Global South contribute to their development. As such, they are constantly evolving. The content of the object of protection here – religious beliefs – is also affected and in turn influences the contours of the right. Crucial factors that are in operation are the prevailing relationships of power between the State and society but, as importantly, socio-economic factors such as poverty or scarce state resources. In that sense legal pluralism becomes even more relevant towards an empowerment analysis as it has expanded "from a concept that refers to the relations between the colonizer and colonized to relations between dominant groups and subordinate groups, such as religious, ethnic or cultural minorities, immigrant groups, and unofficial forms of ordering located in social networks and institutions".[110]

---

107 Natasha Bakht makes this point conversely by arguing that minority religious symbols worn in public are connected more to racism and poverty rather than deliberate lack of integration. See N. Bakht, 'Veiled Objections: Facing Public Opposition to the Niqab', in Lori Beaman (ed.), *Reasonable Accommodation: Managing Religious Diversity*, Vancouver: UBC, 2012, 70–108.

108 ICHR (2009) at v.

109 ICHR (2009) at viii. This point ties in with Habermas's call for a "universally convincing delineation of the borderline" of reciprocal religious toleration. In other words, the setting of 'universally accepted limits of tolerance'. See Juergen Habermas, 'Intolerance and discrimination', *ICON*, 1(1), 2003, 2–12, at 5.

110 Sally Engle Merry, 'Legal Pluralism', *Law and Society Review*, 22, 1998, 869–896 at 872.

When states choose to encourage plural legal orders through recognition, however, one needs to critically assess the State's withdrawal: saving state resources, hidden political motives or even the desire to perpetuate a community's socio-economic disadvantage are at times some of the grounds for such recognition.[111]

Transnationalization of law also contributes to the emergence of legal plurality: without assuming that as a process it advances equality, a State is now influenced not only by States and multilateral bodies but by non-state actors, leading for example to the flourishing of minority faith education institutions. It is hence more and more difficult to separate the local from the global: local actors through participation in transnational networks bring pressure from below and from without.[112] Coupled with globalization and pushed by the media and NGOs, often bypassing states, local cultures attempt to contest the universal.[113] The need for more religiously diverse environments then leads back to claims rooted in multiculturalist policies used as a means to govern multiethnic societies (e.g. as in the UK).

If legal empowerment is currently an integral part of development, within a 'good governance' framework, socio-political factors, such as community mobilization, matter. To the extent that the law on education and religious belief operates as an instrument of exclusion it becomes a peril: "the power of law as well as its attraction and danger lie in its ability to create and impose social reality, meanings and values, and eventually to make them appear natural and self-evident and thus uncontested".[114]

The link between religious difference and law therefore begs consideration of social location (e.g. in de facto segregated schools) as well as identity and values (e.g. core school curricula, values and methodology of teaching religion). Yet human rights are not a culture-free zone, as the case studies of this book have shown. Inversely, culture is compatible with human rights because 'modernity is also a cultural system'.[115] As explored, there are nevertheless a number of obstacles in reconciling the two: these are the fragmented development of legal standards, the perennial issue of balancing competing rights (e.g. religion versus equality) or the persisting reluctance of human rights systems to address culture.[116]

This analysis has also revealed a number of persisting 'grey' zones of regulation: a first example concerns the implications of State recognition for a plural legal order – does recognition signify ossification and stagnation for the religious

111 ICHR (2009) at 11.
112 ICHR (2009) at 12, 21. A good example in this context is the way in which religious fundamentalist groups have campaigned to include conservative norms in the public sphere by instrumentalizing 'strategic secularism' (i.e. the use of secular justification in the defense of religious worldviews).
113 ICHR (2009) at 24.
114 Rajendra Pradhan, 'Negotiating Multiculturalism in Nepal: Law, Hegemony, Contestation and Paradox', 2007, at 3, available at www.uni-bielefeld.de/midea/pdf/Rajendra.pdf.
115 Sally Engle Merry, 'Human Rights Law and the Demonization of Culture (and Anthropology Along the Way)', *Polar: Political and Legal Anthropology Review*, 26(1), 2003, 55–76.
116 ICHR (2009) at 27.

legal order? And to what extent are power disparities within the group accounted for? From the point of view of public education systems, it is still not clear, as faith groups adopt a vast variety of educational approaches when involved in state-sponsored education. The concern over redistribution of access to religiously relevant education in its socio-economic dimension also stands unsolved (e.g. see the case of black South Africans or of Arab Israelis).

A second, much broader gap, relates to the locus of power: who 'speaks for' any community and what are the State's motivations for its relationship with religious legal orders?[117] As often religion (also culture) and law are mobilized in support of political interests, it is essential to critically assess the claims for difference[118] in education as well as elsewhere. Ideally, "the goal of any public policy for the preservation of cultures must be the empowerment of members of cultural groups to appropriate, enrich, and even subvert the terms of their own cultures as they may decide".[119] Without participatory parity, however, this goal becomes unrealistic. More socially relevant religious education legal frameworks can contribute meaningfully towards the achievement of the 'right to be different'.

117 Both questions are addressed in ICHR (2009) at 89.
118 Recognition can serve as a discriminatory treatment to enforce communal boundaries (e.g. religious family law recognition in Israel). See ICHR (2009) at 96.
119 Seyla Benhabib, *The Claims of Culture: Equality and Diversity in the Global Era*, Princeton University Press, 2002, at 58.

References

Adams, Richard. 'OFSTED Finds Serious Failings at Private Faith Schools', *The Guardian*, 24 November 2015, available at www.theguardian.com/education/2015/nov/24/ofsted-finds-serious-failings-at-private-faith-schools

Adelman, Howard. 'Rights and the Hijab: Rationality and Discourse in the Public Sphere', *Human Rights and Human Welfare*, 8, 2008, 43–77

Agerholm, Harriet. 'Government Allows Faith Schools to Split in Two to Avoid Gender Segregation Law', *The Independent*, 11 November 2017, available at www.independent.co.uk/news/education/education-news/government-faith-school-split-hasmonean-high-al-hijrah-two-boys-girls-gender-segregation-law-jewish-a8042386.html

Alexander, H.A. 'Education in the Jewish State', in Ilan Gur-Ze'ev (ed.), *Conflicting Philosophies of Education in Israel/Palestine*, Dordrecht: Kluwer Academic Publishers, 2000, 129–145

Alexander, Wayne. 'Dealing with Diversity in the Classroom: Teachers' Perspectives', PhD Thesis, Faculty of Education and Social Sciences/Cape Peninsula University of Technology, 2009 [in file with the author]

Alibhai-Brown, Yasmin. 'After Multiculturalism', *The Political Quarterly*, 2001, 47–56

Almog, Shulamit and Perry-Hazan, Lotem. 'Contesting Religious Authoriality: The Immanuel "Beis Yaakov" School Segregation Case', *The International Journal for the Semiotics of Law*, 26(1), 2012, 211–225

Almog, Shulamit and Perry-Hazan, Lotem. 'The Ability to Claim and the Opportunity to Imagine: Rights Consciousness and the Education of Ultra-Orthodox Girls', *Journal of Law and Education*, 40(2), 2011, 1–31

Altinok, Nadir. 'The Hidden Crisis: Armed Conflict and Education', Paper commissioned for the Education for All Global Monitoring Report 2011, 2011/ED/EFA/MRT/PI/11, 2011, available at https://news.harvard.edu/wp-content/uploads/2016/02/190743e.pdf

Amaraa, Muhammed, Azaiza, Faisal, Hertz-Lazarowitz, Rachel and Mor-Sommerfeld, Aura. 'A New Bilingual Education in the Conflict-Ridden Israeli Reality: Language Practices', *Language and Education*, 23(1), January 2009, 15–35

Ameen, R. and Hassan, N. 'Are Faith Schools Educationally Defensible?' *Teacher Education*, 3(1), 2013, 11–17

Ammerman, Nancy T. 'The Challenges of Pluralism: Locating Religion in a World of Diversity', *Social Compass*, 57(2), 2010, 154–167

Amoah, Jewel and Bennett, Tom. 'The Freedoms of Religion and Culture Under the South African Constitution: Do Traditional African Religions Enjoy Equal Treatment?' *African Human Rights Journal*, 8, 2008, 357–375

Ansari, H. *The Infidel Within: Muslims in Britain Since 1800*, London: C. Hurst and Co., 2004

Anwarudding, Sardar M. and Gaztambide-Fernandez, Rubén A. 'Religious Pluralism in School Curriculum: A Dangerous Idea or a Necessity? *Curriculum Inquiry*, 45(2), 2015, 147–153

Appadurai, A. *Modernity at Large: Cultural Dimensions of Globalization*, Minneapolis: University of Minnesota Press, 1996

Arthurs, Harry W. 'Law and Learning in an Era of Globalization', *German Law Journal*, 10, 2009, 629

Asad, Talal. *Formations of the Secular: Christianity, Islam, Modernity*, Stanford: Stanford University Press, 2003

Augenstein, Daniel. 'The Contested Polity: Europe's Constitutional Identity Between Religious and Secular Values', University of Edinburg School of Law Working Paper Series, 2009/13

Bader, Veit. 'Post-Secularism or Liberal Democratic Constitutionalism? *Erasmus Law Review*, 5(1), 2012, 5–26

Baer, Susanne. 'A Closer Look at Law: Human Rights as Multi-Level Sites of Struggles Over Multi-Dimensional Equality', *Utrecht Law Review*, 6(2), 2010, 56–76

Baker, Christopher. 'Blurred Encounters? Religious Literacy, Spiritual Capital and Language', in A. Dinholm, R. Furbey and V. Lowndes (eds.), *Faith in the Public Realm*, Bristol: Policy Press, 2009, 105–122

Baker, Christopher and Dinham, Adam. 'New Interdisciplinary Spaces of Religions and Beliefs in Contemporary Though and Practice: An Analysis', *Religions*, 8(2), 2017, 16

Bakht, N. 'Veiled Objections: Facing Public Opposition to the Niqab', in Lori Beaman (ed.), *Reasonable Accommodation: Managing Religious Diversity*, Vancouver: UBC, 2012, 70–108

Ballard, Roger (ed.). *Desh Pardesh: The South Asian Presence in Britain*, London: Hurst & Co, 1994

Barb, A. 'Governing Religious Diversity in a (Post)Secular Age: Teaching About Religion in French and American Public Schools', *Theo-Web*, 16(2), 2017, 204–222

Barry, Brian. *Culture and Equality*, Cambridge, MA: Harvard University Press, 2001

Barzilai, Gad. 'Beyond Relativism: Where Is the Political Power in Legal Pluralism?' *Theoretical Inquiries in Law*, 9(2), 2008, 395–416

Basinger, David. 'Religious Diversity in Public Education', in Chad Meister (ed.), *The Oxford Handbook of Religious Diversity*, New York: Oxford University Press, 2011, 277–288

Batliwala, Srilatha. *When Rights Go Wrong—Distorting the Rights Based Approach to Development*, Harvard University: Hauser Center for Nonprofit Organizations, 2010, available at www.justassociates.org/WhenRightsGoWrong.pdf

Baxi, Upendra. 'The Colonialist Heritage', in Pierre Legrand and Roderick Munday (eds.), *Comparative Legal Studies: Traditions and Transitions*, Cambridge: Cambridge University Press, 2003, 46–75

BBC. 'Archbishop of Canterbury Defends Faith Schools', 4 May 2014, available at www.bbc.com/news/uk-27273053

BBC. 'Grammar Schools and Faith Schools Get Green Light to Expand', 11 May 2018, available at www.bbc.com/news/education-44067719

Becker, Gary. 'The Economic Way of Looking at Behavior', in Ramon Febrero and Pedro Schwartz (eds.), *The Essence of Becker*, Stanford: Hoover Institution Press, 1995, 633–658

Beckford, James A. 'Re-thinking Religious Pluralism', in G. Giordan and E. Pace (eds.), *Religious Pluralism*, New York: Springer, 2014, 15–29

Beckford, James A. 'The Return of Public Religion? A Critical Assessment of a Popular Claim', *Nordic Journal of Religion and Society*, 23(2), 2010, 121–136

Beckford, James A. and Richardson, James A. 'Religion and Regulation', in James A. Beckford and N. Jay Demerth III (eds.), *The Sage Handbook of the Sociology of Religion*, Los Angeles: Sage, 2007, 396–418

Beiter, Klaus Dieter. *The Protection of the Right to Education by International Law*, Leiden: Martinus Nijhoff Publishers, 2005

Benavot, Aaron and Resh, Nura. 'Educational Governance, School Autonomy, and Curriculum Implementation: A Comparative Study of Arab and Jewish Schools in Israel', *Journal of Curriculum Studies*, 35(2), 2003, 171–196

Benavot, Aaron and Resnik, Julia. 'Lessons from the Past: A Comparative Socio-Historical Analysis of Primary and Secondary Education', in Joel E. Cohen, David E. Bloom and Martin B. Malin (eds.), *Educating All Children: A Global Agenda*, Cambridge MA: MIT Press, 2006, 123–229

Bender, Courtney and Klasses, Pamela E. (eds.). *After Pluralism: Reimagining Religious Engagement*, New York: Columbia University Press, 2010

Benhabib, Seyla. *The Claims of Culture: Equality and Diversity in the Global Era*, Princeton, NJ: Princeton University Press, 2002

Bennett, Tom W. 'Law in the Face of Cultural Diversity: South Africa', in M-C. Foblets, J.F. Gaudreault-Des Biens and A. Duntes Renteln (eds.), *Cultural Diversity and the Law: State Responses from Around the World*, Bruxelles: Bruylant, 2010, 17–44

Bennoune, Karima. 'Secularism and Human Rights: A Contextual Analysis of Headscarves, Religious Expression and Women's Equality Under International Law', *Columbia Journal of Transnational Law*, 45(2), 2007, 367–426

Berger, Benjamin L. 'Polygamy and the Predicament of Contemporary Criminal Law', Research Paper Series on Comparative Research in Law and Political Economy, Osgoode Hall Law School, Research Paper No. 36/2012, available at http://ssrn.com/abstract=2081142

Berger, P., Berger, B. and Kellner, H. *The Homeless Mind: Modernisation and Consciousness*, New York: Vintage Books, 1973

Berkeley, R. 'The Runnymede Trust', 11, 2008, available at www.runnymedetrust.org/uploads/publications/pdfs/RightToDivide-2008.pdf/

Berkeley, R. and Vij, S. *Right to Divide? Faith Schools and Community Cohesion*, London: The Runnymede Trust, 2008

Berman, Harold. *The Interaction of Law and Religion*, Nashville & New York: Abingdon Press, 1974

Berman, Paul Schiff. 'Non-State Lawmaking Through the Lens of Global Pluralism', in Michael A. Helfand (ed.), *Negotiating State and Non-State Law: The Challenge of Global and Local Legal Pluralism*, Cambridge: Cambridge University Press, 2015, 15–40

Berman, Paul Schiff. *Global Legal Pluralism: A Jurisprudence of Law Beyond Borders*, New York: Cambridge University Press, 2012

Besson, Samantha. 'European Human Rights Pluralism: Notion and Justification', in M. Maduro, K. Tuori and S. Sankari (eds.), *Transnational Law: Rethinking European Law and Legal Thinking*, Cambridge: Cambridge University Press, 2014, 170–205

Blass, Nachum. 'The Academic Achievements of Arab Israeli Pupils', Taub Center for Social Policy Studies in Israel, Policy Paper No. 04/2017, available at http://taub center.org.il/wp-content/files_mf/academicachievementsofarabisraelipupils.pdf

Blass, Nachum. 'The Israeli Education System—State of the Nation Report 2018', Taub Center for Social Policy Studies in Israel, 2018, available at www.iataskforce. org/sites/default/files/resource/resource-1688.pdf

Blass, Nachum and Bleikh, Haim. *The Determinants of School Budgets: Per Class and Per Students*, Taub Center for Social Policy Studies in Israel, 2018, available at http://taubcenter.org.il/wp-content/files_mf/educationbudget2018en.pdf

Boeve, Lieven. 'Religious Education in a Post-Secular and Post-Christian Context', *Journal of Beliefs and Values*, 33(2), August 2012, 143–156

Boomgaarden, Hajo G. and Freire, André. 'Religion and Euroscepticism: Direct, Indirect or No Effects?' *West European Politics*, 32(6), November 2009, 1240–1265

Bottoni, Rossella, Cristofori, Rinaldo and Ferrari, Silvio (eds.). *Religious Rules, State Law and Normative Pluralism—A Comparative Overview*, Cham, Switzerland: Springer, 2016

Bourdieu, Pierre. *Language and Symbolic Power*, Cambridge, MA: Harvard University Press, 1991

Bourke Martignoni, Joanna. *Echoes from a Distant Shore: The Right to Education in International Development*, Zurich: Schulthess—Editions Romandes, 2012

Bowen, J.R. *Islam, Law and Equality in Indonesia: An Anthropology of Public Reasoning*, Cambridge: Cambridge University Press, 2003

Brown, Wendy. *Regulating Aversion: Tolerance in the Age of Identity and Empire*, Princeton and Oxford: Princeton University Press, 2008

Bryan, Hazel. 'Reconstructing the Teacher as a Post Secular Pedagogue: A Consideration of the New Teachers' Standards', *Journal of Beliefs and Values*, 33(2), 2012, 217–228

Busby, Eleanor. 'Faith Schools: Complaints Over Admission Rise as Number of Selective Religious Schools Set to Increase', *The Independent*, 26 February 2018, available at www.independent.co.uk/news/education/education-news/faith-school-admissions-selective-conservatives-cap-a8225796.html

Çali, Basak. 'Balancing Human Rights? Methodological Problems with Weights, Scales and Proportions', *Human Rights Quarterly*, 29, 2007, 251–270

Campbell, Angela. 'Wives Tales: Reflecting on Research in Bountiful', *Canadian Journal of Law and Society*, 23, 2008, 121–141

Carr, David. 'Post-Secularism, Religious Knowledge and Religious Education', *Journal of Beliefs and Values*, 33(2), 2012, 157–168

Carrera, Sergio and Joanna Parkin, Joanna. 'The Place of Religion in EU Law and Policy: Competing Approaches and Actors Inside the European Commission', Religare Working Document No. 1, September 2010.

Casanova, José. *Public Religions in the Modern World*, Chicago: University of Chicago Press, 1994

Casanova, José. 'Public Religions Revisited', in Hent de Vries (ed.), *Religion: Beyond a Concept*, New York: Fordham University Press, 2008, 101–119

Casanova, Jose. 'Public Religions Revisited', Keynote Speech at the International Conference "Religion Revisited—Women's Rights and the Political Instrumentalisation of Religion", Heinrich-Böll-Foundation & United Nations Research

Institute for Social Development (UNRISD), Berlin, 5–6 June 2009, available at www.gwi-boell.de/sites/default/files/assets/gwi-boell.de/images/downloads/ Religion_Revisited_Keynote_Casanova_June2009.pdf

Castelli, Mike. 'Faith Dialogue as a Pedagogy for a Post Secular Religious Education', *Journal of Beliefs and Values*, 33(2), August 2012, 207–216

Chiba, Masaji (ed.). *Asian Indigenous Law: In Interaction with Received Law*, London: KPI, 1986

Chiba, Masaji. 'Three Dichotomies of Law in Pluralism', in Peter Sack and Jonathan Aleck (eds.), *Law and Anthropology*, New York: New York University Press, 1992, 171–180

Chidester, David. 'Religion Education and the Transformational State in South Africa', *Social Analysis*, 50(3), Winter 2006, 61–83

Chidester, David. 'Religion Education in South Africa', in M. de Souza et al. (eds.), *International Handbook of the Religious, Moral and Spiritual Dimensions in Education*, Dordrecht: Springer, 2009, 433–448

Chidester, David. 'Religion Education in South Africa: Teaching and Learning About Religion, Religions and Religious Diversity', in Lena Larsen and Ingvill T. Plesner (eds.), *Teaching for Tolerance and Freedom of Religion or Belief: Report from the Preparatory Seminar Held in Oslo*, 7–9 December 2002, available at http://folk. uio.no/leirvik/OsloCoalition/DavidChidester.htm

Chidester, David. 'Religious Fundamentalism in South Africa', *Scriptura*, 99, 2008, 350–367

Chidester, David. 'Unity in Diversity: Religion Education and Public Pedagogy in South Africa', *Numen*, 55, 2008, 272–299

Chipkin, Ivon and Leatt, Annie. 'Religion and Revival in Post-Apartheid South Africa', *Focus: The Journal of the Helen Suzman Society*, (62), August 2011, 39–46

Chisholm, L. 'Education Policy in South Africa', Speech Presented to the South African Society of Education, Soweto, 6 February 1993

Chisholm, L. 'The State of South African Schools', in J. Daniel, R. Southall and J. Lutchman (eds.), *State of the Nation: South Africa, 2004–2005*, Cape Town: HSRC Press, 2005, 210–226

Clarke, Charles and Woodhead, Linda. 'A New Settlement: Religion and Belief in Schools', Westminster Faith Debates Report, 2015, available at http://faithde bates.org.uk/wp-content/uploads/2015/06/A-New-Settlement-for-Religion-and-Belief-in-schools.pdf

Coertzen, Pieter. 'Religion and the Constitutional Experience of South Africa', in R. Bottoni et al. (eds.), *Religious Rules, State Law and Normative Pluralism—A Comparative Overview*, Cham, Switzerland: Springer, 2016, 343–355

Cohn, Margit. 'Taking a Bus from Immanuel to Mea Shearim: The Role of Israel's High Court of Justice in Regulating Ethnic and Gender Discrimination in the *Haredi* Ultra-Orthodox Sector', 2012, available at http://ssrn.com/abstract= 2176401

Commision on Religion and Belief in British Public Life. 'Living with Difference: Community, Diversity and the Common Good', Report of the Commission on Religion and Belief in British Public Life, The Woolf Institute, 2015

Connolly, William E. *The Ethos of Pluralization*, Minneapolis: University of Minnesota Press, 1995

Cooling, Trevor. 'Doing God in Education', Theos, 2010, available at www.the osthinktank.co.uk/research/2010/12/02/doing-god-in-education

Cooling, Trevor. 'What Is a Controversial Issue? Implications for the Treatment of Religious Beliefs in Education', *Journal of Beliefs and Values*, 33(2), August 2012, 169–181

Cotterrell, Roger. 'Comparatists and Sociology', in Pierre Legrand and Roderick Munday (eds.), *Comparative Legal Studies: Traditions and Transitions*, Cambridge: Cambridge University Press, 2003, 131–153

Cotterrell, Roger. *Law, Culture and Society: Legal Ideas in the Mirror of Social Theory*, Ashgate: Farnham, 2006

Cotterrell, Roger. 'The Struggle for Law: Some Dilemmas of Cultural Legality', *International Journal of Law in Context*, 4(4), 2009, 373–384

Council of Religious Institutions of the Holy Land. 'Victims of Our Own Narratives? Portrayal of the "Other" in Israeli and Palestinian School Books', Study Report, February 2013, available at https://d7hj1xx5r7f3h.cloudfront.net/Israeli-Palestinian_School_Book_Study_Report-English.pdf [English translation]

Cover, Robert M. 'Nomos and Narrative', in M. Minow, M. Ryan and A. Sarat (eds.), *Narrative, Violence and Law*, Ann Arbor: The University of Michigan Press, 1995, 95–172

Cover, Robert M. 'The Supreme Court 1982 Term—Foreword: Norms and Narrative', *Harvard Law Review*, 97(4), 53, 1983

Cross, M. and Mkwanazi-Twala, Z. 'The Dialectic of Unity and Diversity in Education: Its Implications for a National Curriculum in South Africa', in M. Cross, Z. Mkwanazi-Twala and G. Klein (eds.), *Dealing with Diversity in South African Education*, Cape Town: Juta, 1998, 3–34

Daun, Hager. 'Religious Education and Islam in Europe', in D.B. Holsinger and W.J. Jacob (eds.), *Inequality in Education: Comparative and International Perspectives*, Comparative Education Centre, Dordrecht: Springer, 2009, 348–368

Davie, Grace. *Religion in Britain Since 1945: Believing Without Belonging*, Oxford: Blackwell, 1994

DCSF. *Faith in the System*, London: DCSF, 2007

De Graaf, N.D., De Graaf, P.M. and Kraaykamp, G. 'Parental Cultural Capital and Educational Attainment in the Netherlands: A Refinement of the Cultural Capital Perspective', *Sociology of Education*, 73, 2000, 92–111

de Jong, Johan and Snik, Ger. 'Why Should States Fund Denominational Schools?' *Journal of Philosophy of Education*, 36(4), 2002, 573–587

de Waal, E., Mestry, R. and Russo, C.J. 'Religious and Cultural Dress at School: A Comparative Perspective', *PER/PELJ*, 6(14), 2001, 62–95

de Wet, Corene. 'Religion in Education: An International Perspective', in Carl Wolhuter and Corene de Wet (eds.), *International Comparative Perspectives on Religion and Education*, Bloemfontein: Sun Press, 2014, 1–3

Debray, Régis. *L'Enseignement du fait religieux dans l'école publique*, Paris: Report to the Minister for National Education, 2002

Department for Education. 'School Uniform: Guidance for Governing Bodies, School Leaders, School Staff and Local Authorities', September 2013, available at www.gov.uk/government/publications/school-uniform

Deutsche Welle. 'Where Are "Burqa Bans" in Europe?' 1 August 2019, available at www.dw.com/en/where-are-burqa-bans-in-europe/a-49843292

Dillon, M. 'The Sociology of Religion in Late Modernity', in M. Dillon (ed.), *Handbook of the Sociology of Religion*, Cambridge: Cambridge University Press, 2003, 3–15

Dinham, Adam. 'Public Religion in an Age of Ambivalence: Recovering Religious Literacy After a Century of Secularism', in Lori G. Beaman and Leo Van Arragon (eds.), *Issues in Religion and Education: Whose Religion?*, Leiden: Brill, 2015, 17–33

Dinham, Adam and Jones, Stephen H. 'Religion, Public Policy and the Academy: Brokering Public Faith in a Context of Ambivalence?' *Journal of Contemporary Religion*, 27(2), 2012, 185–201

Dinham, Adam and Martha Shaw, Martha. 'Religious Literacy Through Religious Education: The Future of Teaching and Learning About Religion and Belief', *Religions*, 8, 2017, 119, available at www.mdpi.com/2077-1444/8/7/119

Donlan, Sean Patrick. 'Everything Old Is New Again: Stateless Law, the State of the Law Schools and Comparative Legal/Normative History', in Shauna Van Praagh and Helge Dedek (eds.), *Stateless Law: Evolving Boundaries of a Discipline*, Farnham: Ashgate, 2015, 187–200

Donnelly, Jack and Howard, Rhoda E. 'Assessing National Human Rights Performance: A Theoretical Framework', *Human Rights Quarterly*, 10(2), 1988, 214–248

Dubow, S. *Afrikaner Nationalism, Apartheid and the Conceptualisation of "race"*, University of Witwatersrand/African Studies Institute, 1991

Durkheim, Emile. *The Elementary Forms of Religious Life, 1915*, J.W. Swain (trans.), New York: Free Press, 1962

Dworkin, Ronald. *Taking Rights Seriously*, Cambridge: Harvard University Press, 1978

Eckelaar, John. *Family Law and Personal Life*, Oxford: Oxford University Press, 2007

Egan, Kieran. *Getting It Wrong from the Beginning: Our Progressivist Inheritance from Herbert Spencer*, John Dewey and Jean Piaget, New Haven: Yale University Press, 2003

Ehrlich, Eugen. *Fundamental Principles of the Sociology of Law*, Cambridge MA: Harvard University Press, 1936

El-Or, Tamar. *Educated and Ignorant: Ultra-Orthodox Jewish Women and Their World*, Boulder, CO: Lynne Rienner, 1993, 200

Englard, I. 'Law and Religion in Israel', *American Journal of Comparative Law*, 3571, 1987, 196–203

Engle, Merry. 'Sally Legal Pluralism', *Law & Society Review*, 22, 1988, 869

Ercan, Selen A. 'Democratizing Identity Politics: A Deliberative Approach to the Politics of Recognition', in Dorota A. Gozdecka and Magdalena Kmak (eds.), *Europe at the Edge of Pluralism*, Antwerp: Intersentia, 2015, 13–26

Erricker, Clive. 'Religious Education and Spiritual Development: Pedagogical Insufficiency and Possibility', in M. de Souza et al. (eds.), *International Handbook of the Religious, Moral and Spiritual Dimensions in Education*, Dordrecht: Springer, 2009, 697–715

Estivalezes, Mireille. 'Teaching About Religion at School in France', in M. de Souza et al. (eds.), *International Handbook of the Religious, Moral and Spiritual Dimensions in Education*, Dordrecht: Springer, 2009, 475–486

Evans, Carolyn and Gaze, Beth. 'Between Religious Freedom and Equality: Complexity and Context', *Harvard ILJ Online*, 49, 21 April 2008, 40–49

Evans, Malcolm and Petkoff, Peter. 'A Separation of Convenience? The Concept of Neutrality in the Jurisprudence of the European Court of Human Rights', *Religion, State and Society*, 36(3), September 2008, 205–223

Evans, Rinelle and Cleghorn, Ailie. *Complex Classroom Encounters: A South African Perspective*, Sense Publishers, 2012

Ewald, William. 'Legal History and Comparative Law', *Zeitschrift fuer Europäisches Privatrecht*, 1999, 553

Fancourt, Nigel. 'The Classification and Framing of Religious Dialogues in Two English Schools', *British Journal of Religious Education*, 38(3), 2016, 325–340

Fancourt, Nigel. '"The Safe Forum": Difference, Dialogue and Conflict', in J. Ipgrave, R. Jackson and K. O'Grady (eds.), *Religious Education Research Through a Community of Practice*, Münster: Waxmann, 2009, 201–215

Feniger, Yariv, Shavit, Yossi and Ayalon, Hanna. 'Religiosity, Reading and Educational Achievement Among Jewish Students in Israel', *International Journal of Jewish Education Research*, (7), 2014, 29–67

Ferguson, R. and Roux, C.V. 'Teaching and Learning About Religions in Schools: Responses from a Participation Action Research Project', *Journal for the Study of Religion*, 17(2), 2003, 6–23

Ferrari, Silvio. 'Religious Rules and Legal Pluralism: An Introduction', in R. Bottoni et al. (eds.), *Religious Rules, State Law and Normative Pluralism: A Comparative Overview*, Cham, Switzerland: Springer, 2016, 1–25

Fink, Simon. 'Churches as Society Veto Players: Religious Influence in Actor-Centred Theories of Policy-Making', *West European Politics*, 32(1), 2009, 77–96

Fischer, Louis. 'The Curious Belief in Judicial Supremacy', *Suffolk University Law Review*, 25, 1991, 85, 87

Forsythe, David P. 'Human Rights Studies: On the Dangers of Legalistic Assumptions', in Fons Coomans, Fred Gruenfeld and Menno T. Kamminga (eds.), *Methods of Human Rights Research*, Antwerp: Intersentia, 2009, 59–75

Foucault, Michel. *The History of Sexuality, Vol. 1: An Introduction*, London: Penguin Books, 1978

Foucault, Michel. *Society Must Be Defended: Lectures at the Collège de France, 1975–76*, New York: Picador, 2003

Foucault, Michel. *The Subject and Power in After Modernism*, New York: New York Museum of Contemporary Art Editions, 1984, 417–432

Foucault, Michel. *The Will to Knowledge: History of Sexuality, 1976*, Vol. 1, R. Hurley (trans.), London: Penguin Books, 1998

Fournier, Pascale. 'Halacha, the Jewish State and the Canadian Agunah: Comparative Law at the Intersection of Religious and Secular Orders', *Canadian Journal of Legal Pluralism*, (65), 2012, 165–204

Francis, L.J. *Partnership in Rural Education: Church Schools and Teacher Attitudes*, London: Collins, 1986

Francis, Leslie J. and Robbins, Mandy. 'Teachers at Faith Schools in England and Wales: State of Research', *Theo-Web*, 9(H.1), 2010, 141–159

Frankenberg, Gunter. *Comparative Law as Critique*, Elgar, 2016

Franklin, Shaun. 'Education Rights in Independent Schools', in Faranaaz Veriava, Anso Thom and Tim Fish Hodgson (eds.), *Basic Education Handbook—Education Rights in South Africa*, 2017, 353–371

Fraser, N. and Honneth, A. *Redistribution or Recognition? A Political-Philosophical Exchange*, London and New York: Verso, 2003

Fredman, Sandra. *Human Rights Transformed: Positive Rights and Positive Duties*, Oxford: Oxford University Press, 2008

Gardner, John. *Law as a Leap of Faith*, Oxford: Oxford University Press, 2012

Geertz, Clifford. *Local Knowledge*, New York: Basic Books, 1983

Gibbons, Stephen and Silva, Olmo. 'Faith Primary Schools: Better Schools or Better Pupils?' *Centre Piece*, Summer 2007, 24–25, available at http://cep.lse.ac.uk/pubs/download/cp228.pdf

Giordan, Giuseppe. 'Introduction: Pluralism as Legitimization of Diversity', in G. Giordan and E. Pace (eds.), *Religious Pluralism*, New York: Springer, 2014, 1–12

Giroud, H.A. *Schooling and the Struggle for Public Life: Critical Pedagogy in the Modern Age*, Minneapolis: University of Minnesota, 1988

Glenn, Patrick H. 'The Nationalist Heritage', in Pierre Legrand and Roderick Munday (eds.), *Comparative Legal Studies: Traditions and Transitions*, Cambridge: Cambridge University Press, 2003, 76–99

Gordley, James. 'Comparative Legal Research: Its Function in the Development of Harmonized Law', *The American Journal of Comparative Law*, 43, 1995, 555

Gordon, Robert W. 'Critical Legal Histories', *Stanford Law Review*, 36, 1984, 57, 109

Gozdecka, Dorota A. 'Religion and Legal Boundaries of Democracy in Europe: European Commitment to Democratic Principles', Dissertation University of Helsinki, 2009, available at http://ethesis.helsinki.fi

Gozdecka, Dorota A. and Ercan, Selen. 'What Is Post-Multiculturalism? Recent Trends in Legal and Political Discourse', in D. Gozdecka and M. Kmak (eds.), *Europe at the Edge of Pluralism*, Antwerp: Intersentia, 2015, 27–42

Gray, J. *Gray's Anatomy*, London: Allen Lane, 2009

Graziadei, Michele. 'The Functionalist Heritage', in Pierre Legrand and Roderick Munday (eds.), *Comparative Legal Studies: Traditions and Transitions*, Cambridge: Cambridge University Press, 2003, 100–127

Graziadei, Michele. 'State Norms, Religious Norms and Claims for Plural Normativity Under Democratic Constitutions', in R. Bottoni et al. (eds.), *Religious Rules, State Law and Normative Pluralism: A Comparative Overview*, Cham, Switzerland: Springer, 2016, 29–43

Griffith, John. 'What Is Legal Pluralism?' *Journal of Legal Pluralism*, 24, 1986, 1–55

Grillo, Ralph. 'British and Others: From "Race" to "Faith"', in Steven Vertovec and Susanne Wessendorf (eds.), *The Multiculturalism Backlash: European Discourses, Policies and Practices*, Abingdon: Routledge, 2010, 50–71

Grimmit, Michael. *Religious Education and Human Development*, Great Wakering: McCrimmons, 1987

Gross, Zehavit. 'State-Religious Education in Israel: Between Tradition and Modernity', *Prospects*, 33(2), 2003, 149–164

Grossfeld, Bernhard. 'Comparatists and Languages', in Pierre Legrand and Roderick Munday (eds.), *Comparative Legal Studies: Traditions and Transitions*, Cambridge: Cambridge University Press, 2003, 154–194

Habermas, Juergen. 'Intolerance and Discrimination', *ICON*, 1(1), 2003, 2–12

Habermas, Juergen. 'Notes on a Post-Secular Society', 2008, available at www.signandsight.com/features/1714.html

Hakak, Yohai and Rapoport, Tamar. 'Excellence or Equality in the Name of God? The Case of Ultra-Orthodox Enclave Education in Israel', *The Journal of Religion*, 92, April 2012, 251–276

Hart, H.L.A. *The Concept of Law*, Oxford: Oxford University Press, 1961

Hewer, C. 'Schools for Muslims', *Oxford Review of Education*, 27(4), 2001, 515–527

Hirschl, Ran. 'The Rise of Comparative and Constitutional Law: Thoughts on Substance and Method', *Indian Journal of Constitutional Law*, 2008, 11–37

Hodgson, Douglas. *The Human Right to Education*, Ashgate, 1998

Hodgson, Tim. 'Fish Religion and Culture in Public Education in South Africa', in Faranaaz Veriava, Anso Thom and Tim Fish Hodgson (eds.), *Basic Education Rights Handbook—Education Rights in South Africa*, Braamfontein/Johannesburg: SECTION 27, 2017, 185–203

Hofri-Winogradow, Adam S. 'A Plurality of Discontent: Legal Pluralism, Religious Adjudication and the State', *Journal of Law and Religion*, 26, 2010, 101–133

Holsinger, Donald B. and Jacob, James W. 'Education Inequality and Academic Achievement', in W. James Jacob and Donald B. Holsinger (eds.), *Inequality in Education: Comparative and International Perspectives*, Hong Kong: Springer Comparative Education Research Centre, 2009, 558–567

Howe, R. Brian and Covell, Katherine. *Empowering Children: Children's Rights Education as a Pathway to Citizenship*, Toronto: University of Toronto Press, 2007

Hughes, Philip. 'The Future of Religious Education in the Context of Postmodernity', in M. de Souza et al. (eds.), *International Handbook of the Religious, Moral and Spiritual Dimensions in Education*, Dordrecht: Springer, 2009, 349–362

Human Rights Watch. 'Second Class: Discrimination Against Palestinian Arab Children in Israel's Schools', 30 September 2001, available at www.hrw.org/reports/2001/israel2

Husa, Jaakko. 'Turning the Curriculum Upside Down: Comparative Law as an Educational Too for Constructing Pluralistic Legal Mind', *German Law Journal*, 2009, 913.

International Council on Human Rights. *When Legal Worlds Overlap: Human Rights, State and Non-State Law*, 2009, available at http://www.ichrp.org/files/reports/50/135_report_en.pdf

Ipgrave, Julia. 'Identity and Inter Religious Understanding in Jewish Schools in England', *British Journal of Religious Education*, 38(1), 2016, 47–63

Iram, Yaacov and Schmida, Mirjam. *The Educational System of Israel*, Westport: Greenwood Press, 1988

Israel Periodic Report Submitted to the Committee on the Rights of the Rights of the Child, 20 February 2001, CRC/C/8/Add.44

Jackson, Amy. 'A Critical Legal Pluralist Analysis of the Begum Case', Osgoode Hall Law School Research Paper Series, Research Paper No. 46/2010, 2010

Jackson, Robert. 'Is Diversity Changing Religious Education? Religion, Diversity and Education in Today's Europe', in Geir Skeie (ed.), *Religious Diversity and Education: Nordic Perspectives*, Muenster: Waxmann, 2009, 11–28

Jackson, Robert. *Religious Education: An Interpretive Approach*, London: Hodder & Stoughton, 1997

Jackson, Robert. 'Understanding Religious Diversity in a Plural World: The Interpretive Approach', in M. de Souza et al. (eds.), *International Handbook of the Religious, Moral and Spiritual Dimensions in Education*, Dordrecht: Springer, 2009, 399–414,

Jackson, Robert and Everington, Judith. 'Teaching Inclusive Religious Education Impartially: An English Perspective', *British Journal of Religious Education*, 39, 2017, 7–24

Jackson, Robert and Nesbitt, Eleanor. *Hindu Children in Britain*, Stoke-on-Trent: Trentham Books, 1993

Jackson, Robert and O'Grady, Kevin. 'Religions and Education in England: Social Plurality, Civil Religion and Religious Education Pedagogy', in Robert Jackson, Siebren Miedema, Wolfram Weisse and Jean-Paul Willaime (eds.), *Religion and*

Education in Europe: Developments, Contexts and Debates. Religious Diversity and Education in Europe, Münster: Waxmann, 2007, 181–202

Jacob, James and Holsinger, Donald B. 'Inequality in Education: A Critical Analysis', in Donald B. Holsinger and W. James Jacob (eds.), *Inequality in Education: Comparative and International Perspectives*, Hong Kong: Springer Comparative Education Research Centre, 2009, 1–33

Kahn, Paul W. *Putting Liberalism in Its Place*, Princeton: Princeton University Press, 2005

Karayanni, Michael. 'The "Other" Religion and State Conflict in Israel: On the Nature of Religious Accommodations for the Palestinian-Arab Minority', in Winfried Brugger and Michael Karayanni (eds.), *Religion in the Public Sphere: A Comparative Analysis of German, Israeli, American and International Law*, Berlin: Springer, 2007, 333–377

Kazepov, Yuri and Genova, Angela. 'From Government Fragmentation to Local Governance: Welfare Reforms and Lost Opportunities in Italy', in Paul Henman and Menno Fenger (eds.), *Administering Welfare Reform*, Policy Press, 2006, 233–255

Keck, Margaret E. and Sikking, Kathryn, *Activists Beyond Borders: Advocacy Networks in International Politics*, Ithaca: Cornell University Press, 1998

Kelman, Mark A. *Guide to Critical Legal Studies*, Cambridge: Harvard University Press, 1987

Kennedy, David. 'The Methods and the Politics', in Pierre Legrand and Roderick Munday (eds.), *Comparative Legal Studies: Traditions and Transitions*, Cambridge: Cambridge University Press, 2003, 345–433

Kennedy, Duncan. 'The Critique of Rights in Critical Legal Studies', in W. Brown and J. Halley (eds.), *Left Legalism/Left Critique*, Durham, NC: Duke University Press, 2002, 179–227

Khagram, Sanjeev, Riker, James V. and Sikkink, Kathryn (eds.). *Restructuring World Politics: Transnational Social Movements*, Minneapolis: University of Minnesota Press, 2002

King-Irani, L. 'Women's Rights Are Human Rights', *Al-Raida*, 13(74/75), 1996, 11–12

Kippenberg, Hans G. 'Europe: Area of Pluralization and Diversification of Religions', *Journal of Religion in Europe*, 1, 2008, 133–155

Klare, K. 'Legal Culture and Transformative Constitutionalism', *South African Journal on Human Rights*, 14(1), 1998, 146–188

Kleinhaus, Martha-Marie and Macdonald, Roderick A. 'What Is Critical Legal Pluralism?' *CJLS/RCDS*, 12(2), Fall 1997, 25–46

Koenig, Matthias. 'How Nation-States Respond to Religious Diversity', in P. Bramadat and M. Koenig (eds.), *International Migration and the Governance of Religious Diversity*, Montreal: McGill–Queen's University Press, 2009, 293–317

Koh, Harold. 'Hongju Transnational Legal Processes', *Nebraska Law Review*, 75, 1996, 181

Kukathas, Chandran. 'Education and Citizenship in Diverse Societies', *International Journal of Educational Research*, 35, 2001, 319, 321–322

Kukathas, Chandran. *The Liberal Archipelago: A Theory of Diversity and Freedom*, Oxford: Oxford University Press, 2003

Künkler, Mirjam and Lerner, Hanna. 'A Private Matter? Religious Education and Democracy in Indonesia and Israel', *British Journal of Religious Education*, 2016, 1–29

Kymlicka, Will. 'Education for Citizenship', in M. Halstead and McLaughlin (eds.), *Education in Morality*, Abingdon: Routledge, 1999, 79–102

Kymlicka, Will. *Multicultural Citizenship: A Liberal Theory of Minority Rights*, Oxford: Oxford University Press, 1996

Landsberg, E., *Addressing Barriers to Learning: A South African Perspective*, Pretoria: Van Schaik Publishers, 2005

Lasser, Mitchel De S.-O.-L'E. 'The Question of Understanding', in Pierre Legrand and Roderick Munday (eds.), *Comparative Legal Studies: Traditions and Transitions*, Cambridge: Cambridge University Press, 2003, 197–239

Lawson, I. *Leading Islamic Schools in the UK: A Challenge for Us All*, Nottingham: National College for School Leadership, 2005

Leavy, Alexandra F. 'The Failure of Education Policy in Israel: Politics vs Bureaucracy', 2010, *CUREJ Electronic Journal*, 2010, available at http://repository.upenn.edu/curej/115,Leary

Legrand, Pierre. *Fragments on Law-as-Culture*, Deventer: W.E.J. Tjeenk Willink, 1999

Legrand, Pierre. 'The Impossibility of Legal Transplants', *Maastricht Journal of European and Comparative Law*, 1997, 111–124

Legrand, Pierre. 'John Henry Merryman and Comparative Legal Studies: A Dialogue', *The American Journal of Comparative Law*, 47(3), 1999, 65

Legrand, Pierre. 'The Same and the Different', in Pierre Legrand and Roderick Munday (eds.), *Comparative Legal Studies: Traditions and Transitions*, Cambridge: Cambridge University Press, 2003, 240–311

Lipsky, M. *Street-Level Bureaucracy: Dilemmas of the Individual in Public Services*, New York: Russel Sage Foundation, 1980

Looney, Anne. 'Religious Education in the Public Space: Challenges and Contestations', in M. de Souza et al. (eds.), *International Handbook of the Religious, Moral and Spiritual Dimensions in Education*, Dordrecht: Springer, 2009, 949–966

Macdonald, Roderick A. *Lessons of Everyday Law*, Montreal: McGill University Press, 2002

Mahlmann, Matthias. 'Religion, Secularism and the Origins of Foundational Values of Modern Constitutionalism', Paper presented at the VII World Congress of Constitutional Law: Rethinking the Boundaries of Constitutional Law, 11–16 June 2007 [in file with the author]

Malik, Maleiha. *Minority Legal Orders in the UK: Minorities, Pluralism and the Law*, British Academy Policy Centre, 2012

Maoz, Asher. 'The Application of Religious Law in a Multi-Religion Nation State: The Israeli Model', in R. Bottoni et al. (eds.), *Religious Rules, State Law, and Normative Pluralism—A Comparative Overview*, Cham, Swirzerland: Springer, 2016, 209–227

Maoz, Asher. 'State and Religion in Israel', in M. Mor (ed.), *International Perspectives on Church and State*, Omaha: Creighton University Press and Fordham University Press, 1993, 239–248

Margalit, Avishai and Halbertal, Moshe. 'Liberalism and the Right to Culture', *Social Research*, 71(3), Social Research at Seventy, Fall 2004, 529–548

Maritain, Jacques. 'Truth and Human Fellowship', in *On the Use of Philosophy: Three Essays*, Princeton: Princeton University Press, 1961

Martin, David. *Religion and Power: No Logos Without Mythos*, Farnham: Ashgate, 2014

Mautner, Menachem. 'A Dialogue Between a Liberal and an Ultra-Orthodox on the Exclusion of Women from Torah Study', in S. Lavi and R. Provost (eds.),

Religious Revival in a Post-Multicultural Age, 2013, available at https://ssrn.com/abstract=2169400

Mautner, Menachem. 'The Immanuel Affair and the Problems of Intercultural Encounter', *Democratic Culture in Israel and the World*, 15, 2013, available at http://ssrn.com/abstract=2257217

Maxime St-Hilaire, Maxime. 'The Study of Legal Plurality Outside "Legal Pluralism": The Future of the Discipline?' in Shauna Van Praagh and Helge Dedek (eds.), *Stateless Law: Evolving Boundaries of a Discipline*, Abingdon: Routledge, 2015, 115–132

Mc Connachie, Chris. 'Equality and Unfair Discrimination in Education, Basic Education Rights Handbook: Education Rights in South Africa', in Faranaaz Veriava, Anso Thom and Tim Fish Hodgson (eds.), *Basic Education Rights Handbook: Education Rights in South Africa*, Braamfontein/Johannesburg: SECTION 27, 2017, 91–104

McCrudden, Christopher. 'Judicial Comparativism and Human Rights', in David Nelken and Esin Örücü (eds.), *Comparative Law: A Handbook*, Oxford: Hart Publishing, 2007, 371–398

McCrudden, Christopher. 'Multiculturalism, Freedom of Religion, Equality and the British Constitution: The JFS Case Considered', *International Journal of Constitutional Law (I-CON)*, 2011, 200–229

McDonald, Zahraa. 'The Classroom, an Inadequate Mechanism for Advancing Diversity Via Religion Education in the South African Context', *Journal for the Study of Religion*, 28(2), 2015, 202–219

Medina, Barak. 'Does the Establishment of Religion Justify Regulating Religious Activities? The Israeli Experience', in Winifred Brugger and Michael Karayanni (eds.), *Religion in the Public Sphere: A Comparative Analysis of German Israeli, American and International Law*, Max Planck Institut für auslandisches öffentliches Recht und Völkerrecht, Springer, 2007, 299–332

Medina, Barak. 'Enhancing Freedom of Religion Through Public Provision of Religious Services: The Israeli Experience', *Israeli Law Review*, 39(2), 2006, 127–157

Meek, Christopher B. and Meek, Joshua Y. 'The History and Devolution of Education in South Africa', in D.B. Holsinger and W.J. Jacob (eds.), *Inequality in Education: Comparative and International Perspectives*, Comparative Education Research Centre, 2009, 506–537

Meer, N. and Modood, T. 'The Multicultural State We're in Muslims, "Multiculture" and the "Civic Re-balancing" of British Multiculturalism', *Political Studies*, 57, 2009, 473–497

Meier, C. and Hartell, C. 'Handling Cultural Diversity in Education in South Africa', *SA-eDUC Journal*, 6(2), November 2009, 180–192

Meijer, Wilna A.J. 'Plural Selves and Living Traditions: A Hermeneutical View of Identity and Diversity, Tradition and Historicity', in M. de Souza et al. (eds.), *International Handbook of the Religious, Moral and Spiritual Dimensions in Education*, Dordrecht: Springer, 2009, 321–332

Menski, Werner. 'Beyond Europe', in Esin Orucu and David Nelken (eds.), *Comparative Law: A Handbook*, Oxford: Hart Publishing, 2007, 189–216

Menski, Werner. 'Immigration and Multiculturalism in Britain: New Issues in Research and Policy', *KIAPS: Bulletin of Asian-Pacific Studies*, X, 2002, 43–66

Merry, Sally Engle. 'Human Rights Law and the Demonization of Culture (and Anthropology Along the Way)', *Polar: Political and Legal Anthropology Review*, 26(1), May 2003, 55–76

Merry, Sally Engle. 'International Law and Sociolegal Scholarship: Toward a Spatial Global Legal Pluralism', in M.A. Helfand (ed.), *Negotiating State and Non-State Law: The Challenge of Global and Legal Pluralism*, Cambridge: Cambridge University Press, 2015, 59–80

Merry, Sally Engle. 'Legal Pluralism', *Law and Society Review*, 22, 1998, 869–896

Mestry, Raj. 'The Constitutional Right to Freedom of Religion in South African Primary Schools', *Australia and New Zealand Journal of Law and Education*, 12(2), 2007, 57–68

Michaels, Ralf. 'What Is Non-State Law? A Primer', in Michael A. Helfand (ed.), *Negotiating State and Non-State Law: The Challenge of Global and Local Legal Pluralism*, Cambridge: Cambridge University Press, 2015, 41–58

Miedema, Siebren. 'Educating for Religious Citizenship: Religious Education as Identity Formation', in M. de Souza et al. (eds.), *International Handbook of the Religious, Moral and Spiritual Dimensions in Education*, Dordrecht: Springer, 2009, 967–976

Mikhail, John. 'Dilemmas of Cultural Legality: A Comment on Roger Cotterrell's. "The Struggle for Law" and a Criticism of the House of Lords' Opinions in Begum', *International Journal of Law in Context*, 4(4), 2009, 385–393

Mirza, H., *Multicultural Education in England, International Alliance of Leading Education Institutes (IALEI)*, London: Institute of Education, University of London, 2010

Mirza-Muller, Nathalie. 'Civic Education and Intercultural Issues in Switzerland: Psychosocial Dimensions of an Education to "Otherness"', *Journal of Social Science Education*, 10(4), 2011, 31–40

Modood, Tariq. 'Anti-Essentialism, Multiculturalism and the "Recognition" of Religious Groups', *Journal of Political Philosophy*, 6, 1998, 378–399

Modood, Tariq. 'Multiculturalism and Integration: Struggling with Confusion', EUI RSCAS Accept Pluralism, 2011, available at www.coe.int/t/dg4/cultureheritage/mars/source/resources/references/others/38%20-%20Multiculturalisme%20and%20Integration%20-%20Modood%202011.pdf

Moletsane, R. Beyond Desegregation: Multicultural Education in South African Schools', *Perspectives in Education*, 18(2), 1999, 31–42

Mooney, Cotter. *Anne-Marie Heaven Forbid: An International Legal Analysis of Religious Discrimination*, Farnham: Ashgate, 2009

Moore, Sally Falk. 'Falk Legal Systems of the World: An Introductory Guide to Classifications, Typological Interpretations and Bibliographical Resources', in Leon Lipson and Stanton Wheeler (eds.), *Law and the Social Sciences*, New York: Russell Sage Foundation, 1986, 11–62

Moore, Sally Falk. 'Law and Social Change: The Semi-Autonomous Social Field as an Appropriate Subject of Study', *Law & Society Review*, 7, 1973, 719

Moosa, Ebrahim. 'Tensions in Legal and Religious Values in the 1996 South African Constitution', in Mahmood Mamdani (ed.), *Beyond Rights Talk and Culture Talk*, Cape Town: David Philips Publishers, 2000, 121–135

Moran, Gabriel. 'Religious Education and the Nation-State', in M. de Souza et al. (eds.), *International Handbook of the Religious, Moral and Spiritual Dimensions in Education*, Dordrecht: Springer, 2009, 41–50

Munday, Roderick. 'Accounting for an Encounter', in Pierre Legrand and Roderick Munday (eds.), *Comparative Legal Studies: Traditions and Transitions*, Cambridge: Cambridge University Press, 2003, 3–28

Mustasaari, Sanna. 'Law, Agency and the Intimate Relationships of Young People: From Rights to Duties and Back?' in Dorota A. Gozdecka and Magdalena Kmak (eds.), *Europe at the Edge of Pluralism*, Antwerp: Intersentia, 2015, 133–145

Mutua, M. 'Limitations on Religious Rights: Problematising Religious Freedom in the African Context', *Buffalo Human Rights Law Review*, 5, 1999, 75–105

Naidoo, Marilyn. 'Engaging Difference in Values Education in South African Schools', *Alternation*, Special Edition, 10, 2013, 54–75

Nelken, David. 'Comparatists and Transferability', in Pierre Legrand and Roderick Munday (eds.), *Comparative Legal Studies: Traditions and Transitions*, Cambridge: Cambridge University Press, 2003, 437–466

Nesbitt, Eleanor. 'Ethnography, Religion and Intercultural Education', in M. de Souza et al. (eds.), *International Handbook of the Religious, Moral and Spiritual Dimensions in Education*, Dordrecht: Springer, 2009, 387–398

Niehaus, Inga. 'Emancipation or Disengagement? Islamic Schools in Britain and the Netherlands', in Aurora Alvarez Venguer et al. (eds.), *Islam in Education in European Countries*, Muenster: Waxmann, 2009, 113–130

Norris, Pippa and Inglehart, Ronald. 'Uneven Secularization in the US & Western Europe', in Thomas Banchoff (ed.), *Democracy and the New Religious Pluralism*, Oxford: Oxford University Press, 2007, 31–57

Nowak, Manfred. 'The Right to Education', in A. Eide et al. (eds.), *Economic, Social and Cultural Rights: A Textbook*, Dordrecht: Martinus Nijhoff, 2001, 245–271

Nussbaum, M. *Women and Human Development: The Capabilities Approach.* The Seeley Lectures, Cambridge: Cambridge University Press, 2000

O'Donovan, Oliver. *The Desire of the Nations: Rediscovering the Roots of Political Theology*, Cambridge University Press, 1996

OFSTED. 'OFSTED'S Equality Objectives 2016–2020', No. 160019, April 2016, available at https://assets.publishing.service.gov.uk/government/uploads/system/uploads/attachment_data/file/520134/Ofsted_s_equality_objectives_2016-2020.pdf

OFSTED. 'Religious Education: Realising the Potential', No. 130068, October 2013

Oldfield, Elizabeth, Hartnett, Liane and Bailey, Emma. 'More than an Educated Guess: Assessing Evidence on Faith Schools', Theos Report, 2013, available at www.theosthinktank.co.uk/cmsfiles/archive/files/More%20than%20an%20educated%20guess.pdf

O'Leary, Ryan T. 'The Irony of the Secular: Violent Communication at the Limits of Tolerance', *Journal of Religion, Conflict and Peace*, 3(2), Spring 2010, 2, available at www.religionconflictpeace.org/volume-3-issue-2-spring-2010/irony-secular

Ostberg, Sissel. 'Islamic Nurture and Identity Management: The Lifeworld of Muslim Children and Young People in Norway', in M. de Souza et al. (eds.), *International Handbook of the Religious, Moral and Spiritual Dimensions in Education*, Dordrecht: Springer, 2009, 501–512

Ouellet, Fernand. 'Religious Education and Citizenship in Postmodern Societies', in M. de Souza et al. (eds.), *International Handbook of the Religious, Moral and Spiritual Dimensions in Education*, Dordrecht: Springer, 2009, 363–374

Parekh, Bhikhu. 'The Future of Multi-Ethnic Britain: Reporting on a Report', *The Round Table*, 90(362), 2010, 691–700

Parekh, Bhikhu. *Rethinking Multiculturalism, Cultural Diversity and Political Theory*, London: Macmillan, 2000

Parish, N., Baxter, A. and Sandals, L. *Action Research into the Evolving Role of the Local Authority in Education*, 2012, available at https://assets.publishing.service. gov.uk/government/uploads/system/uploads/attachment_data/file/184055/ DFE-RR224.pdf

Parker-Jenkins, M. *Terms of Engagement: Muslim and Jewish School Communities, Cultural Sustainability and Maintenance*, Derby: University of Derby, 2008, Unpublished Paper

Pedahzur, Ami. 'The Paradox of Civic Education in Non-Liberal Democracies: The Case of Israel', *Journal of Education Policy*, 16(5), 2001, 413–430

Pells, Rachel. 'Faith Schools Academically "No Better" than Any Others, Major New Report Suggests', *The Independent Online*, 2 December 2016, available at www. independent.co.uk/news/education/education-news/faith-schools-academically-no-better-than-any-others-epi-report-religion-catholic-church-england-a7451676. html

Pépin, Luce. *Teaching About Religions in European School Systems: Policy Issues and Trends*, NEF Initiative on Religion and Democracy in Europe, 2009

Perry-Hazan, Lotem. 'From the Constitution to the Classroom: Educational Freedom in Antwerp's Ultra-Orthodox Jewish Schools', *Journal of School Choice*, 8, 2014, 475–502

Perry-Hazan, Lotem, Almog, Shulamit and A'li, Nohad. 'Applying International Human Rights Standards to National Curricula: Insights from Literature Education of Jewish and Arab High Schools', *Northwestern Interdisciplinary Law Review*, VI(1), 2013, 1–20

Peters, Anne. 'The Refinement of International Law: From Fragmentation to Regime Interaction and Politicization', *ICON*, 15(3), 2017, 671–704

Pew Research Center. 'Israel's Religiously Divided Society', 2016, available at www. pewforum.org/2016/03/08/israels-religiously-divided-society/

Pilkington, A. 'Racism in Schools and Ethnic Differentials in Educational Achievement: A Brief Comment on a Recent Debate', *British Journal of Sociology of Education*, 20(3), 1999, 411–417

Poulter, Sebastian. 'Muslim Headscarves in School: Contrasting Legal Approaches in England and France', *Oxford Journal of Legal Studies*, 17(1), 1997, 43–74

Pound, Roscoe. 'Scope and Purpose of Sociological Jurisprudence (Part I)', *Harvard Law Review*, 24, 1911, 591

Pradhan, Rajendra. 'Negotiating Multiculturalism in Nepal: Law, Hegemony, Contestation and Paradox', 2007, available at www.uni-bielefeld.de/midea/pdf/ Rajendra.pdf

Pusztai, Gabriela. 'Schools and Communities of Norm-Awareness', *Religions*, 2, 2011, 372–388

Rabin, Yoram. 'The Many Faces of the Right to Education', in Daphne Erez-Barak and Aeyal Gross (eds.), *Exploring Social Rights—Between Theory and Practice*, Oxford: Hart Publishing, 2008, 265–288

Raday, Frances. 'Claiming Equal Religious Personhood: Women of the Wall's Constitutional Saga', in Winfried Brugger and Michael Karayanni (eds.), *Religion in the Public Sphere: A Comparative Analysis of German, Israeli, American and International Law*, Vol. 190, Berlin: Springer, 2007, 256–298

Raday, Frances. 'Equality, Religion and Gender in Israel', *Jewish Women: A Comprehensive Historical Encyclopedia*, 2009, available at http://jwa.org/encycopedia/ article/equality-religion-and-gender-in-israel

Ramstedt, Martin. 'Anthropological Perspectives on the Normative and Institutional Recognition of Religion by the Law of the State', in R. Bottoni et al. (eds.), *Religious Rules, State Law and Normative Pluralism: A Comparative Overview*, Cham, Switzerland: Springer, 45–59

Randolph, Braham. *Israel: A Modern Education System*, Washington, DC: US Government Printing Office, 1966

Rautenbach, C. 'Deep Legal Pluralism in South Africa: Judicial Accommodation of Non-State Law', *The Journal of Legal Pluralism and Unofficial Law*, 42(60), 2010, 143–177

Rautenbach, C. and Bekker, J.C. *Introduction to Legal Pluralism in South Africa*, 4th ed., Durban: LexisNexis, 2014, 253–263

Rautenbach, C., van Rensburg, F. Jansen and Pienaar, G. 'Culture (and Religion) in Constitutional Adjudication', *PER/PELJ*, 6(1), 2003, available at https://journals.assaf.org.za/per/issue/view/331

Rawls, John. *Justice as Fairness*, Massachusetts: Harvard University Press, 2001

Raz, Joseph. *The Morality of Freedom*, Oxford: Oxford University Press, 1986

Rea, Louise. 'Gender Segregation—Faith-Based Organisation Update', Spring 2018, 7–8, available at http://bateswells.co.uk/wp-content/uploads/2019/06/faith-basedupdate-spring18-pdf.PDF

Reed, Jodie. 'Religion Renewed? The Right Path for English Schools', *Public Policy Research*, 2006, 252–257

Regav, Eitan. *The Challenge of Integrating Haredim into Academic Studies—The State of the Nation Report: Society, Economy and Policy*, Taub Center for Social and Policy Studies, 2016, 219–268

Religious Education Council of England and Wales. 'A Curriculum Framework for Religious Education in England', October 2013

Renteln, Alison Dundes. *The Cultural Defense*, Oxford: Oxford University Press, 2004

Resh, Nura and Benavot, Aaron. 'Educational Governance, School Autonomy, and Curriculum Implementation: Diversity and Uniformity in Knowledge Offerings to Israeli Pupils', *Journal of Curriculum Studies*, 41(1), February 2009, 67–92

Resnik, Judith. 'Living Their Legal Commitments: Paideic Communities, Courts and Robert Cover (an Essay on Racial Segregation at Bob Jones University, Patrilineal Membership Rules, Veiling and Jurisgeneretative Practices)', *Yale Journal of Law and the Humanities*, 17, 2005, 27

Resnik, Julia. 'Particularistic vs. Universalistic Content in the Israeli Education System', *Curriculum Inquiry*, 29(4), Winter 1999, 485–511

Rheinstein, Max. 'Teaching Comparative Law', *University of Chicago Law Review*, 5, 1938, 617

Richard, Adams and Aisha, Gani. ' "Radicalisation Risk" at Six Muslim Schools in London', *The Guardian*, 21 November 2014, available at www.theguardian.com/education/2014/nov/21/ofsted-muslim-schools-london-closure-threat

Richardson, James T. 'Religious Diversity, Social Control, and Legal Pluralism: A Socio-Legal Analysis', in G. Giordan and E. Pace (eds.), *Religious Pluralism*, New York: Springer, 2014, 31–47

Risse-Kappen, Thomas, Ropp, Steve C. and Sikkink, Kathryn (eds.). *The Power of Human Rights: International Norms and Domestic Change*, Cambridge: Cambridge University Press, 1999

Roberts, Robert C. and Wood, Jay W. *Intellectual Virtues: An Essay in Regulative Epistemology*, Oxford: Oxford University Press, 2007

Roos, Clive. 'Public School Governance in South Africa', *The Journal of the Helen Suzman Foundation*, 56, 2010, 57–61

Rosen, Lawrence. 'Beyond Compare', in Pierre Legrand and Roderick Munday (eds.), *Comparative Legal Studies: Traditions and Transitions*, Cambridge: Cambridge University Press, 2003, 493–510

Roux, C. 'Religion in Education: Who Is Responsible?' *Alternation*, Special Edition, 3, 2009, 3–30

Rubinstein, Amnon. 'State and Religion in Israel', *Journal of Contemporary History*, 4, 1967, 107

Rudgard, Olivia. 'Don't Let Faith Schools Take in More Pupils on the Basis of Religion, Leaders Warn', *The Telegraph*, 5 March 2018, available at https://telegraph.co.uk/news/2018/03/05/dont-let-faith-schools-take-pupils-basis-religion-leaders-warn

Runciman, David. *Pluralism and the Personality of the State*, Cambridge: Cambridge University Press, 1997

Sacco, Rodolfo. 'Legal Formants: A Dynamic Approach to Comparative Law', *The American Journal of Comparative Law*, 39, 1991, 1

Sacco, Rodolfo. 'One Hundred Years of Comparative Law', *Tulane Law Review*, 75, 2000, 1159

Sacks, Jonathan. *Not in God's Name*, London: Hodder and Stoughton, 2015

Sajó, A. 'Preliminaries to a Concept of Constitutional Secularism', *Int'l Journal of Constitutional Law*, 6, 2008, 617

Sandberg, Russell. 'Conclusion: In Pursuit of Pluralism', in R. Bottoni et al. (eds.), *Religious Rules, State Law and Normative Pluralism: A Comparative Overview*, Cham, Switzerland: Springer, 2016, 395–420

Sarat, Austin. 'The Law Is All Over: Power, Resistance and the Legal Consciousness of the Welfare Poor', *Yale Journal of Law and the Humanities*, 2(2), 1990, Art. 6, 343–380

Sarat, Austin and Kearns, Thomas R. 'The Unsettled States of Human Rights: An Introduction', in A. Sarat and T.R. Kearns (eds.), *Human Rights: Concepts, Contests, Contingencies*, Ann Arbor: University of Michigan Press, 2001, 1–24

Schiff, Berman and Paul, Schiff. 'Global Legal Pluralism as a Normative Project', *UC Irvine Law Review*, 8, 2018, 149–182

Schlesinger, Rudolf B. (ed.). *Formation of Contracts: A Study of the Common Core of Legal Systems*, Dobbs-Ferry: Oceana, 1968

Schlesinger, Rudolf B. 'The Past and Future of Comparative Law', *The American Journal of Comparative Law*, 43(3), 1995, 477

Schoeman, Willem J. 'South African Religious Demography: The 2013 General Household Survey', *HTS Theologiese Studies/Theological Studies*, 73(2), 2017

Schriewer, J. 'Worldsystem and Interrelationship Networks: The Internationalization of Education and the Role of Comparative Inquiry', in T.S. Popkewitz (ed.), *Educational Knowledge: Changing Relationships Between State, Civil Society, and the Educational Community*, Albany: State University of New York Press, 2000, 305–343

Scott, John Trevitt and Armstrong, Ann Cheryl. 'Faith-Based Schools and the Public Good: Purposes and Perspectives', Paper presented at the AARE Annual Conference, Melbourne, 2010, 1–13

Scott, Sara and McNeish, Di. *Leadership and Faith Schools: Issues and Challenges*, Nottingham: National Centre for School Leadership, 2012, available at www.bristol.ac.uk/media-library/sites/cubec/migrated/documents/leadershipandfaith-schools.pdf

Sela, Neta. 'Yeshivas to Receive State Funds Without Teaching Basic Subjects', *Y Net News*, 24 July 2008, available at http://ynetnews.com/articles/0,7340,L-3572383,00.html

Sen, Amartya. *Development as Freedom*, New York: Anchor Books, 1999

Serfontein, Erika. 'Mariane Education and Religion in South Africa: Policy Analysis and Assessment Against International Law', *Journal of Law and Criminal Justice*, 2(1), March 2014, 117–136

Sezgin, Yuksel. 'A Political Account for Legal Confrontation Between State and Society', *Studies in Law, Politics and Society*, 322, 2004, 199–233

Sezgin, Yüksel. 'Theorizing Formal Pluralism: Quantification of Legal Pluralism for Spatio-Temporal Analysis', *Journal of Legal Pluralism*, 50, 2004, 101–118

Shah, S. and Conchar, C. 'Why Single-Sex Schools? Discourses of Culture/Faith and Achievement', *Cambridge Journal of Education*, 39(2), 2009, 191–204

Shah S. and Iqbal, M. 'Pakistani diaspora in Britain: Intersections of multi-locality and girls' education', *British Journal of Sociology of Education*, 32(5), 2011, 763–783

Shamal, Shmuel. ' "Cultural Shift": The Case of Religion Education in Israel', *British Journal of Sociology of Education*, 21(3), September 2000, 401–417

Shetreet, Shimon. 'State and Religion: Funding of Religious Institutions—The Case of Israel in Comparative Perspective', *Notre Dame Journal of Law, Ethics and Public Policy*, 13(2), 1999, 421–453

Shweder, Richard A. 'What About Female Genital Mutilation? And Why Understanding Culture Matters in the First Place', in R.A. Shweder, M. Minow and H.R. Markus (eds.), *Engaging Cultural: The Multicultural Challenge in Liberal Democracies*, New York: Russell Sage Foundation, 2002, 216–251

Sian, Katy, Law, Ian and Sayyid, Salman. *Debates on Difference and Integration in Education: Monitoring Extremism in the UK—Muslims in School, TOLERACE Project*, Leeds: CERS, University of Leeds, 2011

Siegel, Reva. 'Why Equal Protection No Longer Protects: The Evolving Forms of Status-Enforcing State Action', *Stanford Law Review*, 49, 1996–1997, 1111–1148

Skeie, Geier. 'Plurality and Pluralism in Religious Education', in M. de Souza et al. (eds.), *International Handbook of the Religious, Moral and Spiritual Dimensions in Education*, Dordrecht: Springer, 2009, 307–319

Skop, Yarden. 'Forecast: Only 40% of Israeli Students Will Attend Non-Religious Schools by 2019', *HA'ARETZ DAILY*, 7 August 2013, available at www.haaretz.com/news/national/premium-1.540130

Soudien, C. and Sayed, Y. 'A New Racial State? Exclusion and Inclusion in Education Policy and Practice in South Africa', *Perspectives in Education*, 22(4), 2004, 101–115

'South Africa National Policy on Religion and Education', Government Gazette No. 25459, Vol. 459, 12 September 2003

Spiro, Peter J. 'The Boundaries of Cosmopolitan Pluralism', *Wayne Law Review*, 51, 2005, 1261, 1264

Ssenyonjo, Manisuli. 'The Islamic Veil and Freedom of Religion, the Right to Education and Work: A Survey of Recent International and National Cases', *Chinese Journal of International Law*, 6(3), 2007, 653–710

Starr, J. 'Folk Law in Official Courts in Turkey', in A. Allott and G.R. Woodman (eds.), *People's Law and State Law*, Dordrecht: Foris Publications, 1985, 123–141

Startz, Meredith. 'Income, School Fees and Racial Desegregation in Post-Apartheid South Africa: Evidence from Cape Town Public Secondary Schools', CSSR Working Paper No. 287, December 2010.

Stewart, F. 'Why Horizontal Inequalities Are Important for a Shared Society', *Development*, 57(1), 2014, 46–54

Stopler, Gila. 'The Right to an Exclusively Religious Education—The Ultra-Orthodox Community in Israel in Comparative Perspective', *Georgia Journal of International and Comparative Law*, 42, 2014, 743–796

Suarez, M.M. Orozco and Qin-Hilliard, D.B. 'Globalisation: Culture and Education in the New Millennium', in Suarez-Orozco and Qin-Hilliard (eds.), *Globalisation, Culture and Education in the New Millennium*, Berkeley/Los Angeles: University of California Press, 2004, 1–31

Sullivan, John. 'Faith Schools: A Culture Within a Culture in a Changing World', in M. de Souza et al. (eds.), *International Handbook of the Religious, Moral and Spiritual Dimensions in Education*, Dordrecht: Springer, 2009, 937–947

Sunstein, Cass R. *One Case at a Time: Judicial Minimalism on the Supreme Court*, Cambridge MA: Harvard University Press, 1999

Tamanaha, Brian Z. 'A Framework for Pluralistic Socio-Legal Arenas', in M-C. Foblets, J-F. Gaudreault-DesBiens and A. Dundes-Renteln (eds.), *Cultural Diversity and the Law: State Responses from Around the World*, Bruxelles: Bruylant, 2010, 381–401

Tamanaha, Brian Z. 'A Non-Essentialist Version of Legal Pluralism', *Journal of Law and Society*, 27, 2000, 296

Taylor, Charles. *Multiculturalism and the Politics of Recognition*, Amy Gutman (ed.), Princeton: Princeton University Press, 1992

Taylor, Charles. *A Secular Age*, Cambridge: The Belknap Press of Harvard University Press, 2007

Taylor, Charles. *Sources of the Self*, Cambridge: Cambridge University Press, 1989

Taylor, R.M. 'Indoctrination: A Renewed Threat to Autonomy in Today's Educational Environment', Stanford University, 2012, available at www.philosophy-of-education.org/uploads/papers/Taylor.pdf

Teeger, Chana. 'Ruptures in the Rainbow Nation: How Desegregated South African Schools Deal with Interpersonal and Structural Racism', *Sociology of Education*, 88(3), 2015, 226–243

Teubner, Gunther. *Law as an Autopoietic System*, Oxford: Blackwell, 1993.

Teubner, Gunther. 'Legal Irritants: Good Faith in British Law or How Unifying Law Ends Up in New Differences', *Modern Law Review*, 61, 1998, 11–32

Teubner, Gunter. 'The Two Faces of Janus: Rethinking Legal Pluralism', *Cardozo Law Review*, 13, 1992, 1443

Thio, Li-Ann. 'Relational Constitutionalism and the Management of Religious Disputes: The Singapore. 'Secularism with a Soul Model', *Oxford Journal of Law and Religion*, 1(2), 2012, 446–469

Thomas, P. and Sanderson, P. 'Unwilling Citizens? Muslim Young People and National Identity', *Sociology*, 45(6), 2011, 1028–1044

Thomas, Vinod and Yan, Wang. 'Distribution of Opportunities Key to Development', in Donald B. Holsinger and W. James Jacob (eds.), *Inequality in Education: Comparative and International Perspectives*, Comparative Education Research Centre, Dordrecht: Springer 2009, 34–58

Tomasevski, Katerina. 'Annual Report of the Special Rapporteur on the Right to Education', UN Doc. E/CN.4/2002/60, 13, 2002

Tomasevski, Katerina. *Education Denied: Costs and Remedies*, London: Zen Books, 2003

Tomasevski, Katerina. 'Preliminary Report of the Special Rapporteur on the Right to Education', UN Doc. E/CN.4/1999/49, 1999

Topidi, Kyriaki. *EU Law, Minorities and Enlargement*, Antwerp: Intersentia, 2010

Topidi, Kyriaki. 'Religious Freedom, National Identity, and the Polish Catholic Church: Converging Visions of Nation and God', *Religions*, 10, 2019, 293, available at www.mdpi.com/2077-1444/10/5/293

Topidi, Kyriaki and Fielder, Lauren (eds.). *Religion as Empowerment: Global Legal Perspectives*, Abingdon: Routledge, 2016

Trubek, David. 'Where the Action Is: Critical Legal Studies and Empiricism', *Stanford Law Review*, 36, 1984, 575

Turner, Bryan S. 'Legal Pluralism: Freedom of Religion, Exemptions and the Equality of Citizens', in R. Bottoni et al. (eds.), *Religious Rules, State Law and Normative Pluralism: A Comparative Overview*, Cham, Switzerland: Springer, 2016, 61–73

Turner, Bryan S. and Richardson, James T. 'The Future of Legal Pluralism', in A. Possamai, James T. Richardson and Bryan S. Turner (eds.), *The Sociology of Shari'a: Case Studies from Around the World*, Dordrecht: Springer, 2015, 305–313

Tushnet, Mark. 'Political Power and Judicial Power: Some Observations on the Their Relation', *Fordham Law Review*, 75, 2006, 755

Twining, William (ed.). *Human Rights, Southern Voices-Francis Deng, Abdullahi An-Na'im, Yash Ghori and Upendra Baxi*, Cambridge: Cambridge University Press, 2009

Twining, William. 'Normative and Legal Pluralism: A Global Perspective', *Duke Journal of Comparative and International Law*, 20, 2010, 473–517

UK Department for Education. 'Promoting Fundamental British Values as part of SMSC in Schools: Departmental Advice for Maintained Schools', London, 2014, available at www.gov.uk/government/uploads/system/uploads/attachment_data/file/380595/SMSC_Guidance_Maintained_Schools.pdf

UK Government. 'Improving the Spiritual, Moral, Social and Cultural Development on Pupils: Departmental Advice for Independent Schools, Academies and Free Schools', 2014, available at www.gov.uk/government/uploads/system/uploads/attachment_data/file/380396/Improving_the_spiritual_moral_social_and_cultural_SMSC_development_of_pupils_supplementary_information.pdf

UK Government. *Swann Report, Education for All: Report of the Committee of Enquiry into the Education of Children from Ethnic Minority Groups*, London: Her Majesty's Stationery Office, 1985

UNICEF/Learning for Peace. *Investment in Equity and Peacebuilding: South Africa Case Study-FHI 360*, Washington, DC: Education Policy and Data Center, 2016

Valutyte, Regina and Gailute, Dovilé. 'The Exercise of Religious Freedom in Educational Institutions in the Light of ECtHR Jurisprudence', *Wroclaw Review of Law, Administration and Economics*, 2(2), 2012, 45–62

Van der Veer, Peter. 'Religion and Education in a Secular Age: A Comparative Perspective', *Extrême Orient Extrême Occident*, 33, 2011, 235–245

van Zyl, Andrew E. 'A Historical-Educational Investigation into the Decision to Remove Religious Education from Public Schools in South Africa', *Mediterranean Journal of Social Sciences*, 5(20), September 2014, 1613–1622

Verheyde, Mieke. *Commentary to the UN Convention on the Rights of the Child—Article 28: The Right to Education*, Leiden: Martinus Nijhoff, 2006

Vermeule, Adrian. *Judging Under Uncertainty: An Institutional Theory of Legal Interpretation*, Cambridge MA: Harvard University Press, 2006

Vertovec, Steven and Wessendorf, Susanne. 'Introduction: Assessing the Backlash Against Multiculturalism in Europe', in Steven Vertovec and Susanne Wessendorf (eds.), *The Multiculturalism Backlash: European Discourses, Policies and Practices*, Abingdon: Routledge, 2010, 1–31

von Benda-Beckmann, Franz. 'Who's Afraid of Legal Pluralism? *Journal of Legal Pluralism*, 47, 2002, 37–83.

von Benda-Beckmann, Franz and von Benda-Beckmann, Keebet. 'The Dynamics of Change and Continuity in Plural Legal Orders', *Journal of Legal Pluralism and Unofficial Law*, 53/54, Special Double Issue, 2006, 1–44, Berlin: LIT Verlag

von Benda-Beckmann, Keebet and Turner, Bertram. 'Legal Pluralism, Social Theory and the State', *Journal of Legal Pluralism and Unofficial Law*, 2018, 255–274, doi :10.1080/07329113.2018.1532674

Waldron, Jeremy. 'Legal Pluralism and the Contrast Between Hart's Jurisprudence and Fuller's', in Peter Crane (ed.), *The Hart-Fuller Debate in the Twenty-First Century*, Hart: Oxford, 2010, 135

Walker, Peter. 'OFSTED Targets: "Growing Threat" of Unregistered Schools', *The Guardian*, 11 December 2015, available at www.theguardian.com/education/2015/dec/11/ofsted-unregistered-schools-inspectors-faith

Ward, Ian. 'The Limits of Comparativism: Lessons from UK-EC', *Maastricht Journal of European and Comparative Law*, 2, 1995, 23

Watson, Alan. *Roman Law and Comparative Law*, Athens, GA: University of Georgia Press, 1991

Weller, Paul. 'Religions and Governance in the United Kingdom: Religious Diversity, Established Religion, and Emergent Alternatives', in P. Bramadat and M. Koenig (eds.), *International Migration and the Governance of Religious Diversity*, McGill–Queen's University Press, 2009, 161–194

Whitman, James Q. 'Enforcing Civility and Respect: Three Societies', *Yale Law Journal*, 109, 2009, 1387

Whitman, James Q. 'The Neo-Romantic Turn', in Pierre Legrand and Roderick Munday (eds.), *Comparative Legal Studies: Traditions and Transitions*, Cambridge: Cambridge University Press, 2003, 312–344

Wilcox, C. and Francis, L.J. 'Church of England Schools and Teacher Attitudes: Personal Commitment or Professional Judgement?' in L.J. Francis, W.K. Kay and W.S. Campbell (eds.), *Research in Religious Education*, Leominster: Gracewing, 1996, 311–333

Williams, James. 'How Better Education Has Built a More Secular Britain', *The Conversation*, 13 September 2017, available at http://theconversation.com/how-better-education-has-built-a-more-secular-britain-83656

Willis, P. 'Cultural Production and Theories of Reproduction', in L. Barton and S. Walker (eds.), *Race, Class and Education*, London: Croom Helm, 1983, 106–110

Wolff, Laurence. 'Education in Israel: Divided Schools, Divided Society', 8 May 2017, available at www.momentmag.com/education-in-israel-divided-schools-divided-society

Woodman, G.R. 'Legal Pluralism and Justice', *Journal of African Law*, 40, 1996, 152

World Bank. *World Development Report 2006: Equity and Development*, Oxford University Press, available at http://documents.worldbank.org/curated/en/435331468127174418/pdf/322040World0Development0Report02006.pdf

Wright, Andrew. 'Critical Realism as a Tool for the Interpretation of Cultural Diversity in Liberal Religious Education', in M. de Souza et al. (eds.), *International Handbook of the Religious, Moral and Spiritual Dimensions in Education*, Dordrecht: Springer, 2009, 333–347

Wuthrow, Robert. *America and the Challenge of Religious Diversity*, Princeton NJ: Princeton University Press, 2005

Yonah, Yossi. 'The Palestinian Minority in Israel: Where Common Core Curriculum in Education Meets Conflicting Narratives', *Intercultural Education*, 19(2), April 2008, 105–117

Young, Iris Marion. 'The Ideal of Community and the Politics of Difference', in Linda J. Nicholson (ed.), *Feminism/Postmodernism*, Abingdon: Routledge, 1990, 300–323

Young, Iris Marion. *Inclusion and Democracy*, Oxford: Oxford University Press, 2000

Young, Iris Marion. *Justice and the Politics of Difference*, Princeton: Princeton University Press, 1990

Young, Iris Marion. 'Marion Communication and the Other: Beyond Deliberative Democracy', in S. Benhabib (ed.), *Democracy and Difference Contesting the Boundaries of the Political*, Princeton: Princeton University Press, 1996, 120–137

Zameret, Zvi. 'Fifty Years of Education in the State of Israel', *Ministry of Foreign Affairs*, 14 July 1998, available at www.mfa.gov.il/MFA/History/Modern+History/Israel+at+50/Fifty+Years+of+Education+in+the+State+of+Israel

Zizek, Slavoj. *Living in the End Times*, London: Verso, 2011

Zrinšeak, Siniša. 'Re-thinking Religious Diversity: Diversities and Governance of Diversities in Post-Societies', in G. Giordan and E. Pace (eds.), *Religious Pluralism*, New York: Springer, 2014, 115–131

European Court of Human Rights cases

Dahlab v. Switzerland, Appl. No. 42393/98, 2001

D.H. and Others v. Czech Republic, Appl. No. 57325/00, 2007

Dogru v. France, Appl. No. 27058/05, 2008

Dojan and Others v. Germany (Cases No. 319/08, 2455/08, 7908/10, 8152/10, 8155/10), 2011

Efstratiou v. Greece, Appl. No. 24095/94, 24 Eur. Human Rights Report 294, 1997

Folgero and Others v. Norway, Appl. No. 15472/02, Judgment of 29, June 2007

Hatton and Others v. UK, Appl. No. 36022/97, 2003

Jewish Liturgical Association Cha'are Shalom Ve Tsedek v. France, Appl. No. 2742/95, 2000

Kalac v. Turkey, Appl. No. 20704/92, 1997

Kervanci v. France, Appl. No. 31645/04, 2008

Kjeldsen, Busk Madsen and Pedersen v. Denmark (Cases No. 5095/71, 5920/72, 5926/720), 1976

Kokkinakis v. Greece, Appl. No. 14307/88, 260 ECtHR Ser. A.

Lautsi v. Italy, Appl. No. 30814/06 (Grand Chamber), 2011

Manoussakis and Others v. Greece, Appl. No. 18748/91, 1996

Neulinger and Shuruk v. Switzerland, Appl. No. 41615/07, 2010

Sahin v. Turkey, Appl. No. 44174/98 (Grand Chamber), 2005

Valsamis v. Greece, Appl. No. 21787/93, 24 Eur. Human Rights Report 294, 1997

Zengin v. Turkey, Appl. No. 1448/04, Judgment of 9, October 2007

Domestic case law

Ahmad v. Inner London Education Authority (1978) 1 All ER 574 (UK)

Alexkor Ltd v. Richtersveld Community (2003) (12) BCLR 1301 (CC) (South Africa)

Antonie v. Governing Body Settlers High School (2002) (4) SA378 (C) (South Africa)

AP (Jerusalem) 241/06 *Association for Civil Rights in Israel v. Ministry of Israel* (51 Report 2010, 931–986) (Israel)

Azmi v. Kirklees Metropolitan Council (2007) UKEAT, Appeal No. 0009/97/MAA (25) (UK)

Bagaz 104/87 *Nevo v. The National Labour Court et al.* (22 October 1990) (Israel)

Bagaz 953/87 *Poraz v. Lahat, Mayor of Tel Aviv et al.* (1988) 42(2) P.D. 309 (Israel)

Bhe v. Magistrate, Khayelitsha (Commission for Gender Equality as Amicus Curiae) (South Africa)

CCT 9/97 *Harksen v. Lane No and Others* (1998) (1) SA 3000 (CC) (South Africa)

CCT 11/96 *President of the Republic of South Africa and Another v. Hugo* 1997 ZACC 4; BCLR 708; 1997 (4) SA 1 (18 April 1997) (South Africa)

CCT 60/04 *Minister of Home Affairs and Another v. Fourie and Another* (2005) ZACC19; 2006 (3) BCLR 355 (CC) (South Africa)

Christian Education South Africa v. Minister of Education (2000) (10) BCLR 1051 (CC) (South Africa)

Daniels v. Campbell NO and Others (2004) (5) SA 331(CC) (South Africa)

HCJ 240/98 *Adalah—The Legal Center for the Rights of the Arab Minority in Israel v. The Minister for Religious Affairs* (1999) 52(5) P.D. 167, 178 (Israel)

HCJ 257/89 *Anat Hoffman v. Western Wall Commissioner* (1994) 48(2) P.D. 265 (Israel)

HCJ 1067/08 *Noar Kahalacha Association v. The Ministry of Education* (6 August 2009) (Israel)

HCJ 1113/99 *Adalah—The Legal Center for the Rights of the Arab Minority in Israel v. The Minister for Religious Affairs* (2000) 54(ii) P.D. 164 (Israel)

HCJ 2422/98 *Adalah—The Legal Center for the Rights of the Arab Minority in Israel v. The Minister of Labor and Welfare,* not published (Israel)

HCJ 3358/95 *Anat Hoffman v. The Prime Minister Office,* Tak-Al 2000 (2) 846 (Israel)

HCJ 3752/10 *Rubinstein v. The Knesset* (2014) (Israel)

HCJ 4128/00 *Prime Minister Office v. Anat Hoffman* (2003) P.D. 57(3), 289 (Israel)

HCJ 4805/07 *The Center for Jewish Pluralism v. Ministry of Education* (2008) (Israel)

HCL 4805/07 *The Center for Jewish Pluralism—The Movement for Progressive Judaism in Israel v. Ministry of Education et al.* (unreported), available at http://elyon1.court.gov.il/files_eng/07/050/048/r28/07048050.r28.htm (Israel)

HCJ 8638/03 *Amir v. Rabbinical Court of Appeals,* Jerusalem (6 April 2006) (Israel)

High Schools Teachers Union v. Minister of Education (2004) (Israel)

HM Chief Inspector of Education, Children's Services and Skills v. The Interim Executive Board of Al-Hijrah Schools and Others (2017) EWCA Civ 1426 (UK)

IWN v. Minister of Labor (1998) 52(3) P.D. 630 (Israel)

Kievits Kroon Country Estate (Pty) Ltd v. Mmoledi and Others (LAC) (unreported Case No. JA78/10, 24 July 2012) (South Africa)

London Oratory Case (2015) EWHC 1012 (Admin.) (UK)

Mabena v. Letsoalo 1998 (2) SA 1068 (T) (South Africa)

Mandla v. Dowell Lee (1983) (2) AC 548 (UK)

Miller v. Minister of Defense (1995) 49(4) P.D. (Israel)

Nkosi v. Bührmann (2002) (6) BCLR 574 (SCA) at 578 (South Africa)

Plonit v. Plonit (1997) 51(1) P.D. 198 (Israel)

Prince v. President of the Cape of Good Hope and Others (2002) (2) SA 794 (CC) at 247 [38] (South Africa)

R (on the Application of Watkins-Singh) v. Aberdare Girls' High School Governors (2008) EWHC 1865 (Admin) (UK)

R (on the Application of Williamson) v. Secretary of State for Education and Employ- ment (2005) UKHL 15; (2005) 2 A.C. 246 (UK)

R (on the Application of X) v. Headteachers and Governors of Y School (2007) EWHC (Admin) 298 (UK)

Ryland v. Edros (1997) (2) SA 690 (C) (South Africa)

S v. Negal, S v. Solberg (4) SA 1176 (CC) at 1208F–1209A (South Africa)

Saggers v. British Railways Road (1977) IRLR 266 (UK)

San Antonio Independent School District v. Rodriguez (1973) 411 US 1, 63 (USA)

Shibi v. Sithole (South Africa)

South African Human Rights Commission v. President of the Republic of South Africa (2005) (1) BCLR 1 (CC) (South Africa)

Syndicat Northcrest v. Anselem (2004) SCC 47; (2004) 2 S.C.R. 551 (Canada)

Taylor v. Kurtstag (2004) (4) ALL SA 317 (w); (2005) (1) SA 362 (W); (2005) 7 BCLR 705 (W) (South Africa)

Wisconsin v. Yoder (1972) 406 US 205, 221 (USA)

Wittmann v. Deutscher Schulverein Pretoria and Others (1998) (4) SA 423 (South Africa)

International and European legal texts

Council of Europe 1950 European Convention for the Protection of Human Rights and Fundamental Freedoms, ETS No. 5, 213 U.N.T.S. 222

Council of Europe 1952 First Protocol to the European Convention, ETS No. 9, 213 U.N.T.S. 262

Council of Europe 1961 European Social Charter, ETS No. 35

EU Declaration on the Status of Churches and Non-Confessional Organizations No. 11 to the Last Act of the Treaty of Amsterdam, O.J. 10/111997, 133

EU Directive 2003/86/EC on the Right to Family Reunification, COM(2008)610, 8 October 2008

European Council, Resolution of the Council on the Response of Educational Sys- tems to the Problem of Racism, O.J. C312, 23 November 2005

European Pact on Immigration and Asylum of 2008, Council of the EU, 13440/08, Brussels, 24 September 2008

International Covenant on Civil and Political Rights, Article 18, U.N.T.S. 171, 16 December 1966

Organization of African Unity, 1981 African (Banjul) Charter on Human and Peo- ples' Rights, OAU Doc. CAB/LEG/67/3Rev.5, 1520 U.N.T.S. 217

Organization of American States, 1988 Additional Protocol to the American Con- vention on Human Rights in the Area of Economic, Social and Cultural Rights— Protocol of San Salvador, OAS Treaty Series No. 69

OSCE Office for Democratic Institutions and Human Rights (ODIHR), Toledo Guiding Principles on Teaching About Religions and Beliefs in Public Schools, Warsaw, OSCE-ODIHR, 2007

UN Committee on Economic, Social and Cultural Rights, General Comment No. 21 (2009), The Right of Everyone to Take Part in Cultural Life, UN Doc. E/C.12/ GC/21

UN Convention on the Rights of the Child, General Communet No. 1 (2001), Article 29(1): The Aims of Education, UN Doc. CRC/GC/2001/1, 17 April 2001

UN Committee on the Rights of the Child, CRC General Comment No. 7 (2005): Implementing Child Rights in Early Childhood, UN Doc. CRC/C/GC/7/Rev.1, 20 September 2006

UN Committee on the Rights of the Child, CRC General Comment No. 12 (2009): The Right of the Child to Be Heard, UN Doc. CRC/C/GC/12

UN Convention on the Rights of the Child, UN Doc. A/44/49, 1989, 1577 U.N.T.S. 3

UN Convention on the Rights of the Child, UN Doc. GA Res. 44/25, 20 November 1989

UN The Fight Against Racism, Racial Discrimination, Xenophobia and Related Intolerance and the Comprehensive Implementation of and Follow-Up to the Durban Declaration and Programme of Action, UN Doc. E/CN.4/2005/18

UN Human Rights Committee, General Comment No. 23: The Rights of Minorities, UN Doc. CCPR/C/21/Rev.1/Add.5

UN ICESCR, General Comment No. 13 (1999), Article 13: The Right to Education, UN Doc. E/C.12/1999/10, 8 December 1999

UN International Convention on the Protection of the Rights of All Migrant Workers and Members of Their Families (1990) G.A. Res. 45/158, 45 UN GAOR Supp. (No. 49A) at 262, UN Doc. A/45/49 (1990) 2220 U.N.T.S. 93

UN International Covenant on Civil and Political Rights (1966)

UN Office of the High Commissioner for Human Rights (2008), Report on Indicators for Promoting and Monitoring the Implementation of Human Rights, UN Doc. HRI/MC/20

UN Report of the High-Level Group of the Alliance of Civilizations, 13 November 2006, available at www.unaoc.org/repository/HLG_Report.pdf

UNESCO Convention Against Discrimination in Education, Adopted by the General Conference at Its 11th Session, Paris, 14 December 1960, available at www.unesco.org/education/pdf/DISCRI_E.PDF

UNESCO Dakar Framework for Action, Education for All: Meeting Our Collective Commitments (2000–2015), available at www.unesco.org/education/nfsunesco/pdf/Peace_e.pdf

UNESCO Recommendations Concerning Education for International Understanding, Co-operation and Peace and Education Relating to Human Rights and Fundamental Freedoms (1974), available at www.unesco.org/education/nfsunesco/pdf/Peace_e.pdf

Index